Imagined Orphans

The Rutgers Series in Childhood Studies
Edited by Myra Bluebond-Langner, Rutgers University, Camden

Advisory Board
Joan Jacobs Brumberg, Cornell University, New York City
Perri Klass, Boston University School of Medicine
Jill Korbin, Case Western Reserve University
Bambi Schiefflin, New York University
Enid Schildkraut, American Museum of Natural History

Imagined Orphans

POOR FAMILIES, CHILD WELFARE, AND CONTESTED CITIZENSHIP IN LONDON

LYDIA MURDOCH

Rutgers University Press
New Brunswick, New Jersey, and London

Library of Congress Cataloging-in-Publication Data

Murdoch, Lydia, 1970–
    Imagined orphans : poor families, child welfare, and contested citizenship in London /
Lydia Murdoch.
        p. cm.—(The Rutgers series in childhood studies)
    Includes bibliographical references and index.
    ISBN-13: 978-0-8135-3722-1 (hardcover : alk. paper)
    1. Child welfare—England—London—History—19th century. 2. Child welfare—
England—London—History—20th century. 3. Poor children—Institutional care—
England—London—History—19th century. 4. Poor children—Institutional
care—England—London—History—20th century. 5. Poor families—England—
London—History—19th century. 6. Poor families—England—London—History—
20th century. 7. Dr Barnardo's (Organization)—History. I. Title. II. Series.
HV752.L7M87 2006
305.23'086'940942109034—dc22   2005011351

A British Cataloging-in-Publication record for this book is available from the British Library.

Manufactured in the United States of America

To my mother, Deborah D. Murdock

CONTENTS

LIST OF ILLUSTRATIONS

Figures

Tables

ACKNOWLEDGMENTS

I would like to thank the people who offered the support that sustained me as I worked on this book. M. Jeanne Peterson provided just the right mixture of encouragement and skepticism, opening my mind to new ideas while keeping me grounded in the sources. I am grateful for her contributions at all stages of this project and for her continued friendship. George Alter, Ellen Dwyer, and Andrew Miller also read an earlier version of this text and offered invaluable suggestions, as did Kay McAdams, Timothy Pursell, and Timothy Schmitz. For their advice and encouragement, I also want to thank Ann Carmichael, Katherine Clark, Brian Els, Carol Engelhardt, Patrick Ettinger, Debbie Gershenowitz, Mark Hampton, Patrick Leary, Paul Murphy, Maura O'Connor, Tom Prasch, Steven Stowe, and Valentina Tikoff. Anthony Wohl first introduced me to Victorian history. A model teacher and friend, he helped me polish my prose and clarify my ideas. I am also grateful to Andy Donson, Jon Lawrence, James Marten, Rohan McWilliam, Patricia O'Hara, Pat Thane, and Dror Wahrman, who commented on sections of this work. George Behlmer, Martin Hewitt, and Seth Koven generously shared their research with me. The detailed, judicious comments on the entire manuscript by George Behlmer, Susan Tananbaum, and Susan Thorne have done much to make this a better book.

My colleagues at Vassar have also been a constant source of support. Beth Darlington and Susan Zlotnick remind me why I love the Victorians. I would also like to thank all of my colleagues in the History Department, particularly Robert Brigham, Miriam Cohen, and James Merrell, for their advice and support, and Mita Choudhury, for reading and discussing parts of the manuscript with me over our Wednesday lunches. My students at Vassar, especially those in my History of Childhood seminar, were a constant source of inspiration. I am also deeply grateful to my editor at Rutgers University Press, Melanie Halkias, for her enthusiasm for this project, to my copyeditor, Gretchen Oberfranc, and to the prepress director, Marilyn Campbell.

This book would not have been possible without the support of numerous institutions. I am thankful to the staff and interlibrary loan department at Indiana University and the Lilly Library, and to the librarians and curators at Vassar College, the British Library, the Colindale Newspaper Library, the London Metropolitan Archives, the National Archives, the National Sound Archive, the University College London Archive, and the University of Virginia Library. I am especially grateful to Adrian Allan and Simon Wilson, who helped me navigate the University of Liverpool Library Special Collections and Archives, to Frank Emott and Christopher Reeve at the Barnardo Library, and to Stephen Pover of Barnardo's Photographic and Film Archive. I am also particularly indebted to John Kirkham, the previous archivist at the Barnardo Photographic Archive, for sharing his love of photography and doing so much to make me feel welcome. Grants from Indiana University, the Midwest Victorian Studies Association, the National Endowment for the Humanities, and Vassar College, including an award from the Suzanne Schrier Heimerdinger Junior Faculty Research Fund, provided essential financial assistance. Also, I could not have completed this book when I did without the help of Olivia Moseley, Char Harris, and Lisa Collaco, along with all of the workers at Vassar's Infant and Toddler Center. My thanks to Liverpool University Press for permission to reproduce a revised version of my essay published in *Child Welfare and Social Action in the Nineteenth and Twentieth Centuries* (2001), edited by Jon Lawrence and Pat Starkey.

Pauline and Andrew Phemister provided me with a home away from home in Liverpool, and Rob Sheldon and Debbie Gershenowitz did the same in London. I give my deepest thanks to my family for their support: Deborah Murdock, Robert Bryan, Angus Murdoch, Alice Wakefield, Alec Murdoch, Kris Parker, and Carolyn Evans. My son, Christopher, though hardly cognizant of this book, revived my spirits with his smiles and reminded me of more important things with his cries. More than anyone else, Andy Evans has contributed to this book by editing multiple drafts, discussing my ideas, and taking on his fair share (sometimes more) of childcare. I am profoundly grateful for his good humor, sound historical advice, and partnership. I dedicate this book to my mother, who shared her love of local courthouse records with me early on and showed me how, through her love, families can be strengthened by adversity.

Imagined Orphans

Introduction

❧❦❧

$\mathcal{W}$ith the publication of *Oliver Twist* (1837–39), Charles Dickens created a portrait of the workhouse child that remained the standard image for the Victorian age. Born in an institution, Oliver was "a parish child—the orphan of a workhouse—the humble, half-starved drudge—to be cuffed and buffeted through the world—despised by all, and pitied by none." The workhouse officials knew little about his parents. His father remained entirely unknown, his mother concealed in mystery. She "was found lying in the street. She had walked some distance, for her shoes were worn to pieces; but where she came from, or where she was going to, nobody knows."[1] Old Sally, an adult inmate present at Oliver's birth, stole his mother's locket and ring—the only tokens that could provide clues to his family identity. Not even Oliver's name connected him to his parents. Bumble, the tyrannical workhouse official, picked the name "Twist" from his alphabetical list of possible names for pauper children. Without parents, extended relatives, friends of his own, or even an identifiable place of origin, Oliver lived at the mercy of potentially vindictive or compassionate workhouse officials. The archetypal workhouse child was first and foremost an orphan: alone, without a past, and completely disconnected from his parents.

Throughout the late nineteenth century, middle-class reformers publicly represented most poor children in state and private institutions as being either orphaned, like Oliver, or abandoned by their parents. Late-Victorian welfare and reform literature portrayed such children as isolated in the world, without family or friends, arriving at institutions from unknown or transitory locations. The common phrases used to describe poor children accented their alleged separation from parents and lack of connection to established, stable communities. They were "waifs and strays," or "nobody's children," or "street arabs" who wandered nomadically through the urban landscape, sleeping under archways and on rooftops. According to popular representations, these children lacked homes and any kind of domestic life.

1

When reformers did mention the children's parents, they were usually depicted as abusive and neglectful. Philanthropic tracts, parliamentary investigations, poor law reports, and reform-oriented novels characterized poor parents as vagrants, drunkards, and prostitutes who, if not brutally abusive, were primarily interested in exploiting children for their wages. Public and private officials alike decried "the evil influence" of the children's "own relations,"[2] castigating poor parents as "the worst enemies" of their progeny.[3] If institutionalized children were not already orphans in fact, many welfare reformers hoped to make them orphans in practice by permanently separating them from their indigent parents.

In contrast to this dominant representation of Victorian "waifs and strays," the records of poor law and charitable institutions provide very different narratives of child welfare, in which there were certainly victims, but often no clear villains. The daily workings of the welfare system commonly produced stories quite unlike Oliver's. In one case, the Whitechapel poor law guardians sent three of Sarah Harrison's four illegitimate children to the local poor law school at Forest Gate when she entered the South Grove infirmary in late 1877. Sarah retrieved her children in January 1878, but by the summer the three older girls reentered the Forest Gate school along with their four-year-old brother. Over the course of the next seven years, Sarah spent long periods in the infirmary and workhouse. After several trips to the poor law school, her son eventually returned to her, but the three elder girls entered and left the school ten to fifteen times each, remaining there for periods lasting from nine days to ten months.[4] Institutional care, in this case, was essential to this family's basic survival.

In a second example, a single mother likewise struggled to care for four sons and a daughter after the death of her husband in 1887 from typhoid fever. The mother eventually found work as a servant and secured a variety of placements for her children. The eldest girl entered service, one boy went to the Forest Gate poor law school, another began training for the navy on the *Exmouth* training ship run by the Metropolitan Asylums Board, and a third son became an inmate of Poplar Workhouse. A private charity known as Mr. Austin's Home cared for the youngest son, who was transferred to another charity when Austin's closed in 1891. When the mother refused to consent to her youngest child's emigration to Canada, this charity agreed to restore the boy to her. The assigned caseworker privately acknowledged her to be "a respectable, hard-working woman."[5] Unlike Oliver Twist, none of the children in these accounts was a full orphan. Their lives were certainly characterized by hardship and instability—experiences commonly associated with orphanhood. But the mothers of these children were alive and continued to oversee their welfare.

This book examines the surprising disjunction between the popular representations of Victorian poor children and the ways in which families actually used state and philanthropic welfare services. In fact, most institutionalized children were not orphans. To be sure, some parents were drunkards, prostitutes, and brutal abusers, just as popular reform literature claimed. Moreover, a good number of

Victorian youths were truly full orphans. But on the whole, the popular accounts of child rescue simplified the histories of Victorian and early-twentieth-century social welfare. In each of the above case histories, a single mother struggled to maintain contact with her children despite having to rely on institutional care for long periods of time. Theirs was the more common trajectory of turning to welfare services as the result of illness, death of a partner, or extreme poverty. Yet, until the first decades of the twentieth century, the opposing lines of popular and institutional narratives of child welfare remained startling. The goal of this study is to explore why, if most children in state and charitable institutions were not orphaned or deserted, reformers typically represented them to the public as being either parentless or the victims of parental abuse. What did the erasure or vilification of poor parents in the dominant child welfare narratives suggest about the nature of childhood and the position of the lower working classes within English society?

To address these issues, I focus primarily on two sites of child welfare rhetoric and experience: the charitable institutions run by Thomas Barnardo (1845–1905) and the state-run London poor law institutions for children created under the New Poor Law of 1834. Between the late 1860s and the 1880s, London's most influential children's charities were launched. Barnardo was a key figure in a larger circle of child advocates that included the Methodist minister Thomas Bowman Stephenson (1839–1912), who founded the National Children's Home in 1869, Edward de Montjoie Rudolf (1852–1933), who opened the Church of England Waifs and Strays Society in 1881 (now the Children's Society), and the Reverend Benjamin Waugh (1839–1908), a leader in the London (1884) and National Society for the Prevention of Cruelty to Children (1889).[6]

Within this group, Barnardo was certainly the most widely known, being a prolific writer and avid supporter of photography as a medium for documenting the plight of poor children.[7] Coming to London from Ireland in 1866, he began training as a doctor in hopes of pursuing missionary work, but quit his medical training in 1870 when it became clear that he was no longer considered a candidate for the China Inland Mission. A recently converted member of the Plymouth Brethren, he began evangelizing in the East End as early as 1867, holding regular Sunday sermons, and he briefly taught at a ragged school (free day school for poor children). After an initial failed attempt to found a juvenile mission in 1867, he established the East End Juvenile Mission in 1868, which served as a base for his sermons, children's day and Sunday schools, and boys' labor brigades. Barnardo opened his first children's home in 1870 in Stepney, where, in 1874, he established his own photographic studio. Although other child philanthropists, such as Bowman Stephenson, Annie Macpherson (1825–1904), and J.W.C. Fegan, also photographed children for fund-raising purposes, Barnardo made the most widespread use of photography. He was the first institution director to order the systematic photographing of all children who entered his homes, creating approximately 55,000 photographs for sale and documentary purposes from 1874 until his death in 1905.[8] He later contributed to the movement to replace large military-style barrack schools, which could contain more than one thousand children in the same building, with cottage homes run by foster mothers and fathers. When his Girls' Village Home opened in 1876, it served as an important model for other charities and London poor law authorities. By the time of his death, Barnardo had created several residential homes for poor children within England, established a system of foster care, and built a child emigration program with networks in Canada, Australia, New Zealand, and South Africa. At times extreme in his views and methods, Barnardo, perhaps more than anyone else, shaped late-Victorian debates about child welfare.

Although Barnardo's influence extended far beyond the actual work he did through his organization, children in need of care were much more likely to enter a state-run poor law institution than a private charity. Beginning with the New Poor Law of 1834, nineteenth-century state welfare policies addressed poverty by attacking the rights of poor parents, a trend that accelerated over the course of the century. In an attempt to make the existing poor law system more uniform, more centralized, and, above all else, more cost effective, the 1834 New Poor Law organized local parishes into unions administered by elected local boards of guardians. A central body, the Poor Law Commission (replaced in 1847 by the Poor Law Board and then in 1871 by the Local Government Board), oversaw national poor law policy.[9] The most controversial aim of the New Poor Law was to limit outrelief to paupers—that is, aid traditionally dispersed by parish guardians in the form of food, medical care, or wage supplements—by imposing the so-called workhouse test, which required individuals requesting assistance to enter the workhouse.

The principal founders of the New Poor Law, Nassau Senior (1790–1864), an Oxford economist, and Edwin Chadwick (1800–1890), Jeremy Bentham's former secretary, drew on Bentham's model for panopticon penitentiaries as they conceptualized the new workhouses as places of strict surveillance, discipline, and classification. Architecturally, the workhouses—*bastilles,* as English protesters called them—were not the models of panoptic order that Bentham envisioned, but they did generally contain separate quarters for men, women, and children. This separation of families within workhouses fueled popular protests against the New Poor Law in the 1830s and 1840s, and in practice many local guardians refused to enforce the workhouse test.

During these decades, a common theme in popular representations of the New Poor Law was the suffering of poor parents forced to part with their children. A *Punch* cartoon from 1843, titled "The 'Milk' of Poor-Law 'Kindness,'" condemned the law's separation of families (figure 1).[10] The New Poor Law, in the form of a merciless old workhouse matron, violently pulls an infant from a grief-stricken mother. To remove any doubt about the villains and the victims in this scene, a theatrical, victorious devil stands behind the matron, while an angel behind the mother and child hides its face in shame. In direct contrast to

PUNCH'S PENCILLINGS.——N°· LXII.

THE "MILK" OF POOR-LAW "KINDNESS."

FIGURE 1. A *Punch* cartoon from 1843 (vol. 4, p. 46) critiquing the New Poor Law of 1834, particularly the separation of parents and children within workhouses. *Courtesy of Vassar College Library.*

later representations of poor parents, the mother in this image deserves the public's full sympathy.

Typically, when early critics of the New Poor Law presented workhouse children as orphans, as in *Oliver Twist,* their purpose was to raise awareness about the hardships of urban life in general, not, as later, to divide poor children from their impoverished backgrounds.[11] Oliver's reconstructed family at the end of the novel includes not only Mr. Brownlow, who took in the boy as his son, but also Rose Maylie, his dead mother's sister. The novel closes with the image of Rose and Oliver sharing "their love for one another, and passing whole hours together in picturing the friends whom they had so sadly lost." In the final scene, Oliver's mother, Agnes, her ghost driven by "the love beyond the grave," watches over her child.[12]

If some representations of poor workhouse children in the 1830s and 1840s included a sympathetic view of parents, and even as Oliver became the typical image of the workhouse child, the popular treatment of poor families and parents in reform literature changed drastically by the 1860s and 1870s. A series of economic crises and poor law scandals prompted better state services for children, along with the boom in child welfare charities such as Barnardo's homes, but increased attacks on the adult poor accompanied these improvements. The central Poor Law Board, working in tandem with the Charity Organisation Society (COS), founded in 1869, hoped to limit rising state expenditures by directing the so-called deserving poor to charities and cutting back on poor law outrelief. The policy, in effect, put into practice the original directive of the 1834 New Poor Law.[13] Images such as the 1843 *Punch* cartoon became much less common as welfare reformers seeking to improve conditions for children justified their proposals not by arguing for the reunion of poor families, but by either erasing or vilifying poor parents. The result was a growing geographical as well as discursive separation between poor parents and children.

In London and a few other urban areas, the attack on poor parents had practical effects that went far beyond the New Poor Law's division of children and parents within workhouses. By the 1860s, London poor law guardians tended to favor the plan presented in 1838 by the assistant poor law commissioner, James Kay (1804–1877). Kay proposed to send children away from workhouses to separate schools, which might include children from other parish unions, as a means to promote more efficient education and remove children from the influence of adult paupers in workhouses.[14] In the 1870s, a new group of reformers, many of them women, argued that children's poor law schools needed to do more to remake families for pauper children. These reformers favored building institutions as model villages, complete with individual cottages run by foster parents. Thus, the late-Victorian fascination with "waifs and strays" and parentless "street arabs" coincided with the increased physical separation of children from their actual parents, as well as a broader attack on parental rights. Although much of the scholarship on the poor laws focuses on the New Poor Law of 1834, the reforms of this later period were actually much more drastic in their effects on parent-child relations.

My study of the dynamics of child welfare from the 1870s to the Great War has several wider implications. First, by reconstructing the family backgrounds of institutionalized children and exploring how poor families actually interacted with welfare officials, I present the poor as active, conscious agents who made choices based on their limited resources. In the process, I challenge much of the prevailing literature on child welfare. Most early publications on Victorian child welfare accepted middle-class reformers' representations at face value, claiming that parents were either absent or abusive to their children.[15] Although they look at the issue from a very different perspective, social control

theorists influenced by Michel Foucault and Jacques Donzelot similarly mini-
mize the agency of the poor by presenting them as helpless victims who had no
power to shape or resist onerous welfare policies. Such scholarship, including
Frank Crompton's *Workhouse Children,* the first and only book-length study of
children and the poor law, claims that welfare services easily manipulated and
disciplined the poor within "total institutions."[16] In contrast, by bringing attention to the experiences of a much wider range of institutionalized children, not
only those who were orphaned or deserted, I develop a very different understanding of the process of child welfare, one that recovers the agency and voices of
poor parents. Poor mothers and fathers were not simply manipulated by the system; rather, they negotiated within it to overcome short-term family and economic crises.[17] Reconceptualizing the dynamic of child welfare services
recovers the lost experiences of those families who depended on welfare institutions for survival, especially single parents and, most of all, single mothers.

Second, this book demonstrates that ideals of the family and parental
rights were central to nineteenth- and early-twentieth-century understandings of
citizenship and national identity.[18] Within child welfare disputes, Londoners
debated the very foundations of citizenship well into the late-Victorian period.
In this context, all groups generally defined citizenship in terms of duties and
entitlements, not suffrage, which even after the passage of the Third Reform
Act in 1884 remained a privilege rather than a right. Voting was still limited to
roughly 60 percent of the adult male population.[19]

I argue that the discrepancy between the representation and the reality of
children's experiences within late-Victorian welfare institutions stemmed from
conflicts over middle- and working-class notions of citizenship. The reformers' decision to present poor children as either orphaned or endangered by abusive and "demonic" parents reflected the adult poor's exclusion from the national
community. The public supported charity and state aid to children primarily
because these children were believed to be orphans or the progeny of truly abusive parents. By the 1870s, child welfare reformers increasingly defined citizenship in terms of middle-class domesticity, thereby denying citizenship to large
segments of the working, particularly urban, poor and drawing on the re-created domestic groupings within institutional cottage homes to reclaim poor
children as citizens. By the 1890s, a greater emphasis on poor children's future
roles as members of the British Empire began to overshadow the earlier
emphasis on domesticity, but reformers continued to assert that poor children
needed to be separated from their impoverished parents in order to be fash-
ioned into citizens.

Despite reformers' attempts to erase the existence of parents in public narratives and separate poor children from their parents in practice, impoverished
adults often reasserted claim to their children by using the language of traditional
rights and liberties associated with English citizenship. These guarantees
included the rule of law, the right to petition, and parental rights over children.
Some parents took complaints to welfare officials, demanding that their children

receive a basic standard of care and education; others attended local poor law meetings or petitioned local police court magistrates to defend their custody rights against overzealous reformers. Many parents understood poor law relief as a basic right of citizenship, agreeing with George Goschen, president of the Poor Law Board, when he defined "the fundamental doctrine of the English Poor Laws" to mean that "relief is given not as a matter of charity, but of legal obligation."[20] Even though parents could not legitimately claim a "right" to charitable assistance, they still appealed to magistrates and the popular press when they felt philanthropists had violated their parental rights, demanding due process before the law.

Most of all, poor mothers and fathers defined their powers to oversee the care of their children as an essential element of English liberty. Criticizing this understanding of liberty of the subject, John Stuart Mill noted, "One would almost think that a man's children were supposed to be literally, and not metaphorically, a part of himself, so jealous is opinion of the smallest interference of law with his absolute and exclusive control over them."[21] Thus, even as middle-class reformers increasingly based citizenship on notions of domesticity, respectable work, recognition of one's place in the social hierarchy, and, by the turn of the century, imperial contributions, many working parents continued to assert their status as English citizens based upon the traditional rights and liberties of freeborn Englishmen, among which parental rights were central.

By examining how this dynamic played out in both public and private welfare institutions, this book bridges a common divide in the literature on Victorian child welfare. Too often, histories of charities are considered separately from histories of state welfare services. Recent work suggests that a focus on the "mixed economy" of state services, charity, and self-help organizations more accurately reveals the policies and practices of social welfare.[22] Rather than working in isolation, children's charities and poor law services influenced each other on numerous issues, ranging from architectural design to training programs. Furthermore, although many Victorians feared that unregulated private charities would undermine the efficiency of public agencies, poor law officers often worked in tandem with private organizations. Poor law guardians sometimes relied on charities to emigrate children or to care for youths who were too old to remain in poor law schools. Some branches of the poor law bureaucracy, such as the Metropolitan Association for Befriending Young Servants (MABYS), began as purely voluntary associations and only slowly evolved into government bodies. Most important, it was common for poor families in need to rely on a mixture of self-help, charitable aid, and parish assistance. Barnardo's records frequently document cases of families in receipt of public relief, and some of Barnardo's children had previously been in poor law institutions. Whereas histories of social welfare tend to present private charity work in opposition to public assistance, I suggest that the lines between public and private services were often blurred. That ambiguity is especially apparent when these services are viewed from the perspective of the poor seeking help.

This book is also primarily a study of child welfare in London. England's capital city was not representative of the rest of the country nor of the rest of the world, which remained largely agricultural, but it offers the most dynamic example of how welfare services evolved during a period of intense urban and industrial growth. Other scholars have pointed out the need for regional histories of charity and poor law services, but for my purposes, London provides the best case study documenting the way in which welfare policies developed to deal with a rapidly growing urban population.[23] I focus primarily on children who remained within English institutions instead of concentrating on those who emigrated (mostly with the assistance of private charities) from England to Canada, Australia, New Zealand, and South Africa. The thousands of children who emigrated between 1870 and 1930 were only a small fraction of the total number of children who received aid within English institutions during the same period.[24]

The focus on child welfare developments within London does not, however, exclude a broader examination of London's role within the British Empire. Imperialism helped shape nearly all aspects of child welfare. Fund-raising literature drew on imperial rhetoric to bring attention to London's urban "savages," training programs prepared many children for future military careers, and study of the empire provided poor youths with a common British identity that could potentially overshadow class divisions. Thus, the child welfare system reflected the two-way process of imperialism that scholars have only recently begun to recognize, demonstrating how the empire influenced British institutions, British class relations, and even British notions of national identity.[25]

The structure of this study serves to emphasize the competing perspectives on Victorian child welfare, from reformers to parents to children. The first two chapters concentrate on reformers' debates about child welfare and their public representations of poor children, analyzing the larger causes and consequences of "imagining" these youths as orphans. Chapter 1 focuses on Barnardo's fund-raising literature and photographs, including the infamous "before" and "after" photographs (sometimes taken on the very same day) of children transformed from ragged existence to respectable citizens. Melodrama provided a recognizable format for philanthropic narratives of child rescue and reform in which the endangered child represented pure innocence. The children's parents, however, were either completely absent from these narratives or restricted to the role of fiendish villains. Reform narratives attacked the domesticity of poor families and also represented poor children as a distinctly foreign race of "street arabs" separate from the rest of English society. The children's acceptance into "respectable" English society required a physical, religious, and civic conversion experience to transform them into productive workers.

Chapter 2 also emphasizes the perspectives of welfare workers, exploring reformers' debates in the 1870s regarding the design of children's institutions. A group led by a younger generation of women entering the field of social welfare argued that arrangements of cottage homes with foster mothers and fathers should replace the dominant military-style "barrack" or "monster" schools. Central to these reformers' arguments was the notion that proper domestic environments fostered the growth of individual consciousness and civic responsibility. Thus domesticity and, especially for girls, gender roles became important measurements of poor children's evolution from "street arabs" into potential citizens.

The following three chapters examine child welfare institutions from the perspectives of children and their relatives. Chapter 3 moves to the individual biographical level to investigate the parentage of institutionalized children. Most often, parents decided to institutionalize some or all of their children after experiencing a number of overlapping crises: the inability to find affordable housing suitable for the entire family, death or desertion of a partner, illness, unemployment or casual employment at poor wages, the strains of young children on the family economy, and, in some cases, the challenge of controlling older youths.

The fourth chapter argues that, contrary to popular representations and official policy goals, poor parents by and large did not use welfare institutions as permanent depositories for their children. Furthermore, many parents found ways to oversee the care of their institutionalized children through visits and supervision. When denied access to children, some parents took their complaints to local police courts and the press, sparking a public debate about the rights of poor parents. Inverting philanthropists' use of melodrama, the parents in these accounts appeared to be defending traditional notions of citizenship. They presented themselves as the victims of overzealous reformers, who denied basic English liberties and rights to the poor.

Chapter 5 discusses the training that children received in welfare institutions and the ways in which this training reinforced specific notions of citizenship based on independent labor and a hierarchical class order. By the late nineteenth century, imperial contributions played a greater part in defining children's roles as future citizens.

The final chapter examines how the First World War affected child welfare institutions and promoted new models of citizenship for poor parents and their children. The war brought a new population of children into state and charitable institutions, but it also transformed the public perception of all poor parents. Because of the war, it was no longer necessary for welfare institutions to promote the dominant narrative of children as abandoned "waifs and strays" or as orphans without pasts. Poor parents entered the public discourse because their direct contributions to the war effort—as soldiers, as munitions workers, and as mothers of Britain's current and future soldiers—now outweighed earlier concerns about domesticity and family structure. Furthermore, understandings of the children's own forms of citizenship also began to change during the war, so that the principal model of the reformed child became the male soldier or sailor, rather than the independent artisan or domestic servant of the nineteenth century. Poor children, like their parents, became valued for their direct military contributions to the nation-state, rather than for their ability to re-create preindustrial village life or mirror middle-class domesticity. However, the experiences of institutionalized children during the war were often at odds with the public rhetoric. Far from being model future soldiers or workers, they actually became more rebellious during the war.

The various, competing narratives of child welfare alternately revealed and concealed aspects of child poverty. Victorian reformers' accounts of "waifs and strays," "nobody's children" wandering homeless through the streets of London reflected a growing appreciation of childhood as a stage of life requiring protection. The pathos and pain of the abandoned child in these accounts was undeniable. But what reformers left out and often ignored was a different sort of pain: the pain of parents and relatives forced by poverty to part with their children. Only through other narratives embedded in internal institutional records, police courts, and the local press were the voices of poor parents represented. The following chapters seek to recover the voices of these working mothers and fathers who contested the notion that they lacked the basic rights of citizenship by claiming welfare entitlements, by demanding equal protection under the law, and, most of all, by asserting their parental rights.

CHAPTER 1

"A Little Waif of London, Rescued from the Streets"

MELODRAMA AND POPULAR
REPRESENTATIONS OF POOR CHILDREN

In the summer of 1874 a child named Florence Holder posed for a series of photographs arranged by the Victorian philanthropist Thomas Barnardo in his newly established East London photographic studio. Barnardo mass-produced one of these photographs and distributed it throughout the United Kingdom to advertise his homes for "Orphan and Destitute Children." Portrayed as a newspaper seller in the streets, Florence wore a tattered dress, provocatively raised in the back to expose more of her bare legs and feet (figure 2). Her tangled hair, unkempt dress, and forlorn expression clearly marked her as an abandoned child. Barnardo used similar photographs of Florence's younger sisters—one costumed as a match seller and the other as a destitute child—in other fund-raising materials. The second of these appeared on collection boxes above the text "a little waif of London, rescued from the streets, six years old."

Late-Victorian philanthropists increasingly relied on such melodramatic images because they attracted the attention of the giving public. These particular photographs, however, brought an unexpected reaction. In 1876 the girls' mother recognized her children in Barnardo's advertisements and eventually complained to the local magistrate at the Thames Police Court of what she considered to be "a cruel fraud." Claiming that she had in fact brought her children to Barnardo's two and a half years earlier so that they would be educated and trained as servants, Mrs. Holder insisted that her girls "were sent into the Homes as clean and comfortable as I could make them." They had never been "on the streets," had never worked as newspaper or match sellers, and had never been simply abandoned as the advertisements suggested. Mrs. Holder objected in particular to the photograph of Florence without shoes or stockings, imploring the magistrate to "Look, your worship, how savage she looks! and no wonder." She had only one opinion of Barnardo's manipulation of her daughters' appearances in order to increase donations: "I call it a systematic

FIGURE 2. Florence Holder posed as a newspaper seller in the streets (June 1874). *Courtesy of Barnardo's Photographic and Film Archive (Admission Album 1/1, 16).*

FIGURE 3. Florence Holder as a servant (August 5, 1874). *Courtesy of Barnardo's Photographic and Film Archive (Admission Album 1/1, 18).*

FIGURE 4. The two younger Holder girls (June 1874). *Courtesy of Barnardo's Photographic and Film Archive (Admission Album 1/1, 22).*

fraud upon a benevolent public, to strip them and then take likenesses for such a purpose."[1]

The conflict between Mrs. Holder and Barnardo reveals how late-Victorian child welfare workers manipulated the popular images of poor children in order to promote their cause, even when this meant ignoring or falsifying the children's family backgrounds. Melodrama, a central element of nineteenth-century life, provided a preexisting narrative structure for these philanthropic representations of child poverty. As this chapter will demonstrate, reformers presented poor children to the public as "waifs and strays"—a distinct class and race apart from any recognizable English domestic family structure, history, or national identity—and they drew upon imperial metaphors to describe English urban poverty. As even Florence's mother recognized, the girl's "savage" appearance, more than mere poverty, justified philanthropic intervention. By scripting the evolution of poor children in melodramatic terms of rescue and reformation, philanthropists produced narratives that focused on individual and family pathologies rather than on the broader structural causes of poverty. For Barnardo and other innovative philanthropic reformers who were willing to extend child welfare beyond the services available under the poor law, saving poor children depended on the supposed absence or removal of their parents.

Barnardo's flamboyant fund-raising techniques and photographs of children have inspired several exemplary historical studies. Seth Koven and others have analyzed the court arbitration and public scandal that brought Barnardo's career to its lowest point during the summer of 1877.[2] Backed by the powerful Charity Organisation Society (COS), which had for several years been suspicious of Barnardo's philanthropic activities, the Baptist minister George Reynolds accused Barnardo of serious charges, including neglecting and physically abusing the children in his homes, consorting with a prostitute, claiming the title doctor falsely, and misusing funds. However, it was the issue of Barnardo's artistic photographs that received the most attention during the arbitration. The case focused on a handful of Barnardo's fund-raising photographs similar to the images of the Holder girls, in which he exaggerated the condition of poor children under his care.[3]

After months of hearings, the arbitrators presented their ruling in October 1877. They dismissed most of the accusations against Barnardo, but strongly censored him for the "fictitious representations of destitution" for "the purposes of obtaining money."[4] In Koven's analysis, the dispute between Barnardo and the central office of the COS over whether Barnardo truthfully represented his subjects was part of a wider late-Victorian conflict "between empathic and scientific, religious and secular, approaches to poverty and over who should control the vast apparatus of metropolitan charity."[5] Yet, even as Koven expertly reveals the conflicts and ambiguities in late-nineteenth-century philanthropy, he overlooks the role of parents in Barnardo's representations of child poverty. The end result of Barnardo's philanthropic narratives, which set the tone for much of the literature on child welfare, was to popularize the plight of poor children and successfully raise resources, while simultaneously casting the adult poor out of the English community and calling into question their basic rights to citizenship.

Late-Victorian philanthropic understandings of citizenship focused on two general areas: domesticity and productivity. Child welfare reformers portrayed the poor as lacking both. Accounts of child rescue followed a general format that challenged poor parents' genuine affection for their children as well as their ability to teach children the value of respectable work. Like missionary conversion parables, philanthropic narratives then celebrated the reclamation of poor youths as productive members of English society, citizens in the making, who, according to Barnardo, joined the English community by becoming productive laborers and members of his extended Christian family. Child welfare workers thus defined the foundations and limits of citizenship in Victorian England. To outline this process, I will examine in this chapter how popular images of poor children attacked the domesticity of the poor by presenting child subjects as parentless waifs, as potential victims of sexual abuse, and as racialized "Others" within the heart of England—representations that prompted the salvation of poor children while casting their parents in the role of abusers, unworthy of the rights of English citizenship.

Melodrama and Victorian Child Philanthropy

Melodrama provided various narrative structures and stock characters that proved essential to the construction and reception of Victorian child welfare accounts. A theatrical style that developed in late-eighteenth-century Europe and the United States, melodrama became the dominant theatrical form of the nineteenth century. Popular at first primarily with working-class audiences, melodramatic formulas were so widespread by the end of the century that they shaped the theater of all social classes and permeated most theatrical genres, including comedy, tragedy, pantomime, and music hall performances.[6]

Although popular topics for melodramas changed over the course of the century, ranging from nautical, gothic, and temperance stories to nationalistic and imperial varieties, melodramatic plots typically involved a stark division between unambiguously good and evil forces. According to Rohan McWilliam, the "concerns of melodrama were dominated by the binary oppositions of good and evil, rich and poor, town and country."[7] For example, a female heroine or a child representing pure innocence and virtue was often in danger of being led astray or sexually exploited, typically by an upper-class, urban male villain. The family and the home were also perennial subjects of Victorian melodramas as examples of bourgeois values threatened by industrial disorder. In these domestic melodramas, the family was often divided against itself and then reunited or replaced by a new domestic grouping, resulting in what Martha Vicinus has described as "a temporary resolution of conflicts between the home and the outside world by means of happy endings, however fragile."[8]

The success of a melodramatic performance depended upon close interaction with the audience, requiring actors to improvise their delivery depending on the cheers, gasps, or catcalls coming from the seats.[9] Most of all, melodrama made character traits and internal states immediately visible through the actors' use of heightened emotion and grand physical gestures, so that audiences could always distinguish the good from the bad even if some characters were temporarily misguided.[10]

In the past thirty years, theater historians, literary scholars, and an increasing number of cultural and social historians have argued that the effects of melodrama went far beyond the stage. Citing what she terms the "melodramatic mode," Elaine Hadley writes that "a version of the 'melodramatic' seems to have served as a behavioral and expressive model for several generations of English people."[11] Inspired by Peter Brooks's classic text, *The Melodramatic Imagination* (1976), and Victor Turner's work on social dramas, historians have identified melodramatic narratives and modes of acting in a variety of public settings, including royal scandals, political campaigns, elections, court trials, and popular working-class resistance movements.[12] Melodrama in these contexts was not simply a fictional representation separate from social reality, but a tool for ordering and understanding society. According to McWilliam, "melodrama should be seen as one of the forces that shaped the Victorian frame of mind along with the much discussed categories of class, gender, ethnicity, and national identity. Indeed, melodrama represents a way of getting at these categories."[13] Although some historians interpret melodrama as a trivializing or conservative force promoting the restoration of an old world social order in the face of rapid industrial and social change, others have pointed out its potential to represent the voices of disenfranchised groups, particularly women and the working classes.[14] Above all, however, the common feature in these various social dramas was a theatrical division of the world into good and evil forces directed by clearly visible victims and villains.

By the late nineteenth century, melodrama had an established role in shaping urban social reform work and philanthropic literature. Writers of popular social exposés drew on fictional themes and sensational, melodramatic styles to make their reports more exciting and acceptable to the public.[15] For example, the Reverend Andrew Mearns's tract on working-class housing, William T. Stead's exposé of child prostitution in London, and William Booth's discussion of the Salvation Army's scheme to reform the East End poor through religion and work colonies all sought to rouse public support by casting social problems in terms common to contemporary fiction and theater.[16] Although these social exposés raised awareness about the conditions and broader causes of poverty, their dramatic, popular appeal stemmed from lurid accounts of aristocratic villains, sexual immorality, drunkenness, and the language of imperial exploration applied to the "jungles" of East London. Successful social reform literature divided the world into dark and light forces, unmistakable villains and victims, whom journalists often compared with recognized fictional characters. "Fagin, in 'Oliver Twist,'" wrote one of Barnardo's supporters, "is no mere literary creation. Fagin resided in Spitalfields, and conducted an institution where young persons could be initiated into all the arts of dishonesty."[17] Charles Dickens's famous villain, who snatched up innocent children and trained them in crime, served to capture the attention of sympathizers who might otherwise fail to ponder the extent of child poverty.

Melodrama was central to Barnardo's fund-raising, serving as a tool to structure the details of child poverty in a manner that would resonate with the public and ultimately help shape child welfare policies. Despite public promises that he would no longer employ exaggerated, artistic representations of children, Barnardo incorporated theatrical, staged, and melodramatic elements in his institution's public fund-raising materials and private case records long after the scandal of 1877.[18] Stories with clear victims and villains drew public support while avoiding the more complicated issue of adult poverty and erasing the essential role that many parents played in securing aid for their children.

Domestic Identity and Child Exploitation

The first task of philanthropic narratives, including Barnardo's, was to prove that the children in question were indeed in need of rescue. The best way to make this case was to establish that the parents or guardians were either absent or abusive. Rather than focusing on poverty, reformers attacked the domesticity of the poor by suggesting that the very foundation of these unworthy families (when they existed at all) was economic greed rather than domestic affection. Philanthropic narratives thus demonized poor parents and sought to exclude them from respectable English society on the basis of their supposed lack of domesticity. Except in cases like *Oliver Twist,* where the endangered youth's parents were members of a higher class—a situation usually foretold by a bright gleam in the child's eyes—philanthropic melodramas cast the parents as the main villains.[19] The child represented pure virtue, and the intervening philanthropist played the role of hero or judge who brought the case to public trial.[20] To prove the need for child rescue, Victorian philanthropists highlighted the dangers of inappropriate domestic environments. Their accounts focused on the implicit sexual endangerment of poor children, their explicit involvement in prostitution, and their economic exploitation as beggars and street entertainers. In the very period when middle-class ideals of childhood based on economic dependence, purity, and innocence were beginning to take hold, reformers presented child labor as a form of near slavery closely linked with sexual exploitation.

Barnardo, like other child philanthropists, asserted that most institutionalized children were orphans or "waifs and strays"—purposefully vague terms that nonetheless implied the children had no living parents or had been abandoned.[21] According to Barnardo, the primary causes of child poverty were "*orphanhood*" and "the willful *desertion* of their offspring by unworthy parents."[22] In his famous account of how he first discovered the extent of child poverty in London in the late 1860s, *My First Arab; or, How I Began My Life-Work* (1888), he revealed the parentage of Jim Jarvis, who continued well into the twentieth century to serve as the public image of the Barnardo child. In language that clearly distinguished the child from Barnardo's readers, the boy confessed: "'I never knowed my father, sir. Mother was always sick, an' when I wor a little kid' (he did not look very big now!)—'she went to the 'firmary, an' they put me into the school. I wor all right there, but soon arter, mother died, an' then I runned away from the 'ouse.'" Jim eventually led Barnardo to a rooftop where a host of other "*absolutely homeless and destitute*" boys were sleeping. To Barnardo, "it seemed as though the hand of God himself had suddenly pulled aside the curtain which concealed from my view the untold miseries of forlorn child-life upon the streets of London."[23]

Even when he did not explicitly reveal the details of children's parentage to the public, Barnardo often consigned parents to invisibility. In the case of Florence Holder and her sisters, for example, Barnardo omitted the mother's role in bringing her daughters to his charity for education and training. The public was left with the impression that her youngest was simply "a little waif" who had been "rescued from the streets." Such omissions implied that poor parents played no role in negotiating welfare services for their children and, moreover, that these parents had directly caused their children's suffering through negligence, improvidence, and even immorality.

The story of Jim Jarvis was the first of many melodramatic narratives in which Barnardo played the role of the heroic urban explorer and evangelical missionary who alone was responsible for the salvation of poor children. Barnardo publicized his midnight explorations of East London in search of neglected children, claiming that the youths encountered during these expeditions were the chief residents of his homes.[24] Although the work of reforming children took place during the day, their discovery came at night. "By NIGHT we visit lodging-houses, interview policemen, and fish in waters deep or shallow, stagnant or frozen, for a booty worth winning . . . ," he wrote. "The NIGHT has a work of its own, for it is, we find, the best time, amid scenes repulsive to all but the Christian philanthropist, to seek and find in the most unlikely places precious jewels for the Master's crown."[25]

Barnardo's case records suggest that, at least by the mid-1880s, hardly any of the children in his homes actually arrived there as the bounty of these midnight expeditions; most of the admissions resulted from personal, parental, or some other form of application.[26] Yet the night searches offered a powerful image for fund-raising literature, which fit the melodramatic format of salvation delivered by an external agent.[27] Barnardo was an evangelical prophet who used his bull-lantern to bring light to London in its darkest hour. As he revealed the extent of misery among the poor, he also provided the upper classes with a ready opportunity for their own salvation through charitable giving.

Not all narratives of child rescue involved orphaned or abandoned children, however. In his most dramatic accounts, Barnardo styled himself as an adventurer-evangelist who was ready to do battle in God's name and risk his reputation to save children from living parents or relatives who could only do harm. Pamphlets such as *Kidnapped!* (ca. 1885) recounted cases of child imprisonment and escape from abusive parents or employers. Barnardo presented the parents in these stories as "the worst enemies to the well-being of their unfortunate offspring."[28] Drawing on stage temperance melodramas, philanthropists spoke of innocent children, abused and neglected by monstrous mothers and fathers who turned first to drink and then to violence and vagrancy, and often eventually deserted their children. Unlike the stage melodramas, however, in which the temperance spokesman typically intervened to save the wayward drunk, philanthropic narratives held out little hope of salvation for parents.[29] Barnardo asserted that no fewer than 99 percent of the poor children who attended ragged day schools "were the offspring of parents whose poverty was due to their drinking habits" and that the same was true for the vast majority of children in his homes.[30]

In *A City Waif: How I Fished For and Caught Her* (ca. 1886), Barnardo recounted how he saved Bridget from her abusive and neglectful mother. His confrontation with the drunken parent revealed her true nature: "I have no words at command to describe the ferocious look that came across the woman's face when I spoke of Bridget—how it seemed for a moment to change her from even the besotted-looking creature she seemed at first, to something far more hideous and more repulsive, in which there was little that was womanly or even human left."[31] This episode mirrors a scene described ten years earlier, in which Barnardo condemned a poor mother as "a kind of female fiend, who robbed her child of whatever he possessed, whenever she chanced to catch him."[32] These accounts of demonic, drunken, unwomanly mothers and, less often, brutal fathers justified intervention in homes that the public increasingly understood as not being legitimate families, but rather violent groupings based solely on the economic exploitation and abuse of innocent children.[33] Barnardo's narratives brought the very domesticity of the poor into question. Parents, in these accounts, were "fiends" and monsters undeserving of the most basic of English rights: control over their children.

Descriptions of violent clashes with relatives increased the melodramatic impact of Barnardo's accounts. There was no Victorian philanthropist who so relished detailing the physical abuse he suffered, whether the disfiguring bedbug bites after a night of investigating lodging-house conditions or the wounds from blows hurled by his opponents, who were almost always women.[34] In *Worse Than Orphans: How I Stole Two Girls and Fought for a Boy* (ca. 1885), he first recounted how he "stole" two young girls from a brothel—a clear reference to "The Maiden Tribute" (1885), in which Stead claimed to have bought thirteen-year-old Eliza Armstrong from her mother in order to substantiate the extent of child prostitution in London. The main dramatic appeal of Barnardo's pamphlet lies in the second incident: his battle against "two women—dreadful-looking viragoes" who made their living through crime and prostitution. They were the older sisters of a boy who previously lived at the Stepney Boys' Home. With the help of their mother, the sisters entrapped their brother in order to pawn his Barnardo uniform for alcohol. Learning of the boy's situation, Barnardo heroically broke into the sisters' house, where even the police constables feared to enter without a warrant. With his bull-lantern "full on," he discovered the half-naked boy lying on a heap of rags in the corner. "This boy is mine. Come along, my lad," Barnardo shouted. Hearing this challenge, the sisters attacked Barnardo, who, despite his short stature, valiantly defended himself and the boy: "I placed my back against the door, pushed the boy behind me, and maintained for a few minutes what was almost a stand-up fight with these two infuriated creatures." Late to the scene, constables eventually intervened, but not before Barnardo single-handedly repelled the "half-drunken women," who "raged like wild beasts." Barnardo and the officers took the sisters to the police station, where—in a typical melodramatic moment of chance discovery—they found the boy's mother in the process of being booked for public intoxication. She rested on a stretcher, her gray hair hanging down in a state of "dishonour and shame."[35] The account concludes with the boy returning to the Stepney Home, where he lived for many years and became a true Christian. In this dramatic conflict between good and evil, it was the solitary philanthropic hero, and not the hesitant representatives of the state nor the corrupt adult members of an impoverished family, who restored childhood innocence and effected the boy's religious as well as physical salvation.

In addition to attacking the parents and relatives of poor children directly, philanthropic narratives impugned the domesticity of poor families by highlighting the sexual dangers children faced in poverty-stricken homes. Descriptions of poor children almost universally fixated on their ragged appearance, which signified not only their poverty but also their sexual endangerment.[36] The secretary of the Ragged School Union, for example, complained that child "outcasts . . . run the streets almost in a state of nudity."[37] The frequent emphasis on children's nakedness, especially in the streets, raised fears of prostitution by suggesting that children would soon turn to more profitable means of survival than selling newspapers or matchbooks. Barnardo and his supporters nearly always first introduced children to readers through similar descriptions of disintegrating clothing that failed to cover the child's body, as in the case of a girl wearing a "tattered skirt, which through a dozen rents revealed her limbs."[38] A former official at Barnardo's Girls' Village Home described a thirteen-year-old by contrasting the girl's impoverished upbringing and degraded state with her more refined aspirations. Although she wore a "poor tattered frock," which "could not altogether cover the nakedness that would peep out," she maintained some "true womanly instinct" and tried to cover her naked body.[39] Boys as well as girls were described in a state of semi-nakedness, as reformers implied, albeit in more veiled terms, that they too were in danger of sexual exploitation and corruption. The typical male child in need of rescue was a boy "without shoes or stockings, his nakedness scarcely covered by a few wretched rags."[40] Homeless and friendless, these children were clearly vulnerable to sexual exploitation on the streets of London.

Even more than texts, visual images conveyed the isolation and sexual vulnerability of poor youths. O. G. Rejlander's famous photographic interpretation

"LOST!"
Alone in the streets of London.

For the other side see Appendix.

FIGURE 5. "'Lost!' Alone in the streets of London" (1871).
Barnardo's version of O. G. Rejlander's "Poor Jo" (ca.
1860). *Courtesy of Barnardo's Photographic and Film
Archive (ARC0108/D425).*

of Dickens's street sweep, "Poor Jo" (also known as "Night in Town"; ca. 1860),
was the most widely recognized image of the ragged child: a small, barefoot boy
with ripped trousers and a loosely fitting shirt sits on a doorstep with his head on
his knees. A number of Victorian artists and philanthropists reproduced or modeled their own works on Rejlander's photograph. Barnardo's 1871 photograph
"'Lost!' Alone in the streets of London" (figure 5) closely resembles "Poor Jo,"
and other children's charities, such as the Shaftesbury Society and the National
Refuges for Homeless and Destitute Children, also reproduced versions of
Rejlander's photograph as a powerful icon.[41]

Many of Barnardo's staged photographs focus attention on children's torn,
ripped, or revealing clothing in a way that would have been otherwise unacceptable even in the poorest neighborhoods of London. For example, in a pair of
images eventually entitled "A Midnight Discovery and Its Results," Barnardo

A MIDNIGHT DISCOVERY AND ITS RESULTS.

ON THE STREETS! "SLEEPING OUT."

IN THE HOME! "TUCKED IN."

FIGURE 6. A Barnardo contrast printed in his annual report for 1874–75. Based on earlier photographs, the drawings document a boy's condition before and after being rescued. The boy, Samuel Reed, later testified that Barnardo pressured him to smile for the photograph. *Courtesy of the University of Liverpool Library Special Collections and Archives (D239/A3/1/7).*

made two contrasting photographs of a young boy, Samuel Reed: "On the Streets! 'Sleeping Out'" shows him lying on a doorstep, with large tears in his clothing exposing his bare arms, legs, and feet; then "In the Home! 'Tucked In'" finds him smiling and fully covered by a blanket. Forty to fifty thousand copies of these photographs were printed for sale, and sketched copies of the images illustrated Barnardo's 1874–75 annual report, *Rescue the Perishing* (figure 6).[42]

During the 1877 arbitration, Reed testified that when he first arrived at Barnardo's in 1871, he went to the studio, where Barnardo *"took out his pen-knife and tore my clothes to pieces"* before positioning him for the photographs.[43] The photographer, Thomas Barnes, supported Reed's testimony, noting that the photograph in no way represented the boy's condition when he first arrived at the charity. Describing the first photograph, Barnes claimed, "*His dress had been tampered with.* He could not have come through the streets in the condition that he is here."[44] Barnes's comments imply that viewers would also, on some level, have recognized images of extremely tattered or ragged youths as fictions that could not be found on the actual streets of London. But the symbolic tearing of children's clothing nevertheless reinforced the urgent message that these poor children were alone without parental protection and in danger of sexual exploitation.

Following Stead's 1885 exposé on child prostitution in London, Barnardo became much more explicit in his assertions that he was saving poor children not just from sexually ambiguous or threatening situations, but from a guaranteed life of prostitution. *Night and Day* included numerous references to "The Maiden Tribute" and earlier debates concerning age of consent legislation, and Barnardo's Girls' Village Home was presented as a protective haven for vulnerable girls.[45] Not to be outdone, Barnardo quickly capitalized on the agitation generated by Stead's series of articles by publicizing his own attempts at child abduction. In controversial pamphlets and articles, such as *Kidnapped!* (ca. 1885), *Worse Than Orphans* (ca. 1885), and "Is Philanthropic Abduction Ever Justifiable?" (1885), Barnardo declared that he had abducted forty-seven children in defiance of the law for their protection. "I have myself frequently *bought* little children, and that, too, for a mere trifle," he wrote. "I have also smuggled children quietly away, or I have abducted them almost by force in the face of angry opposition."[46] Like Stead, who after purchasing Eliza had her virginity allegedly confirmed by a doctor, Barnardo claimed that he had medical testimony to prove that one of his abducted children, a four-year-old girl, "was *not* too young to be very seriously affected by her residence in the vile den from whence I rescued her."[47] Barnardo thus created a mirror narrative of "The Maiden Tribute," purposefully repeating and highlighting the most sensational moments. But whereas Stead placed the blame for child prostitution on poor mothers, aristocratic men, and, especially, on a broader society that was unwilling to address the issue of women's inadequate wages, Barnardo singled out dysfunctional families and the "vile den[s]" in which they lived as the source of evil.

For further justification for intervention in poor families, philanthropic narratives frequently portrayed mothers as prostitutes—a charge brandished by Barnardo to discredit mothers who filed custody battles against him.[48] For example, in *Out of an Horrible Pit* (ca. 1892), a fund-raising pamphlet labeled "for ADULT perusal ONLY," Barnardo narrated his rescue of the child Sarah G. from the clutches of her demonic, brothel-keeper mother. The little girl

> had been delivered *only just in time:* "saved, though as by fire." Her home was said to be a veritable "abode of dragons," into which whoever entered must needs bid farewell to purity and innocence. Who would unveil the horrors of such a pestilential den? . . . Sarah's own mother was the keeper of this pest house: she lived upon the ruin of defenseless children, and, alas, alas, one of her early victims had been her own daughter—Sarah's elder sister. . . . [49]

Barnardo used the language of melodrama—dragons and fire, good and evil—to describe the horrors of this home, which only the intervening reformer could safely navigate.[50] The account situated the innocent and defenseless Sarah against her immoral mother, thereby simplifying the complex causes of poverty as the failings of an individual family member.

In many philanthropic narratives, reformers conflated discussions of sexual endangerment and prostitution with criticisms of street entertainment and begging. Critics suggested that begging and hawking were covers for prostitution or similar forms of commerce in which parents exploited innocent children. In *The 1/— Baby: An Incident of the London Slave Trade* (ca. 1889), Barnardo again drew on the fears of child prostitution raised by Stead, this time applying charges of child abuse and exploitation to a much broader group of the poor. Using the language of prostitution to describe begging, he asserted that "a system of white child slavery is to-day in vogue in the metropolis. . . . [A]ny man can *hire or purchase* a child of either sex, for begging purposes, if he only knows where to inquire."[51] In this scenario, child beggars seldom had any relation to the adults they accompanied. "*Tramps buy or borrow little girls of tender age for the purpose of more success-fully soliciting the alms of the benevolent, as they trudge through street and lane in village and town,*" according to Barnardo. "They have been taught to call their owner 'father' or 'mother'; and woe betide such little maids if they dare by so much as a look to suggest that they are not truly related to the wretches who hold their unwilling hands."[52] Like child prostitutes, child beggars and entertainers were vulnerable to adults who controlled the "beggars' market" and treated children as commodities—"a perennial income of coppers, food, and clothing."[53] The parents in these accounts were not actual mothers and fathers at all, but rather owners, experts in street theater who profited from the semblance of a family.

The effect of these philanthropic narratives of parental absence or abuse, child sexualization, prostitution, and theatrical street begging was an over-whelming attack on the domestic identity of the poor. Most philanthropic narra-tives rendered parents invisible or quickly dismissed them in accounts of orphanhood or desertion. When Barnardo did discuss poor families, he generally characterized them as drunken and beastly groupings motivated by mercenary or immoral impulses. Parents allegedly regarded children as commodities to be bought, sold, and sexually exploited for profit. In the case of street beggars and entertainers—often used to represent the poor as a whole—Barnardo described the entire family structure as a form of economic exploitation comparable to child prostitution. In order to gain public support for their much-needed services, philanthropists used melodramatic elements to construct a world clearly divided between good and evil forces, victims and villains, in which any surviving par-ents played the role of unloving and abusive enemies of their children.

The London "Street Arab"

In addition to popularizing accounts of familial disorder, child reform-ers also presented poor children as domestic savages who, like their colonial counterparts, were in need of reclamation. Descriptions of the London "street arab" demonstrate how reformers used the rhetoric of class, race, and nationality to distance children from their families and local communities. By the mid-nineteenth century, paralleling the stories reported by journalists like Henry Mayhew, who characterized the poor as a nomadic race apart from the rest of English society, well-meaning philanthropists increasingly described poor children in racial terms. As Britain became the world's foremost imperial power in the last decades of the century, "street arab" became an ever more common label to signify fears of domestic decline and urban disorder. Yet, as Lindsay Smith insightfully argues, the urban "street arab" was neither fully foreign nor fully irredeemable.[54] Reformers could categorize poor children as a race separate from the English and at the same time suggest that with intervention and assistance these urban youths, unlike their parents, could eventually evolve into English citizens.

The "street arab" became a recognizable type in the second half of the nineteenth century. According to philanthropic reports and waif novels—an increasingly popular genre between the mid-1860s and 1890s, as changing middle-class ideals of childhood brought new attention to the poor—London teemed with shoeblacks, sellers of matches and newspapers, and flower girls who were utterly alone in the world, without relatives or homes of any kind.[55] The first recorded use of the phrase "street arab" dates to the 1840s. In his *First Plea for Ragged Schools* (1847), Thomas Guthrie drew on colonial stereotypes of the Middle East to describe the poor children of Edinburgh: "These Arabs of the city are as wild as those of the desert."[56] In a parliamentary speech of June 6, 1848, Lord Shaftesbury declared, "City Arabs . . . are like tribes of lawless freebooters, bound by no obligations, and utterly ignorant or utterly regardless of social duties."[57] By the late nineteenth century, the "street arab" had become a popular subject for photographs and drawings,[58] and also a well-known literary type. In such books as *The Little London Arabs* (1870), *Little Scrigget, the Street Arab* (1875), and *Mahomet, A. J.: From Street Arab to Evangelist* (2nd ed., 1885) the main character was usually male and potentially more dangerous than the waif.[59]

The term "street arab" implied that poor children were nomadic, alone in the world without homes or families. For example, Barnardo's frequently reprinted account of Jim Jarvis, his "first Arab," opens with Jim's words, "I DON'T LIVE NOWHERE!" After questioning the child, Barnardo determined that Jim was "a GENUINE ARAB BOY, utterly homeless and friendless."[60] By definition, the "street arab" had no parents or guardians. "He is," Barnardo reported, "in the majority of cases, alone; a solitary Ishmaelite, a lonely wayfarer on life's great road."[61] Unlike respectable English citizens who increasingly valued stable domesticity, "street arabs" rejected the middle-class vision of the home and, along with it, the values of English society. According to Barnardo, "they have no certain dwelling-place," preferring to move from lodging houses to temporary shelters under arches, marketplaces, and building entrances.[62] Barnardo described them as "youthful nomades [*sic*], whose only fireside and family circle is the crowded kitchen [of the lodging house], with its vicious assembly."[63] His journal *Night and Day* likened poor children to a dangerous, undomesticated "host of boy Bedouins who roam through our 'province of houses' by day, and curl themselves up at night, like stray, starving dogs."[64] In one of the sample case histories printed in *Night and Day,* Barnardo presented "Fred" as "a life-long Nomad. Not a Nomad of Crim-Tartary or the Russian Steepes [*sic*], if you please, but a Nomad in the England of to-day. Home had never for him a meaning. 'No father, no mother, no friends,' stands in my record as the primary fact of Fred's history."[65] Barnardo implied that with no experience of domesticity of any kind, these youths had no hope of developing into stable English citizens.

Reformers also used racialized language to separate poor children from the broader English social body, drawing on a confused mixture of national, ethnographic, anthropological, biological, and even zoological terminology. Like the urban poor in general, poor children were often construed as a separate race from the English.[66] According to Annie Macpherson, an evangelical advocate of child emigration to Canada who worked closely with Barnardo, poor children were urban savages, "wild 'Arabs'" distinct from the "civilized" English population.[67] The children's author Maud Battersby characterized them as members of a primitive society, a "tribe of national encumbrances which seem never entirely removed, in spite of the good works of philanthropists."[68] In *Gaspar; or, The Story of a Street Arab* (1891), she described a typical fictional meeting in Covent Garden between the "arab" Gaspar (a distinctly un-English name) and a young lady who would be his savior: "She looked at him fixedly, speaking as though he were a strange and somewhat interesting animal, not belonging to the same race as herself. Probably she did not feel as if he were; but Gaspar did not mind, he had not been educated in fine feelings, and it was enough if she noticed him for any reason."[69]

Racial, biological, and even animalistic or subhuman terms classified poor children as physically and morally different from the English. The philanthropist Ellen Barlee described children in a ragged schoolroom as the "most curious motley of zoological specimens possible."[70] Likewise, Barnardo explicitly referred to poor children as a separate "race." He repeatedly presented the public with what he termed "a unique specimen of the *genus* Street-Arab."[71] Racialized descriptions of poor children brought the colonial exotic home to the domestic context. Lord Shaftesbury summed up the popular view of poor children best when he declared that street children constituted a "tribe," "a wild and lawless race" of their own.[72]

Visual representations of poor children reinforced the perception of them as a distinct physical type or even a separate race. Barnardo's standard admission photographs of children posed them in mug shots, a format typically reserved for such social outcasts as prisoners, criminals, and the mentally ill.[73] Before-and-after drawings based on these photographs appeared regularly in *Night and Day* and exaggerated key physical differences, which could be inscribed with racial meaning by darkening the skin color in the before images and making the children's facial features in the after images resemble the classical ideal (figure 7).

FIGURE 7. In this drawing based on photographs the artist accentuated the boy's physiognomic as well as moral transformation by switching from a mug-shot format to a portrait style. Published in *Night and Day* (February 1896): 9. *Courtesy of the University of Liverpool Library Special Collections and Archives.*

A typical drawing of boys at Barnardo's 1887 annual "waifs and strays" tea meeting prompted viewers to see poor youths as racially distinct by depicting the children in the poses of frontal, profile, and three-quarter angles generally used in anthropological photography and sketches (figure 8).[74] Lined up on benches in rows before a plain background, the boys are removed from any community or contextual setting, similar to the arrangements in Francis Galton's anthropometric photographs of criminals and East London Jews. Their faces are likewise drawn at angles meant to emphasize physiognomic qualities that viewers would interpret as signs of physical, moral, and intellectual difference. The impoverished boys' oblong skulls, furrowed brows, large foreheads, accentuated cheekbones, protruding jaws, and vacant stares, in addition to their ragged clothing and visibly malnourished forms, distinguish them as potentially dangerous "street arabs," physically distinct foreigners within domestic England.[75]

In addition to stressing domestic and racial differences, evangelical reformers further characterized the "street arab's" alternative society as one that rejected Christianity. For example, in the melodramatic adventure story *Cleg Kelly: Arab of the City* (1896), young Cleg's atheism identifies him as a social outcast. The story recounts Cleg's dealings with a mad general, his brush with the opium trade, and his recovery from the brink of death, followed by his salvation through the discovery of love and success as a reformed farmer. In the first words of the book Cleg exclaims, "IT's all a dumb lie!—God's dead!"

"CHILDREN WHO WERE *not* CHILDREN."

FIGURE 8. An anthropological-style drawing of boys
attending one of Barnardo's tea meetings. Published in
Night and Day (June 1887): 4. *Courtesy of the University
of Liverpool Library Special Collections and Archives.*

More important, his atheism is the outcome of abuse by his parents: "An' look
at my mother. She just prays lashings. . . . An' me father, he's never a bit the
better. . . . For he thrashes us black and blue when he comes home just the
same." The narrator concludes that "CLEG KELLY was now outcast and alien
from the commonwealth. He had denied the faith, cast aside every known creed,
and defied the Deity Himself. Soon he would defy the policeman and break the
laws of man—which is the natural course of such progression in iniquity, as
every one knows."[76] According to this account of the "street arab's progress,"
parental abuse leads to a rejection of Christianity and English cultural values.
The final stage in the "street arab's" development is direct defiance of the state.
     As the story of Cleg Kelly demonstrates, poor children's alleged
nomadic movements, lack of acceptable family forms, rejection of religion,
and lives of crime raised questions about their citizenship and national identity.

In his autobiographical account, Albert Shakesby likewise claimed that child "street arabs" created their own alternative societies: they "develop into drunkards, hooligans, thieves, and murderers, and have no home besides the lodging-

FIGURE 9. The cover of *Night and Day* (December 1881), displaying the imperial influences on Barnardo's work. *By permission of the British Library (PP.1103cc).*

house or prison." Shakesby hoped that he had "made clear with these few words what a street arab is, and what poor opportunities he has of growing up into an honest and noble citizen."[77] Life outside of bourgeois domestic structures precluded, for Shakesby, the development of civic values. Preferring independence and liberty to the rights of property, the nomadic "street arabs" were commonly called "dwellers in No-Man's-Land."[78] They had no family, religion, or country. Barnardo emphasized: "[T]hese 'Waifs' are *nobody's children.* They live on nobody's land, they pass over the boundary of civilization, eluding, in one way or another, all ordinary efforts to catch them, and it is principally by Institutions such as ours that this class of boys is being constantly sought out, rescued, and saved, for God and for the community."[79]

By comparing poor English children with "arabs," reformers also linked them with other supposedly nomadic groups, such as bedouins, gypsies, Native Americans, and the migratory Irish.[80] These groups existed outside constructions of the nation-state. They literally crossed national boundaries, but also figuratively seemed to belong to a separate community within the state, and thus challenged established national and civic identities. The children's poverty remained dissociated from the general well-being of the English national community and commonwealth. The salvation of the "street arabs" required their reform, not a reevaluation of English society. As Barnardo stressed, their salvation served both to link and reaffirm the values of God and the community.

One of Barnardo's most dramatic cases of child rescue played on constructions of poor children as racial "Others" and highlighted the complex relationships between class, race, and national identity. According to the lead story in the December 1881 issue of *Night and Day,* Barnardo received a group of eight English-born boys whose families had sold them at an early age for a pound each to the tyrannical Arab leader of the acrobatic troupe known as the Beni-Zou-Zougs (figure 9). Raised in Turkey, the boys had lived in a state of near slavery, unpaid for their work, neglected, beaten, uneducated in religious and secular matters, and cut off from all communication with their families and the public. After an investigation by the British consul-general and an English barrister, the children were rescued from Constantinople and brought back to England, where they gradually adopted English ways through training at Barnardo's Stepney Boys' Home.[81]

Although the Beni-Zou-Zougs were by all accounts an exceptional case of child rescue, Barnardo argued that they were thoroughly representative of his daily encounters with London's domestic "street arabs."[82] The case combined contemporary rhetoric concerning "street arabs" with "oriental" melodramatic plots involving imprisoned victims, foreign tyrants, and Turkish settings—imperial themes that late-Victorian audiences began to prefer over the earlier melodramas focused on class conflict.[83] Barnardo's account of the Beni-Zou-Zougs reinforced images of poor, "street arab" children as racial and national foreigners who required internal colonization on an imperial model in order to be reformed into English citizens.

The story of the Beni-Zou-Zougs highlighted the youths' lack of legitimate domestic background and their unstable racial identity. Although one father's application to the Foreign Office for custody of his two boys prompted the investigation, the narrative is the usual one of rescue by government or official investigator, followed by social reintegration through Barnardo's Homes. The article does not pursue one child's request to be reunited with his parents or the entire group's general desire to return "home."[84] As in other philanthropic melodramas, the boys' parents are the absolute villains. Even the Arab leader of the troupe, Hadj Ali Ben Mahomet, a native of Morocco and a French subject, resembles a comic figure rather than a villain. Despite accounts of his brutality, *Night and Day* illustrated Mahomet in a comical, stereotypical manner as a rotund, buck-toothed man wearing spectacles and a large, plumed turban.[85]

The parents, in contrast, were compared with slave traders. In his introduction to the Beni-Zou-Zoug case, Barnardo wrote: "Let us never forget that every month numbers of little children are *sold,* or 'hired,' or 'lent' by their own parents or elder brothers or sisters, or other more distant relatives, into a condition which is practically as bad as any African slavery." Barnardo concluded the article with a reference to threats from parents seeking to retrieve their acrobat sons: "ALREADY I have had to fight more than one battle with relatives who have had the audacity to assert a claim for the lads, notwithstanding the fact that years ago they had 'sold' the poor little creatures into what might have been life-long bondage."[86] As pure villains, the relatives had no claim on the reformed children.

This exposé drew on constructs of race and nationality as well as domesticity to stress the boys' liminal, nomadic social position. The Beni-Zou-Zougs were English-born, yet most could not speak English, having learned instead to communicate in Arabic, French, Spanish, and Italian. The one boy who spoke English was noted for his strange cockney accent, a dialect in itself. They had English given names, such as George Edward Hammond and "Georgie" Bolingbroke, but Barnardo also referred to them by their Arabic names, such as Habashi. Much of the physical description focused on unclear and mixed racial characteristics: the "curly hair" of a "half-caste," the "straight" hair of a "dusky" colored boy, and the "flaxen" hair of the "English boy," who nevertheless, like the others "could not carry on a conversation in his mother-tongue."[87] Despite their English birth, they were illustrated on the journal cover in foreign garb, wearing Turkish clothing and fezzes.

Most significantly, many of the boys had little or no memory of their parents. When asked how he knew he was English, one boy responded: "I know I was taken away from London when I was about five years of age, and my [work] contract shows that I am English. I cannot recollect my parents."[88] Having suppressed all memories of his parents, the child's weak national connection was founded on a work contract—a contract later proved invalid—rather than on the traditional foundations of culture, geography, memory, and family.

The case of the Beni-Zou-Zougs exemplifies how reformers found it increasingly useful to characterize the children of the poor as domestically and racially distinct from other English classes, who, at least in Barnardo's terms, were narrowly conceived as Protestant Anglo-Saxons. Barnardo used this melodramatic case, which played on imperial tensions, to increase support for all of his domestic activities. He presented himself as the defender of "the English law of liberty" against the children's "worst enemies, alas! . . . their own relatives."[89] Even though only one of the eight Beni-Zou-Zoug boys originally brought to Stepney Causeway remained there nine months later, Barnardo boasted that the children would be thoroughly integrated into his "LARGE FAMILY."[90] By racializing poor children, reformers could gain support without bringing attention to the fundamental economic causes of child poverty.

Philanthropists' use of race, however, was extremely fluid. Children's racial characteristics could be modified as they became integrated into English society. Through public and private intervention, "street arabs"—the nomadic, unconnected, and therefore mutable and reformable children of the poor— could be transformed into productive English workers. But without such intervention, the Beni-Zou-Zougs and all poor children would remain internal aliens, a direct challenge to the foundations of the English commonwealth.

The Religious and Civic Conversion Experience

In keeping with the structure of melodrama, the transformation of poor children from waifs and strays and "street arabs" into potential English citizens also carried physical, religious, and civic meanings. Stories of restructuring disorderly families and colonizing the racially distinct children of London's East End merged with models and lessons of religious salvation. The reformed pauper child was a powerful religious symbol, especially among Low Church and Dissenting publishers and readers.[91] The children's salvation placed the intervening philanthropist in a heroic, even Christ-like role, evoking Christian sympathy, forgiveness, and charity that could build cross-class alliances. The reformed child also served as an allegorical model for all individuals in search of religious salvation and a new life.

Combining evangelical and missionary narratives, the fictional and philanthropic accounts of children's reformation traced their spiritual, physical, and civic transformation. Many philanthropic accounts equated acceptance into the Protestant community with a secular conversion into productive membership in the social body, underscoring Barnardo's vision of the English community as not only white, but also Protestant. The assumption was that spiritual awakening as well as industrial values would promote a sense of civic responsibility. The fundamental message of these conversion narratives was that salvation required pauper children's permanent separation from their dysfunctional families and past lives. In theory, their new lives involved not only a physical transformation that was visible to the eye, but also the erasure of their pasts, including all memories of parents and relatives.

Philanthropic accounts and waif stories advanced a religious moral very similar to that of Christian stage melodramas in the 1870s. The philanthropist or upper-class benefactor performed a Christ-like role characterized by self-sacrifice, which sometimes led to death suffered on behalf of the wayward child.[92] Unlike novels such as *Oliver Twist,* where revelation of the child's hidden upper-class background permitted his or her full familial integration, the saved child in most philanthropic narratives was integrated into a new family structure symbolizing the broader Christian community.

The popularity of these accounts of child rescue was partly a product of the late-Victorian evangelical revival, which stressed the importance of acting on behalf of one's Christian beliefs. For example, in the novel *Little Scrigget, the Street Arab* (1875), Scrigget's savior, John Wright, is unusual because he belongs to the working class. Yet Wright practiced the "best sort" of religion: "his religion lies more in deeds than words."[93] Furthermore, the child's transformation symbolized the possibility of spiritual salvation for all people by providing an example, according to one autobiographical account, of "what it means to 'put on the new man; be born again.'"[94] Conversion narratives such as *Mahomet, A. J.: From Street Arab to Evangelist* (2nd ed., 1885), by Salvation Army member Albert Shephard, reinforced this message of spiritual salvation allegorically embodied by the pauper child reclaimed from material want.[95]

Once "discovered" or "rescued," the poor child underwent overlapping civic, religious, and racial conversions in a process similar to the incorporation of imperial subjects, but with the important difference that English youths could usually become "white" again, whereas colonial subjects, including the Irish, remained permanently categorized as racially different. Often the comparison between imperial subjects and domestic poor children was explicit, as in the novel *Ragamuffin Tom* (1903), where the narrative switches back and forth between two stories: Tom's progress from a mud lark to "an honoured citizen" and the adventure story of his benefactors' relative, who escapes from cannibals in Africa.[96] In most narratives of child salvation, youths undergo an initial purification ritual. Reformers describe removing and often burning the children's filthy, vermin-ridden clothing. These acts were often necessary for health purposes, but they also symbolized the child's separation from his or her past and absolution for past sins.[97]

Conversion narratives also lingered on descriptions of children's dark skin coloring as the result of dirt, exposure to the elements, or simply their "natural" appearance. For example, Albert Shephard, inspired to become a Methodist lay preacher after experiencing a vision of Jesus in the Limehouse workhouse, recalled how his old street mates mocked him by pointing to the relative darkness of his skin, yelling "old darkie had become religious; that old darkie had got converted."[98] In *God's Little Girl: A Truthful Narrative of Facts Concerning a Poor "Waif" Admitted into "Dr. Barnardo's Village Home"* (ca. 1885–86), the social purity reformer Ellice Hopkins (1836–1904) referred to the two soot-covered children she had just taken from their father as "my black

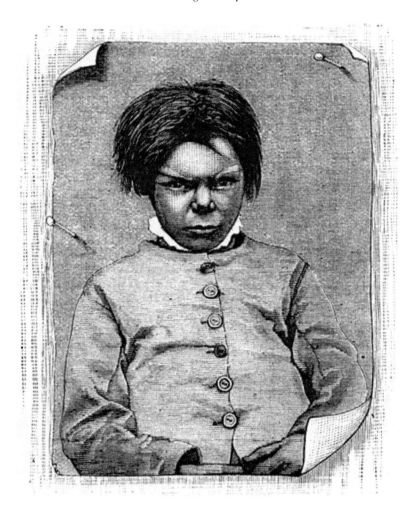

FIGURE 10. "Little Mary." Based on a photograph, this drawing presented poor children as a race separate from the majority of the English population. Published in *Night and Day* (February/March 1881): 25. *Courtesy of the University of Liverpool Library Special Collections and Archives.*

following" and "my two 'wild beasties.'" Like members of some exotic tribe, "[t]hey roared, they danced, they hullaballoed, they punched one another; they behaved like young savages."[99] When a drawing of the younger child, Mary, was published in *Night and Day* with the caption, "*After* the performance of her first toilet," it emphasized her broad nose, coarse hair, and, above all, her dark skin (figure 10).[100]

A child's first bath served as a key turning point in these narratives of salvation, producing the cleanliness associated with middle-class domesticity and symbolizing a spiritual baptism in which racialized "Otherness" vanished or at least diminished, leading to the child's religious awakening and the beginning of a new Protestant and English life.[101] After being rebuked for overzealously splashing her bath water, Mary cried out, "Oh! but I want to get white like the other little gals." This desire was Mary's first step toward leaving her "heathen" and "savage" ways. Not surprisingly, she learned, before her untimely death (so common in children's religious reform tracts), to substitute her pagan reverence for the moon with a Protestant love of God.[102]

After describing this initial phase of purification, narratives of child rescue concentrated on children's religious and civic education. Reform literature suggested that efforts to teach them to read, write, and lose their cockney slang and accents met with remarkable success. The "street arab"-turned-evangelist Albert Shakesby, for instance, wrote and published his autobiography only six years after he began to learn the alphabet.[103] Some critics feared that literacy training held a subversive potential to unleash passions, distract workers from their duties, and, in some cases, promote greater political awareness.[104] In philanthropic reform narratives, however, literacy more often encouraged children to develop a reverence for God, country, and empire.[105] Most important, literacy was necessary for children to partake in evangelical Protestant forms of worship: prayer, personal testimony, missionary work, and, above all else, reading the Bible. Soon after Shakesby's conversion, the Salvation Army sisters taught him proper manners and Scripture by having him read sections of an etiquette book and copy biblical passages each day.[106]

A final stage in accounts of children's conversion was the reorientation of their memories. Already dissociated from their families and communities, poor children were encouraged to forget their past histories, a process that would promote their eventual "depauperization." Barnardo went so far as to forbid the children in his institutions to speak about their pasts, explaining how he made one boy promise that "from the moment he entered our Home, he would never speak to any one except to me of his past life."[107] In one success story, Barnardo recalled how a girl rescued from a common lodging house "happily learned how to *forget!*"[108] Referring to the similar case of Sarah G., the girl saved from her prostitute mother and the "veritable 'abode of dragons,'" Barnardo rejoiced: "[S]he was soon taught to forget. The memories of the young are in some respects blessedly treacherous. . . . She *forgot:* and with the forgetting came a new experience, a pure and innocent and happy life."[109] Barnardo praised the Girls' Village Home for creating an environment that promoted forgetting: "The well-ordered, gentle life of the Village Home at Ilford casts no backward shadows:—'*Forgetting the things which are behind.*'"[110] He hoped that the very environment of child welfare institutions would regenerate childhood innocence and civility. Purity and innocence, the essential elements for the melodramatic happy end, flourished as wayward "street arabs" and waifs evolved into English citizens.

The children's miraculous reform, their development from "savages" into clean, literate, well-mannered, industrious Protestant children, was akin to the extreme transformations characteristic of Victorian melodrama. It is thus not surprising that, as a form of melodrama, the children's religious and civic conversion needed to be demonstrated by a clearly visible physical transformation. Peter Brooks notes that "[t]he melodramatic body is a body seized by meaning." The body's appearance is the most immediate way through which "melodrama's simple, unadulterated messages must be made absolutely clear, visually present, to the audience."[111] The body directly signaled the child's inner state. Reformers often asserted that rescued children underwent complete physical transformations as evidence of their internal changes. As Barnardo claimed:

> IN its effect upon my young *protégés* the life of the Homes performs
> wonderful transformations. It changes even the very expression of their
> faces. Many a time I have observed lads and girls, the lines of whose
> physiognomy have undergone a complete metamorphosis in the course
> of six or eight or twelve months' training.[112]

Barnardo's description is typical of other late-Victorian conversion narratives, especially personal accounts by Salvation Army converts of their religious salvation.[113] Such physical changes, however, also served as a final means of separating poor youths entirely from their past lives by making their bodies literally unrecognizable to parents, relatives, and former associates.[114]

Barnardo's before-and-after photographs from the 1870s provided dramatic evidence for the charitable public of children's conversion experience in its civic, physical, and moral manifestations. Beginning around 1870, he published eighty of these contrasts in pamphlets and as *cartes de visite,* which he freely distributed among the poor to advertise his services and sold to raise funds.[115] Photographs taken within days of each other—and sometimes even on the same day—displayed shocking contrasts that were meant to document the children's literal as well as allegorical transformation. For example, a pair of before-and-after cards advertising Barnardo's Home for Working and Destitute Lads illustrated a boy's change from "Once a Little Vagrant" to "Now a Little Workman" (figure 11). Although these photographs were actually made on the same day, they implied the long-term benefits of Barnardo's homes by supposedly documenting the boy's dramatic physical development over time.[116] In the first image, the gaunt, barefoot, and poorly clad boy is loitering in the streets. In the second, he is working industriously as a brushmaker. The photographs suggested that work was the key to the boy's physical and moral transformation, signified by his seemingly fuller face, new clothes, and altogether industrious appearance. As a newly created "Little Workman," the boy was one step closer to becoming an English citizen and no longer a financial or criminal drain on ratepayers.

In addition to stressing the benefits of work, the before-and-after photographic pairs, like the textual narratives, suggested that children's reform required a clean break from their pasts in order to achieve a truly happy ending. Such images asserted that poor children could be given a completely new identity.

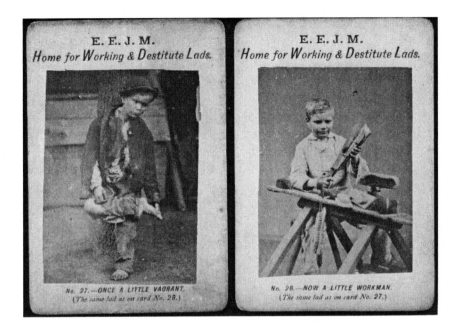

FIGURE 11. "Once a Little Vagrant" and "Now a Little Workman." One of Barnardo's before-and-after contrasts, implying the boy's transformation into a productive worker. *Courtesy of Barnardo's Photographic and Film Archive (ARC0239–0240).*

Philanthropists could retrieve children from "no man's land" and incorporate them into the social order, but this incorporation required a rejection of the past, including all relatives. For example, in the image titled "The Dreadful Past," the ragged, emaciated "nobody's child" looks down abjectly (figure 12). Later, he appears to have totally forgotten his past after entering "The Delightful Present" (figure 13). This second photograph emphasizes the boy's bright eyes and deferential smile; like the "Little Workman," he is shown diligently applying himself to a useful trade.[117] Contrasting with his earlier dark, disheveled dress, the reformed child in "The Delightful Present" wears white clothing (also like the "Little Workman"), symbolizing his newfound purity, religious salvation, and social acceptance. When drawings based on these kinds of photographic contrasts were published in *Night and Day* during the 1890s, they heightened this visual symbolism by cropping and shading the after images to create a halo effect around the reformed child (see figure 7).[118]

Even Barnardo's early admissions photographs, which were not necessarily produced for sale, displayed before-and-after contrasts (figures 14 and 15). In the first image of one new admission, the subject, John, looks more like an adult than a child.[119] Victorians practiced in reading physiognomy would interpret his illiterate expression, slack mouth, vacant, glowering eyes, and heavy brow as immediate signs of racial and social inferiority. John appears to be

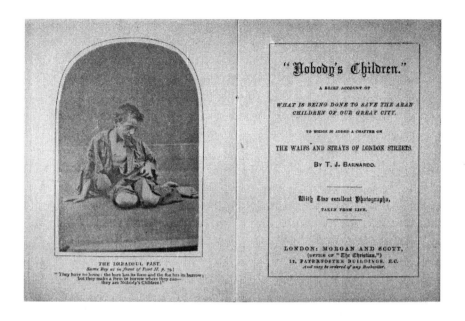

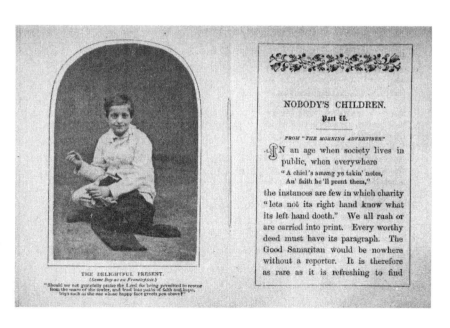

FIGURES 12 AND 13. "The Dreadful Past" and "The Delightful Present" (1872). A rescued "street arab" thrives in before-and-after contrasts from Barnardo's fund-raising literature. *Courtesy of Barnardo's Photographic and Film Archive (ARC0109/D481 and ARC0110/D482).*

FIGURES 14 AND 15. Admission album photographs documenting a boy's condition upon entering Barnardo's (March 14, 1876) and, three days later, his improvement. *Courtesy of Barnardo's Photographic and Film Archive (Admission Album, 1/28, 664 and 666).*

escaping the disciplinary control of the photograph, which is cropped so that his bulky coat, his excessively spiked hair, and the blurred outlines of his torso extend beyond the limits of the image.[120] Three days later, a smaller, childlike, and contained John appears in the uniform of Barnardo's Stepney Causeway, his arms neatly folded across his chest as he sits upright on the chair. This after photograph of John, with a slight smile, recalls the image of Samuel Reed tucked into a hammock at Stepney Causeway (see figure 6). When arranging that photograph, Barnardo had told Reed to "Smile, smile my boy," an expression that both Reed and the photographer felt was unnatural in the circumstances, and it is likely that he did the same with his other child subjects.[121]

Smiles were a common element in philanthropic photographs and drawings of reformed children, as well as in Rejlander's popular photographs of street urchins and Henry Peach Robinson's picturesque photographs of rural female laborers.[122] In her analysis of Rejlander's photograph "Give Us a Copper?" (ca. 1860/63), Jadviga Da Costa Nunes argues that the subject's smile conveyed "both the boy's diligence and contentment with his situation in life."[123] Moreover, the smile diminished signs of coercion, anger, class conflict, and resistance.

In an extreme case of melodramatic theatrics, Barnardo expanded on these photographic contrasts and actually had the children from his homes perform on stage (figure 16). Charitable donors could view the reformed children in a format evocative of evangelical revival meetings known for their testimonial displays. These performances began in the mid-1880s as children's award ceremonies and were combined with singing and short skits at the annual fund-raising meetings;

FIGURE 16. "The Thirty-first Annual Meeting of Dr. Barnardo's Homes" (*Night and Day* [November 1897]: 43). In the 1880s, Barnardo's began holding theatrical fundraising events in which children performed on stage. *Courtesy of the University of Liverpool Library Special Collections and Archives.*

during the 1890s they evolved into full-blown productions at Albert Hall that recounted stories of child rescue and reformation.[124] Although Barnardo condemned the theater as ungodly and refused to accept funds from local theater

groups to avoid having his homes in any way "identified or associated with theatrical performances," his fund-raising events made extensive use of theatrical
traditions.[125] The stage performances combined music, physical drills, tableaux,
skits, and expensive props to dramatize typical melodramatic narratives—salvation from fires and nautical scenes were favorites—along with more domestic
reenactments of life in the institutions.

The contrast between Barnardo's newest recruits and the children trained
in his homes was one of the dramatic highlights of the fund-raising spectacles.
Audiences witnessed children costumed in soiled, torn clothing act out scenes on
sometimes elaborate sets. In 1891, for example, the stage "platform became a
room in an East-end slum, with mother and children slaving at match manufac-
ture."[126] At other times, the action was less scripted, as when dozens of newly
admitted children, "the 'raw material' before it is manufactured," simply stum-
bled around the stage, confused by the bright lights. The audience was "hushed
to sadness and almost to tears by the pathos of the scene before them."[127]

Barnardo directly contrasted such pathetic scenes with displays of industrious, healthy, and joyous children who were embarking on new lives through
his assistance. Skits of the girls from the Girls' Village Home hard at work in
laundries and kitchens complemented the boys' displays of trade and nautical
skills. Declaring that "[p]eople believe in what they see," Barnardo began the
1890 performance with a group of about twenty boys trained in his homes as
brushmakers, bootmakers, carpenters, tailors, and woodchoppers; they entered
the stage and "set vigorously to work to exemplify their respective crafts at separate tables and benches." This scene was followed by another group of young
tradesmen, an interlude of "crippled" boys who, despite their crutches, "exe-
cuted a few simple drill movements with remarkable vigour and precision," and
a display of playful babies. Some very ill children had to be carried on stage by
nurses, eliciting "a sympathetic murmur of pity and encouragement from the
audience." To reassure any onlooker troubled by such a parade of youngsters on
stage, Barnardo pointed to the children's happy faces.[128] *Night and Day* illustrated the 1897 production finale at the Queen's Hall, Langham Place, where
boys preparing to emigrate to Canada rejoiced with song and dance in anticipation of their new lives as farmhands.[129]

These theatrical performances were enormously successful fund-raisers.
Even though Albert Hall was barely two-thirds full for Barnardo's annual meeting in 1892, the organization received £1,677 from donations and an additional
£781 from ticket sales.[130] Barnardo's chaplain for the London Homes, E. M.
Townshend, recounted that the "speeches alone were [a] failure." "The raw
material was numerous & filthy & the Emigrant Lads noisily smart & capitally
drilled & the applause enthusiastic."[131]

The effect of these elaborate theatrical productions was to impress audiences with a melodramatic happy ending: the child, stripped of his or her tar-
nished history had been transformed into a potential citizen, a productive
member of the working class within a regenerated domestic setting based on

affection and Christian love rather than economic exploitation. In classic melo-dramatic style, the audience celebrated the children's restored innocence while condemning the parents. As typical melodramatic villains, the latter were, in the words of Peter Brooks, "expelled from the social realm: driven out, branded as evil, relegated to a space off-stage and outside the civilised world."[132] The stage format ensured that philanthropic donors could witness the children's suffering and progress while remaining distanced observers. Audiences were entertained without the slightest suggestion that child poverty could be the product of broad social inequality or economic dislocation.[133]

Conclusion

Philanthropists' use of the melodramatic format allowed them to produce and reinforce a narrative of child welfare that concentrated on the moral failings of individuals and families rather than on the structural, economic, and communal causes of poverty. Although philanthropists' use of melodrama brought attention to certain recognizable forms of suffering among the poor, particularly material deprivation and spiritual ignorance, it also worked conceptually to divide poor children from their parents and the English poor in general. Philanthropic accounts described poor children as social outcasts at odds with the civic and religious values of English society; but through instruction, hard work, and the creation of alternative family structures they could reclaim their role as future citizens. This process made philanthropic and state intervention in poor families less controversial and ultimately more successful, because support of these programs neither challenged the English family as an institution nor the class order of English society. By ignoring or vilifying the children's parents and presenting poor children as racially and nationally distinct from any recognizable English community, reformers could popularize their heroic conversions of poor children without taking responsibility for the gap between their own privileged lives and the poverty elsewhere in their society. In addition, the narratives allowed reformers to retain their liberal ideals of non-intervention in the lives of "good" English homes and families.

Thus, when philanthropic donors witnessed children such as Florence Holder and her sisters being saved and incorporated into English society, they failed to see Florence's mother and the rest of the adult poor, who were excluded from the philanthropic narratives and denied representation in the late-Victorian social body. Yet, as subsequent chapters will demonstrate, poor parents fiercely contested this exclusion. Mrs. Holder's objection to Florence's "savage" appearance and her charge of "systematic fraud upon a benevolent public" attested to her allegiance with that broader English community as well as her claim to fundamental parental rights concerning the well-being of her daughters.

CHAPTER 2

From Barrack Schools to Family Cottages

CREATING DOMESTIC SPACE AND
CIVIC IDENTITY FOR POOR CHILDREN

❧❧❧

*I*n the opening article for the June 9, 1877, issue of *Chambers's Journal,* journalist William Chambers declared: "The family system is the foundation of everything that is valued in our institutions. Our whole structure of society rests on it. Any attempt to rear children artificially on a wholesale principle, is necessarily defective, will prove abortive, and be attended, one way or another, with bad effects."[1] His comments heralded a momentous change in public opinion about how government and philanthropic organizations should treat the children in their care. Chambers condemned as artificial the grouping of orphaned, deserted, and pauper children in large residential institutions, and he urged England and other parts of the United Kingdom to follow Scotland's more family-based program of boarding-out, or placing children with foster parents. Boarding-out gained support in England from the 1870s through the 1890s, but it nonetheless remained a limited solution, eventually used more by philanthropic societies than by the state.[2]

Instead, in England the emphasis on the family in state and philanthropic programs for children took a different form. Institutions organized into "family cottages"—each containing approximately twenty to forty children who were cared for by foster mothers and sometimes fathers—became popular options. The cottages formed model villages, such as the Girls' Village Home in Ilford (figure 17), founded in 1876 by Thomas Barnardo, and the Kensington and Chelsea Poor Law District School at Banstead, opened in 1880. Although still unavailable to the majority of poor institutionalized children, these family-based institutions quickly became the prevailing ideal for state poor law and philanthropic children's facilities in England, replacing in public favor the workhouse and large block-style residential schools, labeled barrack schools by many for their militaristic structure (figure 18). As Chambers hoped, the family system became the dominant model for teaching children social and political

NIGHT AND DAY.

Edited by Dr. Barnardo.

FIGURE 17. An overview of Barnardo's Girls' Village Home in Ilford, Essex
(1877), which served as a model for children's institutions organized into cottage
homes. *Courtesy of Barnardo's Photographic and Film Archive (ARC0199).*

values. What reformers often overlooked, however, was that the cottage homes
were not necessarily less artificial in their organization than the barrack schools.
The version of the family that they promoted was indeed a peculiar one.

This chapter examines the discursive shift from barrack schools to family
cottages by focusing on the role played by middle-class conceptions of the family, domesticity, and domestic space in late-Victorian debates concerning institutions for poor children. Here I analyze debates among poor law administrators, philanthropists, and middle- and upper-class reformers regarding proper surroundings for poor children, rather than examine from below how the working-class inhabitants of various environments associated these spaces with their own, often distinct, meanings.[3] My study of poor children's institutional environments stems from interdisciplinary work on the political and ideological significance of space that has been developing since the 1970s. Integrating anthropological, architectural, geographical, historical, literary, and psychological approaches,

FIGURE 18. The lavatory of the North Surrey District School (ca. 1908). A typical and, to some, disturbing image of a district school. *Short History of the North Surrey District School* (n.p., ca. 1908), p. 33. *Courtesy of Corporation of London, London Metropolitan Archives.*

scholars have focused on the role of space as a mirror and a constituent of culture and society.[4]

The examination of spatial arrangements is one means to approach not only cultural and social relations in a specific period, including class, race, and gender, but also contemporary conceptions of the individual, the family, and society as a whole.[5] The organization of space also has direct political meanings. During the nineteenth century, as historians such as Leonore Davidoff, Catherine Hall, and F.M.L. Thompson have demonstrated, certain spaces (gardens and children's nurseries, for example) symbolized middle-class domestic values and political ideologies.[6] Meanwhile, other areas of the urban landscape—particularly slums—became causally linked with antisocial behaviors, such as drunkenness, vagrancy, sexual immorality, and political instability.[7]

Underlying the support for children's cottage homes was an ideal of citizenship in which domesticity became a key requirement of Englishness as well as an overall Burkean vision of England as an organic, hierarchical, anti-industrial, individualistic community tied together along the Great Chain of Being through bonds of deference.[8] By "citizen," the reformers did not generally mean a person with full political rights; rather, a citizen was an individual who accepted his or her role as a productive member of the social order, a person who was a threat neither to the state nor to established social relations. Reformers who supported model villages and family cottages for children used middle-class ideals of domesticity and domestic space as means to incorporate pauper children into the English social hierarchy as laborers. Specifically, they asserted that poor children could develop as individuals only within an institutionally re-created domestic space, such as the model village homes. At the same time, welfare workers described the urban dwellings of the poor as intrinsically undomestic and therefore unsuitable for nurturing individual and civic identity in children. Thus, by the 1870s, middle-class notions of domesticity served as an important factor in defining legitimate family relations and even citizenship, competing with coexisting notions of English citizenship based on individual liberty, rule of law, and parental rights.

The first section of this chapter briefly places the debate about poor children's institutions within the broad context of mid- to late-Victorian public debates on working-class housing. This background is followed by an analysis of reformers' attempts to classify and spatially segregate poor children into specialized, disciplinary institutional spaces. I then examine the rise of new generations of female child welfare workers, their attempts to increase their influence in state as well as philanthropic child services, and their specific criticisms of barrack schools. The final section explores how these reformers envisioned institutional model village homes and family cottages as means to promote a distinct form of individual identity and civic responsibility based not on free agency but on maintaining ties to the community. Such institutions presented an organic view of English identity, meaning that the health or well-being of each part within a stable class and social order was dependent on all others. Through the analysis of these topics, I trace how notions of environment and domestic space promoted certain class-based ideals of family, individualism, and citizenship in late-Victorian society.

The Undomestic Poor

Numerous scholars have examined how popular representations of the urban poor contributed to the idea that their very environment precluded all domestic life. Without proper, bourgeois domestic spaces, the poor lacked the physical boundaries linked to middle-class notions of individuality and citizenship. The working-class home could not accommodate the high degree of spatial segregation and the number of specialized rooms that were becoming so important to middle-class concepts of domesticity and individualism.[9] Children and adults, males and females, and even lodgers mixed freely in the homes of the poor. As Felix Driver notes, "The poor were repeatedly said to be housed *en masse* in countless courts and back-alleys, without regard for distinctions of age or sex, and with little differentiation between rooms according to their function."[10]

In addition to raising fears about the lack of appropriate spaces within working-class houses, critics argued that these homes failed to provide a private haven distinct from urban industrial disorder.[11] Working-class homes seemed to contradict the late-nineteenth-century distinction of public and private space as separate spheres with definite boundaries.[12] For example, the working-class home often served as a place for paid labor, or even living quarters for the family pig and other urban livestock, thereby blurring the boundaries between productive and reproductive space and between humans and animals.[13] Furthermore, as Anna Davin has thoroughly chronicled, working-class children ventured unsupervised into streets and courtyards for recreation.[14] Middle-class reformers also viewed the homes of the urban poor not as private sanctums but as sites open to external influences—both the harmful "literal refuse from the streets" and the potentially helpful growing number of religious, sanitary, and philanthropic district visitors.[15]

The supposed lack of private space in working-class living quarters led some middle- and upper-class reformers to argue that it was impossible for poor families to develop any domestic life. Recalling Henry Mayhew's earlier explorations of child poverty, the philanthropist Ellen Barlee wrote: "Alas! in many of the abodes of the poor of our city, there is not space to raise the household hearth—no gathering the members of one family together under the sanctity of a common roof exclusively their own." According to Barlee, these "*brutal*" physical living conditions prevented families from developing affection. "Children are reared," she claimed, "hardly knowing, among the numbers that surround them, who are their kindred." Barlee conjured up visions of poor families that, like animals, "herd together night and day, eating, drinking, sleeping in common" in unsegregated, unspecialized one-room dwellings that "cannot pass under the name of home—it would be but desecration so to term it."[16]

The lodging house became the typical representation of urban living conditions for poor children before their institutionalization. This focus on lodging houses had strong popular appeal, although the actual number of children residing in such places was probably small; fewer still likely lived in them alone, without parents (as Barnardo often represented them).[17] Reformers portrayed lodging houses as centers of filth, vice, and sexual immorality, in which, according to Barnardo, "[i]nmates of all ages and of both sexes were crowded together."[18] Descriptions of lodging houses evoked fantasies of homosexuality as well as more direct references to prostitution.[19] Like Victorian "street arabs," lodgers personified a nomadic life without familial bonds or proper gender roles.[20]

In one dramatic account of his work in lodging houses, Barnardo described his conflict with a group of factory girls. He had settled before the fire, having succeeded in persuading several young boys to come to his Homes, when a "rough-looking factory-girl" from a neighboring lodging house arrived. In a voice "indescribable for its roughness, vulgarity, and unwomanliness," she shouted to her companions, "*here's the bloke as has taken away our pals!*" Giving off "savage" yells comparable to the "whoops of Red Indians on the war-trail," "some twenty or thirty great virago-looking girls" encircled the building, eventually breaking in with an "air of lawless daring" to surround Barnardo and insult him with sharp comments about his appearance, small stature, and spectacles. For all his good work, Barnardo was poorly treated: "pummelled and beaten from head to foot, my spectacles were crushed, my face was cut in one or two places, and in either eye I received perhaps the severest punishment I had ever experienced."[21] Barnardo's account of lodging houses presents a world turned upside down, where women were violent and men frail in comparison, an urban nightmare diametrically opposed to the rural ideal of village life. Even the religious, philanthropic visitor could not create a domestic space by the fireside, safe from the ravages of roaming, lawless bands of unruly, industrial female factory workers.

Many child reformers interpreted the alleged undermining of the domestic order in urban areas as a direct political threat to the state. Some suggested that poorly furnished, impoverished surroundings encouraged socialism and atheism, claiming that the worst of London's communal lodging houses were "well laden with copies of the *British Workman.*"[22] Writing to the *Times* as part of the renewed attack on lodging houses following the 1888 Whitechapel ("Jack the Ripper") murders, the Reverend Lord Sydney Godolphin Osborne used particularly strong language in one of his famous lay sermons to draw a connection between the housing conditions of a growing proportion of the population and the "utter subversion of the very commonest principles of civilisation." Osborne contrasted the "luxury and ease within homes . . . surrounded with all that can promote civilised life" with the chaos and degeneration of the slums. In these areas dwelled "tens of thousands of our fellow creatures begotten and reared in an atmosphere of godless brutality—a species of human sewage, the very drainage of the vilest production of ordinary vice." Osborne warned that "such sewage" was "ever on the increase, and in its increase for ever developing fresh depths of degradation."[23] To Osborne and others, the enclosed, clearly demarcated space of the single-family home had become the essential foundation of English civilization. Without such homes, the aggregate poor lacked all bodily and spatial boundaries associated with classical, bourgeois individualism. Viewed as nonsubjects, the urban poor represented "human sewage," "drainage" whose uncontrollable communal flow threatened to erode all notions of a stable society.[24]

Barnardo and other child advocates argued that in order to protect the interests of the nation, poor children had to be removed from their urban environments. He proclaimed: *"The children must be saved.* To do so they must be rescued from the lodging-houses; from their awful homes, utterly unworthy of the name. . . . They must be transplanted, so to speak, from the wilderness where their existence is every moment in danger, to the fair garden of a Christian Home."[25] This "fair garden of a Christian Home" symbolized middle-class ideals of order, privacy, and religious salvation, as well as the strong English faith in the environment's efficacy to shape the individual.[26] In order to be saved, children had to be transplanted to a new kind of domestic space.

The "Ins and Outs" and Institutional Classification

Child welfare reformers responded to the urban housing crisis by teaching children civic values within institutions theoretically separated from the influence of the adult poor. Yet, although the public generally assumed that orphaned and deserted children were the primary residents in these institutions, the more numerous inmates were the children of the casual poor, popularly called the "ins and outs" because they went in and out of institutions at short intervals.[27] Middle-class reformers viewed the ins and outs as menaces to the institutional order, because they remained connected to the unstable, undomestic ways of their biological families and threatened bourgeois notions of domesticity and individuality. Children who frequently went in and out of institutions came to be regarded as an unreformable source of contamination. By contrast, reformers presented the disproportionately small group of orphaned and deserted children as model inmates, who required protection from the casuals because they were potentially capable of developing bourgeois individualism and other civic values. Many child advocates hoped to segregate the casual children from the more permanent orphaned and deserted inmates. Spatial arrangements thus set the guidelines for citizenship by designating who among the poor was salvageable and who was a threat to the re-created, institutional social order.[28]

Workhouse officials had long tried to separate pauper inmates according to age and gender groups. The 1842 Commissioners' Workhouse Rules Order established a minimum of seven inmate classifications: "aged and infirm men, able-bodied men over fifteen years of age, boys between seven and fifteen, aged and infirm women, able-bodied women over fifteen, girls between seven and fifteen, and children under seven."[29] Each group theoretically had a separate day room, sleeping area, and exercise yard. This separation of husbands from wives and parents from children in workhouses sparked the fiercest opposition to the New Poor Law.[30]

Meanwhile, reformers increasingly relied on architectural design as a means to divide the unindividualized, aggregate poor, separating the so-called deserving from the undeserving. According to one female reformer, spatial segregation was the best way to ensure that all "classes [of the poor were] separated, and each dealt with in the manner most likely to preserve, to purify, or to reclaim it."[31] Architectural specialization of space, intended to avoid indiscriminate mixing in institutions (and in working-class neighborhoods), was the solution adopted by reformers such as Frances Power Cobbe (1822–1904) and Francis Peek, who condemned workhouses as "a huge *omium gatherum* of human want, vice, folly and disease,"[32] the "cesspool into which the drains and dregs of our population trickle," where "the drunkard," the "lazy tramp," and the "abandoned woman," mixed with "a sprinkling of decent poor."[33]

Many poor law unions, however, could not enforce the strict workhouse classifications in practice,[34] and the standard architectural divisions were unsuccessful at preventing interaction among inmates. The senior inspector of metropolitan poor law schools, Edward Carleton Tufnell (1806–86), wrote: "I am confident . . . that architectural arrangements can never effectually secure perfect classification in a workhouse. Conversation, sometimes of the obscenest description, is carried on over walls and through windows. In going to dinner or chapel there are ready means of communication; doors are accidentally left open, and the adults are employed in carrying furniture or other articles from one part to another."[35] Tufnell characterized the workhouse, like the grotesque body of the pauper, by its openings and passageways—empty spaces above walls, open windows, doors, and corridors.[36]

A more effective system of spatial classification came about only gradually and unevenly. Michael Rose argues that a number of crises in the 1860s, including an increase in London poverty, the 1862–64 Lancashire cotton famine, and scandalous reports of workhouses in the *Lancet,* caused authorities to restructure poor relief more in accord with the goals of the New Poor Law of 1834.[37] Throughout the 1870s, poor relief became more effectively centralized, and there was a more concerted attack on outdoor relief for able-bodied men.[38]

The pressure to realize the 1834 principle of no outdoor relief for able-bodied men corresponded with the creation of special policies and isolated quarters for groups believed to be more deserving of relief: children, the sick, the insane, and, by the end of the century, the elderly.[39] As early as the late 1830s, reformers such as James Kay and Tufnell advocated removing children from the "polluting association with the adult inmates" in workhouses and placing them in district schools.[40] Legislation empowering multiple poor law unions to combine into school districts first passed in 1844, but only urban areas, particularly London, made wide use of district schools. Although Kay and Tufnell hoped that London district schools would serve as models for the rest of the country, the bureaucratic difficulties of merging unions and the high cost of building larger schools made it more practical for guardians who wanted to remove children from workhouses to establish single-union schools, called separate schools.[41] By 1870, all poor law unions in London operated some sort of school for children separate from adult paupers in the workhouse.[42]

In addition to separating poor children from adult workhouse inmates, many officials sought to identify and isolate the more permanent inmates from the casual or temporary inmates known as the ins and outs—categories that, as will become clear in later chapters, were often extremely difficult to maintain. Supporters of more stringent segregation became especially vocal in the 1870s as officials cut back on outdoor relief, thus causing an increase in the number of families that resorted to temporary indoor relief.[43] Adults and children thus reaped the material support of poor law institutions without the full benefit of disciplinary training because they maintained irregular contact with external communities and family members. One workhouse official complained in the 1880s that adult inmates frequently discharged themselves (and presumably their children) on days when there was a local fair, a boat race, or a Socialist gathering in London—occasions of popular and political resistance.[44] Ellen Barlee explained that children were "often sent into the [district] school in hard times, and fetched out again by their mothers within a few weeks."[45]

The movement of poor children in and out of institutions contributed to their representation as nonsubjects, members of the aggregate poor who challenged ideals of bourgeois individualism and civic virtue. Descriptions of casual inmates frequently portrayed them as a group that escaped all efforts at spatial and bodily classification. Using the language of the grotesque, investigators represented the ins and outs as fluids or diseases that transmitted the physical and moral qualities of pauperism to more deserving inmates, namely, the orphaned and deserted children.[46] Welfare workers targeted in-and-out children as the source of contagious diseases, particularly the eye infection opthalmia, which was a very real problem in children's institutions but may have been endemic to certain schools rather than introduced by casuals.[47] The rhetoric regarding casual children even suggests that reformers' anxieties extended beyond the desire to control actual physical diseases. For example, one writer denounced casual children as "the plague"—an uncommon yet highly symbolic disease by the 1870s.[48]

Reformers eager to protect the image of the orphan child as the ideal inmate condemned the far more numerous casual children as a "constant influx" and a "foul stream running through the district schools."[49] Joanna Hill (1836/7–1901), who along with her older sisters Florence Davenport Hill (1829–1919) and Rosamond Davenport Hill (1825–1902) dedicated much of her life to prison reform and child welfare, denounced casuals as an "ever swelling stream" that could not be stopped from "pouring through and contaminating by their words and deeds, as well as by the physical diseases they import," the more permanent class of children in welfare institutions.[50] The poet and novelist Menella Smedley (1819–77), an active critic of large children's institutions, argued that casual children were unreformable; the "very milk on which the children are feeding has in it the germs of a fatal disease, and you do not know what they have swallowed until they are dying."[51] Similarly, the architect H. Saxon Snell repeated the common fear that without strict spatial segregation, the ins and outs would return from the "deteriorating influences of their alley homes" to district schools where they would "contaminate the permanent inmates . . . by their impoverished blood."[52] Casual children thus threatened to erode all notions of stable identity and citizenship that sought to exclude the masses.

Common references to casual children as a source of "evil" served as veiled suggestions of their alleged sexual knowledge and accentuated the contrast between morally contaminated casuals and innocent, redeemable orphans.[53] One poor law reformer claimed that the children of the casual poor corrupted the training of orphans and deserted children, arguing that "[t]hese unhappy intruders bring with them a knowledge of evil which it is painful to think of, and impossible to imagine in its full extent."[54] Speech was the primary means of spreading corruption. The casual children "from low homes" spoke of things that "can hardly be imagined," according to an officer in a girls' school— "*things of which* [the officer] *had no idea till she learnt them from the children.*"[55] Jane Elizabeth Nassau Senior (1828–77), the first female poor law inspector, wrote that the in-and-out children "returned each time more and more versed in sin, and exercised a very evident bad influence on the other girls."[56]

Above all, these references to evil imply a knowledge of the external world on the part of the casuals that corrupted the imagined innocence of the permanent children. Inextricably linked to the aggregate poor, casual children spread their physical and moral diseases to the orphaned and deserted children, conceptualized as potential citizens, separate from the rest of the hopeless poor. According to a prominent architect and designer of poor law institutions, children's schools should have a separate building for casuals: "the result would be not only a decrease in the percentage of sickness, but the permanent or long resident children would more surely turn out better citizens."[57]

In more extreme proposals, reformers such as Jane Senior hoped to do away with the casual class of children altogether by removing their parents, rendering them de facto orphans. The Education Commission supported a proposal in the early 1860s that parents who became "chargeable, from whatever cause, should be considered 'disenfranchised'" and "no longer entitled to have control over their own children, whom the Commissioners would remove by Act of Parliament to a distance of not less than three statute miles from the workhouse of which the nominal parents might be inmates."[58] In 1870, Florence Hill also supported abolishing all legal rights of pauper parents over their children. She wanted to prevent parents from removing their children from poor law institutions at will, claiming that "parents who have cast the burden of their children on the State should not be free to interrupt their being made good citizens, for evil purposes of their own."[59] By 1874, Senior wished to detain the parents of ins and outs and send them to agricultural work colonies on the Yorkshire moors—a plan that she put forth with "some hesitation," "knowing the tenderness of the English law with regard to the liberty of the subject."[60] Support for such proposals was by no means uniform or even widespread; poor law inspector Andrew Doyle (1809–88) dismissed the Education Commission's scheme as one of several "extravagant" ideas.[61] But such attacks on the rights of pauper parents reflected a growing trend among child welfare reformers to present an alternative definition of citizenship based not on the liberty of the subject, the rule of law, or the rights of parents, but rather on middle-class ideals of domesticity, bourgeois individualism, and respectable work—values that a rising group of female reformers believed pauper children could best learn in cottage homes rather than district schools.

The Female Critique of Barrack Schools

By the 1870s, a new generation of middle- and upper-class reformers sought to promote institutions that could provide healthy domestic spaces for poor children. Until the 1870s, most support for poor children's institutions in urban areas was directed not toward Barnardo's vision of a "Christian Home," but rather toward the barrack model of large, multiple-union district schools and the potentially equally large single-union separate schools that housed all children in one main building. Critics characterized the barrack schools as uniformly "mass" institutions, but they actually ranged in size from London's smallest separate school at Tooting (174 children) to the South Metropolitan District School at Brighton Road (1,541 children).[62] Supporters of district schools included some of the most controversial leaders of the older generation of poor law reformers, primarily men who remained wedded to the Benthamite principles of uniformity of practice and economy of scale that stood behind the 1834 New Poor Law. Beginning in the 1870s, however, in conjunction with the critique of casual children who went in and out of institutions, significant official as well as unofficial criticism increased not only against the workhouse schools, which allowed for interaction among workhouse children and adults as well as temporary and long-term inmates, but also against the larger barrack-style separate and district schools.[63] The leading opponents of the barrack schools were upper- and middle-class women who argued for a greater female presence in government and philanthropic positions based on women's knowledge of the domestic sphere. These women used domesticity as an important rhetorical tool, superimposing the domestic sphere onto children's institutions—a notably public realm—as a way to legitimize their involvement in public issues.

Drawing on an established tradition of female philanthropic service and district visiting that went back to the eighteenth century, Louisa Twining (1820–1912) led the first generation of women who succeeded in significantly increasing the involvement of upper- and middle-class women in state poor law administration.[64] Louisa was the daughter of the tea merchant Richard Twining, whose own father, Richard, had been a director of the East India Company. Around 1850, Louisa's sister Elizabeth (1805–89) founded what was likely the first of the soon widely copied mothers' meetings, which were instructional and religious gatherings of poor mothers led by middle-class women, who often also served as district visitors.[65] Louisa concentrated her activities on workhouse reform and her duties as secretary of the voluntary Workhouse Visiting Society, established in 1857.[66] She later was a main supporter of the Society for Promoting the Return of Women as Poor Law Guardians and eventually served as a guardian in Kensington (1884–90) and Tunbridge Wells (1893–96).

Throughout her career, Twining called upon women to become involved in the management of poor law institutions, often in the face of direct opposition from local boards of guardians, whom she characterized as men of little perception from a generally lower social class. Drawing a typically sharp distinction between male and female approaches, she asserted in her memoirs that "a great part of the evils which had grown up around the [poor law] system were owing to the fact that it was carried out entirely by men—that the 'female element' . . . had been entirely ignored, and that the fate and control of the thousands of women and children who came under the Poor Law was in the hands of guardians, who could hardly be supposed to know all that was needful on this subject."[67] According to Twining, middle- and upper-class women like herself were in a unique position to shape poor law policies for the benefit of women and children, whose concerns were systematically misunderstood or ignored by male officials.

In addition to pointing out gender tensions in the administration of poor relief, Twining intimated an underlying class strife between public officials and female philanthropists. Critical of the local union boards of guardians, she suggested that their members were "chosen from the lower class of tradesmen in towns, and of farmers in the country."[68] Twining stressed the need to "secure the services of really superior and lady-like women" to supervise the management of children's poor law institutions, women "who would be looked up to with respect by the teachers, male and female (who now feel themselves the superiors in education), as well as by the guardians and other inspectors."[69] Twining hoped that these upper-class women would open a public forum on poor law policies and exert their domestic influence on female and child inmates through the various activities of the Workhouse Visiting Society, such as Bible instruction, Christmas parties, the creation of workhouse libraries, and, especially, the befriending of children during their institutionalization and after their placement in service.[70]

The appointment of Jane Elizabeth Nassau Senior as inspector of workhouses and pauper schools in February 1874 was a major victory for female advocates of workhouse and school reform. Senior was the first female poor law inspector and a great believer in the power of women's influence to reform poor children.[71] In 1874, Senior established her reputation as an authority on poor law administration with the publication of her influential *Report on the Education of Girls in Pauper Schools*. Commissioned in 1873 by James Stansfeld, president of the Local Government Board, the report examined the "physical, moral, and domestic training" of girls in the seventeen London metropolitan poor law schools (the girls' scholastic work was notably exempt from study), along with the condition of girls from poor law schools after they entered domestic service.[72]

Senior's *Report* was significant because it offered an official condemnation of the large barrack district and separate schools. It gave voice and authority to the growing philanthropic literature against large schools in favor of family models for poor children, such as foster homes and institutions composed of separate cottage homes. Among her criticisms, Senior argued that barrack schools were overcrowded to the point that they were unhealthy, facilitating the spread of contagious diseases. She condemned the insufficient separation of temporary and long-term child inmates in metropolitan poor law schools, and identified such intermixing as a major cause of moral corruption and the children's subsequent failures later in life. Like Twining, Senior claimed that women's unique, domestic perspective—as both potential maternal figures and employers of servants—must be consulted and incorporated for the proper training of pauper girls.[73]

Senior met harsh resistance from Edward Tufnell, the senior inspector of poor law schools, who resigned after a long career in 1874, the year Senior's report was published. Along with James Kay, Tufnell was an early supporter of district schools, which he regarded as a cost-effective means for urban unions to segregate children from adult paupers in workhouses. The Tufnell-Senior debate exemplified the conflict between so-called barrack schools and family-based models for children, a conflict that often boiled down to a dispute about gender and professional authority. Reflecting the growing resistance to women philanthropists eager to extend their influence, Tufnell and his supporters, including Edwin Chadwick, portrayed female reformers as dilettantes limited by the narrow prejudices of their class and gender.[74] Tufnell scoffed that Senior and her fellow lady inspectors would cite a girl for unsatisfactory progress after leaving the poor law schools simply because she had been spied "sitting on a door step" or "in the streets with long curls down her back, and not looking respectable."[75] Most important, Tufnell firmly believed that poor boys and girls required similar treatment and that district schools did a commendable job of providing it.[76] He rejected the idea that women were by nature more qualified to administer the care of pauper girls and that institutions organized along domestic lines were better able than the district schools to reform children into artisans, servants, and English citizens.

In spite of Tufnell's arguments, the large barrack schools, which had never gained significant support outside of urban areas, gradually fell out of favor. Poor law authorities began to look more and more to smaller institutions as reformatory models, suggesting the broader influence of women's earlier domestic philanthropy in other fields, such as Elizabeth Fry's visiting work with prisoners and Florence Nightingale's hospital reforms.[77] Also, the colony of cottage homes for French juvenile delinquents founded in 1840 at Mettray near Tours became an important architectural prototype for British reformers.[78] It was not until the 1870s, however, that government and private child welfare workers in England made widespread appeals to build cottage homes for poor children. Barnardo's Girls' Village Home, established outside of London in 1876, served as an innovative example that influenced the direction of state institutions. In addition to Senior's *Report,* other prominent publications and government reports called for the application of the family system to institutions for pauper children, including Florence Hill's *Children of the State* (1868), a favorable poor law report on Mettray (1873), and a parliamentary *Report on Cottage Homes* (1878).[79]

During the 1890s, Henrietta Barnett (1851–1936) and others renewed the assault on the barrack schools. Barnett was active in several movements that focused on housing design and urban planning as solutions to class conflict. She was the co-director of the settlement community Toynbee Hall in East London with her husband, the Reverend Samuel Barnett (1844–1913), and a leader of the garden suburb movement in the early 1900s.[80] From 1875 to 1897, Henrietta Barnett served on the board of managers of Forest Gate District School. Two major disasters at this school—a fire in 1889 that killed twenty-six children and an outbreak of ptomaine poisoning in 1893 that resulted from the use of rotten meat—incited widespread criticism of the barrack system and prompted the Local Government Board to appoint a departmental committee to examine metropolitan poor law schools.[81] The committee was chaired by A. J. Mundella

(1825–97), president of the Board of Trade in William Gladstone's third ministry and longtime education reformer, and included Barnett as a prominent member. Their report helped solidify the strong movement against the aggregation of children in large schools by recommending that the barrack schools be "broken up," that "no more large schools be built," and that new admissions be handled by the expansion of boarding-out programs and institutional cottage homes.[82]

This change in official opinion began to have limited effects. Private charities made the most widespread use of cottage homes. During the year 1877–78, Barnardo housed just over half of all in-care children in cottage homes: 260 girls (51 percent of all Barnardo's institutionalized children) resided at the Girls' Village Home; 253 boys (49 percent of all children) occupied Stepney Causeway, a facility built according to the barrack model. During the 1880s, the proportion of children in Barnardo's family-based institutions increased slightly. Although Barnardo founded additional barrack-style institutions for boys during the late 1870s and 1880s, the Girls' Village Home had more than doubled in size by the early 1880s. By 1885–86, 53 percent of Barnardo's in-care children lived in cottages at the Girls' Village Home or in institutions that housed fewer than forty children in one building.[83] Beginning in 1886, Barnardo increased the proportion of children in family surroundings by boarding-out younger children in village foster homes. In 1895, in testimony before the Mundella committee, he claimed that slightly fewer than one-fifth of the children in his care (including boarded-out children) were in barrack institutions, two-fifths were in cottage homes, and two-fifths were boarded-out.[84]

Poor law authorities were slower to approve the initial costs involved in constructing cottage homes. In 1878, only eight parishes, unions, or school districts in England and Wales had built or planned to build cottage homes for children.[85] The number of poor law institutions structured according to the cottage home system increased to nineteen by 1895 and to twenty-four by 1901–2.[86] Changes within London metropolitan poor law schools best illustrate the growing preference for cottage homes by the turn of the century. In 1894, there were 11,539 in-care children in London poor law schools (as opposed to workhouses, infirmaries, Roman Catholic or other certified schools, the training ship *Exmouth,* and foster homes).[87] Of these children, 90 percent were in large, aggregated institutions and only 10 percent were in London's two groups of cottage homes: the Kensington and Chelsea District School at Banstead and the Shoreditch separate school at Hornchurch.[88] By 1909, however, there were nine metropolitan poor law schools with cottage home facilities. Fifty-seven percent of the children in metropolitan poor law schools were in barrack-style institutions, 39 percent were in cottage homes, and 4 percent were at St. Marylebone's separate school, which operated a mixture of both systems.[89] By the turn of the century, a substantial number of children resided in cottage homes largely as a result of women's growing professional influence as poor law authorities.[90]

"Unfeminine" Masses: Gender, Citizenship, and Individualization

Closer analysis of the critiques of large children's institutions reveals the centrality of the concept of domesticity to these debates. Senior and her supporters asserted that the militaristic barrack schools were doomed to fail in reforming poor children because they were not structured according to the domestic model. The discussion of barrack schools focused overwhelmingly on the condition of girls, often presenting the female child as the model inmate for whom all future policies and institutions should be established. The underlying assumption in the condemnations of mass institutions for girls was that the "normal condition of woman's life is domestic; and that which most closely follows the dictates of nature is almost invariably the most healthy course to pursue."[91] Many reformers—especially women, but also men, such as Barnardo—considered large schools completely inappropriate for girls. Critics of barrack schools characterized them as masculinized spaces that hampered the social development and reformation of pauper girls and ultimately all children. The debates over barrack schools versus cottage homes demonstrated how thoroughly gender ideals had become a key gauge of a child's rise from the pauper class and his or her ultimate development as an individual worthy of citizenship.

The most common criticism of large children's institutions was that they failed to provide girls with the training they needed to become domestic servants, which had long been one of the primary goals of children's philanthropic institutions, but increased in importance during the second half of the century as women became even more involved in child welfare.[92] As F. K. Prochaska has shown, there was an active market for servants from child welfare institutions (and they received exceptionally low wages), but critics of the barrack schools feared that girls from workhouses and mass institutions were completely unprepared for domestic duties in single-family situations.[93] Joanna Hill, who coordinated training for workhouse girls through the Girls' Friendly Society, cautioned:

> The girl may have seen the matron's dinner-table in the Workhouse laid with the ordinary articles, but their names and uses she has not had explained to her. She has seen a large dinner cooked, or perhaps a single chop for an officer, but never a dinner *réchauffé* from yesterday's repast. She has scrubbed a floor, but has had no carpet to shake and put straight; made her bed, but never polished mahogany furniture; washed strong crockery at the Workhouse, but will have many a bitter tear over the unexpected brittleness of the delicate stem of her mistress's best wine-glasses.[94]

A lady from Kent claimed that "[n]o person would come to the Union for servants unless very much in want of them, and then only for servants-of-all-work, at very low wages, not sufficient to buy clothing."[95] On the most basic level, then, reform efforts to improve girls' domestic instruction were an attempt to increase the supply of better-trained servants and to identify respectable employment for poor women. Without proper training, reformers warned, girls would most likely lose their positions and return to the workhouse as adults, after having first attempted to gain an alternative livelihood through prostitution.[96]

Critics of the barrack schools portrayed the girls trained in such institutions as hard, uncontrollable, violent, apathetic, sullen, and unnurturing—traits that contrasted sharply with the middle-class image of working-class respectability, particularly for female servants.[97] Described as "a class proverbial for audacity and shamelessness," pauper girls seemed to contradict all idealized bourgeois feminine qualities.[98] Menella Smedley described the typical girl from poor law schools as "[b]elow average height and development. Well taught in elements of religion, in reading, in writing, and arithmetic. Sullen, violent, and unmanageable in temper. Apathetic when not out of temper. Ignorant of all practical matters, and deficient in aptitude for learning. Self-possessed. Hard. Untruthful. A good-tempered variety is occasionally to be found, but it is very rare."[99]

Reformers who supported Senior's 1874 *Report* dramatized pauper girls' violence as a symbol of their resistance to authority—particularly to fellow servants and mistresses. One of Senior's supporters recounted how a "rather violent" girl broke "a plate on the head of her fellow servant. Another tried to stab the nurse. A third threw herself on the ground when it was attempted to teach her anything." This list of violent behavior eventually ended with the generalization that the "girls were constantly described as seeming like people possessed."[100] Senior likewise recounted how a girl from a London district school had such a "perverse" temper that "the mistress has sometimes tried the experiment of telling her *not* to do the thing she wants to have done, and always with success."[101] In another, more extreme case, the female servant, "violent and obstinate beyond belief, offered to stab her own mother when she came to remonstrate."[102] These commonly accepted representations of the violent nature of girls trained in mass institutions reinforced the view that they were "possessed" by the spirit or will of another, rather than capable as distinct individuals of contributing to the common good.

Another frequent criticism of girls from barrack schools was that they were completely lacking in maternal skills and interest. A female workhouse authority noted that girls raised in the union's large separate school displayed a "strange want of natural affection." When asked why they quit their positions as servants, the girls typically responded, "Oh, there were too many children," or "Oh, I can't suit myself with children."[103] According to female reformers, women trained in mass institutions were even unwilling to care for their own children. They "let their babies fall out of bed, and often take a dislike to them."[104] Critics of barrack schools blamed the girls' lack of nurturing skills on the aggregate structure and routine of the institutions, which made it impossible for officials "to individualise and influence the girls under their care" with affection and personal example.[105]

The alleged lack of domestic bonds among the poor in general was also a common target. Florence Hill reported that adult workhouse inmates raised in barrack schools described their own mothers in only the harshest terms: "My mother left me in a ditch"; "Mine ran off when I was three"; "Mine was always drunk, and I don't know anything about her."[106] Such cases led one female workhouse employee to conclude that there was "a grave and shocking want among the future mothers of the poor; and how, but by placing these poor things in families, are they ever to develop that God-implanted instinct, which, in these girls, I find totally absent?"[107]

On the whole, critics of large institutions blamed the girls' hardness, violence, and lack of mothering on the male-dominated, masculine model of the barrack schools, which did nothing to replace the domestic life that the children allegedly lacked in their natural families. The "monster" schools, as Menella Smedley termed them, came to represent boundless, out-of-control disorder— the direct opposite of what Tufnell and his colleagues claimed was an efficient military model for creating good citizens, be they male or female.[108] The very structure of the large, mass institutions seemed antithetical to the girls' development. A writer for the *Westminster Review* declared, "Females never mass well, either in schools, orphanages, homes, or institutions of any kind, whether as girls or as adults."[109] Barnardo expressed the sentiment best of all. "I do not know why it is," he testified before the Mundella committee, "but when a number of females are massed together, girls or women—it is the same in large factories—they seem to re-act upon each other in a degrading way." Although the massing of boys could develop their sense of "public spirit," the massing of girls produced public disorder and personal degradation.[110] As one poor law official claimed, "very large assemblages of girls are unfeminine."[111]

Some critics argued that domestic arrangements were essential for the development of all children, not only girls, and focused on the lack of individual attention in the barrack schools, making these institutions sound as if they reproduced rather than cured the social ills of urban slums. Many of the practices in large institutions did tend to blur the common divisions of gender and age. Workhouse authorities dressed inmates in uniforms and gave boys and girls similarly styled cropped haircuts upon entering.[112] Within large institutions, there was often no special treatment or cultivation of individual tastes and needs. Unable to remember hundreds of children's names, authorities often simply referred to each as "child." Children received the regulation portion of food, regardless of the "size, appetite, taste, or physical condition" of the individual child.[113]

Critics of the barrack schools argued that the effects of such uniform treatment were soul destroying. The typical girl, according to Smedley, "takes no interest in anything, she cares for nothing, she is like an old person."[114] Barnardo likewise claimed that endless routine, a "hideous uniform and cropped hair," and heavy shoes "changed[d] the natural lightness of the step of youth to the shuffle of old age."[115] Reformers frequently wrote that a family setting encouraged the development of individuals, whereas the "herding together of children" like animals in overcrowded schools promoted nothing but their identification with the aggregate pauper class.[116] By focusing on issues of individuality and, unlike promoters of barrack schools, applying bourgeois expectations of idealized childhood to working-class children as early as the 1870s, these reformers were quite radical. They condemned the necessary discipline of the large schools as stultifying, and instead called for the cultivation of youthful identity and experience at a time when few thought that working-class children should be distinguished from adults.

At the same time, in comparison to Tufnell and his supporters, the critics of barrack schools revealed a heightened fear of class disorder by linking the design of large schools with the production of children who were physically and morally unfit to become English citizens. The spread of disease was a primary concern, and large segments of the reports on these schools concentrated on issues of hygiene and crowding. Opponents of the barrack schools blamed the spread of disease not only on the presence of casual children, but also on the spatial design of these institutions, in which hundreds of children ate together, bathed together, and slept together in overcrowded conditions comparable to the worst slums. Communal washing practices were particularly suspect. School directors might praise the "jet systems" used for washing in large schools as models of efficiency (see figure 18), but critics viewed them as "rather a barbarous system." Children bathed at troughs like animals and sometimes "share[d] the towels promiscuously," thus spreading eye and skin diseases.[117]

For many observers, the barrack schools appeared to reproduce rather than eradicate the physical and moral ills of London's overcrowded slums, turning out youths no more fit for citizenship than their uninstitutionalized peers. To Senior and her supporters, the children reared according to the "unnaturally" uniform and dull routine of mass institutions were "half-formed creatures," "dull, sullen, and mechanical."[118] "One feels," wrote Florence Hill, "as though these children should be little automata instead of human beings, to obey all these clockwork arrangements."[119] Other critics echoed industrial terms, referring to child inmates as "human machines," "a mere cog in an engine of many wheels," "parts of a machine," and "automatons."[120] According to one writer for *Cornhill Magazine,* the final result of mass institutions was to produce children who were "not individuals, but children of the State, machine-made paupers growing up for the market."[121] In the eyes of new generations of reformers, the mass, unspecialized, factory-like architectural spaces of the barrack schools failed to develop recognized forms of domesticity and individuality, the main qualities that would dissociate poor children from the mass of paupers and prepare them for inclusion as citizens in the English community.

By making the issue of individuality one of the key points of the debate, critics of barrack schools demonstrated how age, gender, and class identity were intertwined. Implicit in these discussions of individuality was the notion that the environment, not heredity or free will, created the individual. The child's process of individuation did not come from within; it was imposed from without, as the reformers' common use of the transitive verb "to individualise" implied.[122] In many ways, however, the cottage homes were just as factory-like as the barrack schools. They had similarly strict daily schedules, and their primary goal was to produce good citizens and qualified, deferential laborers. The main difference was that the re-created "family" in the cottage homes served to naturalize the children's transition into their roles as artisans and servants while at the same time it further delegitimized the children's biological family structures.

Family Cottages and Model Village Homes

The assumption underlying the architectural arrangements of model villages and cottage homes was that spatial designs could shape the individual's identity and regulate his or her role in the larger society. In England, proposals for reform colonies such as William Booth's Salvation Army scheme became increasingly popular as means to contain and incorporate the poor into the English community. Model villages for poor children stemmed from a more general European trend to build juvenile reformatories along domestic lines, such as Rauhe Hause in Germany and Mettray in France, which, as Felix Driver has demonstrated, were important models for mid- to late-nineteenth-century British child advocates.[123] The children's villages represented miniature societies, seemingly self-sufficient gated communities that generally included schoolrooms, a chapel, carpentry, shoemaking, ironsmith, and other workshops for boys, laundry and cooking facilities for girls, a village green often surrounded by the children's cottages, and a larger superintendent's or director's house. Reformers argued that cottage homes in open, green spaces away from central London and other cities were the ideal environment in which to "depauperise the children" and train them as artisans and servants.[124] Cottage homes were the cradle of the citizen. They evoked a pastoral, village ideal founded on hierarchical loyalties in sharp contrast to the uncontrollable, undifferentiated urban slums and the factory-like, monstrous barrack schools.

The family cottages simultaneously reinforced a specific version of domesticity and unwittingly undermined the concept of natural domesticity. In spite of repeated demands for institutions based on natural relationships, the domestic arrangements in model villages were artificial in many ways and based on the negation of the children's biological families.[125] For example, describing the case of one child in his Girls' Village Home, Barnardo recounted how she was "removed from a lodging-house and from the care of a tramp whom she called mother, and brought into a cottage home. . . ." Within this home, he continued, "[s]he becomes at once a member of a *family*," surrounded by a "dozen and a half" other girls all under the supervision of the cottage "mother."[126] Left unmentioned was the unusual size this new family—eighteen girls—and the fact that their new mother was of a distinctly higher class and had no legal or biological relation to them.

Reformers seemed never to compare the communal sleeping arrangements in family-based institutions with the overcrowded sleeping areas in urban slums or barrack schools. Poor law relief officers often did not allow children to return to homes deemed overcrowded and unsanitary,[127] but the children at the Girls' Village Home routinely slept four to six in a room.[128] In one of Barnardo's fund-raising appeals, the rhetorical dichotomy between overcrowded, promiscuous, undomestic slums and ordered model villages completely dissolved. Requesting donations to build a new school at the Girls' Village Home, Barnardo described how the current school buildings were in converted stables and coach houses: "the physical and nervous health of the children has already suffered seriously from overcrowding in the ill-lit and ill-ventilated structure now being used as a schoolroom," which by 1891 accommodated 1,200 children instead of the 500 for which it was built.[129]

The re-created domestic order in cottage homes demonstrated the belief of many reformers that notions of family and home were more dependent on class than on blood relations. The class and social positions of the cottage parents supported their privileged domestic status. At Banstead, the first house fathers came from the respectable poor—a baker, plumber/glazier, carpenter, tailor, smith, shoemaker, gardener, and drillmaster. These men were artisans who provided role models and industrial training for the boys.[130] Some institutions also recruited cottage mothers from the working class, generally unmarried women or widows of respectable artisans. Barnardo, however, preferred evangelical abstainers, "educated women, *ladies,*" believing that "the advantages of culture and of fine feeling are inestimable in influencing the girls we rescue."[131]

To accentuate these class and cultural differences spatially, each cottage at the Girls' Village Home contained a separate bedroom for the "mother," in addition to "a separate sitting-room of her own, a private *sanctum* suitably furnished, whither she can retreat for those moments of quietude so necessary for one fulfilling her important duties."[132] (There is no mention of such a distinct space for house "fathers" at Banstead and other cottage homes that recruited men.) This need for private, domestic, specifically female space reflected contemporary trends in middle-class housing.[133] Perhaps more important, this arrangement accustomed the girls to the living conditions that they could anticipate in their expected role as servants: the layout of the bourgeois home and the authority of the female mistress who "ruled" by demanding "loving obedience."[134] Cut off from the external world, the model villages used the domestic arrangement of space and persons to teach children their social roles. A visitor to the Girls' Village Home noted, "The furniture of their rooms, the arrangement of their cottages, are all such as they are likely to meet with in domestic service."[135] Each cottage contained, in addition to the bedrooms and "mother's" sitting room, a living room, playroom, kitchen, and scullery, "such as a girl would meet in service of a medium character."[136]

Supporters of the family system praised cottage homes for dispensing with the worst symbols of routinized institutional life: cropped hair for girls, uniforms, and identification numbers assigned to each child.[137] Yet, clearly, the cottages had a routine of their own that was reinforced by the architectural design. A visitor to the Girls' Village Home remarked how "[e]ach small domestic duty is performed over and over again, till each child learns to be quite an adept at cooking potatoes, or cleaning out a room, or washing and dressing a younger one; and takes pride in her work, so as to be able to do it *as well as Mother.*"[138] According to a former mother at the Girls' Village Home, "The control of the 'Mother' over her household and its internal arrangement is undisputed, and her aim is to train the girls in ways of goodness and practical usefulness, more especially for domestic service."[139]

Parents and children alike generally valued the training they received in welfare institutions.[140] However, by presenting model village homes as idealized visions of domesticity, in spite of their glaring artificialities, reformers naturalized the children's social role as laborers. The contained, clearly divided spaces of model villages presented an organic, anti-industrial model for society, in which poor children were safely incorporated as mediators between the "private sanctum" of their superiors, the house mothers, and the controlled public areas of the community—the village green, the church, and the school.

These naturalized domestic spaces promoted the recognition of poor children as individuals and potential citizens separate from the mass of paupers. Florence Hill argued that the aggregation of large groups of children in the barrack schools prevented the children from "being completely individualized," but the family model provided "individualization, and mutual affection and responsibility." She, like other critics of barrack schools, believed that the domestic union was the "primary group of the body politic."[141] Describing how domestic arrangements contributed to civic identity formation, one female supervisor of children boarded-out in cottage homes imagined she witnessed "'pauper children' becoming Lizzies and Katies, running across the garden." "Lizzie's" transformation from an anonymous pauper child into an individual (suitably located in a garden) with a name was especially marked by her development of nurturing interests appropriate to a servant. "Why, she have all wakened up like," commented her foster mother. "[S]he du sing now o' mornings, and she begins to curl her hair. She's terrible fond o' children. . . . She took to Mrs. Parks' little gel from the first. . . . And Lizzie she du love children. I took her to a prayer-meeting out a-field the other day, and there she gits a baby in her lap, and nurses it a' the time."[142]

Drawing a similar relationship between the development of civic identity and demonstrations of idealized femininity for servants, a visitor to the Girls' Village Home unfavorably compared a girl raised in a workhouse school with the girls at the Village Home. Although the girl from the workhouse was more intelligent in academic matters, she was ignorant in all areas of housework and completely lacking in deference to her mistress: "she knew a smattering of geography, a jumble of history and poetry, but such an amount of bad language and viciousness that we were horrified at her knowledge." The visitor lamented that the "stolid," "indifferent," "insolent" child "stared absently" and "merely acted like a machine" when providing services. The visitor concluded that if the girl "had been subjected to the refining and humanising effects of Home surroundings, [she] might have developed into a thoroughly useful maid."[143] To be counted among humanity, for this female child, depended upon being a good maid, and it was through the regulated structure of the re-created domestic home that she might have acquired the proper attributes. The visitor further explained that Barnardo's village mothers carefully trained the children's "individuality of character" into "usefulness for the benefit of the whole community."[144] In the end, this definition of individuality rested not on ideas of free agency or self-interest, but on the children's perceived usefulness to the greater community as workers who expressed pride in their work and affection for their employers.

Conclusion

When Mary Carpenter (1807–77), leader of the ragged school movement, advocate for juvenile delinquents, campaigner for changes in Indian education, and prison reformer, testified before the 1861 Select Committee on the Education of Destitute Children, she was an influential opponent to the rising view that the homes of the urban poor lacked domesticity. Carpenter asserted that poverty was a monetary rather than a moral condition, and she highlighted the underlying associations among poverty, domesticity, and national citizenship. In particular, Carpenter objected to the Select Committee's accepted definition of ragged day schools as "schools voluntarily established and maintained for children who have no home or no reputable home." The expression "with no home," rebutted Carpenter, "is utterly inapplicable to ragged schools, because if children have no home they cannot attend ragged schools, which are merely day schools. The second term, or those with 'no reputable home,' is an *un-English* prejudging of the home of the children."[145] Although Carpenter was among the earliest advocates of applying domestic models to children's reformatories, her repeated rejection of the broad attack on the homes of the poor as un-English recalled older traditions associating the sanctity of the home with the rights of all freeborn English citizens. In its conclusion, the Select Committee supported Carpenter's defense of the poor, declaring that the existing alternatives to a national system of education, primarily residential industrial schools and reformatories for the poor, were unsatisfactory because they involved an interference with the child's "personal liberty, and his withdrawal from the care of his natural guardians, [which] can only be regarded as a necessary evil."[146]

In the following decades, however, child welfare workers continued to attack the domesticity, and therefore the legitimacy, of poor homes and families. By the 1880s, when support for children's institutions based on the "family system" was secure, reformers overwhelmingly depicted institutions, not parents, as the primary source of domesticity and civic training among the poor. Thus, the Earl of Cairns, president of Barnardo's Homes, could reject with confidence all proposals for poor children's day schools on the grounds that "whatever good is derived from the school is obliterated during the night and the evening when the children return—I will not say *home,* for it seldom is a home they go to, but to the place where they live." Cairns summarized contemporary policies: "our first principle is to take them [children] away from where we find them, to take them out of the surroundings in which they are placed, and then to bring them, not to a barrack, not to a great infirmary or asylum, where they will all be massed together under one roof, but to bring them to something which will as nearly as possible resemble the home which they perhaps have never known, or early lost."[147] Whereas Carpenter argued in 1861 that protecting the English love of liberty required that the homes of all classes—however poor—be respected as legitimate, by the 1870s and 1880s reformers readily dismissed the rights of poor parents to oversee the care of their children.

The increased popularity of family-based institutions over barrack schools corresponded with the growing criticisms of family relations among the poor during the 1860s and 1870s. The semantic conflict over the status of poor dwellings as legitimate homes exemplified the vexed position of the poor within mid- to late-nineteenth-century constructions of the English community, as well as the essential role of the idealized bourgeois home and family as fundamental units of the nation. Despite Victorian exaltations of the family and the home, early welfare and charity programs were aimed (often unsuccessfully) at under-mining the validity and affective bonds of poor families. The promotion of model villages and family cottages for children went hand in hand with the cut-back in outdoor relief during the 1870s, which had made it easier for families to remain intact without resort to philanthropic or poor law institutions for children. By the 1870s, social welfare programs that promoted poor children's integration into the body politic often called for the public erasure of their biological families and the creation of new institutional domestic models. Allegedly without domestic havens of their own, poor children required family-based institutions to teach them key social values: maternalism, affection, deference, individualism, and citizenship.

The preference for family cottages and model villages over barrack schools also demonstrated the growing influence of female reformers, who sought to apply expertise gained through charitable work to state programs for poor children by stressing the importance of women's domestic knowledge. Idealized, re-created domestic models became the primary means to separate poor children from their impoverished surroundings and to naturalize their incorporation into the political body as newly defined individuals. The popularity of children's institutions based on domestic models was the result of middle-class women's growing influence as philanthropists and poor law authorities, which coincided with a greater appreciation of the importance of the home among middle-class men and women. In writing and lobbying campaigns, female reformers validated their expanding public duties by referring to their special domestic knowledge, bringing the language of gender to debates about social reform and stressing that the bourgeois home should serve as the model for all social and political structures.[148] Well-connected women, such as Twining, Cobbe, Senior, the Hill sisters, and Barnett, along with prominent men, such as Barnardo, structured the debates about children's institutions according to gender differences: the militaristic barrack schools versus the domestic family cottages. One of the effects of emphasizing gender in these debates was that domestic ideals became increasingly important measures of poor children's reform and, moreover, of their individual subjectivity as defined by the acceptance of communal values.

Lastly, the reformers' association of domesticity with citizenship suggests the importance of interpreting changes in social welfare within the context of political history. The preference for family cottages over barrack schools first became strong in the 1870s—likely in reaction to public anxiety caused by the wider suffrage resulting from the 1867 Reform Act.[149] Pastoral ideals of deferential communities (as defined in contrast to the undifferentiated urban mob) implied a desire for stability in the face of major challenges to and modifications of the political system. The children's model villages promoted not only social reform but also political stability by defending the organic, hierarchical ideal for all English society, where the rich and the poor replaced industrial class conflict, represented by Barnardo's fistfights with female factory workers and the state-dependent automatons produced by the barrack schools, with domestic affection and deference. Thus, as the Second Reform Act increased suffrage for a new class of urban men, the arguments of child welfare workers revived and modified long-standing conflicts over the construction of English citizenship. Whereas reformers like Mary Carpenter, who remained wary of state interference, held on to notions of individual liberty and parental rights as the primary values of citizenship, it was more common for reformers of the 1870s to disregard the rights of poor parents, representing them as threats to the political body who should be "disenfranchised"— that is, striped of their parental rights—or carted off to the Yorkshire moors to serve in work camps. Even as supporters of cottage homes for poor children made necessary, invaluable improvements in child welfare, they did so in part by relying on a hierarchical construction of Englishness based not on individual rights but on class-based notions of domesticity, thereby facilitating the aid of poor children by depriving their parents of what others considered basic English rights.

CHAPTER 3

The Parents of
"Nobody's Children"

FAMILY BACKGROUNDS AND
THE CAUSES OF POVERTY

In 1896, the journalist William T. Stead
wrote a biographical sketch of Barnardo in which he extolled the child philanthropist as "the father of 'Nobody's Children,'" the head of "the largest family
in the world."[1] Stead's title and article implied that the children's parents played
no role in Barnardo's work. The representative child in Stead's sketch was the
homeless and orphaned (and Roman Catholic) Jim Jarvis, Barnardo's "first
arab."[2] In the place of parents, public and private institutions took on the role of
teaching children their familial identities and civil duties. Yet there was an
important contradiction in Victorian philanthropic and state homes for poor
children: although reformers generally described the children in these institutions as being orphaned or deserted by abusive parents, the children often had
living parents who struggled to maintain contact. This chapter investigates the
parentage of institutionalized children and explores the reasons parents turned
to residential facilities for help. Rather than being "nobody's children," most
children in institutions came from families that had at least one parent and that
were often deeply integrated in their local communities.

Popular images of poor children as waifs and strays have had a tremendous
impact on child welfare literature. Only in the 1990s, after the Barnardo foundation
opened its case histories to researchers, has the British media brought widespread
attention to the practice of separating parents and children.[3] Many earlier studies of
poor children tended to accept uncritically the public images and narratives presented by Victorian reformers. The omission of the children's parents is especially
evident in the early biographies of Barnardo, several of which took their titles
directly from Stead's 1896 biographical sketch.[4] The most popular of these early
biographies was by A. E. Williams, who served as Barnardo's personal secretary
from 1898 until Barnardo's death in 1905. Williams promoted Barnardo's mythic
reputation as a heroic "St. George" fighting on behalf of otherwise abandoned children.[5] Any discussion of parents in these accounts was largely based on Barnardo's

own promotional writings. When mentioned at all, the parents in these early works represented dangerous "dragons" to be vanquished.

More recent critical studies of Barnardo's homes acknowledge that many of the institutionalized children were not actually orphans. In her account of Victorian child emigration schemes, Gillian Wagner notes that fewer than a third of the children admitted to philanthropic children's institutions were "total orphans," even though the institutions rarely referred to parents in their fund-raising literature and commonly described children as "waifs and strays" and "street arabs."[6] In her history of Barnardo's institutions, June Rose describes how their policy of concealing all information from children about parents began under the direction of Barnardo and continued until the 1960s. According to Rose, Barnardo's popular narratives of "rescuing orphans or abandoned children from a ruinous background and restoring them to respectability and a religious faith" were "highly coloured" from the start.[7] Although Wagner and Rose acknowledge the existence of parents, their works maintain an institutional and biographical focus. Wagner discusses children's parents only in the context of select, highly public custody battles filed on behalf of Roman Catholic children against Barnardo in the late 1880s and 1890s. In these cases, the Catholic Church appears to be the active agent seeking custody, while the children's parents emerge as abusive and neglectful.[8] Although Wagner and Rose present important information concerning the parentage of institutionalized children, their heavy use of Barnardo's own writings and their primary attention to the institution have the overall effect of reinforcing the view that parents were not involved in the decisions about their children's welfare.[9]

Like histories of child philanthropy, studies of poor law institutions often ignore parents' roles in finding external aid for their children. For example, in *The Workhouse: A Social History,* Norman Longmate claims that most poor law child inmates were orphans.[10] Similarly, the only extensive history of workhouse children, written by Frank Crompton, focuses on those orphaned and deserted children who were long-term inmates.[11] Crompton provides a valuable history of the local implementation of the New Poor Law in regard to children and the bureaucrats who administered relief. Yet his concentration on the long-term population of orphaned and deserted children within workhouses led him to conclude that these places were "total institutions" in Erving Goffman's sense.[12] Workhouse populations, however, were far less static than Crompton's conclusion suggests. Between 40 and 60 percent of the children in Crompton's study entered workhouses for only temporary stays, returning intermittently or permanently to their families and communities.[13] These transient children constituted a significant proportion of workhouse populations, but their experiences—and the experiences of their parents—do not influence Crompton's overall conclusions or theoretical models. Clearly, the omission and reproach of parents in reformers' public narratives have had a lasting effect on histories of child welfare, which by and large repeat and reinforce the view that parents played mainly negative roles.

As scholars of a wide variety of national and temporal contexts begin to reevaluate the relationship between poor families and children's welfare services and institutions, there is an increased interest in the parents of poor children. Some of the first studies to challenge the popular representations of "nobody's children" are by historians of child emigration from Britain to Canada and other parts of the empire, who are concerned with retelling this story from the perspectives of the children.[14] Like Wagner, Joy Parr notes that only one-third of the eighty thousand child emigrants sent from Britain to Canada between 1868 and 1925 were actually orphans.[15] Although Parr focuses primarily on child emigration policies and the experiences of children after they arrived in Canada, she also briefly examines the hardships that led parents to consent to the emigration of their children. Rather than neglect, it was the eventual inability of kinship networks to sustain individual families through a series of crises—"deaths, illnesses, quarrels and lost jobs"—that most often caused parents to send their children overseas.[16]

In addition to these works on child emigrants and migrants, a number of recent studies have reevaluated the populations within institutions for orphaned, abandoned, and destitute children. Several historians have elucidated the complexities of orphanages, not only demonstrating that many of the children in these institutions were not actually full orphans but also examining parents' interaction with the institutions.[17] In her work on juvenile institutions in eighteenth-century Seville, Valentina Tikoff concludes that some parents, not all of whom were destitute, used charitable institutions publicized as orphanages in a variety of ways, including as naval training and reformatory centers for their children.[18]

Much of the recent scholarship on how parents strategically placed their children in orphanages concentrates on institutions in the United States during the nineteenth and twentieth centuries. Judith Dulberger, for example, concludes that almost 45 percent of the children at the Albany Orphan Asylum in the 1880s and 1890s came from two-parent households, and another 40 percent had one living parent. Parents used the asylum "for temporary refuge during times of destitution and family distress," with the long-term goal of keeping families intact.[19] Timothy Hacsi comes to similar conclusions in his broad, comparative study of orphan asylums in the United States.[20]

In the English context, Lynn Hollen Lees provides the most innovative framework for understanding the interactions of poor families with state welfare institutions. Lees maintains that poor families regularly turned to poor law resources as part of their daily survival strategies. Like other recent scholars working in different contexts, Lees finds that although poor families were broken up in the short term by resorting to institutions for assistance, in the long term they were often able to maintain their family connections.[21]

My account of English child welfare institutions is a contribution to these reevaluations.[22] It is true that in some cases parents were abusive or absent, traumatizing their children in ways worse than even the most sensational philanthropic tracts recounted. In far more cases, however, parents sought out poor law or charitable services and used these institutions as part of their family strategies to survive short-term crises, to overcome longer-term life-cycle stresses, and, as I will explain in chapter 5, to secure important job training for their older children.[23] By necessity, poor law and charitable institutions were integral to parents' coping strategies and essential to the survival of many families struggling with extreme economic hardship.

Institutional Records as Sources

Before I develop these points in greater detail, it is first necessary to consider the intricacies of using the children's case histories and admission and discharge log books that are the main sources for this chapter. On an empirical level, these sources provide invaluable information about the daily workings and clientele of state and charitable children's institutions. Although the details differ depending on the specific year and institution, the poor law log books generally recorded basic information related to each child: name, age, legitimacy, religion, name and address of parent or nearest relative, dates of admission and discharge, the institution to which the child was sent, and, in some cases, the place and circumstances of the child's discharge. Children's admissions registers for Barnardo's institutions document similar information, although without the consistency and completeness of the poor law records.[24] Even more detailed than the poor law records and Barnardo's admissions registers are the Barnardo précis books, written after welfare officers made more involved inquiries concerning each child.[25] These books include a column titled "remarks by the director," where a brief history of the child's circumstances before admission was recorded. Taken together, these registers provide detailed information about the children's family backgrounds and indicate that parents were much more involved in decisions about their children's welfare than the popular fund-raising literature acknowledged.

On another level, it is important to note that children's case histories, like the fund-raising literature, had their own conventions of narrative and style.[26] Welfare workers created these documents for institutional purposes, and the records therefore reflect the values and practical workings of the institutions. Administrators asked certain questions and not others. For example, Barnardo's admission registers were particularly concerned with the children's physical appearance. The height of each child was one of the most consistently recorded facts. A separate column listed the locations of any vaccination marks, and another noted further distinguishing marks on the body. Notations such as "tattoo on left wrist," "mole on right breast," and "scald on left thigh" reveal a careful mapping of the body as potential testimony toward a personal history as well as a future means of identification and regulation.[27] There were columns for the children's hair and eye color, and another for the color of their complexions, categorized as "pale," "fresh," "fair," "ruddy," "olive," "brown," or "dark." Brief physical descriptions of the children's dress upon arrival described their degree of poverty and located them on a moral scale of respectability: "respectably," "tidily," "tidily & amply," "shabby," "shabby but clean," "ragged," "very ragged & dirty," "filthy dirty ragged." Like the color of their skin, the state of the children's clothing featured prominently in the popular literature and imagery as a symbol of their original degradation and subsequent transformation. From the very beginning, Barnardo's admissions records were much more concerned with the children's physical appearance, and the symbolic interpretation of this appearance, than with their family backgrounds. These admission and discharge registers were constructed by welfare institutions, and thus any empirical or factual data contained within them carry inferences of how those institutions conceptualized poverty in Victorian society.

Compared with the brief poor law records and Barnardo's admissions registers, the paragraph-long case histories in the Barnardo précis books contain even more complicated layers of narrative.[28] Each brief history in the director's remarks column most likely summarized a series of interviews with the child and available relatives, friends, workhouse officials, and past employers. Sections of the written director's remarks include direct quotations, presumably taken from earlier interviews. In some instances, the case histories drew directly on literary conventions, thus further complicating the levels of narrative. For example, children's comments at times appear in first-person dialect, as in the case of a seventeen-year-old boy who was said to be "sleeping 'in passages mos'ly, 'cos I can't get enough money for a bed.'"[29] As in Barnardo's fund-raising literature, the use of dialect here immediately distinguishes the speaker as someone of a different class from the interviewer. Such direct use of narrative conventions in the case records suggests that they must be used with caution when attempting to discern details about welfare applicants as distinct from the impressions of welfare officials.

My goal in this chapter is to use children's institutional sources in a multi-layered fashion, first by reading admission registers and initial case reports for details about the children's family backgrounds and ties to the community. The following section surveys the parentage of children in London poor law district schools and Barnardo's homes. The subsequent section offers a closer examination of the reasons why children entered residential institutions. Unlike the public literature on child welfare, the case records confirm that lack of affordable housing, unemployment, illness, the death of one parent, and the strain of young children on the family economy—not alcoholism or wanton cruelty—were the main factors that led to applications for assistance. Parents unable to manage children "beyond parental control" also turned to welfare institutions for help. Lastly, in addition to using the institutional records to reconstruct information about children's family backgrounds, I propose that the very narrative quality of case histories provides important clues about the relationships among children, parents, and officials that are essential for understanding the practical workings of welfare institutions. Contrary to the popular literature, the case histories rarely narrate a story with clear villains and victims or offer a sense of final resolution.

TABLE 3.1 *Parentage of All Permanent Barnardo's Admissions, 1898–1925*

Year	Both Parents Alive		Only Mother Living		Only Father Living		Orphans		Total
	N	*%*	*N*	*%*	*N*	*%*	*N*	*%*	*Total*
1898	260	11	1,183	49	314	13	649	27	2,406
1899	312	10	1,582	53	398	13	719	24	3,011
1900	277	10	1,430	50	272	9	900	31	2,879
1901									
1902	540	15	1,633	47	494	14	834	24	3,501
1903	537	13	2,140	52	534	13	867	21	4,078
1904									
1905	310	13	1,180	49	312	13	610	25	2,412
1906									
1907	387	18	1,077	51	294	14	353	17	2,111
1908	308	16	985	51	244	13	400	21	1,937
1909	372	18	1,096	52	277	13	375	18	2,120
1910	276	12	1,201	54	280	12	486	22	2,243
1911	260	16	890	55	169	10	311	19	1,630
1912	203	17	590	49	136	11	284	23	1,213
1913	167	16	526	50	114	11	253	24	1,060
1914	173	17	544	53	109	11	203	20	1,029
1915	297	25	564	48	161	14	162	14	1,184
1916	363	30	536	44	144	12	163	14	1,206
1917									
1918									
1919									
1920	134	10	853	63	136	10	222	17	1,345
1921	121	9	891	66	111	8	226	17	1,349
1922	140	10	859	64	128	9	224	17	1,351
1923	212	17	736	58	140	11	191	15	1,279
1924	213	15	857	58	185	13	211	14	1,466
1925	233	17	801	60	136	10	173	13	1,343

Source: Compiled from Barnardo's Annual Reports, 1898–1925, Barnardo Archive, D239/A3/1/33–60, ULLSCA.

They were by nature ongoing and incomplete, suggesting a process of negotiation between applicants and officials. Above all, the admissions registers and case histories display a remarkable compassion for parents and children as they highlight the extreme instability of life among the poor.

Family Backgrounds

Only a minority of the children in English public and private welfare institutions were true orphans. According to Barnardo's annual reports from the late 1890s through the early 1900s, the proportion of long-term child inmates who were complete orphans never reached more than one-third of all admissions (table 3.1).[30] From 1898 until the First World War, on average just under a quarter of all children admitted to Barnardo's for long-term stays were orphans. The proportion of orphans decreased significantly during the war, when Barnardo's opened its doors to the children of soldiers fighting abroad, and remained relatively low (under one-fifth of all admissions) in the 1920s. In other words, from 1898 to the First World War, a majority of Barnardo's long-term child admissions had at least one living parent, and this majority reached a high of 86 percent during the war as mothers struggled to provide for their families.

Although comparable data is not available for child admissions before 1898, analysis of Barnardo's case history samples demonstrates similar family backgrounds (table 3.2).[31] Out of the samples of 507 children admitted to Barnardo's in March 1886, January 1887, January 1891, and January 1895, the percentage of children who were total orphans ranged from lows of 14–19 percent in 1886, 1891, and 1895 to a high of 27–30 percent in 1887. The exceptionally high percentage of orphans for the January 1887 sample (though still a minority) is explained by Barnardo's recruiting methods for that month. More than one-third of the admissions for January 1887 arrived after one of Barnardo's East End tea meetings. These admissions tended to be older male youths, generally in their late teens but some as old as twenty-one, who came to the meetings on their own and were more likely to be orphans.[32]

In addition to orphans, Barnardo admissions included children whose parents were both missing or had practically abandoned them. For example, in the late 1880s a mother and father emigrated to Brisbane, Australia, taking with them only four of their eight children. The parents left the other four children in Mr. W. Austin's Home in London under the partial guidance of a family friend. Two of the children soon ran away and moved to another home for working youths; the remaining two arrived at Barnardo's upon the closure of Austin's Home in 1891.[33]

In other cases, the background of the missing parents was much more vague. For example, A.H., a seven-year-old girl, came to Barnardo's in 1887 after her guardian's death. The girl's father, "a seaman, [had] not [been] heard-of since 1883." Her mother, "a prostitute, disappeared about four years ago, leaving [the] chil[d] at her lodgings."[34] Such examples of a child's desertion by

TABLE 3.2   *Parentage of Barnardo Admissions, March 1886, January 1887, January 1891, January 1895*

	Percentage of All Cases (N = 507)	Percentage after Excluding Cases with No Information Reported on		
		Father (N = 474)	*Mother (N = 464)*	*Father and Mother (N = 461)*
Two parents/stepparents alive:				
Both parents alive	11	12	12	12
Father dead, mother and stepfather alive	3	3	3	3
Mother dead, father and stepmother alive	4	4	4	4
Total	18	20	20	20
Lone mother:				
Father dead	20	22	22	22
Father missing/ deserted/ whereabouts unknown	3	3	3	3
Illegitimate child, father unknown/no contact with father/father unmentioned	8	8	9	9
No information about father reported	0		0	
Total	31	33	34	34
Lone father:				
Mother dead	12	13	13	13
Mother missing/ deserted/ whereabouts unknown	1	1	1	1
No information about mother reported	2	2		
Total	15	16	14	14
Both parents dead or missing				
Mother dead; father missing/ deserted/whereabouts unknown	3	3	3	3
Mother dead; illegitimate child, father unknown/no contact with father/father unmentioned	2	2	2	2
Mother dead; no information about father reported	0		0	

(continued)

Table 3.2   Parentage of Barnardo Admissions, March 1886, January 1887, January 1891, January 1895 *(continued)*

	Percentage of All Cases (N = 507)	Percentage after Excluding Cases with No Information Reported on		
		Father *(N = 474)*	*Mother* *(N = 464)*	*Father and Mother* *(N = 461)*
Father dead; mother missing/ deserted/whereabouts unknown	2	2	2	2
Father dead; no information about mother reported	0	0		
Both parents dead	19	20	20	20
Mother missing/deserted/ where-abouts unknown; no information about father reported	0		0	
Father missing/deserted/ where-abouts unknown; no information about mother reported	0	0		
Both parents missing/deserted/ whereabouts unknown	3	3	3	3
No information about mother or father reported	6			
Total	34	30	30	30

Source: Compiled from Précis Books, vols. 1, 5, 10, In-care children's records, Barnardo Archive, D239/D/2/2a/104, 108, 113, ULLSCA.

Note: The percentages for each category are rounded to the nearest whole number.

both parents accounted for a minority of the admissions, on average not more than 3 percent of all sample cases. More common were instances in which one parent had deserted his or her child after the other parent had died (table 3.2). Still, the total percentages of children who were without mother and father, including orphans, were 33 percent, 43 percent, 29 percent, and 25 percent, respectively, for the 1886, 1887, 1891, and 1895 samples of Barnardo's admissions.[35]

In general, the proportion of orphaned and deserted children in poor law schools was very similar to that in Barnardo's institutions. Like Barnardo's admissions, most of the children in poor law district schools had at least one parent living in the area. In 1877, 35 percent of all child inmates in London's five existing district schools were orphaned or deserted.[36] That percentage declined toward the end of the century as the continued cutbacks on outdoor relief forced many parents to seek institutional aid for their children.[37] The director of the Kensington and Chelsea District School at Banstead testified that

TABLE 3.3 *Family Background of Child Admissions to the Kensington and Chelsea District School (Banstead), 1896–97*

	Child Admissions	
	(N)	*(%)*
Child has two living parents with known address(es)	14	7.0
Both parents at residential address	2	1.0
Parent(s) in prison	3	1.5
Father in workhouse, mother in residence	2	1.0
Father in asylum, mother in residence	7	3.5
Child of lone mother with known address (father listed as dead, deserted, or no information given)	113	55.9
Mother at residential address	89	44.1
Mother in workhouse	12	5.9
Mother in infirmary	11	5.4
Mother in service	1	0.5
Child of lone father with known address (mother listed as dead, deserted, or no information given)	28	13.9
Father at residential address	4	2.0
Father in workhouse	13	6.4
Father in infirmary	7	3.5
Father in prison	2	1.0
Father in asylum	1	0.5
Father on ship	1	0.5
Child has no parents listed as nearest relative	47	23.4
Parents listed as dead, deserted, or of unknown address	22	10.9
Sibling(s) listed as only nearest relative (not including siblings in poor law schools)	9	4.5
Grandparent(s) listed as nearest relative	6	3.0
Aunt/uncle listed as nearest relative	3	1.5
"Friend" listed as nearest relative	1	0.5
Blank entry or no information about relatives	6	3.0
Total	202	100.2

Source: Compiled from Admission and Discharge Registers (March 1896–March 1897), Banstead, Kensington and Chelsea School District, KCSD 307, LMA.
Note: The total is slightly over 100% because of rounding up or down for each category.

in 1894 only 14 percent of the institution's child inmates were orphans and 12 percent were deserted.[38] Samples from Banstead's admissions registers in 1896–97 indicate that 23 percent of the children were orphaned or deserted, whereas 77 percent had at least one living parent who could be located (table 3.3).[39] Even these statistics may overestimate the percentages of parentless children. It was common for parents to retrieve their supposedly deserted children when their circumstances improved or when threatened with permanent separation. In one instance, when the Stepney Board of Guardians publicly posted a list of thirty-one deserted children at the Forest Gate District School who were to be emigrated to Canada, parents or relatives reclaimed ten children and removed them from the school.[40]

Concerned that the parents of deserted children too often reappeared when their offspring were old enough to earn wages, reformers such as Florence Hill worked to pass the 1889 Poor Law Act, which empowered poor law guardians to claim custody of deserted boys up to the age of sixteen and girls to the age of eighteen.[41] The 1889 act marked a significant shift in favor of state powers over poor children, but it did not prevent parents from retrieving deserted children in practice from guardians unwilling to claim custody or take disputed cases before the courts. Banstead's director repeatedly noted in the mid-1890s that desertion remained a slippery and often temporary category.[42]

It is possible to make some general conclusions about the family composition of children who were not orphaned or deserted by both parents (tables 3.1–3.3). A minority, although not an insignificant percentage of the children in state and private institutions, came from families with two parents. On average during the 1880s and 1890s, about 20 percent of Barnardo's children had two living parents, including those children whose father or mother had remarried after the death of a spouse. From 1898 to 1915 (when the effects of wartime child admissions became apparent), the percentage of children at Barnardo's institutions who had two living parents ranged from 10 to 18 percent. During the war, Barnardo's, like many poor law institutions, admitted the children of enlisted soldiers. The proportion of Barnardo children with two living parents reached a high of 30 percent in 1916, and declined to prewar levels of 9–17 percent in the years following the war. The Banstead samples suggest that children in poor law schools were less likely to come from families with two living, locatable parents. Among the child admissions to Banstead in 1896–97, only 7 percent had listed addresses for both mother and father. By and large, most children in public and private welfare institutions did not come from two-parent families.

The proportion of institutionalized children coming from father-only homes was roughly comparable to the proportion of children coming from two-parent families. There were many more two-parent homes than father-only homes in the general population, however, which means that sole fathers were much more likely than two-parent families to send their children to an institution. During the 1880s and 1890s, children of lone fathers accounted for 14–16 percent of the sampled Barnardo's admission cases (table 3.2). From 1898 to 1925, the percentage of Barnardo inmates from families with only the father living ranged from 8 to 14 percent (table 3.1). The samples from Banstead indicate that children of lone fathers constituted a comparable proportion of the inmates in poor law schools. In 1896–97, 14 percent of the newly admitted children came from father-only families (table 3.3).[43] Thus, the father's (much more than the mother's) survival and involvement with children clearly served as a bulwark against the need for external aid from welfare or charitable institutions. It is likely that lone fathers, rather than placing their children in welfare institutions, resorted instead to paid boarding homes for their children when home care became too difficult.

The largest group of admissions to state and charitable children's institutions came from families with mothers as the only parent, demonstrating how the loss of the male breadwinner devastated the family economy. The case samples from Barnardo's précis reports of the 1880s and 1890s show that roughly one-third to one-half of all admissions were the children of widowed, deserted, and unmarried mothers. Although the percentage of mother-only child admissions stood at a low of 23 percent in the unusual January 1887 sample, the percentages were significantly higher in the 1886, 1891, and 1895 samples: 47 percent, 32 percent, and 43 percent, respectively. Barnardo's official reports claimed that approximately one-half of all long-term child admissions came from families with solitary mothers. According to the annual reports from 1898 to 1915, 47–55 percent of Barnardo children had only their mothers living. These percentages rose drastically as the First World War increased the number of widows with young children (table 3.1). Children of lone mothers composed the largest single category of Barnardo's child admissions, far outnumbering orphans, deserted children, and the children of lone fathers or two-parent families.

Likewise, solitary mothers appear to be the primary applicants to poor law district schools. Although poor law records generally include information for both parents if both were living and known, in many cases the records simply do not mention the father's whereabouts or status. School officials recorded the main causes of solitary motherhood as the death or desertion of the father, suggesting that, as at Barnardo's, poor law schools were a primary resource for abandoned, unmarried, and especially widowed mothers as they worked to rebuild their households. According to the 1896–97 Banstead samples, 56 percent of the child inmates were committed by solitary mothers, a percentage that is significantly higher than for any other category of children and roughly the same as for Barnardo's admissions (table 3.3). Given that the risks of death were roughly equal for adult men and women in the late nineteenth century, there should have been approximately the same number of children whose fathers had died as children whose mothers had died. The proportion of children who had lost both parents (the product of the probabilities of fathers' and mothers' deaths) was substantially smaller. Thus, although the probability of a child being sent to a state or charitable institution was highest for full orphans, a child was much more likely to enter an institution after the death of a father than after the death of a mother.

In sum, institutional admission registers and initial case history reports clearly document that the majority of institutionalized children were not orphaned or deserted by their parents. Whereas Barnardo and poor law reformers alike represented the orphaned or abandoned child as the typical inmate, two-thirds to three-fourths of the children at Barnardo's homes and poor law district schools had at least one living parent, who often remained in the general locality. (The proportion of children with at least one living parent was surely even higher for short-term inmates at Barnardo's and poor law branch schools, which served as way stations for children between workhouses and district schools.) Of the children who had at least one living parent, a minority came from families headed by two parents or single fathers. Widowed, abandoned, and unmarried mothers were by far the primary applicants requesting institutional care for their children. Although reformers commonly vilified parents or denied their existence to the public, most institutionalized children had at least one living parent. Yet acknowledgment of these parents, and particularly of the large proportion of widowed mothers, would have raised questions about the foundations of poor law and charitable children's institutions, not to mention the entire structure of the Victorian economy.

Unstable Lives

Although it is relatively easy to quantify who used child welfare institutions based on a surface reading of institutional documents, the question of why parents resorted to children's institutions is much more difficult to resolve.[44] Analysis of the various factors that led parents and children to turn to welfare institutions requires a more careful reading of the subtexts of institutional records. Meant to serve as internal documents, admissions registers and children's histories can also provide important information about the lives of the poor. These sources reveal that reformers rescued children from abusive and exploitative parents only in a minority of cases. More generally, parents decided to institutionalize some or all of their children after experiencing a number of often overlapping crises: the inability to find affordable housing suitable for the entire family, death or desertion of a partner, illness, unemployment or casual employment at poor wages, the strains of young children on the family economy, and, in some cases, the challenge of controlling older youths. Parents and children alike drew on a variety of community and family resources in order to survive these crises, and, in the process, they often formed working relationships with welfare officials.

Abuse and Neglect

Even if the popular philanthropic literature tended to focus on child abuse as a primary factor leading to children's institutionalization, documented cases of abuse figure in only a minority of admissions. By the mid-1890s, Barnardo's was receiving referrals from the National Society for the Prevention of Cruelty to Children (NSPCC).[45] These referrals included appalling accounts of violence, which help to explain why Barnardo took such extreme measures to promote his work. For example, a ten-year-old girl ran away from home three times to escape her mother's abuse. According to the girl's case history, "Mother struck her with a poker & hatchet, & also threw knives at her, besides keeping her often without food. [The] Girl's body was in a filthy condition. It was, too, covered with cuts & bruises, the feet being covered with sores."[46] In another case referred to Barnardo's by the NSPCC, the mother's drunken partner abused her nine-year-old daughter. He was said to have "held the child by the leg head downwards, & beat her severely, her screams being described as 'most awful.'"[47] Horrific as these cases were, they were exceptions; accounts of parental violence and willful neglect were rare. Of the 148 children admitted to Barnardo's in January 1895, only 6 (4 percent) had been referred by the NSPCC or had previous family records with the NSPCC known to Barnardo's.[48]

It is possible that differences in policy between the NSPCC and Barnardo's precluded a more active system of referral. Whereas Barnardo clearly supported the separation of children from their parents, resorting at times to "philanthropic kidnapping," the NSPCC generally tried to keep families intact. It sought "to remove the evil from the home, and not the children."[49] In contrast to Barnardo, NSPCC officials expressed great faith in the ability of abusive parents to reform.[50] Furthermore, a public personal dispute in the 1890s between Barnardo and the Reverend Benjamin Waugh, director of the NSPCC, may have prevented wider cooperation between their organizations. Waugh criticized Barnardo's handling of a custody case in which Barnardo sent a Catholic child in his care to Canada against the mother's instructions. Barnardo then accused Waugh (a Congregational minister) of being a pawn of Cardinal Manning, the leader of the English Catholic Church and a great advocate of the poor. According to Barnardo, Manning allegedly lent his support to Waugh and the NSPCC as part of a plot to convert the children of the poor to Catholicism.[51] The extent to which such personal and procedural conflicts affected the frequency of NSPCC referrals to Barnardo's homes remains unclear. Nonetheless, Barnardo's case records document few other instances of clear child abuse. In addition to the six NSPCC-related cases, only two other documented instances of parental violence against children appear in the 1895 sample of 148 case histories.[52] It would be wrong to assume, as many Britons then did, that reformers brought children with living parents to institutions primarily to protect them from abuse.

What is revealed by the examples of child abuse is a sense of shared responsibility for children within poor neighborhoods. When parents failed to care for their children, members of the community often took charge. For example, neighbors appealed to the NSPCC in a case where the father "turned out" his fourteen-year-old son and daughter and neglected the remaining three dependent children in the year after their mother's death following childbirth. The father escaped further investigation only by leaving the neighborhood.[53] In another case, neighbors took more direct action against the single mother of a neglected eleven-year-old son. They deemed her a "drunken & an immoral woman" and said that she "smokes & chews, & has been known to be intoxicated 'from daylight to night.'" Locals demonstrated their disapproval of the woman's behavior, which seemed to threaten communal gender norms in addition to communal morals and parenting standards, by burning the woman's effigy on Guy Fawkes Day. She eventually agreed to admit her son to Barnardo's.[54]

Such anecdotal evidence supports George Behlmer's conclusion that reports of child abuse were most likely to come from the poor, not NSPCC workers or other officials (policemen, school board visitors, poor law relieving officers).[55] In extreme examples of family breakdown, there often remained a sense of communal morality and responsibility for the welfare of children.

Housing

Even if most institutionalized children did not come from physically abusive families, almost all came from backgrounds where poverty and neglect threatened their chances of survival. A common characteristic among poor law and Barnardo children was that almost all of their families struggled to find adequate, sanitary housing.[56] The challenge to find safe, clean, and affordable dwellings with ample space for parents and children proved insurmountable for many parents. Attention to the housing crisis as a factor leading to the placement of children in institutions highlights how thoroughly institutionalization was a symptom of widespread adult poverty and a shortage of housing, rather than simply the result of wanton or absent parents.

Among the best sources for recovering information about housing conditions and the parents of "nobody's children" are Edwin Chadwick's 1883 questionnaires for London Metropolitan Police divisions about child street vendors.[57] Local divisions responded to a set of seven questions concerning child news vendors, match sellers, and fruit sellers, and the potential need for inexpensive children's lodging houses in the area. Like the poor law records and Barnardo's case histories, these police reports indicate that poor street children by and large were not orphaned or deserted, but retained close ties with their families. On the whole, police found few child street vendors in each district, and very few of these were orphaned or deserted—a maximum of 4–5 percent by the estimate of one division.[58] The Islington police reported, "In only one case are any of these [street vendor] children (a brother and a sister) known to be orphans, and they reside with a Grandmother. It is not known that any have been deserted by their parents."[59]

Most child street vendors lived with their parents and contributed to the family income. Overwhelmingly, the police divisions reported that they rarely found children sleeping alone in archways and courts, as Barnardo and other reformers frequently claimed, or in common lodging houses without their parents.[60] One report claimed that newsboys at railroad stations were "children of the respectable working class, & reside with their parents."[61] The Brixton division similarly replied that those child street vendors "known to Police have parents &

remain with them." The Highgate police responded that "boys and girls engaged as newsvendors, fruit sellers, etc. . . . reside with their parents or guardians, who are of the working class."[62] Regarding the usefulness of a children's lodging house, police repeatedly noted that they approved of the idea, but that parents would be extremely unlikely to send their children to such a place. They speculated that parents would be unwilling to lose their children's income and suspicious of any attempts to remove their children, interpreting such actions as an attack on their "so called liberty."[63] The Camberwell police division declared that children would be unlikely to use lodging houses "and separate [themselves] from parents or friends however poor."[64] Contrary to popular representations of poor children as waifs and strays or homeless wanderers in "no-man's land," these police reports confirm that even street children had strong ties to their families and communities. Rather than portraying child street vendors as racially distinct "street arabs" disconnected from their parents, their community, and their nation, the police reports located child poverty within family poverty and broader social issues, such as adult unemployment, casual labor, and the poor conditions of working-class housing.

The strain that overcrowded housing conditions placed on poor families was likely a dominant factor leading parents to place one or more of their children in state or charitable residential institutions. The Chadwick police surveys highlight the dire living conditions among the poor working class. The St. James police surmised that the "boys and girls of this [street vending] class are the offsprings of the poorest and lowest, and their homes are without doubt the most wretched class, and they exist in great Squalor & misery."[65] Other police divisions provided similar accounts of impoverished, crowded dwellings. In Holborn, constables in plain clothes interviewed child street sellers about their living conditions. Most of the children lived with their parents and siblings in dwellings of one or two rooms. The worst cases of overcrowding included that of fourteen-year-old George Pearson, who resided with his father, mother, two brothers, and four sisters in one room.[66]

In some cases, the lack of affordable housing forced several generations of family members to live together in cramped quarters. The Lambeth constable discovered only three child vendors after a day of patrolling (a girl selling fruit and two boys selling newspapers), yet their cases provide important examples of impoverished housing. Describing the living conditions of the two boys, the constable reported:

> The boys were the sons of waterside labourers living with their parents. I visited their homes which in each consisted of two rooms. the families numbering 8 and 10 respectively. a bedstead in each room for two in each, remainder sleeping on the floor. on matresses [sic] which are rolled up during the day and placed under the bedsteads or in a corner of the room. The furniture consisted of a small table and a few chairs in the living-room, but no wash-hand stand, the washing being done from

a basin placed on a chair or on the table. an entire absence of comfort and cleanliness being observable.[67]

The cramped living quarters of these families clearly provided a motive for parents to seek residential care for their children.

The records of poor law schools and Barnardo's homes confirm that the inability of poor families to find adequate housing was a main factor leading to children's institutionalization. One mother struggled for more than a year to maintain her children after their father's death, refusing several offers by the Bethnal Green poor law guardians to take them. She finally agreed to part with her two children when the landlord notified her that she must move "unless she has fewer children at home."[68] Like the poor in general, individuals seeking aid commonly had a history of frequent moves. When Emma Pimm applied with her two children to the Bethnal Green Board of Guardians for relief, she had recently been deserted by her husband, James. During the previous year, Emma and her family had lived in at least six different residences. Their longest stay in one place was for five months, and their shortest was for a two-week period between James's desertion and Emma's application to the guardians.[69] Such frequent moves likely involved attempts to evade angry landlords seeking outstanding rent. Many of Barnardo's case histories indicated that the children's parents were weeks or months overdue in payments.[70]

The housing problem not only drove parents to find residential care for their children, but also prevented them from retrieving children as soon as they may have liked. This was particularly the case after the passage of the 1889 Act for the Prevention of Cruelty to Children, also know as the Children's Charter, which was the first major state limitation on parental powers. The act provided for the punishment of parents found guilty of child abuse and empowered courts to transfer custody of abused children from parents to state or philanthropic officials. After 1889, poor parents who had not abused, intentionally neglected, or deserted their children technically retained the right to retrieve offspring from poor law institutions at will, but in practice local guardians sometimes prohibited them from doing so. The Children's Charter placed pressure on poor law officials to prosecute cases of willful neglect and therefore encouraged closer investigation of the home environment.[71] For example, in 1897 the parents of fifteen-year-old James Driscoll desired to reclaim their son, who had been a patient at the Seaman's Hospital in Greenwich for almost five months. After visiting the parents' house in Rotherhithe, the relieving officer advised against granting them custody. The father was unemployed, and the officer described the home as "in a very dirty state and not fit for the reception of the boy"; two families totaling thirteen people already occupied its six small rooms.[72]

It was common for members of the working classes to live as boarders in shared tenements, a situation that created an additional impediment for many parents and relatives who wished to retrieve children from institutions. When the father of George and Maud Pugh, aged eight and seven, applied to reclaim his children from the Sutton poor law schools, he was renting one of three rooms in a basement tenement occupied by a Mrs. Mitchell. Mrs. Mitchell's adult son may have shared the room with Pugh, and Mrs. Mitchell herself slept in one of the adjoining rooms with her two teenage daughters and twelve-year-old son. When the relieving officer asked Mrs. Mitchell whether she would allow Pugh's children to join him, she claimed she would take the boy but would prefer to have the father without any of his children. Describing Pugh's living situation, the relieving officer concluded: "I do not consider that it is a fit and proper place to allow the boy to live in."[73] Landlords and their other tenants regarded children as an added burden in already overcrowded conditions. Furthermore, welfare officials tended to associate sexual and moral vice with the mixture of men and women, different age groups, and family and nonfamily members that was typical of working-class housing. Such living conditions were a direct threat to middle-class domestic ideals.

Death, Illness, and Unemployment

The search for housing was difficult even when both parents were alive, healthy, and employed. Overlaid and intertwined with the housing crisis as a primary factor contributing to the need for children's residential institutions was the separation of parents and families owing to death, illness, and employment conditions. Cases of true orphanhood reveal the precarious existence of the poor. Parents died from a variety of diseases and environmental or sanitary hazards. The most frequently listed causes of death in Barnardo's children's case records were childbirth and consumption, but a range of other conditions devastated family life among the poor, including alcoholism, asthma, brain disease, bronchitis, cancer, dropsy, epilepsy, influenza, heart failure, liver disease, lung inflammation, pleurisy, pneumonia, typhoid, and, in a very few cases, suicide. Fathers were especially prone to industrial accidents. Typical examples include a blacksmith who died from a fractured skull caused by an accident, and another father who died from lead poisoning.[74] At times, the death of one parent seemed too much for the other to take. For example, the recorder of fourteen-year-old E.W.'s case history at Barnardo's in 1891 wrote that the boy's father, a scavenger working for Mile End parish, died five months after his mother, "it is said from a broken heart."[75]

The death or desertion of one parent was the most common event that led the surviving parent to apply for state or private relief. In the Barnardo samples from the 1880s and 1890s, the children of widows and widowers composed a significant proportion of the admissions, ranging from 27 percent in 1887 to 41 percent in 1891. In the months and years immediately following a spouse's death, the surviving parent usually sought assistance first from friends and extended family, and then turned to poor law and charitable services for help. For example, three-year-old C.H. entered Barnardo's in January 1895. His mother had died three months earlier from bronchitis and pleurisy, leaving the father with seven dependent children. The father, "a respectable man," was a farm laborer in Devon who had lost his own small farm in the 1893 depression. After his wife's death, he remained "weak both in body & in mind," and was able to earn only 10 shillings weekly in addition to the small contributions he received from friends. By the time C.H. entered Barnardo's, relatives had already "taken four children, & could not do more."[76] In this case and others like it, the surviving parent resorted to institutional care for children after exhausting the assistance available from neighbors and extended family members. Institutions, combined with communal resources, could offer the longer-term care necessary to help parents recover from personal and economic crises.

When death did not remove one or both parents, illness often made it impossible for parents to maintain all of their dependent children. Almost one-tenth of the children entering Banstead in 1896–97 had single parents who were in the workhouse infirmary. It was less common, although not rare, for one parent to be institutionalized in an insane asylum, leaving the other to fend for the children as best he or (more likely) she could (table 3.3). Even when parents were not themselves institutionalized because of physical or mental disabilities, they were sometimes too ill or incapacitated to work. The father of one Barnardo child was "a scavenger, but almost past work."[77] Another father had "burnt his right arm a little while ago and has not since been able to work," forcing the family to move from their apartment into a one-room dwelling.[78] Still another, "a furniture-remover," had been "partially crippled from the effects of an accident (both legs were brocken)." He "had no regular work since" and earned only five to seven shillings per week.[79] Long-term illnesses also prevented fathers from working. One report recorded that a ten-year-old's "[f]ather suffers from Bright's Disease, and has only done one month's work in two years."[80] These and similar case histories confirm that poor health and disabilities were common reasons behind fathers' inability to support their children.

Illness also undercut mothers' ability to contribute to the family income. One woman, a domestic servant, had been "seduced by her mistress's son." After giving birth to the child, the woman "lost two situations through ill-health." When she brought her year-old infant to Barnardo's, she was reduced to casual employment "at a jam manufactory, earning only five to six shillings a-week."[81] In many cases, ailing mothers relied on other family members to supplement their meager earnings. The wife of a casual laborer (whom the case worker described as a drunkard) was "unable to work much through ill health." She lived upon the earnings of a married son, and her younger, seventeen-year-old son eventually applied to Barnardo's himself.[82] In the case of a five-year-old boy admitted to Barnardo's, the father was in an insane asylum, and the mother was "'generally too ill to do anything' and is greatly dependent upon her mother," who ran a small business as a wardrobe dealer.[83]

When family members could not provide adequate resources, sick mothers cobbled together support from a broad, although usually insufficient, spectrum of charitable and state services. A widow, "very ill with asthma," was already "dependent upon charity" before bringing one of her two dependent children to Barnardo's.[84] Another widow, "unable to work" because of paralysis, brought her two teenage boys to Barnardo's before she entered the workhouse herself, demonstrating a clear preference for Barnardo's over poor law services for her children.[85] Although an increasingly wide variety of free hospitals, charities, and state services provided the poor—particularly the so-called deserving poor—with medical assistance, accidents and long-term illnesses could still result in the break-up of families.[86]

Even when parents were in good health, Barnardo's case histories show that their wages were often too small and unsteady to maintain all of their children. A mother in service took one of her two children to Barnardo's because she "could not support both her children out of her wages."[87] In another case, a twelve-year-old boy who applied to Barnardo's noted that his widowed mother—"a very respectable woman"—worked at a jam factory where she earned eight shillings a week "but found it impossible to support two children on this amt."[88] From the evidence of case histories, the Victorian concern with the plight of seamstresses appears to have been well founded. The seasonal nature of dressmaking forced many needlewomen to supplement their earnings by pawning household goods, as in the case of the casual seamstress who "parted with almost everything excepting the clothing she & her children are wearing."[89] Of another seamstress "discharged through slackness [of trade]," it was said that "[h]er only hope lies in securing a little charing."[90] Charing and washing—unsteady, poorly paid, and physically demanding work—were the most common occupations listed for mothers bringing their children to Barnardo's. Many fathers were unemployed; when they did have an occupation, it was generally also some form of casual labor: "[f]ather a dock labourer out of employment"; "[f]ather, a bricklayer, now without employment"; and "[f]ather—a sail, sack, & window-blind maker—only gets a job now & then." Such entries tell of the casual, insecure nature of work in late-Victorian London at the height of industrialization.[91]

Life-Cycle Stresses

In conjunction with factors related to housing, health, and employment, life-cycle issues played a major role in parents' decisions to take one or more of their children to a residential institution. Many of the applicants to the poor law guardians and Barnardo's were parents with young children, especially widowed mothers, who after the recent deaths of their husbands remained pregnant and/or with young children at home. Young children strained the family economy because they could not yet earn wages and often prevented parents from working outside the home.[92] As Lynn Hollen Lees has argued, parents often resorted to the short-term separation of their families in poor law institutions with the goal of rebuilding their households in the long term.[93] For example, Emily Bond placed her two girls, Eliza and Ethel, in the Forest Gate District School for the first time in the mid-1880s, when Eliza was six and Ethel was two and a half. Both girls went in and out of schools multiple times during the next several years, staying two weeks to eight months at a time, while their mother was periodically in the workhouse or infirmary. Eventually, their mother seems to have left the workhouse for good by placing her girls in poor law schools for long-term stays: first Eliza for approximately six years and then Ethel for approximately four years. When Emily Bond retrieved her girls in 1893 for the final time, the girls were approximately fourteen and eleven, old enough to take work and contribute to the household economy.[94] In this case and others like it, parents used welfare institutions as way stations while they attempted to regain economic stability, at which point they hoped to retrieve their children.[95]

In cases where it is possible to gain information about the siblings of institutionalized children, important patterns emerge concerning parental motives. There was a popular fear that parents would place their young children in institutions and then retrieve them when they reached the age of twelve or thirteen, at which time youths could care for themselves and begin to contribute to the family income. In fact, however, when parents had several children at home, they were generally more willing to send their older children to a state or private institution. After her father's death, for example, eleven-year-old L.E. entered Barnardo's in March 1886. Her mother, who was pregnant with another child, kept her five remaining children with her, relying on outrelief from the parish for support.[96] In another case, the mother of three illegitimate children chose to admit her eleven-year-old daughter to Barnardo's while she kept her five-year-old boy and two-year-old daughter at home.[97] Likewise, two months after her husband's death, a mother placed her eleven-year-old son with a friend or local philanthropist (a Mr. Phipps) and brought her nine-year-old daughter to Barnardo's in order to retain "three young children at home with her."[98]

Such cases demonstrate how the birth of a child or the presence of young children strained family resources. In many cases, parents were less willing to part with younger children, even though these children could not earn wages and likely impeded parents from finding work outside the home. These examples suggest a degree of parental responsibility and care that directly counters the public representations of mercenary, exploitative mothers and fathers.

Unruly Children
Poor parents also used charitable institutions to train and care for older youths who were unemployed and, in some cases, considered unmanageable.[99] Although poor law schools discharged most children by the time they reached their early teens, Barnardo's accepted older teenagers for industrial training (an issue that will be examined in depth in chapter 5). Unable to provide for their older unemployed children, parents hoped youths might find room, board, and eventual employment through Barnardo's. The widowed father of fifteen-year-old C.S. agreed that Barnardo's could arrange for his son's emigration to Canada, where he might work as a farm laborer. The youth had a blemished history of failed jobs in London. He "lost his first & second situations through being impertinent, his third through staying out late, his fourth through dawdling on his

errands, & his fifth through going off for the day with bad companions." To make matters worse, the boy "[s]moked & drank."[100] In cases such as this, training through Barnardo's institutions and even possible emigration to Canada presented appealing opportunities to parents—and perhaps also to youths unable to find or maintain steady employment in London.

Parents also hoped to discipline unruly children by sending them to welfare institutions for temporary stays or, in some cases, as a last resort. After the death of his estranged wife, a father found his two girls "wayward and unmanageable" and eventually placed them in a private children's institution.[101] In another case, a boy described as being "beyond parental control" joined the *Shaftesbury* training ship, the first of several children's institutions he would enter.[102] One couple of "good character" regretted that their son had gotten "mixed up with bad companions" and was "going to the bad." They claimed to be "quite unable to keep him" and sent the youth to Barnardo's for discipline.[103] In a similar case, a dock laborer's widow with four children sent her twelve-year-old son to the local poor law school. He escaped three months later, however, and returned to his mother, who eventually brought him to Barnardo's. The boy's case report notes, "His mother has tried to manage him but has failed to do so, and he is now quite beyond her control."[104]

Such children frequently had a reputation for truancy or stealing, as in the case of the ten-year-old girl who was "addicted to pilfering, which has made her notorious in the neighborhood."[105] They often left their homes for days or even weeks at a time before requesting admission to an institution on their own or being sent there by parents.[106] In some cases, youths slept on the streets by choice, not because their parents had abandoned them. For example, a teenage boy applying to Barnardo's claimed to be the son of "a poor widow, living in one room, doing washing and charing." Upon further investigation, however, an official discovered that the boy's "mother keeps a grocer's shop in Spitalfields and does a brisk trade . . . and that it is only through the lad's own wilfulness that he is away from home and living in the streets."[107] Such cases hint at underlying family dynamics that left youths feeling neglected and angry. Feeling burdened themselves, some parents readily turned over responsibility for their children to institutions.

In extreme cases, parents rejected any further contact with children who threatened the safety and peace of the family. One mother with dependent children still at home forbade her teenage son from returning to her "on account of the foulness of his talk before the young children."[108] Another mother threw her son out for beating his younger sister. When Barnardo's contacted the mother about what should be done with her boy, she declared that he should not return to her but instead enter the Royal Navy.[109] Lastly, in another clear reversal of the typical popular narrative of the victimized child and the abusive parent, the report of a teenage boy entering Barnardo's noted that he "conducted himself so badly at home that it is believed his mother secretly left her lodgings in order to escape from him."[110] In these cases of unruly youths—almost always males—private institutional records portray parents as the ones in need of protection.

Conclusion

The reports of poor law relieving officers, children's admission and discharge registers, and Barnardo's more detailed précis reports reveal important information about institutionalized children that contemporary reformers tended to erase or condense in their fund-raising narratives of child rescue. The very institutions that produced popular representations of abandoned and orphaned children also produced counternarratives in their day-to-day operations. One particular case history from Barnardo's archives illustrates the multiplicity of factors leading to institutionalization and the complications of child welfare narratives. In January 1895, G.H., a five-year-old boy, became a resident of Barnardo's after arriving at the institution with his mother and aunt. The case worker recorded the following details leading to the boy's admission:

> Father, a builder's labourer, was killed by a fall from a roof, Dec., 1893. Mother (who bears a good character) lives at Islington. Is not very strong, & suffers from spasms around the heart, interfering with her working. She does washing & charing, earning only 4/—per week. Parish relief to the extent of 3/—, three loaves, & three pounds of meat weekly is granted her. Rent 3/6 per week. At the present moment one child only is dependent upon the mother, the youngest having been taken temporarily by a maternal aunt. Mother & children looked pale & weak, through want of sufficient nourishment. G. is not very clear in articulation. New Agreement, with Canada Clauses, signed by mother. Prot[estant].[111]

First, this case history, like thousands of others, demonstrates the extreme instability of life among the poor. The father's death from a workplace accident sent the surviving family members into a spiraling crisis. In just over one year, the mother, sickly and able to earn a mere pittance, broke up her family, placing the youngest child with her sister and G.H. with Barnardo. Unlike the working-class characters in popular narratives, G.H. and his mother appear to have had little control over their plight. The mother did not make a conscious choice to abuse or prostitute her child, or to squander her wages on alcohol (although some parents certainly did).[112] Rather, G.H. and his family were overcome by the larger, seemingly uncontrollable forces that shaped Victorian society: accidental death, the strains of young children, ill health, poor wages, high rent, and an inadequate social safety net. Officials described such parents and youths as having "drifted downward."[113] Their descent was perhaps hastened by bad companions or unwise choices, but, on the whole, institutional welfare records attest to how quickly an unpredictable disaster could lead to the dissolution of the family. Unlike the highly personalized, melodramatic accounts in the popular literature, which emphasized individual moral failures, the disasters in institutional records were largely abstract and impersonal, one blurring into another.

Second, the case history of G.H. is significant for what it tells us about how the poor actually interacted with welfare officials. Stark moral divisions between vicious parents, innocent children, and heroic reformers usually dissolve in the case history records. The Barnardo's official taking down G.H.'s case noted that his mother, like most of the women applying to the institution for assistance, "bears a good character"—a judgment presumably made through observation and interviews with relatives, neighbors, and employers. These records do sometimes contain harshly written references to dissolute parents, such as a father characterized as "a lazy, drunken, foul-mouthed bully" and a mother identified as "a drunken prostitute."[114] More often than not, however, the case histories are remarkable for their degree of sympathy with applicants and a certain flexibility in moral judgments. Officials listed mothers as being respectable or of good character even when they had illegitimate children and, in some cases, continued to live with men out of wedlock.[115] Familiarity with the conditions of life among the poor led many welfare officials to stretch notions of respectability in a way that would have shocked upper- and middle-class reformers.

As the case of G.H. demonstrates, children's admissions to welfare institutions most often involved poor parents' choice and approach, rather than the dramatic story of rescue and reformation recounted in the popular literature. Parents—not reformers—generally took the first step and brought their children to welfare officials, or the children applied directly, as was often the case with older youths. The decision by parents to institutionalize their children was usually carefully considered, arrived at only after appeals to family and friends as well as various forms of public and private outrelief. Once the family members entered the workhouse or Barnardo's headquarters, there were forms to complete and interviews to schedule. G.H.'s silence—the official deemed the boy "not very clear in articulation"—hints at how traumatic this experience must have been for children and parents alike. Barnardo had parents sign a contractual agreement that "the child should be wholly surrendered to our care for training for a term of years, to be stated in each particular case."[116] Although the agreement was not legally binding (unbeknownst to many parents), the perfunctory requirement of parental authorization signified that even Barnardo, the most extreme of the child savers, felt that he could not completely ignore the vast majority of parents in practice, however much he erased them in his public accounts.

Finally, G.H.'s case history illustrates a remarkable sense of community among the urban poor. Far from being a nomadic child of "no man's land," G.H., like most poor children, had ties to neighbors, relatives, and a range of local public and private welfare services, in addition to parents. Before coming to Barnardo's, his mother depended on her sister for both emotional and economic support. In addition to receiving help from her family, G.H.'s mother also relied on outrelief from the parish in the form of food and money. The situation provides a good example of how impoverished parents sought help from a variety of sources at once: family and neighbors, parish relief, and charitable services. Unlike the poor children in popular narratives, who were represented as being separated from traditional English communities, isolated and exploited, the youths and parents who chose to approach welfare institutions were often deeply integrated in their localities. Neighbors protested when parents abused their children, and they knew which children had a reputation for stealing. Parents drew on a variety of welfare services to the best of their abilities, trying to secure a basic standard of care for all of their children. A minority of the children in Barnardo's homes and in poor law institutions were truly "nobody's children." The majority had at least one parent, who, as the next chapter explores, often maintained contact with his or her child after the initial admission to an institution.

CHAPTER 4

"That Most Delicate of All Questions in an Englishman's Mind"

THE RIGHTS OF PARENTS AND THEIR CONTINUED
CONTACT WITH INSTITUTIONALIZED CHILDREN

⟐

On New Year's Eve 1889, a tragic disaster occurred at Forest Gate District School, one of London's largest poor law boarding schools for children. During the night, a fire erupted in a ground floor storage room located below two of the boys' dormitories. The official in charge of one of the boys' dormitories was away on leave for the night, and the remaining supervisor, the yardman, George Hare—"a heavy sleeper, and hard to rouse"—slept deeply as two female officers pounded on his locked bedroom door after they detected the fire.[1] Once awake, Hare, who kept the only key to the staircase leading to the boys' rooms, did not unlock the door or help the children escape onto the roof of the dining hall, where others had safely gathered. Despite early reports of heroic rescue attempts by the school's superintendent, Mr. Duncan, a later parliamentary investigation concluded that he, too, had failed to awaken the sleeping boys or check whether they had escaped.[2] Soon "the building was enveloped in smoke, and boys and women were shrieking from the windows." Only after an officer from another building brought a ladder and broke down the locked door at the bottom of the staircase could the boys begin to exit the burning building. Twenty-six boys aged seven to twelve died, most by suffocation while still in their beds.[3] Even among the annals of poor law and charitable institutions, which are interspersed with horrific accounts of abuse, including brutal officials, mass poisonings resulting from rotten food, and sinking training ships, the Forest Gate fire was one of the deadliest catastrophes ever to occur.[4]

The effects of the fire were immediate and widespread. In the long term, the deaths of the children at Forest Gate School, which could accommodate up to 720 youths, revived criticisms of large barrack schools.[5] Critics suggested that the domestic arrangements of institutional cottage homes or individual foster homes would prevent such blatant disregard for the safety of children.[6] In the days and weeks immediately after the fire, however, attention focused on the children's grieving parents and relatives, who received widespread public recognition and sympathy in the press reports and memorial services following the disaster.

In commiseration with the relatives, the *East End News* printed the dead boys' names and ages along with their parents' addresses. Of the twenty-six boys killed in the fire, only one was an orphan. Most parents lived in residential homes in East London, although some were inmates in the local workhouses or infirmaries of Whitechapel, Poplar, Croydon, and Bow.[7] In melodramatic phrases, the *Police Chronicle* recounted the relatives' agony upon viewing the children's corpses arranged in the school's infirmary hall: "As the day advanced the chamber of death was the scene of some heartrendering [*sic*] incidents. First a mother, then a sister, and occasionally some other relative of a deceased boy, would be conducted to the spot where a body lay, and distressing sobs would penetrate through the closed doors, for none but those connected with the deceased could look on at this solemn moment."[8]

Such outpourings of grief and sympathy for the children's relatives extended well beyond the East End. Queen Victoria expressed "her deep sympathy with the bereaved parents and relatives." The Local Government Board inspector "personally visited the parents, or nearest relatives, of all the deceased children" in order to convey "the sympathy of Her Majesty with them in their bereavement." Perhaps more surprising, the grieving parents displayed gratitude toward the school officials. The inspector was pleased to report that "the mothers of the unfortunate children, without exception, expressed their warm sense of the treatment and care which their children received at Forest Gate School."[9]

The communal burial service took place at St. James's Church, "which was filled to overflowing," and was attended by a number of prominent public men, ranging from members of Parliament and school board authorities to poor law officials. The funeral ceremony that followed at West Ham Cemetery drew "a crowd numbering at least 10,000 of all ages and conditions." Mourners remained long after the service, so that "[i]t was dark before the cemetery was cleared of the people that thronged round the graves."[10]

Early proposals for a memorial involved plans for a stained glass window at St. James's Church. But local East Enders protested: it would be "a rather selfish memorial," because the "lads of the school did not and do not attend the church, [and] neither do their parents, who live in the neighbourhood to which the school belongs—*i.e.*, Poplar and Whitechapel."[11] Responding to the prevailing public sympathy for the dead children's families and the desire for a local memorial, the Forest Gate managers eventually created a site that was elaborate and expensive for a poor law institution: an obelisk encircled by five communal graves at West Ham Cemetery. The monument was inscribed: "In memory of the 26 boys who unhappily lost their lives by the disastrous fire which occurred at the School, Forest Lane, West Ham, 1st January, 1890. Erected, as an expression of sympathy with the bereaved relatives, by the Managers and Staff of the Forest Gate District School."[12]

This official recognition of the dead children's grieving relatives seems the natural response to such a tragedy. Within the overall history of child welfare institutions, however, the repeated public overtures to these children's parents were unusual. District schools gained support in the 1840s as a means to distance poor children from their parents and other adult paupers in workhouses.[13] The stated goal of public poor law schools and many private philanthropic institutions like Barnardo's was to break the cycle of poverty by undermining family relations among the poor. Reform literature often completely erased poor parents from their children's lives by characterizing the children in institutions as being either orphaned or deserted. Even the official history of a district school similar to Forest Gate described the child inmates as "poor orphans and waifs," children "oft-times destitute of father, mother or any friend."[14] When parents were publicly recognized, they were generally denounced as contaminating influences on their children.

Only a disaster on the scale of the Forest Gate fire could reveal—for a fleeting moment—the true circumstances of institutional life: not only did most of these children have parents, but their parents often struggled to maintain contact with them. Parents visited children, supervised their care, and sometimes had frequent interactions with welfare officials on their behalf. Like recent reevaluations of the poor law by Lynn Hollen Lees and others, this chapter argues that the poor were not passive victims of disciplinary policies aimed at destroying poor families.[15] Children's welfare institutions did not function as "total institutions" in which inmates lived completely "cut off from the wider society."[16] Contrary to popular representations and official policy goals, poor parents by and large did not use welfare institutions as permanent depositories for their children, and institutionalization did not mean that all contact between parents and children ended. As chapter 3 showed, most parents relied on institutions for temporary aid as they struggled with strains on the family economy. The public literature portrayed state and private institutions as permanently replacing dissolute parents, but parents and institutions frequently worked together (though often at odds) to care for poor children. In theory, the goal was to separate children from their parents; in practice, short-term stays, visitation policies, parental supervision of the care of institutionalized children, and the reliance of youths on parents both during and after their stays in institutions ensured that the ties between most parents and institutionalized children remained intact.

Furthermore, in the process of supervising the care of their children in state and philanthropic institutions, poor parents asserted a strong sense of their parental rights. Within the sphere of child welfare, the poor claimed what they interpreted as the fundamental rights of freeborn English citizens: liberty of the subject, due process of the law, access to court mediation, and, above all else, the parental right to oversee the care of children. That claim brought them into direct conflict with reformers who sought to redefine citizenship by foregrounding notions of domesticity and class above any claim to such rights. Nevertheless, the poor continued to voice their rights as parents by appealing to those segments of society that were most likely to acknowledge their complaints. They requested support from local guardians, wrote letters to welfare officials, sought the advice of local magistrates, called on the London press for help, and, in extreme cases, organized public protests. Without any direct political voice, many poor parents used the outlets available to them within a civil society to assert their basic rights as English citizens.

Temporary versus Long-Term Institutionalization

Parents most commonly maintained contact with children by sending them to institutions for only short-term stays. After a period of days, weeks, or months, many children returned to their parents, sometimes for only a brief interval before going back to the institution. These children were the dreaded "ins and outs"—the "foul stream running through the district schools."[17] Children admitted for short-term stays accounted for the largest proportion of the populations in most poor law and Barnardo institutions, far outnumbering orphans, deserted children, and other long-term inmates, even though reformers generally conceptualized, popularized, and designed these institutions to serve the needs of the latter. Parents used institutions for temporary assistance as a means to receive aid without permanently losing contact with their children.

Metropolitan Poor Law Institutions

The first step for families seeking indoor state poor law relief was to enter the workhouse. Most workhouses had separate wards for men, women, and children, although reformers constantly noted how difficult it was to maintain these strict divisions. With the growth of metropolitan district and separate schools after the late 1840s, many London unions sent children over two years of age from the workhouse where they were first admitted to the corresponding separate or district school on general admissions days, which were usually held every two weeks. Although London poor law guardians desired to remove all children over two from workhouses as quickly as possible, they were not entirely successful in practice. Even as late as the 1890s, an estimated three thousand children resided in London workhouses, of whom approximately two-thirds were of school age and should have moved on to poor law schools. These children remained in workhouses for longer than two weeks for a variety of reasons: the separate or district schools were full, the schools were quarantined because of disease, or the workhouse children were sick and required a clean bill of health before being sent on to the school.[18]

For poor law officials, the most disturbing reason for the large number of children in workhouses was that parents manipulated their own admissions and discharges to avoid the fortnightly transfers of children to separate schools built outside central London and away from local communities (figure 19). Although the Bethnal Green separate school in Leytonstone was only four miles along the

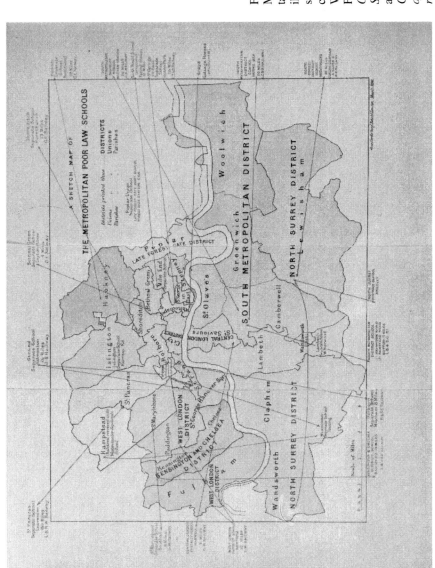

FIGURE 19. "A Sketch Map of the Metropolitan Poor Law Schools," illustrating how most schools were miles from central London. From Walter Monnington and Frederick J. Lampard, *Our London Poor Law Schools* (London: Eyre and Spottiswoode, 1898). *Courtesy of Corporation of London, London Metropolitan Archives.*

Great Eastern Railway from Bethnal Green, the South Metropolitan District School at Herne Bay was a demanding fifty-mile train trip from the locality. Parents wanting to remain in close contact with children necessarily found ways to avoid the transfers. For example, the Greenwich Workhouse master complained of "a girl who for two years has been eligible for the school, but has not been there yet, owing to the fact that her mother continually discharged herself and the child from the workhouse."[19] In a case from Marylebone Workhouse, a family with three children went in and out of the workhouse sixty-two times in a period of just over one year so that the children were never transferred to the poor law school located nine miles to the west in Southall.[20] Many parents manipulated the system so that they could receive basic material aid while at the same time avoiding physical separation from their children.[21]

In 1883, the Kensington and Chelsea poor law school district tried to deal with the problem of readmissions by opening a branch school at Marlesford Lodge in Hammersmith as an intermediate station between union workhouses and the district school at Banstead. Poor law reformers hailed Marlesford Lodge as a model for other institutions because it provided for the speedy transfer of children away from workhouses and effectively decreased the number of readmissions at Banstead, thereby supposedly preventing the ins and outs from endangering the truly orphaned and deserted children. After entering the workhouse, children took baths, received a change of clothes, and then transferred to the branch school later that same day, instead of waiting the normal period of up to two weeks. Children who were ill, who had parents in the workhouse infirmary, or who were known to be ins and outs remained at the branch school, while others went to Banstead on fortnightly admission days.[22]

Despite these structural attempts to remove the more casual class of children from the influence of their families, parents continued to rely on poor law institutions for short-term, intermittent care for their children. There was actually an increase in the number of casual versus more permanent children at the Marlesford Lodge branch school during the 1890s.[23] In 1899, the directors classified only 9 out of the 118 children at Marlesford Lodge as permanent admissions, and only 1 of these 9 children was medically fit to be sent to the district school at Banstead.[24] During the mid-1890s, parents retrieved their children from Marlesford Lodge on average once a month, and one-third of all the children entering the school were classified as readmissions. Most likely, actual readmissions were higher than one-third, because officials classified an admission as a readmission only when it occurred within six months of discharge. In fact, parents moving from parish to parish often brought children to several different poor law schools during any given year.[25]

The branch school managers complained bitterly about these parents who retrieved and then readmitted their children. To give a specific case: Florence and Thomas Smith entered Marlesford Lodge forty-two times between February 1907 and November 1910. Their parents were taking them in and out of the branch school approximately every three weeks. When the children were admitted in November 1910, their father was in the workhouse and their mother was a live-in servant on Fulham Palace Road. Both Florence and Thomas were of "delicate" health, and already "two of the family" had "died of Consumption."[26] Their case is a typical example of how parents used poor law institutions for supplementary assistance during times of extended crisis. Short and repeated stays such as these characterized the majority of admissions to poor law children's institutions, even though most historical accounts concentrate on the longer-term orphaned and deserted child inmates.

Furthermore, even the populations of the district and separate schools, which were meant to house the more permanent class of children, fluctuated to a high degree. These poor law schools did much to foster a sense of common identity and student allegiance, giving the impression that they served a stable student population. Students learned and sang school songs, waved the school flag, joined sports teams, and, in the case of at least one school, received copies of the school magazine even after they were discharged.[27] Many children did remain in the schools for years at a time, particularly in the 1860s, but by the late nineteenth century shorter stays were much more common. In 1860, Edward Carleton Tufnell estimated that 60 percent of district school inmates were orphaned and deserted children and 30 percent were the children of casual paupers, who entered schools for short-term stays.[28] In the 1870s, however, after cutbacks on outrelief, these percentages reversed. By the 1880s and 1890s, officials estimated that approximately two-thirds of all children in metropolitan residential poor law institutions were ins and outs who remained in institutions for stays generally under six months.[29]

The vast majority of children admitted from Whitechapel Workhouse to Forest Gate District School remained at the school for stays of less than one year, and many of these children went back and forth between parents and the school at short intervals.[30] Even Banstead, which, unlike the other London poor law schools, could boast of very few readmissions because of the Marlesford Lodge branch school, retained many children only for periods ranging from one week to several months before they returned to their parents.[31] A survey from Swinton poor law schools in Manchester Union also suggests that many children outside of London remained in schools for stays of less than one year. Of the 700 children in Swinton poor law schools in 1896, 441 (63 percent) had been in the schools for a year or less, 147 (21 percent) for two to three years, 78 (11 percent) for four to five years, 26 (4 percent) for six to seven years, and only 8 (1 percent) for eight to nine years.[32] These various records indicate that most children remained in poor law institutions for short stays—several months, weeks, or even days—before they returned intermittently or permanently to their parents.

Barnardo's Institutions

As private institutions, Barnardo's homes were able to restrict parental access to children in ways that poor law institutions could not. Although they had no legal right to keep children from parents who wanted to reclaim them, Barnardo's institutions often made retrieval difficult and at times impossible. At the initial admission, the parent or guardian usually signed an agreement form stating that the child would remain at Barnardo's for a fixed number of years. These agreements were not legally binding, but they did prevent many parents from reclaiming and perhaps later readmitting their children after short stays.[33] When dealing with private charities, parents simply could not admit and discharge their children at will, as they did with poor law institutions.

Yet, despite Barnardo's restrictions on parental access and his public claim that the children in his institutions were reformed by making a clean break with their relatives, it is doubtful that most children in his British institutions (as opposed to child emigrants) permanently lost contact with parents and relatives. The available documentation for children's length of stay at Barnardo's institutions is not nearly as detailed as it is for poor law institutions.[34] Nevertheless, it is clear from annual reports that most of the children admitted to Barnardo's during the late-Victorian period remained there for short-term, temporary stays. The report for 1895, for example, classified 63 percent of the 3,996 admissions as temporary and 37 percent as permanent. The percentage of temporary admissions remained consistent for the next decade, until Barnardo's death in 1905, after which the organization reversed its earlier policy and began accepting significantly larger numbers of younger children for long-term rather than temporary shelter.[35]

These general distinctions between temporary and permanent children are useful, but they still do not provide any definite information about the average length of stay. Barnardo himself mentioned that it was common for children to remain in his institutions for periods of only several months. In the mid-1870s, he regretted that the Stepney Boys' Home (opened in 1870) did not have enough room to keep boys longer, because of the high demand for his services: *"we are compelled to pass boys very quickly through the house, often giving them but three, four, or six months' training, and then send them out on their life to make room for others."*[36] By the late 1880s, Barnardo estimated that the average length of stay at Stepney was about one year, but that younger boys from ten to thirteen often remained at Leopold House for three years.[37] In a confidential leaflet advising against contributions to Barnardo's, the Charity Organisation Society observed that in 1888 "the average stay of a child under the care of the institution, including the time spent in the colonies, is very little more than a year."[38] It is possible that after being cared for by Barnardo's institutions for a period of a year or more, children returned to their parents or at least had some contact with parents before being transferred to another institution or beginning employment.

"Absconding"

At times children, not parents, limited the length of their stays by "absconding," that is, running away, from both public and private institutions and returning, in many cases, to their parents. Newly established institutions often lacked the organization and discipline, not to mention the secure walls and gates, that discouraged children from running away. Anerley, for example, the North Surrey District School, opened in 1850 with a public celebration for which Charles Dickens, the Archbishop of Canterbury, and the editors of

London's major newspapers had bought tickets.[39] Any hopes of effortlessly reforming poor children vanished, however, with the first transfer of inmates from the workhouses. The school chaplain wrote to Edward Tufnell, "Scarcely a day passed without two or more [children] absconding, either returning to their respective workhouses or prowling about the country."[40]

As institutions became more established, it was less common for children to run away. During the year 1882–83, only a recorded 20 out of a total of 1,351 child residents ran away from Barnardo's homes.[41] But institutions could do little to prevent determined children from escaping. A repeat runaway, Edward Sowden, once escaped the Marlesford Lodge branch school twice in twenty-four hours. He was returned first by his mother at 7 P.M., only to escape again at 1:30 A.M., this time being brought back by a police constable.[42] In the 1910s, one boy ran away from Charles Spurgeon's Stockwell Orphanage nine times, returning on each occasion to his mother, before officials decided he should return permanently to his home.[43]

Often parents or officials sent the runaway children back to the institutions. Edgar and Fred Wood repeatedly ran away from several different poor law schools. When they escaped together from the Marlesford Lodge branch school, their mother returned them.[44] In other cases, children appear to have persuaded parents to keep them at home or place them with other relatives. For example, three days after his admission, W. G. Morey of Chelsea ran away from Marlesford Lodge "to his mother—who then took his discharge."[45] After Ernest Hull absconded from Banstead, his mother sent a police constable to the school "to say [the] lad had arrived home safely."[46] Together with the much more common cases of parents retrieving their children, such examples of running away meant that a child's institutionalization most often did not result in a permanent or even long-term separation from his or her parent(s).

Visits between Parents and Children

When children remained in public or private institutions for stays longer than several months, their parents often maintained contact through periodic visits. State poor law schools and Barnardo's homes established their own mini-societies in the late-Victorian period, but they were far from "total institutions" that secluded children from all contact with the outside world. Even if institutionalization obviously limited and regulated future contact in a way that was extremely painful for many parents and children, it did not, by and large, succeed in destroying the bonds between poor parents and children. Displaying a clear sense of their rights as citizens, parents expected that they would be allowed to visit their children, and they often negotiated with officials for increased visiting opportunities. When officials denied parents access to children, some mothers and fathers responded with a sense of injustice that prompted them to ask their local guardians for help, to write letters, to file formal complaints with the courts, and to appeal to the press for support. Middle-class reformers were often quick to denounce poor parents as noncitizens who did not deserve basic English rights and protections. Yet, despite substantial bureaucratic barriers, poor parents were adept at using the options available to them to oppose treatment that they considered unjust.

Poor law policies certainly did not make it easy for parents to visit their children. Most poor law schools limited visiting days to once a month or once every other month.[47] In the case of the boys' training ship *Goliath,* which was run by the Forest Gate School District, parents and relatives could visit on board the ship only once every four months.[48] Other rules discouraged relatives and friends from making frequent, unregulated visits. Visiting hours were scheduled for weekdays, with all bank holidays excluded,[49] making it difficult for working parents to visit their children. Local guardians often served as advocates for parents, but sometimes were disregarded by school officials. For example, the managers of Ashford, the West London District School, refused a request from the Fulham Board of Guardians to add an additional visiting day on the third Saturday of every month, "which would probably be a very convenient day for both friends and children." The managers claimed that Saturdays were admission days and that "a monthly visiting day affords reasonable facilities to relatives."[50] In addition to working within the school schedules, visitors also had to secure a special visiting order signed by their local union guardians or relieving officer.[51] Furthermore, at least one school forbade visitors from bringing children under seven with them, thereby adding to the burden of visiting parents who still had younger children in their care.[52]

In spite of these regulations, visiting days were popular and at times even festive events. In the early 1890s, the managers of Forest Gate, who limited visiting days to one weekday every other month, found themselves overwhelmed by visitors. On one visiting day alone, more than four hundred friends and relatives showed up at the school, which had a population of roughly seven hundred youths, many of them siblings who would receive visits from the same friends or relatives. The Forest Gate managers disapproved of the "confusion" characteristic of visiting days, noting "the occasional misconduct of some of the visitors, who regarded the matter in the nature of an 'outing.'"[53] Such comments suggest that friends and relatives of the children treated the visiting days as holiday excursions, an opportunity to socialize and escape the worst aspects of their own neighborhoods in Whitechapel and Poplar. In the case of Forest Gate, officials responded by expanding rather than limiting parental access to children. To lessen the crowds of visitors and prevent disruptions to the school routine, they eventually increased the visiting days from once every other month to every Wednesday and Saturday afternoon.[54]

In practice, the school managers at Forest Gate were much more flexible than their official policies suggest. By expanding the visiting days, managers not only improved school discipline by cutting down on the overall "confusion" caused by large groups of visitors, but also recognized and accommodated parents' rights to visit their children. Although unwilling to give parents free access to children, much like boarding schools for middle- and upper-class youths, managers at other poor law schools also worked with parents to ensure that visits were possible without extreme inconveniences. For example, the Ashford superintendent requested a special room where "parents or friends can visit their children."[55] Ashford managers also approved the transfer of a girl from St. John's Home, Ipswich, so that her mother, who lived in the area, could visit more easily.[56] In another case, a mother anxious to see her child complained to her local parish guardians that she wasted needless time waiting at Ashford while school officials searched for the youth's exact whereabouts. The school managers determined that the confusion arose because the child had been sent to the infirmary. In response to the complaint, they recommended that lists of children in the infirmary be posted on visiting days for friends and relatives.[57] Far from being helpless victims of totalizing institutions, parents clearly felt that they had legitimate claims to visit their children without undue burdens and that school officials should accommodate their requests.

It was less common, but not altogether rare, for children to leave poor law institutions to visit parents or relatives under special circumstances. In response to requests from local union guardians, which likely originated with relatives, schools permitted children to visit "dangerously ill" parents in the workhouse infirmary.[58] Managers also arranged for groups of children from Ashford to make regular trips to their parents in the general workhouse.[59] Parents and relatives sometimes requested that children be allowed to leave institutions temporarily in order to attend major family events. The Hackney Board of Guardians, for example, approved an uncle's request for the temporary release of four children so that they could attend their father's funeral, but denied a mother's petition to take her son from the Strand school to "Ongar & Brentwood [other poor law schools] to visit his sister & brothers before he goes into the Army."[60]

Relatives frequently desired that children temporarily leave poor law schools during summer and Christmas holidays, but school directors rarely granted such requests. For example, in 1896 authorities allowed Eliza McCarthy to "take her children from the School [Norwood] in the morning and take them back in [the] evening for the purpose of allowing them to visit Friends & Relatives" during her week of summer vacation.[61] At least through the early 1900s, however, officials generally denied the entreaties steadily flowing in from parents, grandparents, aunts and uncles, and older siblings to release children for Christmas and other holidays.[62]

The reluctance of officials to grant children temporary leaves from poor law institutions did not stop the onslaught of requests from parents and other family members. The *East London Observer* reported in 1889 that the December meeting of the Stepney Board of Guardians was primarily "occupied in listening to the applications of parents who were desirous of having their children with them on Christmas Day." To all of these requests, "the Chairman was compelled to return a negative answer, owing to the prevalence of diphtheria and fever, and the risk of infection."[63] Noting that the refusal of requests for children's temporary leaves was "sometimes regarded as a hardship" by relatives, the managers of Forest Gate likewise made an extra effort to outline their policy to the public. They prepared and sent a notice to the relatives explaining why children in the school could not have temporary leaves. Children discharged by parents for temporary visits could reenter the school only after the normal process of probation in the workhouse and the reception ward at Forest Gate. The policy, managers stressed, was intended to prevent "the introduction of disease into the School, and not from any want of sympathy with relatives."[64]

Many authorities conflated fears of disease with fears of immorality associated with pauperism, but at least the Forest Gate managers acknowledged that parents had a legitimate claim to see their children and that only a more pressing concern—the fear of actual disease—could interfere with this claim. Perhaps the Forest Gate managers' assertion of "sympathy with relatives" was simply an attempt to prevent more forceful protests from relatives who viewed restrictions on the children's leave as a "hardship." But the notice was also an admission that parents were anxious to see their children. The frequent requests by parents for children's leave, their visits to the institutions, and their complaints over relatively minor matters such as a long wait affirm that parents wanted to remain in contact with their children and that many thought they had the right to negotiate the terms of this contact.

Barnardo's stated visiting policies were similar to those of poor law institutions, but they eventually became the subject of many more disputes between parents and officials. Visiting policies at Barnardo's various central London institutions were less strict than those at the Barkingside Girls' Village Home, where there was a greater effort to isolate girls characterized as being in moral danger, and it followed that boys gained more access to parents and relatives than girls. Relatives and friends could visit the Girls' Village Home only once every three months, and they had to apply for an admission card at least one week in advance.[65] Officials monitored meetings between children and parents,[66] but at times youths could go on excursions to visit relatives. When he was nine years old, Arthur Harding (b. 1886) entered Barnardo's Leopold House on Mile End Road after the police found him "sleeping rough" in the streets. Leopold House was "a penny tram ride" from Harding's home. He recalled, "We were allowed out on Saturdays about 1 o'clock and I went home and stayed a few hours."[67] Harding claimed that "Dr. Barnardo's seemed to occupy the largest part of my childhood from nine until I was nearly twelve years old," when he returned to live with his family. In his memoirs, however, there are few references to Barnardo's, and these focus not on his experiences within the institution but on his visits with relatives. Harding described his weekly trips back to Leopold House with his sister, who gave him money for candy, and his first and only visit to his grandparents in Hoxton Workhouse with his mother, who wanted to show off his "smart," soldierlike Barnardo uniform.[68] At least in memory, Harding's time at Barnardo's worked to accentuate rather than undermine his family bonds.

Other children saw their parents less regularly, but in some cases enjoyed extended holiday visits with relatives. Charles Gough (b. 1886) entered Barnardo's with his older brother when he was four and remained under the institution's care for more than fourteen years. When Gough's widowed mother pleaded to have the boys visit her at Swindon, officials agreed and made arrangements for the boys' travel, which their aunt supervised.[69] By admitting their children to a private rather than a state institution, parents were more likely to have their access to children restricted or even denied; but even Barnardo's allowed many parents to have periodic contact with children.

Although it was not uncommon for Barnardo's institutions to allow parents access to institutionalized children, the organization restricted visitation on a level that would have been impossible within the poor law system. After a child's admission to one of his homes, Barnardo often personally refused visits from parents whom he judged to be not "of good character." This practice sparked a barrage of complaints in the late 1880s and early 1890s. Pointing to the violation of their parental rights, parents protested that Barnardo misled them and, moreover, that his actions were illegal. Yet, unlike the poor law institutions, Barnardo's organization was not subject to oversight by a parallel bureaucracy and network of local outposts through which parents could file complaints. If Barnardo or another official denied relatives access to their children, there was no local parish guardian or relieving officer who might serve as an advocate, no local board of guardians' meetings before which to present a case, no formally recognized system through which to voice complaints and receive a response. Thus, when relatives wanted to pursue complaints that the charity had ignored or dismissed, they tended to turn to the most readily available and familiar authorities outside of the private institution: local police court magistrates and the press.

Local metropolitan police courts, or "petty sessions," first created in the late eighteenth century, provided the primary legal services for the poor when it came to criminal charges not requiring a trial before a jury.[70] By the mid-nineteenth century, London's twenty-three magistrates typically heard cases that revealed the strains of urban life: rental disputes, petty theft, truancy, vagrancy, drunkenness, gambling, licensing violations, food adulteration, domestic violence, sexual assault, and attempted suicide.[71] Magistrates personally decided whether to dismiss a case, to pass it on to a higher court, or to rule on the case themselves. They had the power to award damages and punishments, which were usually in the form of fines or hard labor and could at times be shockingly harsh, as in the 1889 case of a man sentenced to two months' hard labor for stealing a piece of bacon.[72] As the only courts to which most working people had access, the police courts frequently supported workers in complaints against poor law guardians, the police, and school board authorities.[73]

Like the earlier justices of the peace, police court magistrates also served as general resources for the poor, offering advice, informally negotiating disputes, and, when appropriate, doling out funds from the poor boxes kept in each of London's thirteen police courts. Individuals often sought general guidance from their local magistrates concerning family matters. For example, a man appeared before the Woolwich magistrate requesting "advice respecting his son, aged 17, who forsook his work and gave him great trouble." On learning that the son was tall, the magistrate suggested the boy become a soldier—a solution that pleased the father if not the son.[74] At times, family melodramas unfolded before the courts. One father appealed to the Worship Street magistrate for advice in dealing with his eighteen-year-old daughter, a repeat runaway charged with stealing a shawl from her father. Most recently, the warrant officer had discovered the girl at a Birmingham brothel with her younger sister. The father had wanted to send the girl to a "home" to keep her from "a dissolute life," but he now recanted before the court: "crying, [he] said that he had a good home, and should like to have his daughter if she would promise to behave well" and "act a daughter's part." The magistrate "at length yielded and, advising the prisoner for her good, allowed her to be discharged."[75]

When magistrates could offer no immediate solution, either because the case was outside of their jurisdiction or involved a private rather than criminal matter, parents in dispute with private institutions often drew on the influence of the local press to raise public awareness and support. Journalists, who regularly sat in on police court proceedings in wait for sensational cases, consciously provided a public forum in which the working classes could have some sort of dialogue, however limited, with welfare and state officials. Press reports, albeit highly selective, provide the only record of cases before police courts that did not result in formal criminal trials. Individuals brought reports of missing persons and charity appeals before magistrates with the expectation that the press would publicize their cause.[76] In November 1876, the London *Times* printed a magistrate's charitable appeal for donations to help the surviving daughter of Sebastian Pether, a landscape painter, who was destitute after ruining her eyesight working as a needlewoman. The magistrate requested that "if the Press would only make this case known," he "was sure either that some society would come forward and aid Miss Pether or that the charitably disposed would do something that would make a permanent provision for her." Within a week, the paper reported the receipt of numerous generous donations.[77] The press thus served as an advocate for poor Londoners, an outlet for their complaints, and a reminder to the broader society of their rights and liberties.

Parents and relatives of institutionalized children who objected to Barnardo's visitation policies had few alternatives than to turn to the police courts. Although magistrates generally denied having any legal powers to intervene in these cases, they often voiced support for poor parents and in some cases suggested that the press take up their cause in hopes of pressuring Barnardo to respond. In December 1889, for example, the *Standard* reported that "[a] young woman who applied for advice [at the Thames Police Court] stated she took her little girl to Dr. Barnardo's Home three months ago, and although she had made four applications to see her, she was unable to do so.

They refused to let her have her."[78] The magistrate determined that Barnardo was improperly detaining the child and sent an officer of the court with the applicant to the Girls' Village Home.

In a similar case, a woman appealing to the Thames Police Court testified that "she had two children in Dr. Barnardo's Home, and the rules were that the children could be visited once in three months or be written to once a month, but the authorities of the Home declined to tell her where they were."[79] The magistrate regretted that he had no jurisdiction, but suggested that the press publicize the recent conflicts in hopes of pressuring Barnardo to explain his actions. He referred the woman and her husband to the High Court for a writ of *habeas corpus*—a process requiring legal counsel that was prohibitively expensive for impoverished parents.[80] These parents desired to maintain contact with their children and expected that visits would be allowed within certain reasonable restrictions. Shocked and angered that Barnardo had jettisoned "the rules" and denied them access to their children, parents seeking visitation rights, like the parents demanding custody rights discussed later in this chapter, protested in the courts available to them.

Parental Supervision of Institutionalized Children

In addition to having direct contact with their institutionalized children, parents also supervised the children's care in significant ways. In cases where children required exceptional medical treatment, it was common for poor law authorities first to seek parental consent. Parents also complained when they believed authorities mistreated children and at times pressed for the punishment of guilty employees. Finally, parental supervision of children was most generally apparent, although at times highly contested, in decisions about children's religious instruction. Important differences emerge between public and private institutions in their policies concerning these issues. Whereas poor law authorities generally accepted parents' rights to oversee their children in these areas, Barnardo's, like many other private children's charities, increasingly sought to limit parental involvement.

Medical Supervision

Poor law institutions, in particular, reaffirmed parental rights by requesting parents' consent in cases where children required extensive or controversial medical treatment. Parents were required to give their consent verbally or in the form of a signed document for operations performed on their children.[81] For example, in the late 1890s poor law authorities temporarily transferred nine-year-old Mary Driscall from the Orpington poor law school to a hospital ship at Dartford when she was diagnosed with smallpox. While on board the ship, she developed a complication in one eye that required surgery. The Bermondsey relieving officer took steps to confirm that Mary's father, a resident of the Rotherhithe infirmary, had visited Mary and, upon the advice of the medical officer, given his consent prior to her surgery.[82] Operations were not the only medical reasons for officials to confer with parents. By 1916, the Ashford school recommended that the superintendent inform parents and local guardians when children suffered from any serious accident, such as a fractured bone.[83] Interactions between poor law officials and parents because of children's serious medical conditions were a rare but important way that parents maintained their ties to children.

Perhaps the most significant area in which parents supervised their children's medical care involved the controversial issue of smallpox vaccination. After Edward Jenner developed an effective vaccine in the 1790s, Parliament passed a series of acts aimed at establishing free, national, and compulsory vaccination.[84] There was widespread resistance to compulsory vaccination, however, and several anti-vaccination organizations developed between the 1860s and 1890s. The organized resistance took several forms, but it was centered primarily in the working class and largely motivated by an appeal to parental rights. Many individuals disputed vaccination on scientific as well as moral grounds (largely because of the injection of calf lymph into the human body), and protesters believed that parents, not the state, should decide whether to vaccinate their children.

Most important, the resistance movement linked working-class parental rights with the rights of national citizenship. At the 1885 Leicester anti-vaccination demonstration, where Jenner's hanged effigy was paraded and a spirited rendition of *Rule Britannia* sung, a London protester stated "[t]hat the principle of the compulsory Vaccination Acts is subversive of that personal liberty which is the birthright of every Briton; that they are destructive of parental right, tyrannical, [and] unjust in their operation."[85] By 1898, Lord Salisbury argued that compulsory vaccination might be acceptable for imperial subjects, but that such state regulation challenged the intrinsic, traditional liberties of freeborn English citizens. "It is idle to tell me that the people [anti-vaccinationists] are wrong or that they are deceived; as long as they have feelings they will resist," he declared. "They are Englishmen, and it is no use to quote to me the precedents of India and Ceylon to show the way in which their prejudices can be overcome."[86]

In this context, institutional policies concerning smallpox vaccination could be an especially charged issue. Although, as Nadja Durbach demonstrates, working-class anti-vaccinationists often sought to distinguish themselves from "unrespectable" paupers, the poorest of the working class also asserted their right to supervise their children's medical care.[87] Barnardo's institutions, which were generally less willing to keep parents informed about their children's welfare than poor law institutions, seem to have routinely vaccinated children without parental consent after frequent outbreaks of smallpox in 1901.[88] Poor law schools also responded to the outbreak of smallpox in London in 1901, but their handling of children's vaccination reveals a much greater general concern for parental consent. In November 1901 the managers of the Ashford District School requested that local guardians approve the re-vaccination of all children over seven in the school.[89] The guardians from Hammersmith, Paddington, and St. George's unions replied that children over ten could be re-vaccinated, "subject to the consent of the parents being obtained."[90] The Paddington guardians later forwarded to the Ashford managers "lists of children whose parents consent to their re-vaccination, or who may be re-vaccinated without such consent, being [orphaned, deserted, or abused children] under the control of the Guardians"; accompanying the lists were "particulars of cases in which the consent of the parents has been refused."[91]

The re-vaccination of children was not required by legislation, but it is nevertheless significant that officials were so careful to pursue parental consent for this medical procedure. Given the intensity of the debate over compulsory vaccination, poor law officials felt compelled to recognize the rights of poor parents to dictate the treatment of their children's bodies.

Complaints of Abuse

Parental supervision of institutionalized children extended beyond the relatively nonconfrontational, bureaucratic requests for parental consent in cases of medical treatment. Parents protested when they thought officials unjustly punished, neglected, or otherwise abused their children. Some poor law schools had specific guidelines regarding the punishment of children. Banstead, organized according to the cottage home system, directed that "[t]he [cottage] fathers and mothers are on no pretense to inflict corporal punishment, or deprive the children of their food, and no child is to be punished by confinement in a dark room."[92] School officials sometimes ignored such guidelines, however, and frequently dismissed parental complaints after a brief investigation.

In cases of extreme abuse, parents as well as local communities staged public protests. When the nurse at Hackney's Brentwood infants' school "pushed [a girl] down [a] stone staircase," causing her death, it was the mother's outrage that sparked an investigation revealing a history of horrific abuses at the school.[93] The nurse, Ella Gillespie, received five years' penal servitude for abusing children from 1886 to 1893. She was accused of hitting children with various objects and of requiring "basket drill" at night—a sadistic exercise in which she forced children to "walk round the dormitory in their bare feet, and with a basket on their heads containing their day clothes." Among other instances of cruelty, she deprived infants of sufficient water, so that if "it was raining they went into the playground and drank the water out of the puddles."[94]

In the aftermath of the Gillespie case, the superintendent and matron of Brentwood resigned. But when the Hackney Board of Guardians supported giving them pensions despite the abuses that had occurred under their authority, locals organized a "crowded meeting of Hackney ratepayers" that "became of a noisy character." They eventually passed a "resolution of protest" against the pensions "by an overwhelming majority."[95] A local cleric later dismissed the meeting as "a gathering of rowdies," and one of the guardians regretted the "board's yielding to public clamour." But other board members took the local protest more seriously, voting nine to eight in favor of rescinding the pensions.

If the Brentwood case demonstrates how entire communities rallied to protect pauper children in the face of public scandal, the more mundane, everyday inquiries and protests provide the most comprehensive evidence of parents' desire to oversee the care of their children. For example, a mother protested that her son was "not kindly treated" at the Working Boys' Home where the Bermondsey Board of Guardians had sent him, and she requested that the boy be discharged. A relieving officer investigated the complaint, though he concluded that "the Superintendent is more than kind (having of course a due regard to discipline) to those placed under his charge."[96] Parents wrote letters to their local guardians and school officials as a means of monitoring and, they hoped, influencing the treatment of their children, often requesting explanations when children had been hurt. One mother demanded to know why officials gave her son a punishment of six strokes. The school managers replied that the boy was guilty of "generally unsatisfactory conduct, taking the keys from the Chargemaster's room, unlocking noors [sic] and climbing on the roof of the building."[97] Whether the mother believed the punishment fit her child's actions remains unclear, but she at least felt justified in questioning the school officials about the treatment of her son, and the managers were willing to explain their actions.

In other cases, parental complaints prompted school directors to reprimand abusive staff. After a mother wrote to complain that her son "had been boxed on the ear" by a school official, managers warned the man against striking children.[98] A letter to the Fulham Board of Guardians from a Mrs. Winfield claimed that "on examining her [recently discharged] boys, she found the youngest, Fred, had a bruise on his back caused by the Yardmaster striking him with a walking stick." After the managers discovered that the master had also hit several other boys, they "severely reprimanded" him and sent an oblique apology to the mother, professing to "regret the incident, if such took place, it being contrary to orders."[99] Parents criticized officials for mistreating children not only physically but also emotionally. After one of her sons ran home to her from Ashford, a mother protested that the child had been cruelly treated by a porter who unjustly confiscated the boy's flute, given to him by his dead father, and hit his two younger brothers on the head.[100]

In order to make such complaints, parents required a substantial knowledge of the poor law bureaucracy and its workings. In fact, the parents of children in poor law institutions had significant access to officials and procedural outlets for complaints. They could file protests with their local guardians or directly with school managers. Although poor law officials eventually dismissed many parental charges, they at least maintained the pretense of investigating serious as well as more minor complaints and responded to parents. By writing letters and appealing to their local officials, parents exercised their rights to remain informed about the treatment of their children and to demand a standard of decent care.

In contrast, parents with children at Barnardo's institutions had few outlets for protest. Barnardo often dismissed parental charges of abuse outright, forcing parents to turn directly to the press and the courts for assistance. In the midst of Barnardo's conflict with the Reverend George Reynolds during the late 1870s, the press reported numerous charges of abuse against Barnardo. Reynolds's sensationalist attack on Barnardo, *Dr. Barnardo's Homes, Containing Startling Revelations,* included charges of solitary confinement of children for days at a time, child neglect, and physical abuse. According to Reynolds, admittedly an extremely problematic source, parents were horrified by the treatment of their children at Barnardo's institutions. Reynolds recounted that a Mrs. Wallbridge, "now a Bible woman," had placed her two boys and two girls in Barnardo's homes. She later complained that the children found the food inedible and suffered from ill health. They were overworked, treated unkindly, and forced to write false letters stating that "they were very happy and comfortable." After visiting her children, Mrs. Wallbridge protested that they were in fact sickly and neglected; their "shirts were filthy, their clothes greasy, and their language vile."[101]

Reynolds's accusations may have been the product of a disgruntled evangelical losing power to Barnardo in the East End, but it is less easy to dismiss the barrage of attacks from parents against Barnardo that surfaced in the Thames Police Court and the press a decade later. Barnardo tried to dismiss these complaints by suggesting that "[m]uch of the Police Court reporting of the metropolis is in the hands of a small number of Irish Roman Catholic pressmen, and to such, it need hardly be said, the name of our [Protestant] Homes is at all times obnoxious."[102] The number and nature of the complaints, however, cast serious doubts on Barnardo's claim of a Catholic conspiracy.

In one case before the Thames magistrate, for example, William Pratt requested assistance in finding his fifteen-year-old disabled son Harry, who had recently run away from Barnardo's Stepney Causeway Home after a six-month stay. As reported by the *Standard,* the father "believed the boy left in consequence of the ill-treatment he was subjected to, as every time he came on a visit to [the] Applicant he complained of having been struck by the officials." William Pratt's most damning and ultimately contested piece of evidence was a letter written by Harry to his mother:

> Dear mother,—I write to let you know how I am treated in the home. On Thursday one of the officers hit me because I could not walk quick enough for him, and so I answered him back. On the night I wanted to go in the bath he would not let me. He knocked me down in the bath, and I ran outside naked. He took me in the towel-room, and kicked and punched me till I could not move. They are going to birch me because I lifted up my crutch to him. Would you come on Monday and see about it? I shall run away from here next week if they do it. So good-bye, from your loving son, HARRY PRATT.[103]

According to Barnardo, the letter contained "an utterly baseless and trumped up charge," and he declared that even the boy's mother had admitted it to be "groundless" and had requested that Harry be allowed to remain at Stepney Causeway because she could not keep him in her one-room dwelling.[104]

No matter what the truth was, Harry Pratt's case demonstrates how parents continued to meet and negotiate, even battle, with officials. Furthermore, motivated by the boy's disappearance and a belated sense of outrage at his treatment, William Pratt eventually brought his case to the public by appealing to the police magistrate. On some level, this father believed that Barnardo had mistreated his son and should be held accountable.

Such charges of abuse against poor law and Barnardo's officials were likely not representative of the general treatment of children in these institutions. There are many equally compelling testimonies about kind, even loving officials. Rather, these cases prove that many poor parents struggled to maintain supervision over their children and, when necessary, held welfare providers accountable for abusive treatment.

Religious Instruction

More than parental medical supervision or concerns about abuse, the issue of religious instruction brought to the forefront a connection—either symbolic or active—between children and their parents. At times, Barnardo blatantly ignored the religious wishes of parents, and he gained notoriety for training Catholic children in his homes as Protestants. Unlike Barnardo's, poor law institutions were more attuned to parents' religious wishes and in some cases made special provisions to ensure that children received the proper religious instruction.

As poor law children's institutions became more specialized over the course of the nineteenth century, separate institutions developed to serve children of different religions. Reflecting the larger debate over national education, an issue charged with religious tension, Catholic advocates in the 1860s lamented that the state denied Catholic poor law children religious instruction in their faith. One critic likened the care of Catholic children in poor law institutions to "kidnapping and forcible proselytizing on a gigantic scale."[105] In response to such complaints, poor law authorities gradually made better provisions for the religious instruction of non-Anglican children. After 1868, poor law authorities were required by law to keep creed registers of all pauper inmates. Children in state-run poor law schools attended Church of England services, but by the 1860s guardians could send non-Anglican children to privately established denominational schools certified by the central Poor Law Board, and, after 1871, by the Local Government Board. By the 1890s, there were sixteen Roman Catholic certified schools in London serving 2,265 children.[106] In contrast to the situation in the 1860s and even 1870s, it was generally rare by the end of the century to find non-Anglican children in the poor law schools. Local guardians tended to transfer Jewish children directly from the workhouse to the Norwood Jewish Orphanage and Roman Catholic children to Catholic certified schools.[107]

Guardians paid the certified schools a weekly sum for these children's upkeep and, whenever possible, sought parental approval before transferring

children. In many cases, parents' wishes about their children's religious affiliation had more to do with familial identification than religious practice. One
mother told the relieving officer that she was a Protestant and that her five children had "been sent to the Goeling Street Protestant Mission Hall when any-
where." After her husband entered the infirmary, however, she requested that
three of their children be sent to a Roman Catholic school because he was
Catholic.[108]

In cases where non-Anglican children entered poor law institutions, officials were occasionally willing to provide special arrangements. After receiving
pressure from the central Poor Law Board in 1871, the directors of the *Goliath*
training ship, managed by the Forest Gate School District, eventually allowed
boys to attend Roman Catholic services on land when the weather permitted. It
is doubtful, however, that officials encouraged the boys to attend Catholic
masses; in the following years a number of youths sought conversion to the
Church of England so that they could attend services on board the ship. Yet
even in these cases, poor law officials approved the boys' conversions only if
they were over twelve years old (the age by which they were considered able to
make their own religious decisions) and, in many cases, if they had been
orphaned or deserted by their parents.[109]

Most poor law institutions seem to have been increasingly willing to provide for non-Anglican children as the century progressed. Before the opening of
the Banstead cottage homes in 1880, the managers considered establishing separate cottages for Roman Catholic children, who would attend Catholic services
at the school and be cared for by Catholic officers.[110] Even the special
Opthalmia School run by the Central London School District welcomed visits
from Roman Catholic nurses by the late 1890s.[111] In early-twentieth-century
instances, the managers of Marlesford Lodge arranged for a rabbi to visit a
child inmate, and officials supported a Jewish mother's request that her daughter move from the Ashford District School to a Jewish certified school so that
"the child may be brought up in the Jewish religion."[112] In the decades after the
1860s, poor law institutions came to respect children's religious instruction as
an important symbolic and sometimes active link connecting children with their
parents.

Custody Conflicts and the Rights of Poor Parents

As the director of private, and specifically Protestant, institutions,
Barnardo was under no obligation to respect children's religious backgrounds.
Parents who signed his admission agreement forms knew that the children
would receive instruction in the Protestant faith, although Catholic as well as
Protestant parents sometimes admitted their children but refused to sign the
agreements.[113] When parents requested to remove their children from
Barnardo's for religious reasons, he typically refused. Critical of Barnardo's
decisions, the Bishop of Salford compared his homes unfavorably with the

more flexible poor law institutions: "In every way the State seems to respect the religion of the subject. The opposite of this is the case in some of our great philanthropic institutions."[114]

On religious issues—as in other areas, such as parental visitation and general freedom of removal—Barnardo restricted parental controls over children that were for the most part routine under the poor law. Parents did not passively accept these limitations, however. They responded in the late 1880s and early 1890s by pursuing several highly public custody suits against Barnardo, which in turn sparked the numerous parental complaints against him before local police court magistrates.[115]

The most prominent custody cases to reach the High Court in 1889 involved three Catholic children: Harry Gossage, Martha Tye, and John James Roddy. Barnardo had weathered similar custody disputes, especially ones regarding Catholic children, since the founding of his first homes in the 1870s, but never before had these conflicts reached the High Court.[116] In 1885, he boasted that *"in no fewer than forty-seven well-marked cases"* he had "invaded the legal domain of parental control" and ignored the "cuckoo cry of 'Liberty of the subject!'" Adhering to *"moral* law" above *"judicial* law," Barnardo advocated *"philanthropic abduction"* in *"defiance* of the law of the land" when a child's welfare was at stake.[117] He openly acknowledged that the court system allowed him to take such actions without penalty, because poor parents filing cases against him were unlikely able to afford the required appearance before a judge in chambers.

In each of the three 1889 custody cases, the children's parents (whom the Catholic solicitors Leathley and Co. eventually represented) requested that the children be transferred to a Catholic institution within the year after their admission to Barnardo's homes. Barnardo refused to discharge the children and instead sent two abroad and one to stay in the countryside. The courts eventually issued writs of *habeus corpus* against Barnardo in all three cases, but he claimed to be unable to track down the children (and it appears that the children were never transferred to Catholic institutions or returned to their parents). Barnardo was forced to pay the court costs, which likely contributed to his institution's 1893 financial crisis, but he still effectively succeeded with his plan of "philanthropic abduction."[118]

In all three custody trials, Barnardo highlighted the parents' immorality and represented them as part of a greater Catholic threat to the English nation. In *Night and Day* he described how Gossage's mother sold him to organ-grinders (a disputed charge) and falsified evidence to claim that Roddy arrived "clothed in mere rags and looking half starved" (even though his admission photograph showed a healthy child "neatly and cleanly dressed").[119] At the same time, Barnardo developed an additional argument that denied parents' agency. He claimed that the "poor relatives" demanding custody were "but pawns on the chessboard, to be pushed forward frequently as mere cover for the secret designs of the real parties," namely, the Catholic Church.[120] Barnardo decried the "secret

Romish attempts to lay hands on my children" and made a general "*appeal to the Nation*" for the "English people" to join him against "Romish intolerance and aggression."[121] He argued that the custody battles did not stem from "that most delicate of all questions in an Englishman's mind—THE RIGHTS OF PARENTS," but were instead the product of "the stealthy steps of a crafty, unscrupulous, and usurping ecclesiastical tyranny."[122] In regard to Catholics, Barnardo asserted that religious affiliation had no real relation to familial identity.

The parents of Gossage, Tye, and Roddy undoubtedly received assistance from the Catholic Church in their custody claims, and, at least in the cases of Gossage and Tye, there were worrisome signs that their mothers had been abusive and neglectful. Yet, Barnardo's accusation that a Catholic conspiracy was behind these parents' charges simply does not explain the flood of other custody complaints rising against him. In December 1889, the clerk of the Thames Police Court noted that in response to the highly publicized custody cases, "a panic seemed to have arisen among parents who had children in the home" and "complaints [against Barnardo] were now frequent."[123] These grassroots protests, which often had nothing to do with religion per se, demonstrate how reluctant many poor parents were to relinquish complete control of their children. Perhaps because of their knowledge of the poor law system, many parents expected that they would at the very least be able to supervise their children's health and training. They were surprised and at times outraged when Barnardo used deceptive tactics to prevent all contact with their children. But rather than passively accepting complete separation, many parents filed complaints with the institution and eventually brought their protests to the courts.

Press coverage of police court custody claims against Barnardo often placed the plaintiffs in a sympathetic light while asserting parents' basic right to oversee the care of their children. In one case, the *Times* reported that a widowed, "respectably-dressed woman" who was the mother of eight children told the magistrate that she admitted her "quite healthy and strong" fourteen-year-old son to Barnardo's home three months earlier so that he would be taught a trade. When the mother visited her boy, she found that he was very ill. Barnardo refused her request to reclaim the boy. Although the magistrate recognized the woman's right to her child, he was legally unable to help her.[124] Reporting on the same case, the *Standard* stressed the importance of parental rights and printed the magistrate's proclamation that "Dr. Barnardo had no right to keep a child against the parent's wish."[125]

In other similar cases, magistrates used their authority to advise philanthropists to relinquish children to relatives.[126] But when overzealous reformers failed to regard such advice, parents and relatives were left with few options other than the hope that the press would print accounts of their complaints and pressure the managers of private institutions to act in their favor. The most critical press reports made Barnardo appear more like a slave trader than a heroic philanthropist. The *Standard* recounted how one father "stepped into the witness-box, and said [his] children were taken away without his knowledge, and he objected to Dr. Barnardo detaining them. He would like to know if it were the law of the land that Dr. Barnardo should be allowed to barter children, and do what he liked with them."[127] Likewise appealing to higher standards of legal justice, the local *East End News* reported that a "respectably attired woman" applied to the Thames Police Court magistrate, Mr. Saunders, for help in retrieving her son from Barnardo. When the magistrate replied that "he could not help her," and "she had better go back to Dr. Barnardo's and make another application," the following dialogue took place:

> *Applicant:* Is there no protection for poor women? Can't you help me?
> *Mr. Saunders:* You must go to some other court if you want possession of your boy.
> *Applicant:* This is a court of justice, isn't it?
> *Mr. Saunders:* Yes, but I can't help you.
> Applicant then left the court, saying it was a shame a poor woman was unable to get any redress.[128]

In capturing the theatrics of courtroom melodramas, this exchange reveals how poor families used the courts and the press to assert their own sense of justice and legal rights. According to this applicant, justice should be within reach of all individuals, not only the rich. Although unsuccessful, she demanded that the magistrate protect her parental rights. To fail to do so was to acknowledge that there was one law for the rich and another for the poor. This mother, like the father questioning whether the "law of the land" permitted Barnardo to "barter children" and like the scores of other applicants filing before the Thames Police Court, insisted that Barnardo should not be above the law and that, as a citizen of England, she should have equal access to justice. Denied such access, these parents nonetheless sought every available means within a civil society to regain custody of their children.

Parent-Child Relations after Institutionalization

Parents succeeded in maintaining contact with children while they were institutionalized by temporarily removing them, visiting them on prescribed days, and generally supervising their care. After leaving English public or private institutions for the final time, many children again managed to reconnect with their relatives. Some younger children and even older youths went directly from institutions to the care of their parents. Other youths left the residential institutions after several years to begin work as servants or in some other employment, but they too regularly relied on relatives for economic and emotional support. Although poor law reformers and Barnardo publicly hoped to separate children from their "dreadful pasts," many children returned to parents as young adults and continued to depend on their relatives after institutionalization.

After one admission or several readmissions for a few weeks, months, or years, many children eventually returned from institutions to the care of parents who had regained their health or a certain degree of economic stability. Even among the poor law schools meant for the more "permanent" inmates, children leaving the school to join a mother, father, or both parents represented a significant proportion of discharges. For example, 86 (41 percent) of the 210 discharges from Banstead in 1896–97 were children who returned directly to the care of a parent.[129]

Nineteenth-century anecdotal evidence from Barnardo's institutions suggests that those children who did not emigrate also commonly returned to parents. After fourteen years in Barnardo's homes, Charles Gough recalled "bracing myself for the biggest challenge of my life so far": "the thrill and excitement of going home to my own mother."[130] Eventually in the twentieth century the charity effectively pursued a policy of separating parents and children, but in the early 1900s the Executive Committee resolved to "take the initiative in suggesting or if necessary urging restoration" of children to parents when their circumstances had improved.[131] The extent to which the organization followed this policy is uncertain, but at least in the nineteenth century, when most children entered Barnardo's for relatively temporary, short-term stays, it is likely that many of these children regained contact with relatives after being discharged. In their published letters to welfare officials, discharged children included references to appreciative siblings and parents, highlighting the cooperation between poor relatives and public and private institutions rather than the antagonism that dominated popular fund-raising literature.[132]

Other youths did not return directly to their parents after leaving residential institutions, but instead began working as servants or entered some other employment. The Metropolitan Association for Befriending Young Servants (MABYS), a voluntary organization of upper- and middle-class women founded by Jane Nassau Senior and Henrietta Barnett in the mid-1870s, provided systematic follow-up reports of children who left institutions. The role and authority of MABYS remained highly contested in the 1870s, but by the 1880s and 1890s it was an accepted auxiliary of the poor law, with more than one thousand volunteers and a publishing record in the annual reports of the Local Government Board and various poor law school districts.[133] The MABYS ladies regularly visited discharged poor law girls in their places of service and helped them seek new employment and housing until the girls reached twenty, finding domestic service positions for more than five thousand girls each year by the mid-1880s.[134]

The MABYS reports offer anecdotal evidence of youths desiring and seeking contact with their relatives. For instance, fifteen-year-old E.B. from Whitechapel "[d]id nothing but cry in her first place, as she wanted to be near her mother."[135] In some cases, the girls left their MABYS placement in order to return to relatives. Sixteen-year-old Agnes Farley, a student at the Ashford District School for three and a half years, "[r]an away from her last place and went to her mother." Agnes continued to live with her "bad mother" at least until she was eighteen.[136] After seven years at the Forest Gate District School, fifteen-year-old J.A. from Poplar "[r]an away from a very good situation after 6 months and went to her mother."[137] Nineteen-year-old Mary Ball returned to her mother after over six years' residence in Ashford and three in service. Clara Maystone, a resident of Ashford for twelve years, "[l]eft her place [of service] in June," when she was also nineteen, "with over a year's character, quite suddenly, as her mother wanted her home."[138]

Girls who had been in poor law schools for years left service to care for sick parents and also returned to parents when they were ill themselves. After two and a half years in service and "an excellent character," Alice Knowles became ill and went "home to be nursed by her good mother."[139] Those youths who remained in institutions the longest often still had strong emotional connections with their parents and relatives. The MABYS visitor reported that Ellen Kett, who had been a resident of Ashford for seven and a half of her nineteen years, had "lately lost her mother, which she feels deeply."[140]

Many of the girls leaving poor law schools also found employment through their relatives, preferring these placements to the ones offered by MABYS. Minnie Moody left her first place of service in order to be a "housemaid where her mother is [a] cook." After six years in Ashford, Maud Wadsworth was "doing very well as [a] housemaid in the same place where her mother is housekeeper." E. Jones worked at a German restaurant, "a place found for her by her mother." Ada Carter was "[p]laced by her mother as [an] accountant in a shop in Oxford Street." Jane Lang's mother "placed her at a shop in the Fulham Road," and Ada Stallion's stepmother "apprenticed her to book-binding," work that she could do at home. Nineteen-year-old E.J., who had been a resident of the Forest Gate District School for four years, worked at the same jam factory as her mother. Eager to supervise her daughter, Florence Deer's mother was "anxious to get her into the sorting room of the Laundry at which she herself works." This mother's plan does not seem to have succeeded. Florence remained in service for some time, eventually returning home to her mother to help her brother in his shop—work that she preferred to domestic service. In a case realizing the fears of the MABYS ladies, thirteen-year-old Annie Woolcock was "removed from her first place by her relations, and when last heard of was in the country fruit-picking."[141] Parents sought out employment for their children that would promote close supervision and contact, in many cases preferring daily service or other work that would allow girls to live at home over positions as live-in domestic servants.

Many reformers, but especially those from the upper and middle classes, reviled the children's parents and voiced the often repeated "wish [that] all the girls were foundlings; [since] we no sooner get a girl a good place, where she is going on well, than somebody comes forward to take possession of her and her earnings."[142] MABYS workers considered any contact with relatives suspect. As Tufnell critically observed of its precursor organization, the MABYS classifications for the girls' progress ("satisfactory," "fairly satisfactory," "unsatisfactory," "bad," "in Homes," "dead," "unfit for service," "lost") included a separate category for "gone to relations," which necessarily excluded girls who had returned to relatives from being classified as doing well.[143] Senior originally argued that guardians should have legal custody of children who spent more than five years in poor law schools until they were eighteen or twenty—an extension of state powers over parental rights that many poor law reformers and child philanthropists, including Barnardo, supported at the end of the century. According to Senior, such custody reforms would protect the youths from "ill-treatment by their employers" and, moreover, from "the evil influence" of the children's "own relations."[144]

In spite of the attempts to restrict parent-child contact after youths left institutions, parents remained principal participants in their children's lives, often limiting interaction with welfare officials. Girls and their relatives at times refused all MABYS visits and withheld current addresses. Fifteen-year-old Edith Q., a resident of Forest Gate District School for almost five years, left her first MABYS position after two weeks in order to be closer to her sisters. Her aunt told the visitor, "'Edith will be looked after by her sisters and requires no help from MABYS.'"[145] Elizabeth Simmonds had been in the Ashford District School for almost eight years before beginning a domestic service position arranged by MABYS. Soon, however, she was "taken away from her place by her mother, who refused to let her go to a Training Home, for which she was passed by MABYS, and is now lost sight of."[146]

A common narrative in MABYS reports was that girls became "unsettled" or "upset" by relatives who visited and sometimes removed them from service. In a typical example, the MABYS visitor reported that the mother of C.G. "has unsettled her, wants her to get a place nearer home, and tries to get the girl's money."[147] A similar report on eighteen-year-old Kate Saville, a resident of a district school for five years, gave the following description of her progress after leaving the school: "Left her place [of service] in February, where she had been eighteen months, and done well, and went to her aunt at Ealing. When visited it was found that this aunt and uncle were really her parents; but as she was a 'deserted child' they would not appear as parents. They spent all her money and pawned her clothes. In July she was placed again [by MABYS], and taken away. [She is] Now lost sight of."[148] Philanthropic ladies and parents in disguise battled over the girl's fate. Not even the combined efforts of the state and the voluntary MABYS workers could prevent the reappearance of Kate's parents, who perhaps did want nothing more than their daughter's wages and clothes to pawn. Yet many parents and youths welcomed the support, both financial and emotional, that only family could provide after years of separation.

Conclusion

Looking back on their time at the Ashford District School, two sisters wrote to officials to report the death of their brother in the First World War and thanked them for making Ashford "the home which we look to in our trouble."[149] As a supplementary "home" in times of need, the poor law school provided essential, much appreciated support that ultimately did not sever the connections uniting a family, but rather allowed it to survive periods of crisis. Although there were severe limits on their powers of influence, most parents did not simply abandon their children to institutions. The same poor parents disparaged or omitted in the popular reform literature made broad use of various means of protest within a civil society to modify institutional practices and policies. When children were harshly disciplined, abused, denied appropriate medical care or religious instruction, or illegally detained, parents protested, appealing to those in power most likely to be sympathetic to their cause. They pressured local bureaucrats, wrote letters to welfare officials, organized public protests, and presented their complaints before police courts and the press. In the few cases where funding was available, parents took their accusations against Barnardo's illegal activities to the High Court.

Far from being passive recipients of welfare or victims of "total institutions" who simply deserted their children to institutional care, many parents worked with welfare officials to watch over their children, believing that, despite their poverty, their parental right to do so was a fundamental right of citizenship. Barnardo and other reformers hoped to undermine parents' claim to their children by emphasizing the worst cases of abuse, but the poor nonetheless continued to hold their parental rights as "that most delicate of all questions in an Englishman's mind."

CHAPTER 5

Training "Street Arabs" into British Citizens

MAKING ARTISANS AND
MEMBERS OF EMPIRE

⚜

*I*n 1870 the Forest Gate School District purchased a broken-down ship, the *Goliath,* to serve as a training vessel for boys. The *Goliath* was built as a man-of-war around 1835, converted to a steamer during the Crimean War, and then outfitted as the first ship of a new program to train poor law children for careers in the Royal Navy and mercantile marine.[1] In 1871 a writer for the London *Times* vividly recounted the physical and moral transformation of youths on board the *Goliath:*

> We are told, and we can well believe, that the training supplied on board the "Goliath,"—education not only in books, but in work,—transforms with astonishing rapidity and completeness even the facial and bodily characteristics of the street arabs who have the good fortune to be drafted to the School Ship at Gravesend. Dull eyes brighten, narrow chests expand, stunted figures erect themselves, and the mental and moral nature partakes of the healthy change. In this metamorphosis we have a promise for the future. An addition of energy to the national life, an improvement of the physical type of the race, rescue of thousands from a life of squalor and dependence,—these are gains worth purchasing at a higher price than a few out-of-date wooden men-of-war.[2]

Drawing on a tradition of training poor children for the military that went back to the eighteenth century, reformers emphasized the hard work and moral instruction that theoretically transformed these youths from "street arabs" into productive citizens.[3] Praising the use of training ships for poor law children, Florence Nightingale later wrote: "Every so trained, and so depauperised boy, is a bequest to England worth making."[4] Striking the same note, *Punch* in 1876 devised a "Motto for our Training Ships": "Teaching promotes the vigour of the seed, / And a right training hearts of oak will breed."[5] The desire to create such "hearts of oak"—loyal British citizens—was not only a key theme in reformers' popular fund-raising narratives of child rescue and conversion, but also a primary factor shaping youths' instruction in welfare institutions.

This chapter examines the training children received in public and private institutions and the various models of citizenship that reformers sought to promote. Although parents and welfare officials alike generally valued the training, I argue that they had very different views of its purpose. Welfare officials tended to place greater emphasis on training as a means to teach poor children the values of citizenship. For example, the *Goliath* training ship program drew on older models of citizenship in which the military served as the primary means to integrate poor youths into the nation. Although this military approach to citizenship remained an important element of Victorian child welfare programs, two new citizen ideals came to have even greater influence over children's training: the anti-industrial idealization of independent artisans, which dominated children's instruction in the 1870s and 1880s, and the imperial model of citizenship, which took prominence in the 1890s.

A unifying factor in all Victorian approaches to teaching youths how to be citizens, whether through the inculcation of military, artisanal, or imperial knowledge and values, was that their ultimate employment should physically and morally distance them from their impoverished parents. Yet poor parents often had different goals in mind, bringing their children to institutions so that they could be trained as servants or taught a trade. Economic motives were paramount for these parents as they sought to provide a future for their children that would enable them not only to escape the "squalor and dependence" of poverty, but also to keep their families intact in the long term. In the end, the parents' and children's economic and personal motives were often at odds with the officials' ideological concerns. Basing their training programs on ideals of citizenship rather than practical economic concerns, many institutions prepared children for professions that were ill suited to the late-Victorian and Edwardian industrial economy.

Work, Discipline, and the Artisan Ideal of Citizenship

All child welfare institutions placed great importance on discipline and work as the key values that would enable poor youths to escape the fates of their parents. The earlier generation of poor law reformers—men such as Edwin Chadwick, James Kay, and Edward Tufnell, who promoted the large barrack schools instead of domesticated cottage homes—believed that military training and time discipline were the best means to transform pauper children into productive members of the labor force. Officials sought to discipline children through a variety of daily practices. For example, even at the Banstead cottage homes, the children submitted to an inspection every morning by the cottage "mother" or "father," who checked the children's "cleanliness of person and clothing, to see that their boots are clean, hair and clothes brushed, and buttons and strings on." The day's events—inspection, meals, prayers, recreational breaks, school, professional training, parades, drills, swimming, and the occasional game of cricket or football—proceeded according to strict timetables divided by increments as short as ten minutes from the time the children rose at 6:00 A.M. in summer until their bedtimes between 7:00 and 9:00 P.M.[6] Children's institutions, like adult wards in workhouses, aimed to instill in youths the punctuality, discipline, and deference of industrious laborers.

Beginning with the creation of large children's institutions in the 1840s, reformers lauded physical and military drill exercises as one of the best methods to discipline the minds and bodies of poor children. Tufnell, the inspector of metropolitan poor law schools from the late 1840s until 1874, first popularized the practice of military drill and band training in the schools he oversaw.[7] Chadwick also became a great supporter of children's military drill, successfully campaigning to make drill an accepted part of the curriculum for girls as well as boys in most poor law and board schools by the 1880s.[8] According to Chadwick, drill promoted "sanitary" benefits by improving the children's health; furthermore, it provided important "moral" benefits. "[S]ystematised drill," he wrote, encouraged "all that is implied in the term discipline—viz., Duty, Self-restraint, Order, Punctuality, Obedience to command, Patience." The physical and moral effects of drill combined in what Chadwick termed the "economic" benefits: "by suppleing the joints, rendering the action prompt as well as easy, [and] by giving promptitude in concurrent and punctual action with others," drill contributed "to the efficiency and productive value of the pupils as labourers or as foremen in after life."[9] In contrast to reformers who favored training youths as independent skilled artisans, Chadwick valued how drill developed supple, efficient, "punctual action" in relation to other workers, like a well-oiled machine.

Even Barnardo, who strongly opposed factory and industrial labor, linking such forms of work with social rebellion, praised the "disciplinary" as well as the "physical advantages" of drill. He exercised his male "raw recruits" three times daily in the drill yard with the aim of creating productive workers. "The precision and definiteness of this training," he wrote in 1888, "imprints itself deeply into the character of the boy whose life has hitherto too often been wild and aimless, and its lessons leave their mark on the whole round of his work."[10]

The process of training poor children as orderly laborers also involved teaching them to respect the rights of private property. At times, children's attacks on school property threatened to demolish entire institutions, signifying how the youths' objections to school discipline could develop into more serious expressions of class-based protest. The chaplain of the North Surrey District School at Anerley, one of the first district schools opened in 1850, wrote to Tufnell to complain about the behavior of the school's initial group of pupils: "The slightest restraint exercised over them was immediately revenged by destruction of property, a trait peculiarly workhouse."[11] Tufnell later described these disruptions as "a riot," in which the children destroyed £100 worth of property during the month after the school opened. The example of youths setting fire to a newly opened poor law school in Manchester contributed to Tufnell's generalization in 1860 that "on the opening of a district school we have almost invariably had a riot and great destruction of property."[12] Reformers identified this lack of respect for property—"a trait peculiarly workhouse"—as one of the main vices that prevented paupers from becoming independent laborers.

Officials used various approaches to instill in children a respect for property. Tufnell spoke in military terms. After the initial chaos following a school opening, the children, he believed, would "get under proper control, and then all the new comers who are as vicious as the first portion will soon fall into the moral tone of the school." Confident that children would respect school property as soon as officials established the institutional routine, Tufnell praised the order prevailing at London's three existing district schools in 1860: "At the present time I should as soon expect a riot in any district school as amongst a flock of sheep."[13]

Subsequent reformers stressed that children learned to respect property and become disciplined, self-reliant workers when required to care for their own belongings. Boys' training ships and institutions that operated on the cottage home model as did Barnardo's Girls' Village Home and Banstead at first required children to wash much of their own laundry, and many schools attempted to produce all goods, such as shoes and clothing, on site.[14] The captain of the *Goliath* requested a sewing machine so that the boys would be prepared "to materially help themselves by making and repairing their clothing," skills that would help make them "useful in future life."[15] Boys as well as girls did housework and expressed pride in the appearance of their domestic surroundings. Barnardo claimed, for example, "that all the *household work* of the Homes is done by the boys themselves. They are their own cooks and waiters, their own boot-blacks and house- and chamber-maids. They scrub the floors (and we pride ourselves on the floors at Stepney)."[16] Whether reformers favored military-style discipline or the cultivation of a domestic identification with property, the ideological goal was the same: to transform pauper children into self-reliant, independent workers who respected property rights.

The emphasis on respect for property remained a constant factor in children's institutions, as did military training, but there was a general shift in the 1870s and 1880s as the rising number of public and private residential institutions for children increasingly aimed to provide youths with training as skilled artisans. Work had more than economic worth; it inculcated the values that would lead children to become "depauperised" individuals, "disciplined into orderly citizens and useful servants."[17] In a period of intensifying labor unrest, reformers hoped that the training provided to girls as servants and to boys as artisans would reinforce hierarchical communal ties. Domestic service and artisan trades, such as shoemaker, tailor, blacksmith, and carpenter, recalled the English preindustrial past, just as the debates about the architectural design of children's institutions sought to recapture the social harmony of village life. English reformers ignored the history of protest by artisans on the European continent in 1848, which arose as a response to their declining status, and instead envisioned artisans as respectable individuals contributing to their communities and strengthening the national and economic order. By training poor youths to become servants and skilled laborers, reformers strove to recapture a preindustrial ideal of self-sufficiency, craftsmanship, and social harmony.

There were important age-related institutional differences in the professional training children received. Most poor law schools engaged children in a mixture of academic and professional training, the latter increasing with the child's age. The school managers at Ashford, a barrack school, decided that children over thirteen would focus on full-time professional training. The managers at Banstead likewise determined in 1882 that all children over thirteen who had passed the fourth standard in national educational levels should cease their studies and devote themselves entirely to professional training.[18] Youths could no longer attend poor law schools once they reached the age of sixteen.

In general, children who were not discharged to their parents left poor law schools for employment or further training when they reached fourteen to sixteen years of age, although some left for work when they were as young as twelve years old. Many of these youths went directly to employers or the military (particularly as recruits for army and navy bands), but they also might enter a privately funded lodging home, such as the several Working Boys' Homes and the homes operated by the Metropolitan Association for the Befriending of Young Servants (MABYS) in London.[19] It was also common for boys between twelve and fifteen leaving metropolitan poor law schools to join the *Goliath* training ship and, after it burned in 1875, the *Exmouth,* which prepared boys for careers in the Royal Navy and mercantile marine.[20] Most children in institutions received some professional training at all ages, but this training increased as they grew older.

Compared with poor law schools, Barnardo's institutions served an older population of youths, particularly those no longer eligible for poor law services, and thus were even more focused on professional training. From the founding in 1870 of Stepney Causeway, Barnardo's first residential institution, to his death in 1905, the majority of his admissions were older youths. Voluntary societies were urgently needed, Barnardo claimed, because the "arab class" was mostly between thirteen and a half and fifteen years old, yet poor law assistance often ceased at fourteen.[21] Barnardo's fund-raising literature and photographs often portrayed younger children, but those actually admitted tended to be in their mid to late teens. For example, the fifty-three boys admitted following Barnardo's East End tea meetings in 1884 were all over ten years old: the youngest was eleven, two were thirteen, three were fourteen, four were fifteen, fifteen were sixteen, twenty-two were seventeen, five were eighteen, and one was nineteen.[22]

Barnardo's general admission statistics also support the impression that his institutions (during his lifetime) served mainly older youths. In 1898, 118 of the total annual 2,406 "permanent" admissions were infants of two years and younger, 103 were between two and five years old, 415 were between five and ten, 522 were between ten and fourteen, 464 were between fourteen and sixteen, and a startling 784 (33 percent) were over sixteen.[23] The age ratios remain roughly similar until Barnardo's death in 1905, when the organization became more concerned with infant welfare and ceased to admit as many older youths.[24] Although upper-class donors may have been attracted to the home life offered by Barnardo's institutions for supposedly orphaned and abandoned children, many poor parents and welfare officials viewed the homes as professional training centers for older youths. For instance, a father who worked as a prison guard stated that he had brought his fourteen-year-old son to Barnardo's because he "had no means of learning his son a trade and desired that he should be trained at 'Dr. Barnardo's Homes,' and sent out to Canada"—a service for which the father was willing to pay the expenses.[25]

Despite the age differences of the populations of poor law schools and Barnardo's institutions, the training was generally very similar. Initially, poor law schools looked to private institutions as models. An 1878 parliamentary report examined six private children's institutions, including Barnardo's Girls' Village Home (opened in 1876), and determined that professional training was the best means to transform poor law children into "useful and respectable members of society."[26] Such training, reformers argued in the 1870s and 1880s, was even more important than religious or educational instruction as a means to integrate poor children into the national community.

The training provided in the large barrack schools was very similar to that in institutions based on the cottage home system. Although there were some variations, poor law institutions generally instructed small groups of older girls in skills required for domestic service: housework, cooking, laundry, and needlework. Boys trained in a variety of artisanal skills. Most children's institutions included tailoring, shoemaking, baking, and carpentry shops, and some also provided training in blacksmithing, farmwork, gardening, painting, plumbing, and engineering.[27] By the late 1880s, Barnardo was preparing girls to be domestic servants and laundry workers, and boys to be tailors, shoemakers, carpenters, brushmakers, engineers, bakers, wheelwrights, and blacksmiths.[28] Most poor law schools and Barnardo's homes also continued to shape boys for careers in the military by offering instruction in marching bands and nautical skills, either on actual training ships or on land-based reproductions of ships.[29]

A new genre of photographs published in annual reports and fund-raising literature glorified the children's experience of work and the bountiful products of their labor.[30] Groups of child workers—typically occupied at non-industrial, skilled activities—were carefully posed and arranged, their motion stopped so as to illustrate the various stages of work. In a photograph of the shoemakers' workshop at Anerley, the North Surrey District School, rows of boys displayed finished boots on the corners of their workbenches. The back of the shop, behind the two adult supervisors, displayed more rows of finished or soon-to-be-repaired boots and shoes.[31]

FIGURE 20. Barnardo's tinsmiths. *Courtesy of Barnardo's Photographic and Film Archive (ARC0021/D93).*

FIGURE 21. The blacksmith workshop at Banstead, the Kensington and Chelsea District Dchool (ca. 1899). *The Sixth Report of the Managers of the Kensington and Chelsea School District* (London: J. W. Wakeham, 1899), 44. *Courtesy of Corporation of London, London Metropolitan Archives.*

Barnardo's courtyard photograph of tinsmiths at work is one of the most stylized versions of these photographs and clearly demonstrates how they extolled craftsmanship by careful construction (figure 20). In this case, the workshop was transported outside (likely for lighting purposes) and arranged so as to convey a sense of abundance and social harmony. The entire composition is a balanced, mirror image. The left and right sides contain similar background windows, vertical building supports, storage trunks, and workbench displays. On each side of the image, seven child tinsmiths of various sizes and physical abilities go about their work. A circular coil of wire occupies the center foreground for aesthetic unity; behind it, a child worker steadfastly hammers his piece of tin, while in the background the workshop master, one of only two subjects to gaze directly at the viewer, represents the model craftsman the children might aspire to become. The scene overflows with tin products created not in a factory but by hand: teapots, coffee urns, watering cans, washtubs, and tin cups and pails of all sizes. The overall narrative of this photograph implies social integration and harmony through labor, property, and deference. Unlike the children rioting in early poor law schools, these young apprentices appear to identify wholly with the consumer goods they are producing with their own hands.

Photographs of boys working at trades and girls performing domestic tasks suggested that labor situated poor children within a hierarchical national community. More than any other skilled professional, the blacksmith embodied noble values, prompting institutions to publicize their attempts to train boys as blacksmiths through the early 1900s—long after economic demand for such work had evaporated. Banstead's 1899 managers' report, for example, extolled the virtues of the ironsmith shop above all others. The managers admitted that the boys were more likely to find work as bakers, but they claimed that the bakery offered "not so wholesome a trade for boys" as smithing. The report included a photograph of three boys working in the smith shop, overseen by the master (figure 21). The caption emphasized that "boys are taught to forge and make various articles, both useful and ornamental, under efficient instructors. They develop strength, and become very useful and efficient sons of Vulcan."[32] As the boys acquired the efficiency of their instructors, they came to identify with the "useful," handcrafted, and solid objects they created. Their usefulness to society was based on the usefulness of the products they produced. No longer the sons of paupers, they became the "sons of Vulcan," practically mythic workers prepared to serve the needs of local communities.

The glorification of smiths and other craftsmen underlined officials' widespread distaste for mechanized, industrial factory labor. Barnardo was most virulent in his attacks on factory workers, especially female ones, whom he described as lawless bands of violent infidels determined to undermine his philanthropic work.[33] Yet, most of the artisan trades taught at children's institutions were clearly in decline by the 1870s and 1880s. Barnardo's wheelwrights, perhaps the most extreme example, were nostalgic symbols of preindustrial life.

As early as 1860, Tufnell objected to the common practice among poor law schools of training children as tailors and shoemakers, because these were typically low-paying jobs that mechanical production methods were already replacing. It would be better, he suggested, to train boys as railway engineers, in addition to preparing them for careers in the military.[34] Few institutions followed Tufnell's advice, however, and most continued to disregard the expanding industries of the second industrial revolution. According to a 1901 survey of professional training in poor law schools, shoemaking and tailoring remained the most popular trades taught at the turn of the century, with baking and carpentry in second place. Only one of the poor law schools that replied to the 1901 survey, the Mitcham school in Holborn, routinely trained boys as engineers.[35] In 1913 the managers of Ashford, the West London District School, were still debating whether to continue its tailoring and shoemaking shops. Later that same year, the school's education committee rejected a recommendation that boys be instructed in engineering and electrical work on the grounds that such training would "be beneficial neither to the lad nor to the Institution."[36] Children's institutions held on to the ideal of the independent artisan, a recognized and respected individual within the imagined, organic national community, long after the economic demand for such forms of labor declined.

Furthermore, public and private institutions continued to publicize the benefits of their artisan workshops through the early 1900s, even as it became increasingly clear that the actual training was extremely poor. Internal reports suggested that, instead of receiving proper technical training, boys as well as girls primarily worked as manual, unskilled laborers for general institutional upkeep. A 1901 report on professional training at Ashford, for example, found much to criticize. The investigators discovered that the boys made few complete products themselves. At the tailor's shop, "a partially made coat was exhibited, but it was ascertained that the number of new garments actually made did not average one a month." The boys spent most of their time patching old garments. Moreover, children often worked without any supervision. Inspectors lamented that the paid carpenter at Ashford "is almost always, if not quite, engaged in doing necessary repairs about the premises, and can devote little, or no time, to training the boys." The report observed that most boys were "employed in domestic work, viz., scrubbing floors and tables, cleaning knives and forks, working for officers, etc.," work that had little value in terms of professional training. The Ashford committee concluded that "the results of the so-called industrial training are exceedingly poor."[37] Few of the boys at Ashford were even placed in school training workshops, and it was not uncommon for subsequent employers to return these children to the institution because they had been so poorly trained.[38]

By the mid- to late 1890s, the growing criticism of the quality of professional training joined with the much broader reconceptualization of working-class childhood. Public and private children's institutions were gradually transformed from professional training centers for poor youths into schools where the primary purpose was education. Moreover, after the passage of the Education Act and the creation of the London School Board, both in 1870, general educational requirements increased for all English children. The next year, the London School Board established a minimum age of ten years for children leaving school. National legislation followed. In 1880, Parliament made full-time school attendance compulsory until the age of ten, and raised the minimum age to eleven in 1893 (excluding child agricultural workers) and to twelve in 1899. David Rubinstein notes that by the early 1900s, the London School Board required that almost all London children remain in school full-time until age fourteen.[39] These acts at first did not apply to poor law schools. Although the Local Government Board school inspector complained in the mid-1880s that the academic work of older girls in poor law schools suffered because of "the heavy pressure of industrial work," no attempts were made to regulate the professional training of poor children in institutions until the late 1890s.[40] Even in the mid-1890s, some poor law schools continued to place children as young as eight in part-time professional training, and the typical age for poor law children to begin part-time professional training was from ten to eleven years old. (Some institutions defined "part-time" loosely, so that some children worked part-time at professional training for as long as ten hours a day.)[41]

Eventually, however, the national redefinition of childhood as a life stage characterized by school rather than work transformed the structure of children's poor law and charitable institutions. In 1897, the Local Government Board established strict guidelines for the ages and hours of school attendance and professional training in poor law institutions. The board directed that children under eleven years could be subjected to no more than one hour daily of professional training or manual work, children in half-time school could receive no more than five hours of professional training a day, and only children over fourteen years could be entirely withdrawn from school for professional training, but for no more than eight hours per day.[42]

There was some resistance to these limitations, but by the early 1900s, most institutions for poor children had made the transition from training center to school. The Banstead managers, as well as other school managers, at first resented the board's regulation from above and repeatedly defied the 1897 order, claiming that professional training and manual labor were essential for the children's future and for the survival of the "cottage home" foundation of the institution.[43] By 1900, however, the majority of children studied academics rather than professional skills, and the average number of older children in school versus professional training at Banstead reversed in proportion as children began to stay in school classes longer.[44]

By 1905, most institutions had drastically reduced the amount of manual labor required of children. At Banstead, boys began part-time instruction three days a week in a trade of their choice only after they reached age twelve. Boys could begin full-time professional work when they turned fourteen. All Banstead girls remained in school full-time until they reached fourteen (or the sixth standard), when they began a year of training as domestic servants.[45] Whereas at least some professional training had been an essential component of most poor children's training in the 1870s and 1880s, by the turn of the century it was strictly reserved for older youths.

Like the poor law schools, Barnardo's institutions underwent a transformation at the turn of the century. The charity had primarily served as a professional training center for older youths, but after Barnardo's death in 1905, the proportion of younger admissions grew. Whereas youths older than sixteen commonly accounted for a third of admissions in the nineteenth century, in 1907 they represented only 3 percent of the annual admissions.[46] The transition was swift. In its 1905 annual report, the charity still stressed the need to help youths over sixteen, but the 1907 report declared that "[t]hese are Homes for Orphan and Destitute *Children*." The 1908 report reaffirmed the statement: "Our Homes are for *young people*—not adults." By 1911 Barnardo's defined a new focus: "If it were possible, we should prefer receiving *all* our children as *babies;* for then we should have a much greater certainty of success in obliterating the first evil impressions of the slum or the bad results of neglect and destitution, and we might expect even better results than now we can show."[47]

A growing appreciation of childhood as a distinct life stage for all social classes transformed the structure and basic tenets of institutions for poor children. Welfare officials and reformers like Barnardo initially conceived of their institutions primarily as professional training centers. Moral depravity, they stressed, was the main cause of poverty; consequently, the purpose of institutions should be to instill in children, via practical training, the values that would make them good workers and respectable, useful citizens, namely, industry, punctuality, deference, self-reliance, respect for private property, and a sense of social cohesion and harmony. The ideal of the artisan as a model working-class citizen remained important into the early twentieth century, but reached its peak during the period of heightened industrial tension in the 1880s. By the 1890s, reformers increasingly argued that children should not be treated as young workers. As institutions shifted their emphasis from professional training to general education, new ideologies replaced the importance of work as the defining element of British citizenship. The children's identity not only as independent workers grounded in their local communities, but also as representatives of the British Empire came to define their progress from "street arabs" to British citizens.

Imperial Citizenship

By the 1890s, the language of child welfare began to emphasize poor children's roles as representatives of the British Empire more than their value as preindustrial workers who cultivated and preserved traditional, localized village social relations. Several factors contributed to this transition, including the growing criticism of children's professional training, a recognition of the changing economy, a spreading belief that working-class children, like the children of the upper classes, deserved a "childhood" free from work, the continued debate about national citizenship linked with the Second and Third Reform Acts, and, most important, the rapid expansion of the British Empire in the 1880s and 1890s.[48] Reformers increasingly sought to incorporate poor children into the national community through notions of imperial citizenship that stressed a common British identity based on racial constructions. Stephen Heathorn suggests a similar trend in his study of English elementary school reading books from 1880 to 1914. He notes that a "sense of communal solidarity was offered to those at the bottom of society by emphasizing a shared cultural heritage—expressed largely in a language of 'race'—that might compete with other, potentially dangerous and fragmenting social identities, like class."[49]

Institutions for poor children reflected this broader social trend as they encouraged children to think of themselves as members of the British nation and race, in contrast to colonial subjects. In a manner much more explicit than the earlier citizen model, which sought to integrate poor children into the organic national community through their work as skilled artisans, notions of imperial citizenship stressed poor children's direct link and ensuing responsibility to the nation. At the same time, ideals of imperial citizenship continued to imply that the redemption of poor children required their separation from parents and relatives.

From the 1890s to the early 1900s, the culture of empire infiltrated children's institutions. In his study of turn-of-the-century London, Jonathan Schneer explores the many, often contradictory ways in which the empire shaped London's architecture, economy, social life, politics, and culture. London's popular entertainments, for example, encouraged audiences to believe that "British imperialists were heroes, the colonized peoples were inferior, [and] imperialism benefited all Britons."[50] Although institutionalized children, unlike the general London public, were a captive audience, unable to select their forms of entertainment, they too learned of the empire through educational and recreational activities. Along with the general public, poor school children in the 1910s participated in annual Empire Day celebrations. Institutions organized the celebrations either on the school grounds or at other London locales, such as St. Paul's Cathedral, where Barnardo boys attended a special Empire Day service.[51]

Children also learned of the empire in more subtle ways. For example, the *Ashford School Magazine,* distributed beginning in 1906 to children in the West London District School and recent graduates, included updates on animals at the Regent's Park Zoo, a principal site of imperial power in the metropolis. Schneer notes that the "very notion that one could list and classify, let alone cage, all species of animals was an inherently imperial project."[52] Children read of Britain's imperial power in reports of newly added chimpanzees and other exotic animals. They experienced the limits of this imperial enterprise by following the progress of Martha, the baby gorilla that died (despite the efforts of a

female doctor) from a bout of melancholy following her transport to London—
a case of trauma with which many of the children could surely relate.[53]

Children's institutions also celebrated the empire by creating their own
imperial displays and exhibitions. In the early 1900s, as imperial museum displays proliferated throughout London, the Ashford District School established
its own school museum, which soon divided into two separate museums, one
for boys and one for girls.[54] The museums contained objects from around the
world, donated by patrons of the school and old scholars (former students of the
poor law schools) who had emigrated or traveled beyond Britain. These haphaz-
ard, often personal collections served to familiarize children with the world, to
catalogue the material resources of the empire, and to highlight differences
between British and imperial subjects. Objects such as "bullets," "a badge of the
Devonshire Regiment," and "a portable coffee-pot picked up on the battle-field
of Sedan" celebrated military exploits.[55] A list of donations to the museum,
printed in the *Ashford School Magazine,* suggests that patrons and old scholars
typically sent samples of valuable raw materials from around the globe. The
magazine editors thanked "Miss Masham for gold quartz from the Phoenix
Mine, Rhodesia," "Mr. Chennells for cocoa beans from Jamaica," and "Mr.
Cooper for sugar cane from Gin Gin, Queensland."[56]

Other museum objects emphasized cultural differences by illustrating
what donors thought to be native customs. Shells from Tasmania were said to be
"probably used for money."[57] Religious practices of diverse traditions were presented in implicit opposition to English Protestantism. A "Zambesi Bean" was
described as an amulet worn by natives, and a "Soudanese charm" as "consisting of a box containing a verse from the Mahommedan Scriptures, the Korân,
reminding one of the phylacteries worn by the Jews in ancient times."[58] Other
materials demonstrated supposed racial differences, broadly conceived,
between "civilized" and "savage" peoples. One donor described a "Soudanese
dagger" as having a "wooden handle [that] would only fit a very narrow hand,
but the Soudanese, as well as many other savages, have such hands."[59]

The museum collections categorized and displayed the material benefits of
empire and promoted a common sense of Britishness based on imperial strength,
common customs, and racial identity. At the same time, the process of creating
the collections served to celebrate the success of old scholars. Once poor children themselves, these contributors publicized their worldly achievements by
sending materials back to the Ashford museums for other children to view.

Children's institutions also encouraged a shared sense of British identity,
often based on racial constructions, through special entertainment and lecture
series. Magic lantern shows were a common form of entertainment in poor law
schools.[60] Records do not indicate the content of the shows, but missionary activities, explorers, and imperial campaigns were popular topics in the late nineteenth
century. Collections of missionary slides for sale in the 1890s had titles such as
"Celestials and Barbarians," "Glimpses of India," and "Heroes and Fanatics of the
Sudan."[61] Sometimes the contrasts between British citizens and imperial subjects

were much more direct. Two illustrated lectures at Banstead by G. H. Lord on the Holy Land, Egypt, and Syria, for example, included "living representations and the native costumes," giving children spectacular, controlled examples of orientalized subjects with which to compare themselves.[62] At Ashford, moreover, select youths regularly performed in blackface minstrels. A 1906 notice in the school magazine posted a farewell to Ernest Jones, "a scholar for several years" who enlisted in the band of the King's Royal Rifles. A popular boy, Jones had been active in the school's "Entertainment work, both in the farces and as cornerman—Bones—in the Nigger Troupe."[63] Popular at the turn of the century, blackface troupes sang such blatantly racist songs such as "Il Africano Imbecilio" and "The Funny Little Nigger," which served to blur class divisions and advance a common sense of white, British superiority over the colonial "Other."[64]

As noted above, the *Ashford School Magazine* was another vehicle that promoted a common sense of British identity. Officials at Ashford hoped the publication would create a "feeling of fellowship and mutual interest between the past and present children of our Schools,"[65] and it is likely that the editors' strategy of placing details about the school on the inside covers encouraged Ashford's youths to read each issue's generic articles. Similar to the elementary textbooks described by Heathorn, the *Ashford School Magazine* linked earlier liberal definitions of British citizenship, based on constitutional liberties, with the growing emphasis on a common Anglo-Saxon racial heritage.[66] The first year's issues, for example, featured a series of lead articles on "The Far East." Each article documented a particular region's geography, climate, agricultural practices, natural resources, trade, and government, presenting a general picture of foreigners, in contrast to the British, as tyrannical leaders and poor workers. The author attributed the small population of Burma, for instance, to the "tyrannical nature of its government," and claimed that the population began to increase only after the beginning of formal British rule in 1885.[67] Likewise, "The King of Siam [Indochina] is an absolute monarch, so that the common people have no rights which the nobility are bound to respect. A considerable army is kept, in which service is compulsory."[68]

The "Far East" articles implied and at times explicitly stated that British rule was required to establish "law and order" as well as an efficient system of trade. On their own, the Burmese were "good traders, but unpunctual and wanting in method." Under British administration, the "trade of the country has been enormously increased."[69] In contrast, the French in Indochina were men of "little commercial enterprise," who "seem to be unable to deal with the semi-civilised inhabitants of countries under their rule."[70] According to these articles, successful trade as well as liberal constitutional government were natural British qualities. The author also posited clear racial distinctions between colonizers and colonized. The article on Malaysia, for example, asserted that the "Malays are the brown race, just as Europeans are of the white race, negroes are the black race, while Chinese and Japanese belong to the yellow race."[71] Such articles extended the promise of assimilation and even social advancement to poor children through the material benefits of Britain's empire and encouraged them to identify with British constitutional and racial traditions rather than class loyalties.

The late-nineteenth-century emphasis on imperial citizenship corresponded with the increased militarization of children's institutions. Although charitable organizations had a long history of training poor youths for military service, poor law institutions did not begin to make concerted efforts to prepare boys for military careers until the 1850s. After the disastrous revelations of Britain's military weaknesses in the Crimean War, Chadwick and Tufnell pushed to establish drill, band, and naval training in schools.[72] As early as 1859, Chadwick argued that Britain's imperial status as an economic power, not to mention the fate of the "Anglo-Saxon race," depended on children's military training. The growth of the British Empire, he claimed, required that civilian traders around the world be prepared to "clear Wilds and contend against Savagery and wild beasts." A Lancashireman conducting business in the first quarter of the century was not required to leave his parish, Chadwick noted, but his sons should be prepared to protect their trading interests abroad:

> One Son enters a Commercial house to labour at the Desk at home but an occasion arises which sends him as a Merchant to China, and there he suddenly finds himself compelled to take up a musquet and submit to an extempored drill with other Anglo Saxon Mercantile Men to defend their lives against a furious Canton Mob[.] Another is led from the Desk to India and is there suddenly compelled as one of the whites doomed to Masacre [*sic*], to fight for his life as he may[.] Another agriculturally disposed takes fair looking land at Natal, but he finds his crops trampled down by Elephants and he has to contend against beasts of the Tiger Kind.[73]

The new generation of British traders required military skills in order to protect their commercial interests. In the late 1850s, following the imperial trauma of the 1857 Indian Revolt, Chadwick still defined these interests in individual, rather than national, terms; but the overall message was clear: without proper military training of children, the British Empire was at risk.

Although children's institutions gradually incorporated various forms of military training, including drills, bands, and training ships for boys from poor law schools, the transformation from pauper to artisan rather than to soldier or sailor remained the dominant model until the 1890s. The growth of Barnardo's institutions best illustrates the gradual shift to notions of imperial citizenship that led to the increasing importance of training ships. Beginning in the mid-1870s, Barnardo made intermittent public appeals for funds to build a training ship connected with his homes.[74] By the late 1890s, having failed to obtain an old man-of-war from the Admiralty, he decided to build a naval training area on land instead.[75] In 1901 ship owner Edmund Watts donated money for Barnardo to build the Watts Naval School in Norfolk, which soon replaced the Girls'

Village Home as the primary institution represented in Barnardo's fund-raising literature.[76] Notions of citizenship that emphasized military strength and global, imperial relations rapidly overshadowed those based on the localized village ideal and domesticity. Even images of the Girls' Village Home from the first decades of the twentieth century project the new militaristic theme. In place of earlier domestic scenes centered around individual cottages, photographs from the 1920s feature rows of Girl Guides in uniform, marching with flags.[77]

Institutions continued to train children as workers, but they increasingly justified this training by referring to the imperial rather than the village context. For example, at Ashford's first Sport's Day in 1906, the school's vice chairman declared that the boys and girls should "[c]onsider the expenses incurred" by their training as carpenters, tailors, shoemakers, cooks, and laundry workers. "We call upon you boys and girls to justify those expenses," he admonished. "We want you to understand that each one of you is an individual unit of King Edward VII's Empire, that each has his or her own separate work to do, which, when done heartily, will not only be beneficial to you in particular, but to the Nation in general."[78] By the early twentieth century, as in the eighteenth and early nineteenth centuries, imperial service replaced the reconstructed domesticity of the village model as the best means through which to incorporate poor children into the nation.[79]

At the turn of the twentieth century, reformers often referred to children as the raw material of the nation.[80] The previously suspect language of machinery and mass production became celebrated. In the 1870s and 1880s, reformers had condemned the mass barrack schools for churning out uniform automatons. These reformers had feared that children raised in large schools would lack the domestic affection necessary to promote the sense of local responsibility and individuality that served as the basis of national citizenship. By the early 1900s, however, reformers were much more likely to present in a positive light the mass production of youths for the service of the nation. One of the most explicit uses of such metaphors appeared in the 1910 annual report of Barnardo's institutions: "The Watts Naval School may tersely be defined as the 'Handy-man's factory.' The raw material is sent to our breezy Norfolk Home in the shape of promising boys of good physical physique, and then, stage by stage, smart little Jack Tars are evolved and drafted into the sea services of the Empire."[81] This efficient assembly line transformed boys into citizens defined by their duty to protect the empire. The metaphor extended to photographic representation as well. By the First World War, mass composite images of hundreds of children, which first appeared in fund-raising materials in the early 1900s, had replaced the earlier individual before-and-after pairs. These images assuaged fears of population decline and, later, war casualties by stressing the vast numbers of children saved for the future strength of the nation.[82]

The Ashford school song exemplifies the extreme militarization of children's institutions by the early 1900s. The first three verses emphasize children's overall importance as representatives of the British Empire:

Ashford! Home and School in one,
When our day of learning's done,
We will bear thy name afar
Be it peace, or be it war.
Love thee in the days to come,
Sound the trumpets, beat the drum.

Ashford! We will ne'er forget
How beneath thy flag we met.
Ne'er forget the dear old home
Wheresoever we may roam;
Forward! with thy flag unfurled
We will win our race—the world.

England's work can never rest,
To the South, and East, and West.
To the bitter frowning North
Ashford! we will wander forth.
Bear the motto of our School
Wheresoever Britons rule.[83]

The song encouraged children to identify themselves as representatives of the empire, standard-bearers of Britain's national might throughout the world. School authorities hoped that association with the British nation and the Anglo-Saxon race would diminish separate class identities.[84] The children's separation from their families and their potential class interests was most evident in the repeated description of Ashford as the children's home—not a temporary home in times of trouble, which would imply serious class inequalities, but their only home.

The Employment of Youths from London Poor Law Schools

If most reformers valued the ideological aspects of children's training as a means to integrate them as citizens, parents and youths placed greater emphasis on the practical, economic value of training. It was not uncommon for parents and youths to praise the training and education offered by welfare institutions, which in almost all cases was superior to that available to most working-class children.[85] By the end of the century, however, male youths struggled to find employment in the artisan-style positions for which they had trained. The majority of them eventually became unskilled, manual laborers. The army, Royal Navy, and mercantile marine remained the most popular options for boys leaving institutions. But their popularity perhaps more accurately reflected the limited opportunities for young males, rather than a general acceptance of national duty, and parents often objected to the decision. Similarly, domestic service was practically the only option for girls leaving institutions, but they too displayed a preference for other forms of employment that allowed them more freedom and interaction with relatives and friends. The goal of children's institutions may have been to produce "orderly citizens and useful servants," but in practice the economy and interests of youths and their relatives worked against reformers' conception of the ideal citizen-worker.

In relation to the overall number of children served, poor law institutions placed very few youths directly in employment and even fewer of these in positions for which they had trained. Officials claimed to prepare boys for careers as independent blacksmiths, shoemakers, and tailors, but most boys found work in other areas. Among the 139 boys leaving Ashford for service between 1888 and 1893, for example, there were only two blacksmiths, eleven tailors, and nine shoemakers. Band training offered significantly greater opportunities; nineteen (14 percent) boys left Ashford to join army bands. The school had relatively good success at placing bakers (twenty-two, 16 percent), but the positions most frequently accepted did not conform to the artisan ideal. Thirty-one (22 percent) of the Ashford boys became fishermen, and another twenty-six (19 percent) embarked on working life as page boys.[86] At Banstead in the 1880s, more boys were leaving to become hairdressers and page boys than shoemakers, tailors, and blacksmiths.[87] Although the Banstead managers extolled blacksmithing as the most wholesome employment for boys, the school placed a mere eighteen boys in that profession in the 1880s and 1890s.[88] By the turn of the century, mining— the form of work most often associated with exploitative conditions and industrial unrest—had become an important area of employment for youths, third only to army bands and positions as pages and messengers.[89] The Banstead managers voiced a common concern when they stated in 1905, "[I]t is very discouraging to find that the trades naturally chosen by our smartest and most intelligent lads present the fewest opportunities for following them up on their leaving school."[90] The "smartest" youths followed their instructors' advice and trained as artisans, but there were few jobs in these fields by the late nineteenth century.

The military remained the only area where institutional training strongly corresponded with boys' employment prospects. London metropolitan poor law and certified schools placed 644 boys in employment in 1884. Of these, 129 (20 percent) joined naval and army bands. An additional 159 (25 percent) left the training ship *Exmouth* to join the navy and mercantile marine, and 8 boys (1 percent) enlisted directly as soldiers in the army.[91] By the mid-1890s, there was a very slight increase in the percentage of boys leaving metropolitan poor law and certified schools for the military. Out of the 773 boys sent to employment in 1895, 174 (23 percent) joined bands, 101 (13 percent) entered the navy, and 91 (12 percent) left for the mercantile marine; in effect, just under half of the boys placed in positions were pursuing careers in the military.[92] Reformers who favored the increasing militarization of children's institutions argued that military service for boys was the best way for the youths to contribute to the national strength.

Furthermore, many reformers valued military service as the most efficient means to separate poor children from their relatives. As early as 1867, Tufnell claimed:

> All persons who have had much experience in pauper schools are well aware that when the children are launched into the world it is of the utmost importance that they should see as little of their relations as possible. If a well-trained pauper boy fails to become independent, or falls into crime and misery, in nine cases out of ten the cause may be traced to the influence of pauper parents or relations. . . . Now boys engaged in the army or navy are at once removed from the evil influences I have alluded to. . . . If I had my will I would bring up every pauper boy to be a musician for the army or navy bands, or to be a sailor for the royal navy or merchant service.[93]

By extending male youths' time in a distant and highly regulated form of service, reformers hoped to dissociate poor children further from their parents, the alleged cause of all poverty and misfortune.

Likely for this same reason, many parents opposed school officials' decisions to train boys for military careers. One mother wrote to the Kensington and Chelsea School District managers in 1879, requesting that her son "may be taken out of the Band and taught a trade."[94] In this case, the managers refused the mother's request, but by the early 1900s institutions generally consulted with parents concerning their children's instruction.[95] All boys who were not orphaned or deserted needed the consent of their parents before joining the *Exmouth* training ship. Parents signed consent forms agreeing not only to a son's training on the *Exmouth,* but also to "his entering the Royal Navy and engaging to serve until he shall have completed twelve years' continuous service from the age of eighteen, or to his entering the Mercantile Marine service."[96] Given this extended time commitment, many parents were understandably reluctant to sign the consent forms. In 1909, the chairman of the Kensington and Chelsea School District noted, "Our numbers on the *Exmouth* have much increased, and one would like to see it still further taken advantage of, but, unfortunately, the parents of the boys often object, however much the boys themselves wish to go."[97]

During the First World War, in an attempt to fill vacancies on the training ship, the Local Government Board wrote to poor law school managers praising "the advantages of a sea career for boys," but schools still had trouble convincing parents.[98] The managers of Ashford resorted to more coercive tactics. They hoped to increase their recruits by recommending that local parish guardians "be asked to bring their influence to bear upon the parents of boys suitable for the 'Exmouth.'"[99] There were other cases during the war when guardians pressured parents to consent to the enlistment of their boys. The Paddington Board of Guardians, for example, promised the Ashford managers in 1915 "to use their influence at the proper time to obtain the mother's consent to the enlistment" of her son.[100]

The repeated appeals to increase recruits and the eventual recourse to coercion demonstrate that parents clearly objected to the dangers involved in a naval or army career, which in many cases would take boys far away from London. The burning of the *Goliath* training ship in 1875, which resulted in the deaths of sixteen or seventeen boys, had left a lasting public memory of potential dangers even in times of peace.[101] The enforced separation between parents and children was also a common complaint. Youths who spoke well of their military experiences still felt a longing for relatives. The bandsman H. Latham left Ashford in 1898 for the *Exmouth* and then enlisted with the Lancashire Fusiliers, 3rd Battalion. After more than five years of service, he wrote from South Africa to his schoolmasters at Ashford, "I like the Army, but do not like being away from home so long without seeing my relatives."[102] The extreme geographical distances were among the greatest, non-life-threatening drawbacks of military careers. When in 1919 the public learned that the War Office had a long-standing practice of sending young army band recruits from poor law schools to stations in India, even the Ashford officials were distraught.[103] Ashford children may have sung songs proclaiming their desire to "Bear the motto of our School / Wheresoever Britons rule," but many of them wanted to remain closer to home.

Even more than military service for boys, domestic service was the primary source of employment for girls leaving institutions, a form of work that also prompted resistance when it required long-term separation from relatives. A handful of the girls placed by public and private institutions found immediate employment as dressmakers and laundry workers, but the vast majority became general servants, reflecting overall female employment patterns.[104] However, after-care reports by the Metropolitan Association for Befriending Young Servants (MABYS) documented a substantial resistance to service among girls from poor law schools in the years following their initial placement. One MABYS lady visitor regretted that seventeen-year-old H.M. simply "[p]refers being at home and running about the streets to being in service."[105] Many girls refused to work as live-in servants, preferring daily work instead.[106] Some girls rejected domestic service completely. A MABYS visitor reported in 1891 that Annie Towle lived at home with relations and worked in a laundry. The lady visitor described Annie as a "steady girl, but quite determined never to go to service."[107] A.D. from Whitechapel also returned from service to her relations. She refused "all help" from MABYS and "now works at a factory."[108] Twenty-year-old H.B., a resident of Forest Gate District School for five years, similarly "[r]efuses to go to service, lives with her married sister, and goes to daily work." A.B. from Whitechapel "quite refuses to enter service again, and goes to daily work." In 1892, the MABYS visitor regretted that E.S. of Poplar was "[s]till at factory work and refuses to go to service." Work was "slack" for nineteen-year-old A.S., who lived with relatives and did tailoring, but she would "not hear of going back to service."[109] Margaret Murphy probably gained an overall rating of "unsatisfactory" from her MABYS visitor because she worked at a coffee shop and would "not go to regular service." After bouts of illness and several placements as a live-in servant, Ada

Wilson desperately wanted to return home to her mother. In an extreme expression of her antipathy to service, she was "found cutting up all her aprons" before leaving her last position.[110]

The strong opposition to service is unmistakable in these instances. Although such cases do not represent the majority, they document a common trend. Instead of domestic service, many girls preferred working in factories, laundries, shops, public houses, and restaurants, along with other, less typical work for females, which could often be done from home, such as tailoring, shoemaking, machine work, bookbinding, and accounting.[111] Such employment allowed them more independence and did not require living separately, often at far distances, from relatives.

The MABYS ladies viewed service as ideal work for poor girls because it limited their interactions with "unrespectable" parents and relatives, much as military service did for boys. Proper training followed by respectable employment with the families they served theoretically meant that girls would cast off impoverished relatives, who constantly threatened to unravel the reformers' work. Yet the MABYS reports highlight the fragility of these reform efforts. For example, a MABYS visitor noted in 1891 that seventeen-year-old Alice Coleman, a student at the Ashford District School for three years, was "[d]oing well in her first place, and has had a prize for good service." By the following year, however, Alice was a lost cause. MABYS had "[l]ost sight of" her. The visitor reported that Alice was "troublesome in service." She "spent all her money on fine clothes, and painted her face." Alice left service to be with her mother, who then moved without leaving MABYS a forwarding address. When a MABYS lady found Alice again in 1893, she was still living with relations, presumably her mother. The visitor reported with disappointment that Alice "[w]as employed at Capt. Boyton's Water Show, and is now ill from [the] effects of being so constantly in the water, and staying with friends. She will never settle to service again, we fear."[112] Once an ideal servant, Alice reached beyond her status by wearing "fine clothes," material goods meant to satisfy her personal desires. The MABYS lady blamed Alice's downfall equally on her abandonment of service and her reunion with relatives, so that her illness could be understood to have been caused both by the effects of water and the effects of staying with her friends (a common term for relatives). Having entered a topsy-turvy world in which the captain was commander of a water show rather than a battleship, Alice, the MABYS lady feared, was completely unsettled and rootless. The fear that she "will never settle to service again" reflected a much greater fear of social and economic subversion.

Conclusion

Changes in the institutional training of poor children revealed significant shifts in ideals of childhood and citizenship during the late nineteenth century. Viewed as workers in the 1870s and 1880s, poor children could demonstrate their reform by adopting the values and skills of independent artisans and respectable servants. The village and the properly domestic family served as the basic units of the nation. Training boys as artisans and girls as servants firmly established them within the organic national community. By the end of the century, however, school, not work, characterized the lives of children. Institutions still sought to teach poor children the basic values of citizenship, but they increasingly did so by stressing youths' communal British identity as representatives of the empire. The common thread tying both forms of citizenship was reformers' definition of the virtues of the reformed child in contrast to the vices of the parents and, in the case of imperial citizenship, to colonial subjects. To achieve transformation from "street arab" into British citizen, the poor child theoretically needed to cut all contact with relatives and abandon the economic claims of class.

In practice, however, institutional training was much more a process of cooperation and bargaining among parents, children, and welfare officials. Parents turned to public and private institutions partly because they provided professional and educational instruction for children; and, in most cases, parents were thankful for that training. Annie Warren, for example, wrote to the *Ashford School Magazine* to report that she was working as a cook and that her brother, also a former resident of Ashford, was a bandsman on the HMS *Good Hope*. "All our relations are very proud of us both," she stated, "and know that we owe it all to the untiring energy of all those who taught us."[113] But even as parents appreciated training services that they felt benefited their children, they also rejected services that did not fit with their desires. The significant resistance on the part of parents and youths to military training for boys and live-in domestic positions for girls suggests that parents and youths were not always willing to undergo long-term family separation and restrictions on their independence for the sake of employment.

CHAPTER 6

"Their Charge and Ours"

CHANGING NOTIONS OF CHILD
WELFARE AND CITIZENSHIP

≈✵◎✵≈

*I*n its annual report for 1917, Barnardo's
homes published an illustration, "Their Charge and Ours," that illuminates the pro-
found effects of the First World War on British understandings of citizenship.[1]
Within the outline of a flying Union Jack, hundreds of children's faces peer out at
the viewer (figure 22). In its depiction of the core of the British nation, the future to
be protected and nurtured, this photographic collage emphasizes the vast the number of children saved in wartime. Even though the features of individual children
are discernible, it is the mass that matters here. Superimposed on the left side of the
flag, a British soldier and sailor look steadfastly off into the distance, a pugnacious
English bulldog by their side, their weapons drawn and ready to meet the enemy.
Linking the children directly with the military men, the caption explains, "These
Children[:] Babies, Boys and Girls—are War Admissions to the Homes. Their
fathers are Soldiers or Sailors in the fighting front." For the first time, Barnardo's
organization explicitly identified and hailed the fathers of the youths in its homes
in heroic terms. "Their Charge and Ours" suggested that, just as British men were
charged to serve the nation with duty, loyalty, and, if necessary, self-sacrifice, child
welfare institutions were obligated to serve the nation by caring for poor youths,
who, if they survived, would become the future forces of Britain.

Barnardo's organization began experimenting with composite photographs
in the decade before the war, shifting away from the Victorian before-and-after
contrasts of individual children, but it had never before used a composite photograph that included so many children or made such a direct link between the children and the nation.[2] "Their Charge and Ours" became typical of wartime child
welfare rhetoric and imagery. Philanthropic and state officials promoted child welfare programs by stressing the patriotic and nationalistic importance of their work
above all else, drawing connections between Britain's national strength, its military
forces, and the health of its children. Directly after the outbreak of war, even the
cover of *Night and Day* changed to promote a new image of child welfare that

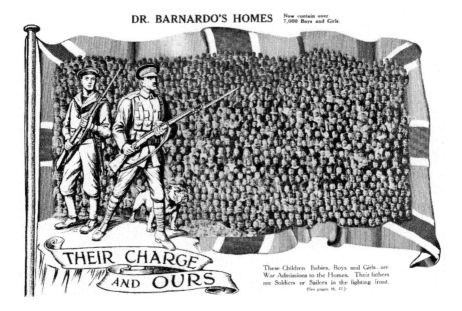

FIGURE 22. The centerfold image (pp. 12–13) from Barnardo's 1917 *Annual Report* promotes a connection between the war effort and child welfare. *Courtesy of the University of Liverpool Library Special Collections and Archives (D239/A3/52).*

stressed the children's importance as future soldiers and future citizens of the nation. Replacing the image used since the late nineteenth century, which contrasted scenes of street life and crime with ones of successful reformation through Barnardo's homes, the new color cover, first published in October 1914, featured a boy dressed in a sailor's uniform and holding a flag. The mottoes surrounding him reinforced the message: "FOR GOD AND COUNTRY," "Under one Flag. Some useful citizens in the making."[3]

Britain's first total war profoundly affected child welfare institutions and promoted new models of citizenship for poor parents and their children. The war not only brought a different population of children into state and charitable institutions, but also precipitated a transformation in the public perception of all poor parents. In contrast to the elision or demonization of previous decades, poor parents were much more likely to be recognized and even valorized by welfare workers in the public realm. Welfare institutions no longer needed the dominant narrative of children as abandoned "waifs and strays" or as orphans without pasts. Poor parents' direct contributions to the war effort as soldiers, as munitions workers, and as mothers of Britain's current and future soldiers began to outweigh reformers' concern about the morality and domesticity of poor families.

At the same time, changes to suffrage laws codified the greatest transformation in understandings of citizenship. The war, much more than any of the nineteenth-century reform acts, caused voting to be recognized as a right rather than a privilege for most Britons. The 1918 Representation of the People Act extended suffrage to women over thirty and nearly all adult men, thereby increasing the total portion of the adult population with voting privileges from 28 to 78 percent.[4] As Nicoletta Gullace has argued, "patriotism, rather than manhood" became "the fundamental qualification for citizenship."[5] When child welfare reformers stressed service to the nation rather than bourgeois domesticity or artisanal self-sufficiency as the primary means to incorporate the poor as citizens, they were articulating an understanding of citizenship that was actually much more in line with the concept that the poor themselves had advocated since the nineteenth century. Rather than inclusion or exclusion, new notions of citizenship emphasized connections among English men and women and the common rights that bound them to the nation.

Reformers' ideals of children's role as future citizens also began to change during the war. Based on earlier models of imperial citizenship, the principal wartime public face of the reformed child evolved into that of the male soldier or sailor, rather than the independent artisan or domesticated servant of the nineteenth century. The experiences of institutionalized children during the war, however, were often at odds with the public rhetoric. A series of crises within children's institutions involving challenges to adult authority revealed child welfare workers' anxieties about soldiers at the front and the security of state authority over the home front, proving how thoroughly the lives of children had become intertwined with notions of Britain's military and national strength.

War and Child Welfare Institutions

Total war transformed the British home front, and child welfare institutions were compelled to modify their mission and structure in a number of ways. War forced some families to resort to poor law and charitable institutions for the first time, bringing a new population of children into these institutions. Furthermore, the institutions' daily routines changed in both small and significant ways. In some cases, the state directly drew on the resources of child welfare institutions for military purposes; in others, youths faced unprecedented wartime conditions along with the rest of the British population. Finally, both state and philanthropic child welfare organizations experimented with new types of institutions, demonstrating a greater willingness to recognize, accept, and in some cases even support poor parents along with their children. Although the changes brought by war were in many cases temporary, they nonetheless prompted child welfare officials to define their mission as one undertaken in tandem with rather than in opposition to Britain's impoverished mothers and fathers.

Many families sought institutional care for their children for the first time during the war. In a handful of cases, local guardians sent the children of interned alien enemies to poor law schools for the "duration of the war."[6] In addition, air raids in London's East End destroyed the homes of the city's working poor, prompting state poor law schools to provide temporary accommodation for displaced children.[7] Although officers sent by Barnardo's organization to areas affected by a particularly destructive Zeppelin raid in 1915 found only one child in need of care,[8] the charity made a point to publicize such instances in *Night and Day*. In the case of two young boys whose "diligent," "honest" father was killed in a 1917 air raid, the charity claimed that its care was a service in support of the "National economy."[9] The shared experience of war on the home front, combined with the expectation that child welfare work supported Britain's national strength, created a new context in which child welfare workers were more likely to praise than condemn Britain's poor mothers and fathers.

By far the most important factor influencing the populations of child welfare institutions was the voluntary enlistment and, after 1916, conscription of men for the military. Over the course of the war, Barnardo's institutions claimed to have sheltered almost 1,000 children of soldiers.[10] This is a significant number, considering that Barnardo's annual "permanent" admissions for 1914–1916 ranged from 1,029 to 1,206.[11] The image of children of soldiers and sailors became Barnardo's favorite symbol of its national contribution during the war years. In addition to fund-raising advertisements like "Their Charge and Ours," the organization regularly publicized its aid to these children in *Night and Day* and in specially prepared pamphlets, such as *Tommy's Bairns,* which the charity's director praised in particular for having "stirred up sympathy."[12] The director reminded the readers of *Night and Day* that "[m]any a man in the trenches or on the deep has been cheered and comforted by the knowledge that we were caring for his children, and that whatever happened to him, they would be safe in our keeping."[13]

Condemnations of poor parents, typical of the Victorian era, also diminished as child welfare institutions increasingly contributed facilities and personnel to the general war effort. For example, the War Office refurbished the rifle range at Ashford, the West London poor law school, increasing its size and adding artificial lighting so that troops could train there.[14] Youth bands from state and charitable institutions rallied support for the war. Soon after war began, youths at Banstead, the Kensington and Chelsea poor law school, held a concert that raised more than £40 for the Belgian Relief Fund, and the *Times* reported that the band from Barnardo's homes went "daily to various parts of London to march at the head of recruits."[15] In November 1914, Ashford officials rejected a proposal to volunteer the school band to the War Office for recruiting purposes, not for lack of patriotism, but because the band was rapidly losing members directly to the war effort. Five boys had recently enlisted, and three more were expected to join the military within days.[16] For a brief period from the fall of 1915 to the spring of 1916, Barnardo's organization even sent boys from the Stepney Home to work in munitions factories.[17]

In addition to drawing upon the resources of active institutions, the state requisitioned underutilized schools for new purposes. During the first months of war, the Local Government Board converted the West London school for infants into a refugee center for the thousands of Belgians fleeing to London. By the beginning of 1915, the board had also arranged for the school to receive approximately three hundred wounded soldiers under the care of the King Albert Relief Hospital.[18] Such changes in the populations of child welfare institutions and the alignment of these institutions with the general war effort helped to decrease the stigma of poverty. No longer housing only the children of the "unrespectable" poor, poor law schools and Barnardo's served air raid victims, wounded soldiers, and refugees along with the sons and daughters of British soldiers fighting at the front.

In addition to bringing new populations into child welfare institutions, the war prompted poor law schools and Barnardo's to reevaluate policies concerning the separation of poor parents from their children and the practice of boarding-out or placing children with foster parents, especially in cases involving unmarried mothers. The typical late-Victorian charity for unwed mothers sent the mother first to a rescue home and then to service, while placing the child in foster care. The mother generally paid part or all of the fees for foster care—a periodic penance that served as a reminder of her sin—yet was allowed only limited contact with her child.[19] Barnardo's organization originally followed this punitive pattern. In the 1890s, the charity started a special boarding-out program for unmarried mothers' first children and, in a very few cases, the children of poor widows. The organization placed these children with "respectable foster mother[s]" and agreed to share the costs of boarding-out with those natural mothers who had proven themselves to be "penitent and desirous of leading a better life," while helping them to find positions as servants.[20] A tragic problem associated with such programs, however, was that the mortality rates for these boarded-out children tended to be exceptionally high—60 to 90 percent, according to the most distressing parliamentary and medical studies conducted in the late nineteenth century, although the mortality rates for Barnardo's Auxiliary Boarding-Out program were never so high.[21]

Such high infant mortality rates had long been an issue of national concern. Well before the Great War, European countries associated expanding populations with military strength. Especially in France, but also in Britain, politicians and medical professionals expressed concern about the steady decline in national populations and birthrates since the late nineteenth century.[22] Late-nineteenth- and early-twentieth-century British public health workers became especially concerned with high infant mortality rates, which, reformers argued, threatened national security in an age of European imperialism.[23] With the experience of total war, a war of attrition, public anxiety about the population level increased. As the war dragged on, welfare reformers began to link child deaths on the home front with the deaths of soldiers on the battle front to suggest that the children were Britain's future soldiers and that their deaths contributed to the weakening of the nation's military force.[24]

Shifting the focus of the population debate from deaths to births, politicians, doctors, and welfare reformers described procreation as a patriotic duty.

In one popular magazine, for example, A. M. Richardson appealed to married couples to have more children: "I think what the Spirit of Britain, if she could speak, would say, at least to the younger married members of the community, is 'Give me sons and daughters—sons to take the place of the gallant dead, daughters to bear and train the coming generations for their country's good.'"[25] This and other pronatalist rallying calls valued children in terms of their potential service to the state as soldiers or mothers of soldiers, apostles of the "Spirit of Britain."

The public clamor over "war babies" soon challenged the Victorian notion that appeals for more British babies should be limited to married couples. In the spring of 1915, Conservative M.P. Robert McNeill announced that a "large number of unmarried girls, in districts where masses of troops have been quartered, are about to become mothers."[26] In one country borough alone, McNeill estimated, more than two thousand single women would soon be mothers of war babies—a claim that the *Observer* later proved to be "grossly exaggerated" (although illegitimacy rates did temporarily rise during the war).[27] Nevertheless, by presenting illegitimate children in the highest possible patriotic terms as "the offspring of the heroes of the Marne, of Ypres, [and] of Neuve Chapelle," McNeill sparked a national campaign to provide state allowances for illegitimate and legitimate children of soldiers.[28]

Ultimately, McNeill hoped to revise Britain's legitimacy laws. Attempts to change the bastardy laws in England were generally limited to proposals for the legitimization of children whose parents subsequently married, as was allowed in Scotland.[29] Although some proposals for state allowances to unmarried mothers would limit aid to the companions of soldiers,[30] others asserted that state maternity allowances should be universal, separate from the poor law, and make no distinction between married and unmarried mothers.[31]

This increase in wartime pronatalist propaganda had significant effects on national welfare programs.[32] Although child welfare institutions by no means completely jettisoned earlier policies, they were willing to experiment during the war with different programs that supported the state's pronatalist goals and in some cases allowed mothers, married and unmarried alike, to remain in contact with their children. The most extensive experiments involved crèches, or nurseries, where working mothers could leave their children during daytime or nighttime shifts, and hostels where women lived with their children. Areas with munitions factories, which increasingly relied on female employees, had the greatest need for aid to working mothers. In 1916 the Welfare Department of the Ministry of Munitions promised to subsidize more than three-quarters of the cost of day- and nighttime crèches operated by private charities and businesses in munitions areas. Angela Woollacott estimates that by the summer of 1918, the Board of Education and the Ministry of Munitions together oversaw upwards of 160 nurseries for working mothers.[33] Largely following the example of private charities, and in some cases drawing on their resources, the state also established a number of hostels for unmarried and working mothers and their children by the end the war.[34] Eventually, the need for such hostels declined, because the government extended its support of impoverished mothers with such legislation as the 1918 Maternity and Child Welfare Act, which empowered local authorities to offer food supplements and other aid to married and unmarried women. By 1929, boards of guardians could give unmarried mothers monetary relief outside of the workhouse for the first time since the passage of the 1834 New Poor Law.[35]

As early as the spring of 1915, Barnardo's also became involved in the issue of "war babies," devising new pronatalist programs for mothers and children.[36] The organization criticized the state for not providing allowances for the illegitimate children of soldiers and pressed for the reform of legitimacy and adoption laws.[37] In part because of its continuing difficulty in finding foster parents and in part because of the shifting attitudes toward unmarried mothers, Barnardo's followed the trend of many other children's charities and began to supplement its growing Auxiliary Boarding-Out program with a system of crèches where mothers could leave their children during working hours.[38] Barnardo's considered either taking over existing crèches or founding new crèches for the children of female munitions workers in various places, including Kent, Carlisle, Newcastle, Crayford, and Woolwich.

The wartime crèches brought about significant cooperation among state organizations, private charities, and business interests. Medical officers of health concerned with high infant mortality rates were often the first to press Barnardo's to build crèches in their localities, but the charity also received support and promises of grants from philanthropists like Lady Henry Grosvenor, from government officials representing the Board of Education and the Ministry of Munitions, and from munitions manufacturers, including Vickers, one of England's two dominant arms producers, which had already spent thousands of pounds building hostels for male and female munitions workers.[39] Barnardo's eventually opened separate crèches for married and unmarried female workers at Woolwich Arsenal and ran a number of other crèches in Barnsbury, Stepney, and Willesden.[40] During the war years, the organization claimed to have logged 18,960 admissions into its crèches.[41] Although most state and philanthropic experiments with crèches and hostels for women and their children were temporary wartime arrangements, they nonetheless exemplified an overall willingness to recognize and structurally accommodate the connections between poor parents and children.

From "Nobody's Children" to "Somebody's Bairns"

Popular representations of poor parents and their children underwent dramatic transformation with the start of war, demonstrating growing appreciation of the poor as essential members of the British nation. For the most part, the children in Barnardo's wartime fund-raising literature needed no saving from evil parents who would sell them to foreign lands or engage Barnardo's officials in drunken brawls. Instead, articles in *Night and Day* were more likely to rely on stark realism to recount the details of poverty. In one account, for example, nine-year-old Bernard's industrious parents "of good character" struggled with poverty for ten years before seeking his admission. The father suffered from serious "gastric trouble" that had required four operations. Once a robust "engine-fitter," he was eventually forced to hawk vegetables, at which he "earned little." Bernard's mother was also in "poor health," but earned what she could at charing.[42] Another article told how the parents of recently admitted seven-year-old Ethel had been "happy together" living in East London, "despite the father's small earnings as a casual labourer, and the rapidly increasing family." But the "respectable and willing" father died suddenly, having fallen "when trying to board a train in motion." Given no compensation and lacking insurance to support her four dependent children, Ethel's mother turned first to her parents—"good-hearted people"—but they were themselves living "in very great poverty." Only after seeking parish relief and earning a small sum at charing did the mother apply to Barnardo's for Ethel's admission.[43]

The charity's fund-raising literature thus described cases of kind, hard-working parents who struggled to find livable earnings, suffered from disease, died on the battlefield or in accidents, and often failed, even with the support of the parish and relatives, to provide for all of their children without turning to charity for help. The section within wartime issues of *Night and Day* that detailed specific case histories soon took the title "Somebody's Bairns," a specific reference to the children's parents that directly challenged the Victorian assertion that new admissions were "Nobody's Children."[44] The journal's style and format of reporting departed from its former melodramatic accounts of child rescue and came to resemble the much more realistic and often sympathetic private case history records of the nineteenth century.

Wartime representations of poor parents never made a complete break with the past, however. Especially after the first years of war, accounts of negligent mothers resurfaced in Barnardo's public fund-raising materials. *Night and Day* reported cases of soldiers who returned home to find their unfaithful wives corrupted by state allowances, which they spent at the local pub rather than on their children.[45] In such cases, the fathers remained heroic, but the mothers became popular scapegoats, for whom "the new and often risky conditions of an unfettered life . . . proved too much."[46]

Yet alongside these castigations of irresponsible mothers, child welfare groups also praised Britain's mothers as being essential to the war effort. The public perceptions of unmarried mothers underwent the most extreme change, as a few prominent reformers came forward to represent these women not as sinners who should relinquish their children, but as patriotic contributors to Britain's military future. According to the 1915 resolution of one London Women's Conference on "war babies," "it was in the highest interest of the State that the bond of mutual affection and responsibility between mother and child should be preserved."[47] Although hostility toward unmarried mothers and the poor in general certainly persisted, the war placed a greater value on mothers' ability to raise healthy children for the nation.

The public perception of poor children changed along with the image of their parents. Previously viewed as a potential drain on the national economy, poor children were suddenly valuable resources. Prewar pronatalism became even more pronounced as Barnardo's organization justified its mission in nationalistic, militaristic terms. Privately, the charity's council minutes emphasized in 1917 that aid to the children of soldiers and sailors, as well as to poor children in general, was work of the highest patriotic order: "We *must* look after the children—child life is the Nation's greatest asset."[48] Publicly, Barnardo's reminded potential donors that each child saved would contribute to the strength of Britain's military forces. For example, a pamphlet published in late 1915, appropriately titled *Child Life: The Nation's Greatest Asset,* asked, *"Who shall fill the places of those who are gone?"* After fanning fears of Britain's declining population, the author concluded that the "puniest atom of humanity that ever wailed its advent in a London slum, weighed to-day in the scales of national life, becomes of untold value. A potential citizen is born into the world; it is *our* business that he grows and does his national work."[49] All children, regardless of class, were potential citizens, and Barnardo's charity reaffirmed its purpose by defining its work in terms of service to the state. Again and again, the charity reminded readers that it provided an essential national service by saving the "children who will, in course of time, take the place of the fallen."[50]

In Barnardo's institutions and in state poor law schools, the soldier was idealized as the dominant citizen model for reformed slum children, replacing the domesticated female servant and the male artisan, who had been the most popular points of reference for nineteenth-century reformers. The lives of institutionalized children intertwined with those of soldiers in very real as well as symbolic ways. After the first months of war, it soon became clear that thousands of youths from poor law schools and Barnardo's institutions were already serving in Britain's military forces (figure 23). Over the course of the war, 10,715 "Barnardo Boys" served in the army and navy, including 520 who were killed.[51] The majority of these recruits—more than 6,000—had been child emigrants to Canada, but Barnardo's representatives in the war also included 19 soldiers from Australasia, 7 from India, 1 from Jamaica, and 1 from China, in addition to the thousands from Britain.[52] The charity boasted that "Barnardo boys have been in almost every naval engagement of the War," and two young men had died with Lord Kitchener on the *Hampshire.*[53] "[B]oy after boy trained in the Watts Naval School is serving in our Navy," the organization claimed, and "in the trenches, . . . the sons of the Homes are showing themselves true Britons in the firing line."[54]

State poor law schools also focused on the soldier as the model of good citizenship for reformed poor children, the ideal Briton, who placed duty, discipline, and sacrifice for the nation above individual needs and desires. Like Barnardo's charity, state poor law schools highlighted the contributions of former pupils to Britain's armed forces. During the war, boys as young as twelve and thirteen signed up for the training ship *Exmouth* in preparation for the navy, and fourteen- and fifteen-year-old boys joined a number of military band regiments in England,

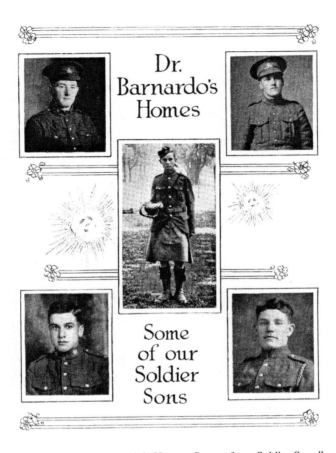

FIGURE 23. "Dr. Barnardo's Homes, Some of our Soldier Sons."
During the First World War, Barnardo's promoted the idea that it
was training Britain's future soldiers, as in this image from the
charity's 1917 *Annual Report* (p. 11). *Courtesy of the University of
Liverpool Library Special Collections and Archives (D239/A3/52).*

Ireland, and Scotland.[55] Like Barnardo's charity, some poor law schools kept
accounts of the number of former students who had enlisted and died during the
war. Ashford, the West London poor law school, honored more than four hundred
former pupils who enlisted, and mourned the deaths of approximately fifty men
who died in combat.[56]

Both during and after the war, the children who remained in welfare institutions lived with the knowledge that they, too, must soon contribute to Britain's
military strength. Aspects of school routines directly linked to military service,
such as physical drills, band, and naval training, received even greater emphasis. Hiring a "competent fleet Instructor" for the Watts Naval Training School
became an issue of "urgent National Importance," according to Barnardo's

executive committee.[57] Continuing the trend of the previous decade, Barnardo's fund-raising materials focused primarily on the naval school and allowed the Girls' Village Home to recede from public view. Nearly every issue of *Night and Day* included portraits of recent recruits in military uniform, alongside images of boys training at the schools. "The Art of Taking Cover, as Practiced by Our Watts Naval School Boys" displays a group of boys in a distant field, marching with flag held high, while other youths run ahead to take cover from imaginary gunfire. A similar photograph, "Marines in the Making, Watts Naval Boys Out with the Guns," poses two rows of Barnardo boys, lined up to face each other with rifles and a canon on either side of a re-created trench.[58]

The symbolic presence of soldiers infiltrated all aspects of child welfare institutions. In perhaps the strangest of all wartime associations between poor children and soldiers, Barnardo's established what was called the Cot Endowment Fund. Beginning in 1915, donors who gave a lump sum in addition to an annual maintenance fee could hang plaques memorializing soldiers killed in action above the beds of individual children, who in some cases were said to resemble the men who died.[59] After the war, children's institutions dedicated monuments, plaques, and stained glass windows to their war dead, as did so many of Britain's schools, universities, and churches.[60] School officials constantly reminded youths of the heroic actions of former students, and the Ashford District School even created a special holiday so that its students could commemorate all "honours earned in the war by Old Scholars."[61]

Letters from soldiers published in two sources, Barnardo's *Night and Day* and the *Ashford School Magazine,* also linked soldiers with children in welfare institutions, providing youths with a model of citizenship based on direct knowledge of soldiers' hardships and heroism. Although these magazines were published primarily for former pupils and donors, children and adult officials in the institutions likely read them as well. In many cases, the writers sent regards to school officers and directly addressed the behavior of institutionalized youths. Other letters gave news of relatives and former schoolmates who had enlisted, recording deaths, injuries, and daily conditions. Soldiers and sailors provided realistic accounts of the brutality and banality of war, and in some cases criticized what they saw as a useless conflict. In 1915, for example, Lance Corporal Alfred Twelftree wrote to his old school at Ashford from Flanders: "You cannot imagine what modern warfare is like, and, of course, shell fire does a lot to upset nerves, etc., and what with burrowing under ground, I think we must be going back to the Stone Age again." He pleaded, "Hurry up the end of the war and [bring] civilization once again."[62] In his frank admission of fear experienced in battle, Twelftree not only critiqued the methods of modern warfare, but also challenged the then still popular association of the war with civilized values and ideals.

In most cases, however, the thoroughly censored letters testified to the soldiers' sense of national duty and service, which they often associated with their early training at Ashford or Barnardo's homes. Soldiers' letters were sometimes remarkably upbeat. A fortnight before Private James Kerr was killed in action, the former member of the Stepney Boys' Home sent "a lively letter from the front, bubbling over with the zest of life." He reported that being in the trenches "was rather exciting the first time" and "not half so bad as I though it would be," despite the casualties his unit had already suffered. Although clearly shaken by shell explosions, Kerr enthused: "I like being up in the trenches. There is hardly any danger if we keep our heads down, or unless a shell finds us: otherwise it is quite like a picnic. We cook our own food while we are in them."[63]

If other soldiers did not always join in Private Kerr's youthful enthusiasm, they did share his sense of duty. Upon finally entering the army after six failed medical inspections, Frederick Wyatt wrote to Ashford, "I must see if I cannot bring a little honour, on my part, to the old School; at any rate, I shall try."[64] Similarly, a survivor of Gallipoli, who had left Ashford eighteen years previously, declared from his current station on the Western Front, "All I earnestly hope to do is 'My Duty,' and trust to be always a credit to Ashford."[65] In another case, two sisters informed the school of the death of their brother, Thomas Lester, whom the director remembered as a youth who "did his duty as a scholar, [and] was ever ready to render cheerful and willing obedience." The sisters wrote that even after being seriously wounded and sent back to England, their brother returned to France to fulfill "his duty which he did not shirk." While mourning his death at "only 19 years of age," they still sought to "bear in mind that he died willingly for King and Country, the same as a good many of the other Old Boys, for whose relatives we have great sympathy."[66] In all of these cases, the institutions served as a moral guide and a source of inspiration for soldiers and sailors in battle. As a former "Barnardo Boy" wrote to *Night and Day* in a letter about the conditions in German prisoner of war camps, "Good luck to our dear old Homes, the makers of so many brave lads."[67] Published letters such as these validated the national importance of child welfare institutions, which had produced such "brave lads" willing to fight and die for king and country.

Going beyond simple affirmations of doing a citizen's duty, many letters from soldiers acknowledged the horrors of war while setting a high standard of physical and mental perseverance, restraint, and, if necessary, self-sacrifice. John Roberts, fighting for a Canadian regiment, wrote to Ashford just days before returning to the trenches. Having survived being stuck in a mud hole up to his waist while out on a wiring party, he could still remark, "if it were not for the awful mud, life would not be too bad."[68] Another private was glad to be "still in the land of the living" after a failed advance resulted in the deaths of 75 percent of his battalion and all of the officers except two. "The most trying thing to the men who were left," he wrote, "was to stay in the trenches and hear the wounded calling for help." His only solace was the chaplain's last words before battle: "Greater love hath no man than this, that a man lay down his life for his friend."[69] In another account of extreme fortitude expressed with self-deprecating reserve, Lance Corporal F. Ivey wrote to the school officers at Ashford in the summer of

1917: "I sincerely hope you will forgive me for deserting you for such a long time; to tell you the truth I have had rather a rough time of it lately." The army had sent him home the previous fall after a serious leg injury suffered in the Somme. Ivey recalled, "I had rather a rough time when I was wounded, as I had to lie in 'No Man's Land' three days." Commenting on Ivey's letter, the magazine editors declared, "It is wonderful to note the uncomplaining and even cheerful tone of the letters from our brave wounded. . . . Can any of us, living comfortably at home, even faintly imagine the terrible sufferings, both mental and physical, endured by those who are compelled to stay for any length of time wounded and untended in that desolate strip of land between the two lines?"[70]

Clearly, the horror of "No Man's Land" was far removed from the home front, yet children's welfare institutions, the caretakers and makers of the "nation's greatest asset," had the charge of preparing young males for such conditions. They did so, in part, by publishing and praising the heroic deeds of men such as Ivey, who modeled how to meet extreme hardships with unflinching duty, discipline, and even cheer.

Wartime Disruptions

As the war progressed, it became increasingly clear to child welfare officials that many of the youths residing in their institutions seriously lacked the discipline, obedience, and certainly the good cheer of the idealized soldier. A number of London's child welfare institutions, which were struggling to accommodate new populations while dealing with wartime cutbacks, experienced serious disruptions and, in some cases, youth rebellions. Normal routines broke down, especially after 1916, when many of the regular staff members were recruited.[71] At the same time, parents' complaints to welfare officials about staff mistreatment of their children increased, as some inexperienced officers physically abused children and resorted to corporal punishment far exceeding normal practices.[72] Managers at Ashford repeatedly had to remind staff members to follow school guidelines regarding corporal punishment. Official investigations of complaints, which were surely just a small sampling of actual cases, reported that several wardswomen had "occasionally given a saucy boy a slap," that the temporary boys' attendant kicked a child, and that the shoemaker hit a boy with a strap "for disobeying instructions to submit his boots for repair."[73] In addition to dealing with inexperienced staff, the institutions faced a number of other wartime dislocations along with the rest of London. Youths practiced fire drills at night and in some cases, because of the threat of air raids, had to move their dormitories down from the upper floors.[74] In sum, children's welfare institutions endured many of the major home front disruptions caused by the war, including air raids, food rationing, and, by the summer of 1918, illnesses and deaths from the rampant influenza epidemic.[75]

All of these factors—not to mention the ongoing news of the war itself—contributed to a general atmosphere of disorder in many child welfare institutions.

Within several months after the outbreak of war, officials voiced unprecedented complaints about youths' unruly behavior, signifying that the wartime disruptions provided more opportunities as well as reasons for children to misbehave just as the general tolerance for misconduct was declining. At Ashford, where children's behavioral problems seemed to be extreme but not entirely exceptional, the school chaplain, J. Victor H. Reade, viewed youths' rebelliousness as a serious problem. He began his 1915 annual address, published in the *Ashford School Magazine,* by praising British forces for their "righteous cause" as well as their "courage and endurance unequalled in the world's history." Reade directly contrasted these military qualities with the sins of the home front, which revealed Britain's potential weaknesses: "Drunkenness, impurity, lax morals, dishonourable behaviour even in high places, self-indulgence, [and] culpable ignorance of our religious duties." Children, more than anyone else, appeared to be linked to many of these sins: "We, in this dear Old School at Ashford—and I feel I am but voicing the feelings of most of the Officers here—are anxious to see among the children greater self-control, more real and willing obedience, more desire for goodness and not the flabby, selfish, irresponsible spirit which is too often observable among so many of the younger generation."[76] Reade's estimate changed little over time. In 1918, in reply to a questioner who asked whether recent spiritual efforts and the events of the Great War had reformed the youths at Ashford, he regretted that he simply had not "perceived what I consider an adequate response on the part of the children to these special and extraordinary efforts."[77]

As the chaplain suggested, he was not alone in remarking on such poor discipline and attitudes. In the fall of 1916, Ashford's superintendent issued a special report on the "Behaviour of the Children," which stated in no uncertain terms that the "general behaviour of the children is not by any means satisfactory, and the Superintendent and Matron are very much concerned at the increasing disregard by the children to those in authority."[78] Disregarding the model soldiers and sailors paraded before them, the actual children in welfare institutions often proved unwilling to submit to the duty and obedience expected of them as Britain's future military forces and supporters of the home front.

Three examples of children's unruly behavior at Ashford demonstrate how youths began to act more rebelliously and how long-standing patterns of behavior became more threatening in the context of war. First, the number of children running away from Ashford, as well as from other poor law schools, increased dramatically during the war, to levels unprecedented since the founding of the very first large poor law schools in the mid-nineteenth century. One month after writing the report on children's behavior, Ashford's superintendent submitted an alarmed chronicle of a spate of recent escapes. From September 17 to October 8, 1916, there were forty cases of boys as young as eight running away from the school. Ten-year-old William Rothman escaped four times during that three-week period, and on one of these occasions he was accompanied by thirteen other boys, including his older brother Thomas. Only a few of the youths returned to the school on their own. Most were brought back by the police, four by the relieving officer from Fulham, two by relatives. At the time of the report, four boys were still missing. In attempting to explain "this most unusual outbreak," the superintendent cited a number of factors, ranging from staff changes to a lack of amusements during a recent holiday, darker evenings owing to lighting restrictions, and even "the circulation of a large amount of exciting and undesirable literature" among the boys.[79] As children continued to run away throughout the fall, school officials eventually ended all approved leaves of absences for boys and girls, removed William and Thomas Rothman from the school, and increased the punishments for running away to seven strokes with a birch for boys under ten years old and twelve strokes for those over ten. Some members of the school's board of managers, obviously blaming the children's parents and relatives for inspiring the escapes, proposed to end all visits to the school from relatives. Their amendment failed to pass by three votes.[80]

The boys who ran away from poor law schools often did return to parents or relatives, who in many cases brought them back to the schools, sometimes repeatedly.[81] In other cases, however, parents agreed to keep the child or make other arrangements for one who could no longer bear institutional life. When, for example, in October 1917 Robert and William Biggs ran away from the Marlesford Lodge branch school in Hammersmith to see their father, who was home on leave, the father arranged for the brothers to stay with relatives after he returned to war.[82] Even though children's desire to see relatives or simply escape the school routine was understandable, the increased number of escapes during the war raised fears about youth rebellion and the decline of institutional order. Like soldiers who deserted their posts, the children who ran away demonstrated an unwillingness to obey authorities that was unacceptable during wartime.

Another wartime disruption at Ashford proved that girls as well as boys shared in the unruly behavior that so worried school officials. In 1916 the superintendent reported that the school was once "again experiencing a condition of things where insolence and disobedience on the part of the girls whilst under the Chargemistress are developing to an alarming extent."[83] Twenty years earlier, the inspector of poor law schools had mildly criticized the girls at Ashford for their extreme shyness, which verged on unresponsiveness. Now the Ashford girls appeared to be an uncontrollable bunch.[84] The main problem seemed to be the girls' behavior during meals, when they all gathered together and refused to follow the school's normal policy of eating in silence. Officials removed the offending girls from the main dining hall into a separate room, but this segregation made matters worse. "For five, ten, or more minutes," the superintendent recounted, "the girls would refuse silence, and as a consequence were kept waiting for their meals," so that the younger, better behaved girls had almost finished eating before older girls had even received their plates. Conditions degenerated until at one evening meal "the disorder was extreme, and the girls positively refused to obey." The superintendent described the events that followed: "At varying intervals five girls were expelled from the room, and the conduct of these girls was coarse and insolent. They shouted, kicked the door, and mimicked the Mistress, who was continuously appealing for silence." The superintendent hoped to improve the situation by temporarily removing the chargemistress, who had obviously become a figure of ridicule for some of the more outspoken girls. Admitting this to be only a temporary solution, he expressed his fear of "this insubordination spreading and unsettling classes of instruction elsewhere."[85] The girls' insolence and failure to respect adult authorities were particularly worrisome in wartime, when such youthful actions raised fears of a more widespread breakdown of order on the home front.

The third and most complicated and pervasive example of youth disorder at Ashford involved cases of children, both boys and girls, who suffered from incontinence. Bed-wetting had always been a problem for all sorts of children's institutions, but child enuresis both increased in frequency during the war and took on new meanings. By 1916, child incontinence—never before an issue of major official concern at Ashford—arose as a prime topic in reports of the medical officer, the school visiting committee, the education committee, and the superintendent, and figured as an important subject at the board of managers' meetings.[86] A separate ladies' committee of the board of managers was formed in November 1917 with the sole purpose of investigating the treatment of incontinent children.[87]

Bed-wetting did indeed become an endemic problem for the school during the war years. By 1917, the school's medical officer reported having examined 119 children who experienced regular nocturnal incontinence, including 50 girls and 69 boys. He estimated that more than 60 percent of these youths first entered the school after January 1916 and believed that on the whole "their early training has been greatly neglected."[88] Six months later, in the spring of 1918, the superintendent noted that cases of incontinent children continued to increase. Although he denied that the war was the cause, he nonetheless recorded that the "great influx of dirty children" came to the school in 1914 and the following years.[89]

Cases of children's incontinence not only rose in frequency during the war, but also took on new, disturbing forms that went beyond nocturnal bed-wetting. School officials expressed particular shock at those children who participated in what they called "flagrant cases."[90] In March 1918, for example, the ladies' committee reported the following "proofs of [the children's] dirty habits." A supervisor witnessed a girl, who lacked all shame in her condition, "putting on her stockings while sitting on her bed in a pool on the macintosh." In an even more outrageous case, "A boy was noticed trying to pass a parcel from his own pocket to his neighbour's at breakfast. It was found to contain the faeces which he had taken from his bed."[91] The school punishment log books list similar incidents of a boy disciplined for "[m]essing his bed and holding his nightshirt up with the solid lumps inside and put[ting] it on to another boy's bed."[92] Although most of the cases in the punishment books involve nighttime incontinence, there are also a number of cases of "Dirty Habits in School."[93] The ladies' committee reported that many of the children were "thoroughly dirty in their habits by day as well as by night," and the members were especially upset that these youths seemingly demonstrated "no feeling of discomfort."[94] Staff members complained bitterly about having to clean some of the "filthy boys so frequently."[95]

As early as 1917, school officers suspected that many of the cases of nocturnal and daytime incontinence resulted from the children's "negligence" rather than any sort of physical infirmity.[96] The superintendent concluded that in many cases the children were "helpless" to change their patterns, but other acts of incontinence were "consciously done" out of "sheer laziness."[97] His judgment confirmed the evaluation of the ladies' committee: "fault is not due to physical infirmity. Will power seems to be wanting. The children have got into lazy habits, and it is very difficult to make them feel ashamed, while there are so many at fault. Some strong notice is wanted to rouse them to habits of self-control."[98] Over the course of the war, school officials began to interpret child incontinence—both older patterns of nighttime bed-wetting and the more recent "flagrant" cases—as a willful act of disobedience, a challenge to authority that if not directly comparable to running away and disobeying regulations at least confirmed a child's refusal to conform to the institutional order. Certainly child incontinence did not show respect for the physical self-control and perseverance displayed by heroic soldiers and sailors.

There occurred among child welfare officials a marked shift in theories about the root causes of incontinence. Increasingly, they argued that it was a social rather than strictly a medical disorder. Before the Great War, children's bed-wetting was primarily a concern for the medical officer, not a topic of detailed discussion for other nonmedical poor law officials, and certainly not an issue for school boards of managers. The pre-1914 treatments for incontinence tended to focus on children's physical condition. In serious, prolonged cases of urinal incontinence, doctors would sometimes recommend surgery, as in the case of two fifteen-year-old band boys at Ashford who underwent circumcision in 1912.[99] Articles in the *Lancet* recommended the use of electric shock therapy or faradism for incontinence, but there is no evidence that poor law medical officers used such specialized and experimental treatments.[100] Drugs, especially belladonna, but also lycopodium, thyroid extract, iron, arsenic, and a variety of other concoctions, were by far the most common medical treatments recommended by doctors for use in poor law schools.[101] Child welfare institutions also tended to rely on treatments involving the interruption of children's regular sleep patterns. Procedures still common at the beginning of the war included "[r]aising the foot of the [child's] bed slightly higher than the head," "[w]ithholding liquids for varying periods before the child goes to bed," "[r]ousing the child from sleep at stated intervals of time," attaching a "mechanical contrivance" such as reel to the child in order to prevent sleeping on the back, and dousing the child in a "[c]old spray bath in the early morning."[102] At the beginning of 1916, it was still common practice at Ashford to label incontinence a "physical defect" and send child sufferers to the medical infirmary for treatment.[103]

As the war progressed, the care of incontinent children shifted from the medical officer to nonmedical administrators, such as the members of Ashford's ladies' committee. Treatments likewise came to focus on children's social behavior rather than their physical bodies. In the summer of 1917, the Ashford medical officer reported with regret that belladonna was having no effect on incontinent children, and he declared the following spring that he could "find nothing physically wrong with the children reported to him."[104] With this news, school officials agreed to adopt corporal punishment as the principal response to child nocturnal and daytime incontinence.[105] From the spring through the summer of 1918, cases of incontinence dominate the school punishment log books. Before the war, the most common offenses resulting in corporal punishment for boys clearly involved a failure to obey school authorities, such as running away, stealing, hitting another child, destroying property, or disobeying teachers. Beginning in April 1918, these earlier types of offences practically disappear as cases of incontinence fill punishment log books. Daily entries list multiple, often repeat instances of boys, generally between seven and ten years old, who suffered "3 good smacks with [the] Slipper" or four to six strokes of the birch for their "dirty" or "filthy" habits or for generally "[d]isgracing their beds."[106] What officials had once perceived as a medical problem came to be understood as a willful act of disobedience on the part of youths. Such disobedience was particularly unacceptable in schools that were expected to be training Britain's future military men.

In addition to corporal punishment, Ashford officials imposed a variety of other penalties aimed at shaming and disciplining incontinent youths: sending children to talk with school officials, reducing the amount of cocoa given at tea time, having the girls wash their own sheets, forcing incontinent children to sleep on the floor, and not allowing children who wet their beds to use sheets or blankets.[107] Authorities also banned incontinent children from joining in all school games. Instead, in a clear example of treatment reflecting the militarization of the home front, the youths participated in extra daily "open air exercise in the form of drill," in addition to another drill session before going to bed. As if to accentuate the exclusion from games, the "elder boys" suffering from incontinence had "to tidy the field and playground."[108] The superintendent favored small rewards for improvement, but also advocated "badging the children" as a way to make them "ashamed of their dirty habit."[109]

Most of these responses were departures from the earlier medical approach to the problem, but some proposals drew on medical practices as a form of punishment. For example, doctors had long suggested changes in children's diets as cure for enuresis. At Ashford, however, the superintendent hoped to gain the medical officer's approval for a change in children's diet not because he believed in any physical link between certain foods and bed-wetting, but because he wanted to use food as a form of punishment by giving incontinent children a "diet that would prove less palatable."[110] In a similar example, the school matron sent six of the worst cases of incontinent girls to the infirmary with the explicit intent of shaming them. The infirmary became a site of punishment and surveillance rather than healing, where "[n]o medical treatment was given, but the girls understood that they were under medical supervision."[111]

The new understanding of incontinence as a social problem to be punished rather than medicated in part resulted from the increase in the clearly rebellious, "flagrant" cases during the war. Yet the use of punishment in all cases, not just the "flagrant" ones, and the subsequent ban against punishing children for incontinence soon after the war ended, signified that the war gave new meanings to the physical functioning of children's bodies.[112] Nocturnal and daytime incontinence represented in all too physical terms youths' failure to conform to the institutional order. The war created the context in which it seemed fitting to explain incontinence as an authority issue—a sort of home front "shell shock"—that called for increased regimentation and punishment. Amid cases of actual soldiers who suffered from shell shock, exhibiting tremors, failing eyesight or hearing, and even in some cases what doctors labeled "false or hysterical incontinence," children suffering from incontinence presented a difficult obstacle to officials determined to turn these youths into a fighting force.

The outbreak of child incontinence within the institution perhaps even raised concern about British soldiers' ability to sustain the horrors of trench warfare.[113] Even among the vast majority of soldiers who never experienced shell shock symptoms, doctors recognized enuresis as a serious problem. The *Index to the Surgeon General's Library* identified three main groups who suffered from enuresis: children, women, and soldiers.[114] The many cases of incontinence at Ashford challenged the model of youths as duty-bound, self-sacrificing citizens in the making and perhaps became such an important issue in official reports because of underlying fears about similar breakdowns within Britain's military forces.

These cases of unruly youths—runaways, boisterous girls who refused to eat in silence, and, perhaps most of all, individuals who by choice, physical affliction, or trauma were unwilling or unable to control their most basic bodily functions—challenged the notion that child welfare institutions were producing Britain's ideal future citizens. School managers admitted early in 1917 that "[i]t is true that at Ashford, as well as at other places, there have been numerous cases of children being out of hand." "The causes," they claimed, were "well known" and "of almost universal application. A restless spirit has pervaded the boys and girls of the country, and it is not to be expected that the Ashford Schools should remain unaffected."[115] Again and again, school officials condemned in particular the youths' lack of will power, self-control, and respect for adults in authority.[116] These were the very qualities necessary for unity on the home front and for success in battle, as demonstrated by the patriotic letters from former scholars fighting on the front. In contrast to these letters, the actions of the "flabby, selfish, irresponsible" youths at Ashford raised fears of mutiny. Despite the official praise in fund-raising materials and school magazines, by 1916 the daily experiences within child welfare institutions were causing serious concern among officials about the soundness of Britain's future military forces, concern about the overall stability of the home front, and, most of all, concern about the ability of child welfare institutions to produce model citizens who would willingly accept and display the loyalty, discipline, obedience, self-sacrifice, and self-control necessary for modern warfare.

Conclusion

The Great War resulted in the militarization of child welfare institutions along with the rest of the British home front. War brought new populations of children and untrained staff into institutions, disrupting normal routines and shifting the meanings of welfare. In the context of war, child welfare institutions promoted new notions of citizenship based on direct service to the nation, an approach that incorporated the adult poor and valued children for their potential to contribute to Britain's military strength. War prompted charities such as Barnardo's and the state to experiment with new types of institutions, such as crèches and hostels that allowed working mothers, married and unmarried, to have greater contact with their children. In public reform literature, the British Tommy and the female munitions worker or struggling soldier's wife replaced the wayward drunkard or prostitute as typical parents. The war also changed expectations for children's future citizenship. Military values trumped domestic values as the state directly took on the role usually played by individual family units in forming good citizens. When Barnardo's Girls' Village Home first started a group of the Girl Guides in 1920, the director feared that the movement's popularity undermined the domestic life of the cottages, claiming "it took the girls away from home and transferred the seat of authority to the Parade Ground."[117] Ironically, the decreased emphasis on re-created domestic structures allowed for greater recognition of the children's biological parents in ways that had never been acceptable in the nineteenth century.

Youthful acts of rebellion during the war also provide a brief glimpse into how children experienced life within such institutions. Underneath the spirit of rebellion evident in nighttime escapes and challenges to specific teachers lurked more disturbing signs of child trauma. The cases of repeat runaways, girls' violent outbursts, and, most of all, widespread bed-wetting suggest that these were children deeply in need of attention and care, love and affection. Although, within the context of their time, most would not have suffered from outright abuse, they certainly suffered from the emotional and physical neglect that came with poverty and the strains of war.

Conclusion

❧⦿❧

On the Day of His Admission," a fund-raising photograph for Barnardo's charity dating from after the First World War, graphically illustrates the remarkable shift in Britons' understanding of poverty that had occurred since images of street waifs like Florence Holder and her sisters dominated child welfare literature (see chapter 1). Printed on the back covers of Barnardo's annual report for 1920 and in *Night and Day,* the photograph shows a young boy holding the hand of an adult woman, who was likely a relative (figure 24). They stand on the steps of the "city slums" against a bleak background of crumbling walls. However, the child, in contrast to images of the late nineteenth century, is not threatened by any of the dangers traditionally associated with poverty. He is respectably and neatly dressed and appears small and childlike compared with the woman next to him. His face reveals neither the dangerous, roguelike expression of the unreformed poor nor the reassuring smile of the rescued child, which were standard types in Victorian images of poor children. Instead, both adult and child have a fearful, tentative look about them, perhaps in anticipation of what is to come. Whereas Victorian narratives of child welfare typically closed with boys happily marching offstage on their way to Canada or to a reformed life as contented laborers, this photograph hints that the future, not only the past, will be difficult. Most important, the clasped hands of the boy and woman provide the central focal point for the photograph, suggesting an intimacy and a connection.

Largely because of the experiences of the First World War, but also because of reforms of the previous decades, attitudes in Britain toward child poverty had changed enough to permit this unusual illustration by the 1920s.[1] The causes of poverty remained similar: death, illness, unemployment, insufficient housing. But unlike Victorian images of child poverty, this representation is not one of imagined orphans, waifs and strays separated from their parents as well as from the entire English community.

162

DR BARNARDO'S HOMES.

ON THE DAY OF
HIS ADMISSION

"I was an hungred, and ye gave Me meat: I was thirsty, and ye gave Me drink: I was a stranger, and ye took Me in: naked, and ye clothed Me: I was sick, and ye visited Me."—"Inasmuch———"

FIGURE 24. "Dr. Barnardo's Homes. On the Day of His Admission." A postwar photograph from the charity's 1920 *Annual Report* (back cover). *Courtesy of the University of Liverpool Library Special Collections and Archives (D239/A3/55).*

In the late nineteenth century, class played a dominant role in shaping popular representations of child poverty. The entire structure of public and private children's welfare institutions was conceived for orphaned and deserted children. When faced with the reality that most of the children who resided in institutions had at least one living parent, many middle-class reformers did their best to ensure that the ties between parent and child would be severed. Reformers geographically removed children to suburban institutions, even foreign countries, and in extreme cases practiced "philanthropic abduction" or argued that poor parents should be sent away to work camps. Many reformers claimed that the role of institutions was to provide poor children not only with material aid and practical instruction, but also with the domestic environment and affective relationships that they supposedly lacked.

By the 1870s and 1880s, the implicit goal of many children's institutions was to create an alternative world to the existing culture, which was riven with industrial class conflict. Within the children's model villages, boys and girls still trained to be workers; but unlike their parents, they were to become workers who experienced a pride in their work, an identification with artisanal values, and a family-like affection for their social superiors. These were the qualities that transformed waifs and strays and "street arabs" into recognized individuals and citizens.

The hope that institutions could remake poor children into useful citizens was common among most reformers. Yet an analysis of how child welfare workers sought to reach this goal reveals important differences as well as similarities. There were significant rifts among various groups of reformers: differences of gender and generation, as in the conflict between Edward Tufnell and Jane Senior over district schools versus cottage homes; differences of class, which become clear in Louisa Twining's critique of local poor law guardians; and differences of religion, most apparent in Barnardo's conflicts with Catholics and even evangelicals in his own East End. Uniting these middle- and upper-class reformers, however, was the general belief that poor children would have a better chance in life if they severed all connections with their parents and relatives.

Despite these attempts to separate them from their children, many poor parents and relatives tried their best to remain involved in children's lives both during and after their institutionalization. Children's residential institutions more often served as short-term, intermittent support for children during times of family crisis, not permanent replacements for the children's homes and families. Parents and relatives visited children within institutions and remained involved, as much as they could, in supervising their care. After leaving institutions, many older youths relied on their relatives for emotional support, care in times of sickness, housing, and employment. Although welfare reformers demonized and omitted poor parents in their popular representations of child poverty, they were frequently forced to deal with children's relatives in the day-to-day functioning of institutions.

The conflict between the public narratives and practical workings of welfare institutions grew out of the contested nature of citizenship and, in particular, the position of the poor in the late nineteenth century. Victorian reformers challenged poor people's basic status as citizens by attacking their domesticity. Yet many poor mothers and fathers sought to maintain contact with their children in ways that revealed an alternate understanding of citizenship founded on traditional rights and liberties, among which parental rights were essential. Displaying a developed knowledge of welfare bureaucracy, poor parents demanded due process and the right to petition, and they took their appeals to parish guardians, police court magistrates, and local London newspapers.

By the turn of the century, however, the conflict between middle- and working-class notions of citizenship began to give way to new citizen models based on imperial contributions—a sign of rising imperial competition and military concerns that gained much greater force during the First World War. Total war encouraged welfare reformers to recognize and even praise poor parents in their public as well as private writings. The war redefined citizenship in terms of each individual's direct contribution to the nation, making it much more difficult to erase or vilify the parents of poor children.

The Great War replaced melodrama with social realism as the dominant mode for representing child poverty. But throughout the late-Victorian period, melodrama provided the language, characters, and narratives that shaped child welfare. The poor orphan child was the ultimate innocent victim, eliciting public sympathy and donations while representing hope for a new beginning. Just as reformers used melodrama to shape their public appeals, parents, too, drew on melodramatic formats. They presented themselves as members of the respectable poor whose rights were being trampled by overzealous reformers.

At their worst, relations between parents and welfare officials were characterized by disdain, exploitation, and resistance, as when Barnardo illegally retained children against their parents' wishes or when benevolent agencies struggled to keep girls from leaving their positions as domestics and returning home. But at their best, relations between parents and lower-level officials demonstrated cooperation and negotiation in the face of extreme hardship. Aware of their limited options, many poor parents welcomed the shelter, nourishment, education, and professional training that their children received from public and private services.

Even Barnardo, who openly expressed his contempt for poor parents, could be remembered as a heroic figure by many people in London's East End. When he died in 1905, his body lay in state in the People's Mission Church at Edinburgh Castle, the East End coffeehouse that he founded in the early 1870s. The organization's journal reported that in the following days "[t]housands of the East End who had learned to love him paid . . . their last tributes of respect." His funeral procession through the East End to Liverpool Station, where the group boarded a train to the Girls' Village Home at Barkingside, was a scene of communal mourning: "All along to Liverpool Street the way was lined by a dense crowd of hushed and reverent people, many of them sobbing, the roughest and poorest men among them standing with bared heads as the long procession went by."[2]

Only at Barnardo's funeral scene did the charity present the poorest of the poor as being connected to the larger community through their grief over Barnardo's death. Yet these adults, including the "roughest and poorest," must be reintegrated into the history of Victorian child welfare. Despised or erased in public reform narratives, they often grieved over the separation from their children and struggled to maintain parent-child relations. Recognition of their pain, alongside that of their children, begins to reveal, albeit in somewhat melodramatic terms, the devastating effects of poverty.

NOTES

Abbreviations

BBG	Bermondsey Board of Guardians
BPFA	Barnardo Photographic and Film Archive
CLSD	Central London School District
COS	Charity Organisation Society
FGDS	Forest Gate School District
KCSD	Kensington and Chelsea School District
LMA	London Metropolitan Archives
MABYS	Metropolitan Association for Befriending Young Servants
NSA	National Sound Archive
NSPCC	National Society for the Prevention of Cruelty to Children
PP	Parliamentary Papers
UCL	University College London Archives
ULLSCA	University of Liverpool Library Special Collections and Archive
WLSD	West London School District

Introduction

1. Charles Dickens, *The Adventures of Oliver Twist* (Oxford: Oxford University Press, 1987), 3. On the melodramatic elements of *Oliver Twist* and resistance to the New Poor Law (1834), see Laura C. Berry, *The Child, the State, and the Victorian Novel* (Charlottesville: University Press of Virginia, 1999), 28–62, and Elaine Hadley, *Melodramatic Tactics: Theatricalized Dissent in the English Marketplace, 1800–1885* (Stanford: Stanford University Press, 1995), 77–132.
2. Jane Nassau Senior, *Report on the Education of Girls in Pauper Schools* (January 1, 1874), reprinted in Menella B. Smedley, *Boarding-Out and Pauper Schools Especially for Girls: Being a Reprint of the Principal Reports on Pauper Education in the Blue Book for 1873–4* (London: Henry S. King and Co., 1875), 113.
3. T. J. Barnardo, "The Continued Necessity for Voluntary Agencies in Reclaiming the Children of the Streets," *Night and Day* (November 1881): 204.

4. Admission and Discharge Registers, Stepney Board of Guardians, Whitechapel, Children from Whitechapel at Forest Gate, Roman Catholic Schools, T. S. Exmouth, etc., vol. 1 (1871–1891), St.B.G.Wh/138/1–2, London Metropolitan Archives (LMA). See entries for Agnes, Elizabeth, Sarah, and John Harrison.

5. A.D. (male, age 7), admitted January 12, 1891, Précis Books, vol. 5, In-care children's records, Barnardo Archive, D239/D/2/2a/108, University of Liverpool Library Special Collections and Archive (ULLSCA).

6. See George Behlmer, *Child Abuse and Moral Reform in England, 1870–1908* (Stanford: Stanford University Press, 1982); George Behlmer, *Friends of the Family: The English Home and Its Guardians, 1850–1940* (Stanford: Stanford University Press, 1998), 104–16, 289–93; June Rose, *For the Sake of the Children: Inside Dr. Barnardo's, 120 Years of Caring for Children* (London: Hodder and Stroughton, 1987); Gillian Wagner, *Barnardo* (London: Weidenfeld and Nicholson, 1979); Harriet Ward, "The Charitable Relationship: Parents, Children and the Waifs and Strays Society" (Ph.D. diss., University of Bristol, 1990).

7. On Barnardo's early life and career, see Wagner, *Barnardo*, 1–69.

8. Valerie Lloyd, *The Camera and Dr. Barnardo* (Hertford: Barnardo School of Printing, 1974), 11. Barnardo's first main photographer, Thomas Barnes, photographed children for Bowman Stephenson's Children's Home (founded in 1869) before coming to work for Barnardo in the early 1870s. Likewise, Annie Macpherson sold photographs of children to advertise her Home of Industry in London as well as her homes for child emigrants to Canada. See Gillian Wagner, *Children of the Empire* (London: Weidenfeld and Nicholson, 1982), 60, 108. On the photographs of children by J.W.C. Fegan and others, see Seth Koven, "Dr. Barnardo's 'Artistic Fictions': Photography, Sexuality, and the Ragged Child in Victorian London," *Radical History Review* 69 (1997): 45n88. On Victorian debates about photography as an objective versus artistic medium, see Elizabeth Edwards, ed., *Anthropology and Photography, 1860–1920* (New Haven and London: Yale University Press, 1992), 4; Jennifer Green-Lewis, *Framing the Victorians: Photography and the Culture of Realism* (Ithaca and London: Cornell University Press, 1996), 227–34 and passim; Allan Sekula, "The Body and the Archive," *October* 39 (Winter 1986): 6, 17, 30, and passim; John Tagg, "Power and Photography: Part One, A Means of Surveillance: The Photograph as Evidence in Law," *Screen Education* 36 (Autumn 1980): 52.

9. For an excellent review of the poor laws, see Lynn Hollen Lees, *The Solidarities of Strangers: The English Poor Laws and the People, 1700–1948* (Cambridge: Cambridge University Press, 1998).

10. *Punch* 4 (1843): 46. For a discussion of the melodramatic elements of this image, see Hadley, *Melodramatic Tactics,* 104–5.

11. See Hadley, *Melodramatic Tactics,* 77–132, and Baruch Hochman and Ilja Wachs, *Dickens: The Orphan Condition* (Madison, NJ: Fairleigh Dickinson University Press; London: Associated University Press, 1999).

12. Dickens, *Oliver Twist,* 479–80.

13. Alan Kidd, *State, Society and the Poor in Nineteenth-Century England* (London: Macmillan Press Ltd.; New York: St. Martin's Press, 1999), 45–52.

14. For a review of the debates and practices surrounding proposals to send children to workhouses, district schools, and cottage homes, see William Chance, *Children under the Poor Law: Their Education, Training and After-Care, Together with a*

Criticism of the Report of the Departmental Committee on Metropolitan Poor Law Schools (London: Swan Sonnenschein and Co., 1897), 1–45.

15. See chapter 3 for a detailed discussion of this literature.

16. Foucault presents children as the victims of disciplinary schools, reformatories, and workshops. He uses the French colony for juvenile delinquents at Mettray, a model for British reformers, to illustrate "the disciplinary form at its most extreme." See *Discipline and Punish: The Birth of the Prison,* trans. Alan Sheridan (New York: Vintage Books, 1979), 293. Jacques Donzelot wrote the most influential adaptation of Foucault's ideas in the context of the family and social welfare: *The Policing of Families,* trans. Robert Hurley (New York: Pantheon Books, 1979). Other social control theorists draw on Erving Goffman's model of "total institutions" in their analyses of child welfare. See Goffman, *Asylums: Essays on the Social Situation of Mental Patients and Other Inmates* (1961; New York: Doubleday, 1990), and Frank Crompton, *Workhouse Children: Infant and Child Paupers under the Worcestershire Poor Law, 1780–1871* (Stroud: Sutton Publishing, 1997).

17. For studies that also approach social welfare as a bargaining process, see Behlmer, *Friends of the Family*; Linda Gordon, "Family Violence, Feminism, and Social Control," in *Women, the State, and Welfare,* ed. Linda Gordon (Madison: University of Wisconsin Press, 1990), 192; Timothy Hitchcock, Peter King, and Pamela Sharpe, eds., *Chronicling Poverty: The Voices and Strategies of the English Poor, 1640–1840* (New York: St. Martin's Press, 1997); Colin Jones, "Some Recent Trends in the History of Charity," in *Charity, Self-Interest and Welfare in the English Past,* ed. Martin Daunton (New York: St. Martin's Press, 1996), 53–54; Michael Katz, *The Undeserving Poor: From the War on Poverty to the War on Welfare* (New York: Pantheon Books, 1989); Lees, *Solidarities of Strangers*; Marco H. D. van Leeuwen, "Logic of Charity: Poor Relief in Preindustrial Europe," *Journal of Interdisciplinary History* 24 (1994), 589–613; Katherine Lynch, *Family, Class, and Ideology in Early Industrial France: Social Policy and the Working-Class Family, 1825–1848* (Madison: University of Wisconsin Press, 1988); Peter Mandler, ed., *The Uses of Charity: The Poor on Relief in the Nineteenth-Century Metropolis* (Philadelphia: University of Pennsylvania Press, 1990); Lara Marks, *Model Mothers: Jewish Mothers and Maternity Provision in East London, 1870–1939* (Oxford: Clarendon Press, 1994); Ellen Ross, *Love and Toil: Motherhood in Outcast London, 1870–1918* (New York and Oxford: Oxford University Press, 1993).

18. On the family as a basic unit of national citizenship, see Behlmer, *Friends of the Family,* 1–2, 9–14, 22, and passim. In *Solidarities of Strangers,* Lees notes that "the poor laws set the limits of membership [in English and Welsh communities] and pushed some people out. They defined the meaning of social citizenship for a period of over three hundred years" (9). For the eighteenth and early nineteenth centuries, Linda Colley's *Britons: Forging the Nation, 1707–1837* (New Haven: Yale University Press, 1992) is now the standard work on national identity.

19. Nicoletta F. Gullace, *"The Blood of Our Sons": Men, Women, and the Renegotiation of British Citizenship during the Great War* (New York: Palgrave Macmillan, 2002), 7. On the Victorian understanding of voting as a privilege, see Colin Matthew, "Public Life and Politics," in *The Nineteenth Century: The British Isles, 1815–1901,* ed. Colin Matthew (Oxford: Oxford University Press, 2000), 93.

20. Goschen, quoted in Gareth Stedman Jones, *Outcast London: A Study in the Relationship between Classes in Victorian Society* (1971; New York: Pantheon Books, 1984), 254. At the same time, Goschen worked to limit the scope of this "right" through his campaign against outrelief.
21. John Stuart Mill, *On Liberty,* ed. Edward Alexander (Toronto: Broadview, 1999), 155.
22. See Geoffrey Finlayson, *Citizen, State, and Social Welfare in Britain, 1830–1990* (Oxford: Clarendon Press, 1994); Colin Jones, "Recent Trends," 51–52; and Kidd, *State, Society and the Poor.* There is, of course, the danger of ignoring the dissimilarities between private and public institutions. I point out key differences in the chapters that follow.
23. For regional studies of the poor law, see Crompton, *Workhouse Children*; Anne Digby, "The Rural Poor Law," in *The New Poor Law in the Nineteenth Century,* ed. Derek Fraser (New York: St. Martin's Press, 1976), 149–70; Anne Digby, *Pauper Palaces: The Economy and Poor Law of Nineteenth-Century Norfolk* (London: Routledge, 1978). On the nineteenth-century growth of London, see H. J. Dyos and Michael Wolff, eds., *The Victorian City: Images and Realities* (London and Boston: Routledge and Kegan Paul, 1973).
24. On child emigration, see Elaine Hadley, "Natives in a Strange Land: The Philanthropic Discourse of Juvenile Emigration in Mid-Nineteenth-Century England," *Victorian Studies* 33, no. 3 (1990): 411–39; Phyllis Harrison, ed., *The Home Children* (Winnipeg, Manitoba: Watson and Dwyer Publishing Ltd., 1979); Joy Parr, *Labouring Children: British Immigrant Apprentices to Canada, 1869–1924* (London: Croom Helm; Montreal: McGill-Queen's University Press, 1980); Laura Peters, *Orphan Texts: Victorian Orphans, Culture, and Empire* (Manchester: Manchester University Press, 2000), 79–121; Geoffrey Sherington and Chris Jeffery, *Fairbridge: Empire and Child Migration* (Ilford, Essex: Woburn Press, 1998); and Wagner, *Children of the Empire.* Wagner estimates that philanthropic organizations emigrated 87,699 children to Canada between 1868 and 1928. In comparison, 54,255 children under sixteen received indoor poor law relief within institutions in just one year, 1884–85, in England and Wales. Thousands more were cared for by domestic philanthropic institutions. See Wagner, *Children of the Empire,* 259, and *Local Government Board: Fourteenth Report, 1884–85,* Parliamentary Papers (PP) (1884–85) xxxii, Appendix D, 148.
25. For notable studies of the empire's influence on Britain, see Antoinette Burton, *At the Heart of the Empire: Indians and the Colonial Encounter in Late-Victorian Britain* (Berkeley: University of California Press, 1998); Catherine Hall, *Civilising Subjects: Metropole and Colony in the English Imagination, 1830–1867* (Chicago: University of Chicago Press, 2002); Catherine Hall, *White, Male and Middle Class: Explorations in Feminism and History* (New York: Routledge, 1992); Jonathan Schneer, *London 1900: The Imperial Metropolis* (New Haven and London: Yale University Press, 1999); and Susan Thorne, *Congregational Missions and the Making of an Imperial Culture in Nineteenth-Century England* (Stanford: Stanford University Press, 1999).

CHAPTER 1 *"A Little Waif of London, Rescued from the Streets"*

1. For the account of the Holder girls, see "Mrs. Holder's Case. Deceptive Photographs. Thames Police Court—November 30, 1876" (unlabeled newspaper

clipping) and "George Collins Questioned re. Mrs. Holder's Children," Reynolds-Barnardo Arbitration, COS's Dr. Barnardo Sub-Committee Minutes, 1877–78, Family Welfare Association [Charity Organisation Society (COS)] Papers, A/FWA/C/D10/3, LMA. For Barnardo's defense, see *Night and Day* (November 1, 1877): 125.

2. On the 1877 arbitration, see Koven, "Dr. Barnardo's 'Artistic Fictions,'" 6–45; Koven, *Slumming: Sexual and Social Politics in Victorian London* (Princeton: Princeton University Press, 2004), 88–139; Thomas Prasch, "Fixed Positions: Working-Class Subjects and Photographic Hegemony in Victorian Britain" (Ph.D. diss., Indiana University, 1994); Lindsay Smith, "The Shoe-Black to the Crossing Sweeper: Victorian Street Arabs and Photography," *Textual Practice* 10, no. 1 (1996): 29–55; and Wagner, *Barnardo*, 86–172.

3. For details on the photographs of Kitty Smith, see "Questioning George Collins re. Kitty Smith," Dr. Barnardo's Homes, Reynolds-Barnardo Arbitration, COS's Dr. Barnardo Sub-Committee Minutes, 1877–78, A/FWA/C/D10/3, LMA; and the Barnardo Photographic and Film Archive (BPFA), Admission Album, 1/7, 157–62 (January 20, 1875). On the photographs of William Fletcher and the Williams children ("Out of the Depths"), see Barnardo's Trustees' Evidence on William Fletcher and George Collins's sworn testimony re. "Out of the Depths" (July 9, 1877), in Dr. Barnardo's Homes, Reynolds-Barnardo Arbitration, COS's Dr. Barnardo Sub-Committee Minutes, 1877–78, A/FWA/C/D10/3, LMA; "Out of the Depths" (1875), BPFA D298; Koven, *Slumming*, 122–25; and Smith, "Shoe-Black to the Crossing Sweeper," 40–44.

4. *Times*, October 19, 1877, quoted in Koven, *Slumming*, 113.

5. Koven, *Slumming*, 92–93. Koven also notes important similarities between Barnardo's work and that of the COS. See *Slumming*, 100–103.

6. For thematic discussions of melodrama, see Michael R. Booth, *English Melodrama* (London: Herbert Jenkins, 1965); Robert Bechtold Heilman, *Tragedy and Melodrama: Versions of Experience* (Seattle and London: University of Washington Press, 1968); Rohan McWilliam, "The Licensed Stare: Melodrama and the Culture of Spectacle," *Nineteenth Century Studies* 13 (1999): 156–61; Rohan McWilliam, "Melodrama and the Historians," *Radical History Review* 78 (2000): 59–62; Martin Meisel, *Realizations: Narrative, Pictorial, and Theatrical Arts in Nineteenth-Century England* (Princeton: Princeton University Press, 1983); Frank Rahill, *The World of Melodrama* (University Park and London: Pennsylvania State University Press, 1967); and Martha Vicinus, "'Helpless and Unfriended': Nineteenth-Century Domestic Melodrama," *New Literary History* 13, no. 1 (Autumn 1981): 127–43. Peter Brooks's *The Melodramatic Imagination: Balzac, Henry James, Melodrama, and the Mode of Excess* (New Haven and London: Yale University Press, 1976) is the classic work on this topic.

7. McWilliam, "Melodrama and the Historians," 59.

8. Vicinus, "'Helpless and Unfriended,'" 129.

9. Hadley, *Melodramatic Tactics*, 67–69.

10. McWilliam, "Licensed Stare," 157. Also see Brooks, *Melodramatic Imagination*.

11. Hadley, *Melodramatic Tactics*, 3.

12. In a review of scholarship on Victorian social melodramas, Rohan McWilliam labels historians' widespread interest in this topic the "melodramatic turn." McWilliam, "Melodrama and the Historians," 58. See, for example, Marc Baer,

Theatre and Disorder in Late Georgian London (Oxford: Clarendon Press, 1992); Brooks, *Melodramatic Imagination*; Anna Clark, "The Politics of Seduction in English Popular Culture, 1748–1848," in *The Progress of Romance: The Politics of Popular Fiction*, ed. Jean Radford (London: Routledge and Kegan Paul, 1986), 47–70; Anna Clark, "Queen Caroline and the Sexual Politics of Popular Culture in London, 1820," *Representations* 31 (1990): 47–68; Kali Israel, "French Vices and British Liberties: Gender, Class, and Narrative Competition in a Late Victorian Sex Scandal," *Social History* 22 (1997): 1–26; Patrick Joyce, *Democratic Subjects: The Self and the Social in Nineteenth-Century England* (Cambridge: Cambridge University Press, 1994); Patrick Joyce, *Visions of the People: Industrial England and the Question of Class, 1848–1914* (Cambridge: Cambridge University Press, 1990); Thomas Laqueur, "The Queen Caroline Affair: Politics as Art in the Reign of George IV," *Journal of Modern History* 54, no. 3 (1982): 417–66; Sarah Maza, "Domestic Melodrama as Political Ideology: The Case of the Comte de Sanois," *American Historical Review* 94 (1989): 1249–64; Rohan McWilliam, "Radicalism and Popular Culture: The Tichborne Case and the Politics of 'Fair Play,' 1867–1886," in *Currents of Radicalism: Popular Radicalism, Organised Labour and Party Politics in Britain, 1850–1914*, ed. Eugenio F. Biagini and Alastair J. Reid (Cambridge: Cambridge University Press, 1991), 44–64; Patrice Petro, *Joyless Streets: Women and Melodramatic Representation in Weimar Germany* (Princeton: Princeton University Press, 1989); Susie L. Steinbach, "The Melodramatic Contract: Breach of Promise and the Performance of Virtue," *Nineteenth Century Studies* 14 (2000): 1–34; Victor Turner, "Social Dramas and Stories about Them," *Critical Inquiry* 7 (Autumn 1980): 141–68; James Vernon, *Politics and the People: A Study in English Political Culture, c. 1815–1867* (Cambridge: Cambridge University Press, 1993); and Judith Walkowitz, *City of Dreadful Delight: Narratives of Sexual Danger in Late-Victorian London* (Chicago: University of Chicago Press, 1992).

13. McWilliam, "Licensed Stare," 171.

14. For example, Laqueur, Walkowitz, and, to a lesser extent, Hadley focus on melodrama's conservative effects, whereas Clark, Joyce, McWilliam, and Steinbach bring attention to its radical potential. For another study of melodrama as a source of working-class resistance, see Kristen Leaver, "Victorian Melodrama and the Performance of Poverty," *Victorian Literature and Culture* (1999): 443–56.

15. See especially Walkowitz's widely influential *City of Dreadful Delight*, 15–39. Perry L. Curtis provides an excellent review of how late-Victorian social reform literature presented a polarized vision of East and West London in *Jack the Ripper and the London Press* (New Haven and London: Yale University Press, 2001), 32–47.

16. Andrew Mearns, *The Bitter Cry of Outcast London . . .* , ed. Anthony S. Wohl (New York: Humanities Press, 1970); W. T. Stead, "The Maiden Tribute of Modern Babylon," *Pall Mall Gazette* (July 6, 1885): 1–6, (July 7, 1885): 1–6, (July 8, 1885): 1–5, (July 10, 1885): 1–6; William Booth, *In Darkest England and the Way Out* (New York and London: Funk and Wagnalls, 1891). Also see Peter Keating, ed., *Into Unknown England, 1866–1913: Selections from the Social Explorers* (Manchester: Manchester University Press; Totowa, NJ: Rowman and Littlefield, 1976).

17. G. H. Pike ["A London Rambler"], *The Romance of the Streets* (London: Hodder and Stroughton, 1872), 8.

18. In admission photographs, children continued to wear many of the same outfits and hold the same props. There are also later examples and reproductions of the much more obviously staged fund-raising photographs, including "The Dreadful Past," a depiction of a "street arab," which reappeared in the 1918 film *From Cradle to Citizenship*. Barnardo's organization continued to draw on theatrical representations of poverty long after his death in 1905; in 1912 it asked the editor of *Punch* to recommend a "strong literary man" who might become the new editor of the fund-raising journal *Night and Day*. See Executive Committee, Committee Minutes (July 10, 1912), Council Papers, Barnardo Archive, D239/B3/1, ULLSCA.

19. For other examples of poor children revealed to have upper-class parents, see Maud C. Battersby, *Gaspar: or, The Story of a Street Arab* (London: George Cauldwell, 1891), and Augustus Mayhew, *Paved with Gold: or The Romance and Reality of the London Streets* (London: Chapman and Hill, 1857).

20. I have drawn on Brooks's explanation of the melodramatic format in *Melodramatic Imagination*, 30–31. On the child as the signifier of innocent virtue, see Vicinus, "'Helpless and Unfriended,'" 130.

21. The common portrayal of children as orphaned or deserted by parents reappeared in most of Barnardo's publications. See, for example, Barnardo, "Preventive Homes: A Paper Read before the Social Science Congress at Liverpool, October, 1876," *Night and Day* (January 15, 1877): 2–3; Barnardo, *"Something Attempted, Something Done": Dr. Barnardo's Homes* (London: John F. Shaw and Co., 1889), 84; "The Keepers of Our Gates," review of Charles Booth, *Labour and Life of the People*, vol. 1, *East London*, *Night and Day* (November 1890): 182; "Wastrels," *Night and Day* (June 16, 1877): 70. Barnardo's emphasis on orphaned/deserted children is also apparent in the samples of case histories published in his monthly fund-raising magazine, *Night and Day*.

22. Barnardo, *"The King's Business Requireth Haste": A Year's Work in "Dr. Barnardo's Homes"* (London: J. F. Shaw and Co., 1885), 41 (emphasis in original).

23. Barnardo, *My First Arab; or How I began My Life-Work* (1888; London: Stepney Causeway, 1917), 9, 15 (emphasis in original). Barnardo published many versions of this account, starting with the one that appeared in *The Christian* in 1872. Although later versions dated Barnardo's meeting with Jarvis to 1866, the year he first arrived in London, earlier ones situate the event in the winter of 1869–70. See Wagner, *Barnardo*, 30.

24. *"Rescue the Perishing": Being the Report for the Ninth Year of the East-End Juvenile Mission, and for the Fifth Year of the Homes for Reclaiming Destitute Children of Both Sexes: A Statement of Accounts, 1874–75* (London: Morgan and Scott; Haughton and Co., 1876), xlvi (copy available as D239/A3/7, ULLSCA). By 1885, Barnardo had hired a children's beadle to conduct these midnight searches in his place. See *"The King's Business Requireth Haste,"* 20.

25. *Night and Day* (January 15, 1877): 2. For other fictional and philanthropic accounts highlighting the role of the intervening upper-class benefactor, see Ellen Barlee, *Pantomime Waifs: or, A Plea for Our City Children* (London: S. W. Partridge and Co., 1884), 15; Battersby, *Gaspar*; Brenda [Mrs. G. Castle Smith], *Froggy's Little Brother* (London: John F. Shaw and Co., 1875); G. Crockford, "Little Nat," *Good Words for the Young* (June 1, 1869): 365–70; Henry Holbeach, "My Little Gipsy Cousin," *Good Words for the Young* (March 1, 1871): 294–96;

Ellice Hopkins, *God's Little Girl: A Truthful Narrative of Facts Concerning a Poor "Waif" Admitted to "Dr. Barnardo's Village Home"* (London: J. F. Shaw and Co., ca. 1885); J. E. Partridge, *Ragamuffin Tom* (London: Wells Gardner, Darton and Co., 1903); and Albert Shakesby, *From Street Arab to Evangelist: The Life Story of Albert Shakesby, a Converted Athlete, by Himself* (Hull: Burtt Brothers, 1910). Mary Royce's *Little Scrigget, the Street Arab* (Leicester: J. and T. Spencer, 1875) is an unusual example of the poor child's salvation through the efforts of a respectable working-class Christ figure, John Wright.

26. See chapter 3. In the précis records for 1886, there are only three clear cases of children "Found in the Streets by Brockfield [an agent of Barnardo's] and brought to the Home": C.J. (May 25); D.O. (May 25); and E.M. (May 27). See Précis Books (1886), vol. 1, In-care children's records, Barnardo Archive, D239/D/2/2a/104, ULLSCA.

27. See McWilliam's discussion of Christina Crosby's work, "Melodrama and the Historians," 68.

28. Barnardo, "The Continued Necessity for Voluntary Agencies in Reclaiming the Children of the Streets," *Night and Day* (November 1881): 204.

29. See Booth, *English Melodrama*, 33, 131–36, 152–53, for descriptions of temperance melodramas that remained popular on the stage through the late nineteenth century.

30. Barnardo, *"Something Attempted Something Done, Being the Annual Report of Dr. Barnardo's Homes, East End Juvenile Mission"* (London: John F. Shaw and Co., 1888), 13. Alcohol was also the focus of many "street arab" and waif novels. Like Barnardo, the Reverend J. E. Shephard claimed that alcohol "robs the mother of her motherliness, and the father of his truest manhood." See J. E. Shephard, *Mahomet, A. J.: From Street Arab to Evangelist*, 2nd ed. (London: W. H. Tomkins, 1885), 12. Also see Barlee, *Pantomime Waifs*, 46, 226; James Greenwood, *The True History of a Little Ragamuffin* (London: S. O. Beeton, 1866), in which a child runs away from home after being abused by his Irish stepmother, a gin drinker; and Shakesby, *From Street Arab to Evangelist*, 2, 14, 28, 36.

31. Barnardo, *A City Waif: How I Fished For and Caught Her* (London: J. F. Shaw and Co., ca. 1886), 25–26.

32. G. H. Pike, *Children Reclaimed for Life: The Story of Dr. Barnardo's Work in London* (London: Hodder and Stroughton, 1875), 61.

33. There are some rare, self-contradictory exceptions to these monstrous portrayals of parents in Barnardo's writings. In one pamphlet he stated: "NOTHING vexes me more than to hear people talk of my children as if they were the 'scum of the earth,' . . . such Pariahs of society as to be dubbed by the scornful, 'gutter children,' or by the pitiful, 'waifs and strays.'" He insisted that many of his children came from the "*decent* poor," although he did not often present this aspect of his work to the public. Furthermore, Barnardo's examples of children from the respectable poor were usually orphans. See Barnardo, *"The Seed of the Righteous" among the Children of the Poorest* (London: J. F. Shaw and Co., ca. 1887), 1–2, and "Our Annual Meeting in Exeter Hall," *Night and Day* (October 1883): 63.

34. See Barnardo, "A Very Restless Night," *Night and Day* (April 16, 1877): 41–42, and Koven's analysis of this text in *Slumming*, 109–11. For accounts of Barnardo's fights with unruly women, see "A Thrashing," *Night and Day* (August 1877): 85–87, and *Kidnapped! A Narrative of Fact* (London: J. F. Shaw and Co., ca.

1885), 15–18, in addition to *Worse Than Orphans: How I Stole Two Girls and Fought for a Boy* (London: J. F. Shaw and Co., ca. 1885), discussed below.

35. *Worse Than Orphans*, 26–29, quotations at 27–29.

36. See Koven, *Slumming*, 112–24.

37. J. G. Gent, Esq., secretary to the Ragged School Union (June 10, 1861), *Report from the Select Committee on the Education of Destitute Children; Together with the Proceedings of the Committee, Minutes of Evidence, and Appendix*, PP (1861) vii, 428, para. 329.

38. Barnardo, *Episodes in Humble Lives* (London: J. F. Shaw and Co., ca. 1894), 3. Also see Barnardo, *A City Waif*, 6, and *Never Had a Home: A Very Commonplace History* (London: J. F. Shaw and Co., 1890).

39. [A Late "Holiday Mother"], *My Cottage: A Story of Dr. Barnardo's Village Home for Orphan and Destitute Girls* (London: J. F. Shaw and Co., ca. 1885), 44.

40. Barnardo, *"Taken Out of the Gutter": A True Incident of Child Life on the Streets of London* (London: Haughton and Co., ca. 1881), 8–9. In a much more explicit, pornographic photograph, a reclining teenage male holds his shirt open in the position of sexual provocateur. See Admission Album, 1/3, 71 (August 25, 1874), BPFA.

41. Lloyd, *The Camera and Dr. Barnardo*, 13, and "Lost!" D425/ARC0108, BPFA. See also Smith, "Shoe-Black to the Crossing Sweeper," 36, and Koven, "Dr. Barnardo's 'Artistic Fictions,'" 28–29. The Shaftesbury Society used Rejlander's photograph for publicity advertisements, and the National Refuges for Homeless and Destitute Children included a drawing of "Poor Jo" on the cover of its monthly magazine, *Our Log Book*, from 1899 to 1903.

42. Questioning of Thomas Barnes re. Photographs of Samuel Reed, Dr. Barnardo's Homes, Reynolds-Barnardo Arbitration, COS's Dr. Barnardo Sub-Committee Minutes, 1877–78, Family Welfare Association Papers [COS], A/FWA/D10/3, LMA. Koven also discusses the photographs of Samuel Reed in *Slumming*, 120–22.

43. Testimony of Samuel Reed, Dr. Barnardo's Homes, Reynolds-Barnardo Arbitration, COS's Dr. Barnardo Sub-Committee Minutes, 1877–78, Family Welfare Association Papers [COS], A/FWA/D10/3, LMA (emphasis in original). Also see George Reynolds, *Dr. Barnardo's Homes, Containing Startling Revelations* (London: n.p., 1877), 7.

44. Questioning of Thomas Barnes, Dr. Barnardo's Homes, Reynolds-Barnardo Arbitration, COS's Dr. Barnardo Sub-Committee Minutes, 1877–78, Family Welfare Association Papers [COS], A/FWA/D10/3, LMA (emphasis in original). Barnes came to Barnardo's weekly beginning in 1871 and was Barnardo's main photographer by the late 1870s. An entry in the Children's Admission Registers for September 5, 1878, notes, "til further notice all photos are taken by Barnes." Barnardo's second main photographer, Roderick Johnstone, began working in the studio in the early 1880s. He probably headed the studio after 1888 until 1906. See Children's Admission Registers (September 5, 1878), Children's Records, In-care children's records, Barnardo Archive, D239/D/2/2a/2, ULLSCA, and Lloyd, *The Camera and Dr. Barnardo*, 13, 15.

45. See, for example, "The House of Lords and the Protection of Young Girls," *Night and Day* (September 1881): 161–63, and *Night and Day* (December 1887): 127. Also see Barnardo, *A City Waif*, 17, 27–30. The president of Barnardo's Homes,

the Earl of Cairns, presided over the 1881 House of Lords Select Committee investigation of child prostitution. On "The Maiden Tribute," see Deborah Gorham, "The 'Maiden Tribute of Modern Babylon' Re-examined: Child Prostitution and the Idea of Childhood in Late-Victorian England," *Victorian Studies* 21, no. 3 (1978): 353–79; Wagner, *Barnardo*, 206–8; and Walkowitz, *City of Dreadful Delight*, 81–134.

46. "Is Philanthropic Abduction Ever Justifiable?" *Night and Day* (November 1885): 149–52, quotation at 149 (emphasis in original).

47. *Night and Day* (March 1886): 42 (emphasis in original).

48. For example, see the following articles in *Night and Day*: "Is Philanthropic Abduction Ever Justifiable?" (November 1885): 150; "The Roman Catholics and My Children" (November 1889): 125; and "Dr. Barnardo Again!" (June 1890): 126. For general descriptions of mothers as prostitutes, see *Night and Day* (April/May 1882): 53; *Night and Day* (October 1883): 74; Barnardo, *A Year's Work in the Institution Known as "Dr. Barnardo's Homes"* (London: J. F. Shaw and Co., ca. 1884), 8; Barnardo, *"The King's Business Requireth Haste,"* 60.

49. Barnardo, *Out of an Horrible Pit* (London: J. F. Shaw and Co., ca. 1892), 2 (emphasis in original).

50. On melodrama's dreamlike qualities, see Booth, *English Melodrama*, 14, 120, and Brooks, *Melodramatic Imagination*, 41–43.

51. Barnardo, *The 1/— Baby: An Incident of the London Slave Trade* (London: Stepney Causeway, ca. 1889), 1 (emphasis in original).

52. *"Rescue the Perishing,"* lviii (emphasis in original). This account is repeated almost word for word in *"The King's Business Requireth Haste,"* 23–24, and *Worse Than Orphans*, 2–3. For similar accounts of children bought and sold for begging/entertaining purposes, see Barlee, *Pantomime Waifs*, 103–11; Barnardo, *Kidnapped!* 4; *The Cruelty Man: Actual Experiences of an Inspector of the N.S.P.C.C. Graphically Told by Himself* (London: National Society for the Prevention of Cruelty to Children, 1912), 67; Norman Flower, *The Boy Who Did Grow Up*, with an introduction by J. M. Barrie (London, New York, Toronto, and Melbourne: Cassell and Co., Ltd., 1919), 129–30; Thor Fredur, *Sketches from Shady Places* (London: Smith, Elder, and Co., 1879), 11; *Night and Day* (June 1887): 13, (December 1887): 124, and (September 1891): 121; and Pike, *Romance of the Streets*, 53–55.

53. *Night and Day* (December 1887): 124.

54. Smith, "Shoe-Black to the Crossing Sweeper," 29, 33.

55. On waif and "street arab" novels, see Anna Davin, *Growing Up Poor: Home, School and Street in London, 1870–1914* (London: Rivers Oram Press, 1996), 90–91, 161–64, and Davin, "Waif Stories in Late Nineteenth-Century England," *History Workshop Journal* 52 (2001): 67–98.

56. Thomas Guthrie, *First Plea for Ragged Schools* (1847), quoted in Smith, "Shoe-Black to the Crossing Sweeper," 30. Also see Hugh Cunningham, *The Children of the Poor: Representations of Childhood since the Seventeenth Century* (Oxford: Blackwell, 1991), 106.

57. Lord Shaftesbury, speech in Parliament (June 6, 1848), quoted in *Oxford English Dictionary*, s.v. "street Arab."

58. See Smith, "Shoe-Black to the Crossing Sweeper." H. M. Stanley [Dorothy Tennant], *London Street Arabs* (London, Paris, and Melbourne: Cassell and

Company, Ltd., 1890), gives a detailed account of how Tennant dressed her child models in rags and darkened their faces.

59. Also see Barlee, *Pantomime Waifs*; Barnardo, *My First Arab*; Battersby, *Gaspar*; S. R. Crockett, *Cleg Kelly: Arab of the City* (London: Smith, Elder, and Co., 1896); J.W.C. Fegan, *A Plea for Our Street-Arabs: Grace Triumphant, or the Dying Match-Seller* (London: Boys' Home, 1895); Pike, *Children Reclaimed for Life*; Shakesby, *From Street Arab to Evangelist*; and Stanley, *London Street Arabs*. One consequence of the term's widespread use is that many scholars uncritically adopt it. See, for example, Lionel Rose, *The Erosion of Childhood: Child Oppression in Great Britain, 1860–1918* (London and New York: Routledge, 1991). For perceptive examinations of the term "street arab," see Smith, "Shoe-Black to the Crossing Sweeper," and Cunningham, *Children of the Poor*, 97–132.

60. Barnardo, *My First Arab*, 1–2. Anna Davin, in "Waif Stories," likewise notes that "the failure of the family is essential to the plot structure of the waif story, with rare exceptions" (88).

61. *Night and Day* (June 1887): 3. Also see "Preventive Homes," *Night and Day* (January 15, 1877): 3.

62. "Preventive Homes," *Night and Day* (January 15, 1877): 3. Also see *"Rescuing the Perishing,"* xi–xii.

63. "London Lodging Houses, V.—Boys Found in Them," *Night and Day* (June 16, 1877): 83.

64. "Street Boys Rescued," by the author of "Episodes in an Obscure Life," *Night and Day* (September 1, 1877): 106.

65. "Personal Notes," *Night and Day* (September 1891): 121.

66. On the construction of the urban poor as a race apart, see Gertrude Himmelfarb, *The Idea of Poverty: England in the Early Industrial Age* (New York: Knopf, 1985); Deborah Epstein Nord, "The Social Explorer as Anthropologist: Victorian Travellers among the Urban Poor," in *Visions of the Modern City: Essays in History, Art, and Literature*, ed. William Sharpe and Leonard Wallock (New York: Columbia University Press, 1983), 118–30; Thorne, *Congregational Missions*, esp. chs. 2 and 3; and Walkowitz, *City of Dreadful Delight*, 19. On the particular racialization of the Irish, see Perry L. Curtis, *Apes and Angels: The Irishman in Victorian Caricature*, rev. ed. (Washington, DC: Smithsonian Institution Press, 1997). For contemporary examples, see William Booth, *In Darkest England and the Way Out* (1890); Henry Mayhew, *London Labour and the London Poor* (1861–62; London: Penguin Books, 1987); and Watts Phillips, *The Wild Tribes of London* (London: Ward and Lock, 1855).

67. Annie Macpherson, *The Little London Arabs* (London: Morgan and Chase, 1870), 37. For a comparison of poor children to "tribes of savages," see Howard J. Goldsmith, *Dottings of a Dosser: Being Revelations of the Inner Life of Low London Lodging-Houses* (London: T. Fisher Unwin, 1886), 45.

68. Battersby, *Gaspar*, 8.

69. Ibid., 21–22.

70. Ellen Barlee, *Our Homeless Poor; And What We Can Do To Help Them* (London: James Nisbet and Co., 1860), 194.

71. Barnardo, *China-John: or "What's the Good?"* (London: Stepney Causeway, 1902), 2. Also see Barnardo, *My First Arab*, 2; "London Lodging Houses, V.—

Boys Found in Them," *Night and Day* (June 16, 1877): 84; *Night and Day* (June 1887): 4.
72. Lord Ashley, *Quarterly Review* article (1846), quoted in Cunningham, *Children of the Poor*, 106.
73. Green-Lewis, *Framing the Victorians*, 187–226; Tagg, "Power and Photography," 24–45; John Tagg, *The Burden of Representation: Essays on Photographies and Histories* (Amherst: University of Massachusetts Press, 1988), 3–64.
74. *Night and Day* (June 1887): 4. On anthropological uses of photography, see Edwards, ed., *Anthropology and Photography*, and Andrew D. Evans, "Capturing Race: Anthropology and Photography in German and Austrian Prisoner-of-War Camps during World War I," in *Colonialist Photography: Imag(in)ing Race and Place*, ed. Eleanor M. Hight and Gary D. Sampson (London and New York: Routledge, 2002), 228–35.
75. See [A Late "Holiday Mother"], *My Cottage*, 16, for a similar description of a poor girl's physiognomy upon entering the Girls' Village Home.
76. Crockett, *Cleg Kelly*, 1, 5, 6.
77. Shakesby, *From Street Arab to Evangelist*, 29. See also Pike, *Romance of the Streets*, 8.
78. Barnardo, *China-John*, 3.
79. "Personal Notes," *Night and Day* (March 1890): 62 (emphasis in original).
80. See Barnardo's description of Native Americans in *Night and Day* (February 1885): 24–25.
81. "The Beni-Zou-Zougs!" *Night and Day* (December 1881): 216–17, 221.
82. Ibid., 215.
83. Booth, *English Melodrama*, 88, and John M. MacKenzie, *Propaganda and Empire: The Manipulation of British Public Opinion, 1880–1960* (Manchester: Manchester University Press, 1984), 45.
84. "The Beni-Zou-Zougs!" *Night and Day* (December 1881): 220.
85. See illustration, ibid., 215.
86. Ibid., 215, 221.
87. Ibid., 216, 217, 218. Also see 220.
88. Ibid., 216–17, quotation at 216.
89. Ibid., 215.
90. Ibid., 221. The other seven "were placed under proper care in other parts of the country, either in public institutions or under some other proper kind of supervision." See "Our Annual Meeting," *Night and Day* (September 1882): 71.
91. Davin, "Waif Stories," 72.
92. Royce, *Little Scrigget*, 67–72, 89–90. On the format of Christian stage melodramas, see Michael Kilgarriff, ed., *The Golden Age of Melodrama: Twelve Nineteenth-Century Melodramas* (London: Wolfe Publishing Ltd., 1974), 26.
93. Royce, *Little Scrigget*, 39.
94. I. W. Ventnor, preface to Shephard, *Mahomet*, 2.
95. Also see Fegan, *A Plea for Our Street-Arabs*, and Shakesby, *From Street Arab to Evangelist*. On Salvation Army conversion narratives, see Pamela J. Walker, *Pulling the Devil's Kingdom Down: The Salvation Army in Victorian Britain* (Berkeley: University of California Press, 2001), 64–93.
96. Partridge, *Ragamuffin Tom*, 83.
97. Hopkins, *God's Little Girl*, 15; Partridge, *Ragamuffin Tom*, 7.

98. Shephard, *Mahomet*, 61.
99. Hopkins, *God's Little Girl*, 14.
100. *Night and Day* (February/March 1881): 25.
101. For examples, see Barnardo's, *Annual Report*, 1880–81, 16, D239/A3/13, ULLSCA; Barnardo, *"The King's Business Requireth Haste,"* 14 (example of bath ritual for Roman Catholic child); Battersby, *Gaspar*, 39; Hopkins, *God's Little Girl*, 15; Hume Nisbet, "The Life of a Waif," in *Tales for the Homes*, ed. James Marchant (London: Chatto and Windus, 1907), 158; Patridge, *Ragamuffin Tom*, 7, 9; Pike, *Romance of the Streets*, 31.
102. Hopkins, *God's Little Girl*, 19, 20–21, 28–29, quotation at 19.
103. Shakesby, *From Street Arab to Evangelist*, 188.
104. Thor Fredur wrote, "Reading . . . is one of the darling vices of the shady classes. . . . I have seen men so infatuated with reading that they would do nothing else, thus allowing themselves to be ruined utterly by their passion." *Sketches from Shady Places*, 116–17. On the political awareness derived from reading, see George Haw, *From Workhouse to Westminster: The Life Story of Will Crooks, M.P.*, with an introduction by G. K. Chesterton (London, Paris, New York, and Melbourne: Cassell and Company, Ltd., 1907), 18–22.
105. For accounts that focus on children's literacy as a means of their conversion, see, for example, Barnardo, *China-John*, 7; Barnardo, *Rescued for Life: The True Story of a Young Thief . . .* (London: J. F. Shaw and Co., ca. 1885), 15–18, 31–32; Hopkins, *God's Little Girl*, 6, 21; Macpherson, *Little London Arabs*, 14; Nisbet, "Life of a Waif," 162; Partridge, *Ragamuffin Tom*, 7, 27–34, 68; Pike, *Romance of the Streets*, 38–39; "Personal Notes," *Night and Day* (March 1890): 62; Royce, *Little Scrigget*, 11, 41.
106. Shakesby, *From Street Arab to Evangelist*, 194. On Shakesby's etiquette training, also see 50, 179, 194–95.
107. Barnardo, *Rescued for Life*, 21. Also see Barnardo, "Preventive Homes," *Night and Day* (January 15, 1877): 4, and Flower, *Boy Who Did Grow Up*, 148–49.
108. Barnardo, *Two Rescues!* (London: Stepney Causeway, n.d.), 16 (emphasis in original).
109. Barnardo, *Out of an Horrible Pit*, 3 (emphasis in original).
110. Barnardo, *Episodes in Humble Lives*, 7 (emphasis in original).
111. Peter Brooks, "Melodrama, Body, Revolution," in *Melodrama: Stage, Picture, Screen*, ed. Jacky Bratton, Jim Cook, and Christine Gledhill (London: British Film Institute, 1994), 18.
112. "Personal Notes," *Night and Day* (June 1890): 101 (emphasis in original).
113. Walker, *Pulling the Devil's Kingdom Down*, 88–91.
114. See, for example, Barnardo, *Rescued for Life*, 38; Shakesby, *From Street Arab to Evangelist*, 211.
115. Lloyd, *The Camera and Dr. Barnardo*, 11–12. Barnardo also used photographs to solicit larger donations. An 1889 advertisement for foster parents in *Night and Day* offered individual photographs of children along with full case histories in exchange for £16, the cost of one year's maintenance. See "'Somebody's Bairns': Wanted—Foster Parents!" *Night and Day* (April 1889): 53–54, and similar advertisements in 1891 editions of *Night and Day*.
116. Lloyd, *The Camera and Dr. Barnardo*, 20; "Once a Little Vagrant" and "Now a Little Workman," D422/ARC0239–40, BPFA.

117. "The Dreadful Past," D481/ARC0109, and "The Delightful Present," D482/ARC0110, BPFA.
118. See, for example, before-and-after drawings of Charles Cooker and Matthew Hodder in *Night and Day* (February 1896): 9.
119. Admission Album, 1/28, 664 (March 14, 1876) and 666 (March 17, 1876), BPFA.
120. John's tousled hair was a characteristic of the "street arab." The artist Dorothy Tennant, known for her realistic drawings of poor children, described how the hair of the child model who tidied himself in anticipation of a sitting could be "worried up into a mop again if vigorously shampooed by his friend." See Stanley, *London Street Arabs*, 7.
121. Testimony of Samuel Reed and Questioning of Thomas Barnes, A/FWA/D10/3, Dr. Barnardo's Homes, Reynolds-Barnardo Arbitration, COS's Dr. Barnardo Sub-Committee Minutes, 1877–78, Family Welfare Association Papers [COS], LMA.
122. Robinson was often infuriated at his inability to coerce rural female subjects to smile and usually resorted to photographing middle-class models dressed as rural workers. See Henry Peach Robinson, *Picture-Making by Photography*, 5th ed. (1897; New York: Arno Press, 1973), 52, 96–97; Robinson, *The Elements of a Pictorial Photograph* (1896; New York: Arno Press, 1973), 104.
123. Jadviga M. Da Costa Nunes, "O. G. Rejlander's Photographs of Ragged Children: Reflections on the Idea of Urban Poverty in Mid-Victorian Society," *Nineteenth Century Studies* 4 (1990): 125. Also see Sarah Greenough, "The Curious Contagion of the Camera," in *On the Art of Fixing a Shadow: One Hundred and Fifty Years of Photography* (Boston, Toronto, London: National Gallery of Art and Art Institute of Chicago in Association with Bulfinch Press/Little, Brown and Co., 1989), 137.
124. See the following articles in *Night and Day*: "Our Annual Meeting" (July 1886): 105–25; "A Year's Work and a Day's Witness" (July 1890): 140–56; "After Twenty-five Years" (July 1891): 85–97; "Our Twenty-Sixth Anniversary" (July 1892): 65–80; and "A Royal Visit" (August 1896): 51–59. June Rose presents a critical analysis of Barnardo's before-and-after presentations at annual meetings in the 1880s in *For the Sake of the Children*, 66–67. After Barnardo's death in 1905, the organization was more hesitant to have the children perform. In March 1909, the Executive Committee declined an offer for exhibition space at the Earl's Court Exhibition for "fear of the effect on the boys and interfering with the work of the shops." An offer to partake in the Pageant of Empire at the Crystal Palace was also declined in 1910, although boys from Stepney and the Watts Naval Training School did continue to perform in the downscaled Albert Hall meetings as well as in the Lord Mayor's Shows of 1913 and 1916. See Executive Committee, Committee Minutes, vol. 1 (December 14, 1908–February 10, 1915), 15–17, 67–68, 78, 229; vol. 2 (November 1, 1916), Council Papers, Barnardo Archive, D239/B3/1/1 and D239/B3/121, ULLSCA.
125. "Theatricals," *Night and Day* (January 1893): 13.
126. "After Twenty-five Years," *Night and Day* (July 1891): 87.
127. Ibid., 90. Also see *Night and Day* (July 1892): 73.
128. "A Year's Work and a Day's Witness," *Night and Day* (July 1890): 146–47.
129. *Night and Day* (November 1897): 43.
130. Barnardo's Committee Meeting (July 15, 1892), Council Minutes including information on individual children and residency statistics (February 1891–October

1899), 40, Council Papers, Barnardo Archive, D239/B1/6, ULLSCA; E. M. Townshend to Jessie Young, June 24, 1892, Barnardo Archive, D239/A4/5, ULLSCA.

131. E. M. Townshend to Jessie Young, June 24, 1892, Barnardo Archive, D239/A4/5, ULLSCA.

132. Brooks, "Melodrama, Body, Revolution," 19.

133. See Deborah Epstein Nord, *Walking the Victorian Streets: Women, Representation, and the City* (Ithaca and London: Cornell University Press, 1995), 20, and Maren Stange, "Gotham's Crime and Misery: Ideology and Entertainment in Jacob Riis's Lantern Slide Exhibitions," *Views: The Journal of Photography in New England* 8, no. 3 (Spring 1987): 7–11.

CHAPTER 2 *From Barrack Schools to Family Cottages*

1. William Chambers, "The Boarding-Out System," *Chambers's Journal of Popular Literature, Science, and Art,* 4th ser., 14 (June 9, 1877): 353.

2. On boarding-out in England, see Henry Aveling, *The Boarding-Out System and Legislation Relating to the Protection of Children and Infant Life: A Manual for Poor-Law Guardians, Boarding-Out Committees, and Practical Workers* (London: Swan Sonnenschein and Co., 1890); Behlmer, *Friends of the Family*, 285–89, 293–94; Florence Davenport Hill, *Children of the State* (1868; London: Macmillan and Co., 1889); Francis Duke, "Pauper Education," in *New Poor Law*, ed. Fraser, 81; Danby Palmer Fry, *The Boarding Out of Pauper Children: Containing the General Order of the Poor Law Board, and the Accompanying Circular, with Notes & Introduction* (London: Knight and Co., 1870); Wilhelmina L. Hall, *Boarding-Out, as a Method of Pauper Education and Check on Hereditary Pauperism* (London: Hatchards, 1887); Richard Humble, *Boarding-Out of Orphan and Deserted Pauper Children versus Workhouse Schools* (Adel, Leeds: n.p., 1883); and Smedley, Boarding-Out. On boarding-out and general child welfare policies in Scotland, see Lynn Abrams, *The Orphan Country: Children of Scotland's Broken Homes from 1845 to the Present Day* (Edinburgh: John Donald Publishers, Ltd., 1998).

3. For case studies that explore the meanings of space from the inhabitants' perspectives, see *The Cultural Meaning of Urban Space,* ed. Robert Rotenberg and Gary McDonogh (Westport, CT, and London: Bergin and Garvey, 1993). M. J. Daunton discusses working-class conceptions of domesticity in *House and Home in the Victorian City: Working-Class Housing, 1850–1914* (London: Edward Arnold, 1983), 263–85, as does Martin Hewitt in "District Visiting and the Constitution of Domestic Space in the Mid-Nineteenth Century," in *Domestic Space: Reading the Nineteenth-Century Interior,* ed. Inga Bryden and Janet Floyd (Manchester: Manchester University Press, 1999), 121–41.

4. See Elizabeth Grosz, "Bodies-Cities," in *Sexuality and Space,* ed. Beatriz Colomina (New York: Princeton Architectural Press, 1992), 244–49, and Setha M. Low, "Cultural Meaning of the Plaza: The History of the Spanish-American Gridplan-Plaza Urban Design," in *Cultural Meaning of Urban Space,* ed. Rotenberg and McDonogh, 75.

5. For examples of such historical studies of space, see Annmarie Adams, *Architecture in the Family Way: Doctors, Houses, and Women* (Montreal: McGill-Queen's University Press, 1996); Clifford E. Clark Jr., "Domestic Architecture as

an Index to Social History: The Romantic Revival and the Cult of Domesticity in America, 1840–1870," *Journal of Interdisciplinary History* 7, no. 1 (Summer 1976): 33–56; Colomina, ed., *Sexuality and Space*; Felix Driver, "Moral Geographies: Social Science and the Urban Environment in Mid-Nineteenth Century England," *Transactions of the Institute of British Geographers,* n.s., 13 (1988): 275–87; Foucault, *Discipline and Punish*; Mary Poovey, *Making a Social Body: British Cultural Formation, 1830–1864* (Chicago: University of Chicago Press, 1995); Rotenberg and McDonogh, eds., *Cultural Meaning of Urban Space*; Dell Upton, "Lancasterian Schools, Republican Citizenship, and the Spatial Imagination in Early Nineteenth-Century America," *Journal of the Society of Architectural Historians* 55, no. 3 (September 1996): 238–53.

6. Leonore Davidoff and Catherine Hall, *Family Fortunes: Men and Women of the English Middle Class, 1780–1850* (Chicago: University of Chicago Press, 1987), 357–64 and passim; F.M.L. Thompson, *The Rise of Respectable Society: A Social History of Victorian Britain, 1830–1900* (London: Fontana Press, 1988), 152–96.

7. Felix Driver, "Discipline Without Frontiers? Representations of the Mettray Reformatory Colony in Britain, 1840–1880," *Journal of Historical Sociology* 3, no. 3 (1990): 273; Driver, "Moral Geographies," 277 and passim.

8. The continued support for communities envisioned according to the Great Chain of Being alongside the rising class conflict of the late nineteenth century adds support to David Cannadine's argument that three different social models coexisted in Britain: "the hierarchical view of society as a seamless web; the triadic version with upper, middle, and lower collective groups; and the dichotomous, adversarial picture, where society is sundered between 'us' and 'them'" (20). See Cannadine, *The Rise and Fall of Class in Britain* (New York: Columbia University Press, 1999).

9. Adams, *Architecture in the Family Way,* 136–42; Clifford Clark, "Domestic Architecture," 49–53; Davidoff and Hall, *Family Fortunes,* 364–70, 375–80.

10. Driver, "Moral Geographies," 281.

11. On the resilience of working-class privacy, see Hewitt, "District Visiting," 121–23, 129–34, 137–38.

12. Daunton, *House and Home,* 12–15, 35.

13. Peter Stallybrass and Allon White, *The Politics and Poetics of Transgression* (Ithaca: Cornell University Press, 1986), 48–50, 132, 147.

14. Davin, *Growing Up Poor,* 57, 63–68, and passim.

15. Poovey, *Making a Social Body,* 144. Also see Martin Hewitt "The Travails of Domestic Visiting: Manchester, 1830–70," *Historical Research* 71 (June 1998): 196–227, and Hewitt, "District Visiting."

16. Barlee, *Our Homeless Poor,* 217 (emphasis in original), 218.

17. Barnardo often claimed that many of the children in his homes came from lodging houses. See, for example, "The Continued Necessity for Voluntary Agencies in Reclaiming the Children of the Streets," *Night and Day* (November 1881): 204, and "Waifs and Strays at Supper," *Night and Day* (February/March 1882): 32–33.

18. Barnardo, "London Lodging Houses," *Night and Day* (January 1877): 11. Also see Goldsmith, *Dottings of a Dosser,* 40–43; Viscount Ingestre, ed., *Meliora: or, Better Times to Come* (London: John W. Parker and Son, 1852), 185.

19. Seth Koven astutely analyzes Barnardo's narrative of slumming in a lodging house, suggesting that the account involves homosexual fantasies as well as a reversal of

identity. See Barnardo, "A Very Restless Night," *Night and Day* (April 16, 1877): 40–43, and Koven, "Dr. Barnardo's 'Artistic Fictions,'" 22–24. For a later account of "personal contamination caused by even one night" in a lodging house, see "A Lady," *Five Days and Five Nights as a Tramp among Tramps: Social Investigation by A Lady* (Manchester: John Heywood, 1904), 14.

20. Barnardo, *Night and Day* (June 1887): 15.
21. Barnardo, "A Thrashing," *Night and Day* (August 1877): 85 (emphasis in original), 87. For an illustration of this "thrashing," see *"Something Attempted Something Done"* (1888), 146.
22. Macpherson, *Little London Arabs*, 8. See "Bare Walls, Little Furniture, and Other Scenes," *Our Log Book* (April 15, 1899): 315, and Goldsmith, *Dottings of a Dosser*, 50.
23. Osborne, quoted in *"Something Attempted Something Done"* (1888), 12.
24. Stallybrass and White, *Politics and Poetics of Transgression*, 125–48, skillfully summarize Victorian reformers' association of the poor with dirt, sewage, disease, and moral depravity. For discussions of the aggregate, embodied rhetoric used to describe the poor, see Poovey, *Making a Social Body*, 37, and Moira Gatens, "Corporeal Representation in/and the Body Politic," in *Writing on the Body: Female Embodiment and Feminist Theory*, ed. Kate Conboy, Nadia Medina, and Sarah Stanbury (New York: Columbia University Press, 1997), 83. Mikhail Bakhtin's distinction between the "grotesque body" and the "classical body" is also useful. According to Bakhtin, "the grotesque body is not separated from the rest of the world. It is not a closed, complete unit; it is unfinished, outgrows itself, transgresses its own limits." Unlike the grotesque body, the classical body is "isolated, alone, fenced off from all other bodies," in sum, the ideal of bourgeois individualism. See Bakhtin, *Rabelais and His World*, trans. Helene Iswolsky (Cambridge, MA: MIT Press, 1968), 26, 29.
25. *Barnardo's Annual Reports, 1883–84*, 9, D239/A3/16, ULLSCA (emphasis in original).
26. On the symbolic meaning of the garden as a site of bourgeois values, see Davidoff and Hall, *Family Fortunes*, 370–75, and Walter E. Houghton, *The Victorian Frame of Mind, 1830–1870* (New Haven and London: Yale University Press, 1957), 343.
27. See chapters 3 and 4.
28. On the connections between spatial design and citizenship, see Elizabeth Grosz, "Bodies-Cities," 250, and Upton, "Lancasterian Schools," 243–51. For a general discussion of how Victorian social scientists sought to reform individuals through model environments, including institutional spaces, see Driver, "Moral Geographies," 279–84.
29. Felix Driver, *Power and Pauperism: The Workhouse System, 1834–1884* (Cambridge: Cambridge University Press, 1993), 64. Also see Anne Digby, *The Poor Law in Nineteenth-Century England and Wales* (London: Historical Association, 1982), 17. For an illustration of a workhouse design with strict spatial divisions for distinct classifications of the poor, see S. H. Brooks, *Select Designs for Public Buildings; Consisting of Plans, Elevations, Perspective Views, Sections, and Details, of Churches, Chapels, Schools, Alms-Houses, Gas-Works, Markets, and Other Buildings Erected for Public Purposes* (London: Thomas Kelly, Paternoster Row, 1842), plate 83.
30. Derek Fraser, *The Evolution of the British Welfare State: A History of Social Policy since the Industrial Revolution* (London: Macmillan Press, Ltd., 1973), 47;

Dorothy Thompson, *The Chartists: Popular Politics in the Industrial Revolution* (New York: Pantheon Books, 1984), 29. Digby notes that children under two were allowed to be with their mothers always and that children under four slept with their mothers. Mothers also had daily access to their children under seven, but were restricted to short weekly meetings when children were over seven. See Digby, *Pauper Palaces*, 156.

31. Smedley, *Boarding-Out*, 4.
32. Frances Power Cobbe, "The Philosophy of the Poor Laws," *Fraser's Magazine* 70 (1864): 386.
33. Francis Peek, "Hereditary Pauperism and Pauper Education," *Contemporary Review* 31 (1877): 137.
34. See Digby, *Poor Law*, 23; Fraser, *Evolution of the British Welfare State*, 48; Michael Rose, "The Crisis of Poor Relief in England, 1860–1890," in *The Emergence of the Welfare State in Britain and Germany, 1850–1950*, ed. W. J. Mommsen (London: Croom Helm, 1981), 53–54.
35. Edward Carleton Tufnell, quoted in Florence Hill, *Children of the State*, 19. Also see S. E. DeMorgan, "The Workhouse Girl," *Good Words* 10 (1869): 285. In a rare objection to demands for strict architectural segregation, T. H. Murray Browne wrote: "The *geographical* proximity of the children to adult paupers is an objection which has been much exaggerated. Children do not catch pauperism as they do the measles, by passing someone on the stairs." Browne, *The Education and Future of Workhouse Children: A Paper Read at the West Midland District Poor Law Conference* (London: Knight and Co., 1883), 7–8.
36. See Bakhtin, *Rabelais and His World*, 318.
37. Rose, "Crisis of Poor Relief," 52, 54–58.
38. Digby, *Poor Law*, 25; Rose, "Crisis of Poor Relief," 59, 62; Peter Wood, *Poverty and the Workhouse in Victorian Britain* (Wolfeboro Falls, NH: Alan Sutton Publishing Inc., 1991), 126.
39. Felix Driver, "The Historical Geography of the Workhouse System in England and Wales, 1834–1883," *Journal of Historical Geography* 15, no. 3 (1989): 278, 282–84; Driver, *Power and Pauperism*, 69–72; Rose, "Crisis of Poor Relief," 60–62; Wood, *Poverty and the Workhouse*, 46, 142ff, 188.
40. Chance, *Children under the Poor Law*, 6.
41. On the creation of district schools, see Berry, *Child, State, and Victorian Novel*, 30–44; Driver, *Power and Pauperism*, 97; Duke, "Pauper Education," 67–86; Derek Fraser, "The English Poor Law and the Origins of the British Welfare State," in *Emergence of the Welfare State*, ed. Mommsen, 15; Federic J. Mouat, "On the Education and Training of Children of the Poor," *Journal of the Statistical Society* 43 (1880): 206–7; and Edward Carleton Tufnell, *Training of Pauper Children* (London: Eyre and Spottiswoode, 1880), 2. From 1844 to 1930, London had the following poor law school districts: Brentwood School District (1877–85), Central London School District (1849–1930), Finsbury School District (1868–69), Forest Gate School District (1868–97), Kensington and Chelsea School District (1876–1930), North Surrey School District (1849–1930), South Metropolitan School District (1849–1902), and West London School District (1868–1930).
42. Duke, "Pauper Education," 74. Although removal of children from workhouses became the trend in urban unions, the vast majority of rural unions continued to maintain child paupers within workhouses.

43. Jane Nassau Senior noted this association between outdoor relief and casuals. See Senior, *Report on the Education of Girls in Pauper Schools* (January 1, 1874), reprinted in Smedley, *Boarding-Out*, 60.
44. Louisa Twining, *A Letter on Some Matters of Poor Law Administration* (London: William Ridgway, 1887), 41–42. These events recalled early-nineteenth-century uses of relatively unregulated public space. See Daunton, *House and Home*, 13–14, 269–70.
45. Barlee, *Friendless and Helpless* (London: Emily Faithfull, 1863), 227. Also see Twining, *A Letter*, 46.
46. On the grotesque, see Bakhtin, *Rabelais and His World*, esp. 25–27, 303–22.
47. Forest Gate District School, *Annual Reports of Managers, 1894*, 5, FGSD 19, LMA; H. Saxon Snell, *Charitable and Parochial Establishments* (London: B. T. Batsford, 1881), 39; "Summary of Medical Reports by Dr. Bridges and Dr. Mouat, with Special Reference to Opthalmia," in Smedley, *Boarding-Out*, 32–34. For accounts suggesting that diseases were endemic to certain schools, infecting children who had previously been healthy, see Robert Brudenell Carter, "On Contagious Ophthalmia, as Influenced by the Arrangements of Workhouses and Pauper Schools," *Lancet* (December 20, 1873): 871, and "Ophthalmia and Scarlet Fever at Barrack Schools," *British Medical Journal* (May 16, 1896): 1223.
48. Menella Smedley, "Workhouse Schools for Girls," *Macmillan's Magazine* 31 (1874): 31. For fears of physical and moral contamination from casual children, also see "Little Pauper Boarders," *All the Year Round*, n.s., 2 (1869): 301, and M.O.H., quoted in *Fourth Report of the Local Government Board* (1875), quoted in Eric T. Evans, ed., *Social Policy, 1830–1914: Individualism, Collectivism and the Origins of the Welfare State* (London: Routledge and Kegan Paul, 1978), 186.
49. Hall, *Boarding-Out*, 9; Smedley, *Boarding-Out*, 4; Grant, Birmingham, 1870, quoted in "Summary of Medical Reports by Dr. Bridges and Dr. Mouat," in Smedley, *Boarding-Out*, 33.
50. Joanna Hill, "The Pseudo and the Real 'Cottage Homes' for Pauper Children," *Westminster Review* 146 (1896): 661. Also see Hall, *Boarding-Out*, 42.
51. Menella Smedley, "Pauper Homes," *Good Words* 17 (1876): 49. For another account of pauperism being imbibed, see Peek, "Hereditary Pauperism," 135.
52. H. Saxon Snell, letter to the *Times*, quoted in Snell, *Charitable and Parochial Establishments*, 39.
53. For references to casual children as "evil," see Barlee, *Friendless and Helpless*, 227–28; Joanna Hill, "Workhouse Girls: What They Are and How to Help Them," *Macmillan's Magazine* 28 (1873): 132; "Pauper Girls," *Westminster Review* 93 (1870): 488–89; Senior, *Report*, in Smedley, *Boarding-Out*, 63–64; Smedley, *Boarding-Out*, v–vii, xix; Smedley, "Workhouse Schools for Girls," 31; Snell, *Charitable and Parochial Establishments*, 39; Henrietta Synnot, "Little Paupers," *Contemporary Review* 24 (1874): 970. On the orphaned child as the ultimate signifier of innocent virtue, see Martha Vicinus, "'Helpless and Unfriended,'" 130.
54. Smedley, *Boarding-Out*, v.
55. Ibid., vi (emphasis in original).
56. Senior, *Report*, in Smedley, *Boarding-Out*, 63.
57. Snell, *Charitable and Parochial Establishments*, 39. See "Kensington District Schools, Design for Ground Plan of Main Buildings," plate between 40 and 41. The growing concern with the spatial separation of casual children seems to parallel the

attempt to isolate adult casual inmates. Compare, for example, two designs of adult casual wards that were exemplary models from the 1860s and 1870s. In the first, St. Marylebone Temporary Casual Wards (1867), inmates slept and worked side by side in common areas. By the 1870s, however, the "cellular" system of St. Olave's Union casual wards was the model for London. Inmates slept and worked in individual cells. The goal was the "entire separation of the Inmates from each other from the time they enter to the time they leave the building" (27). For the designs, see plates between 34 and 35 (St. Marylebone) and between 28 and 29 (St. Olave's).

58. Report of A. Doyle in *Return from Unions in England and Wales of the Number of Children in Workhouses*, PP (1862) xlix, 583. Also quoted in Peters, *Orphan Texts*, 13.
59. Florence Hill, "The Family System for Workhouse Children," *Contemporary Review* 15 (1870): 273.
60. Jane Senior, quoted in Chance, *Children under the Poor Law*, 319.
61. Report of A. Doyle, PP (1862) xlix, 583.
62. Chance, *Children under the Poor Law*, 82.
63. Driver, *Power and Pauperism*, 96–101.
64. On Twining, see Janet E. Grenier, "Twining, Louisa (1820–1912)," *Oxford Dictionary of National Biography* (Oxford University Press, 2004); Julia Parker, *Women and Welfare: Ten Victorian Women in Public Social Service* (New York: St. Martin's Press, 1989), 53, 157; and F. K. Prochaska, *Women and Philanthropy in Nineteenth-Century England* (Oxford: Clarendon Press, 1980), 175–81.
65. F. Prochaska, "A Mother's Country: Mothers' Meetings and Family Welfare in Britain, 1850–1950," *History* 74 (October 1989): 380–82.
66. Louisa Twining, "Recollections of Workhouse Visiting and Management," reprinted in Twining, *Recollections of Workhouse Visiting and Management during Twenty-Five Years* (London: C. Kegan Paul and Co., 1880), 22–25.
67. Twining, *Recollections*, ix, xi, 10, 31, 33, 152, 171–72, 181–82, quotation at 64–65.
68. Louisa Twining, "Workhouses and Woman's Work," reprinted from *Church of England Monthly Review* (1857) in Twining, *Recollections*, 169.
69. Ibid., 152. She noted that poor law administration was an appropriate activity not only for ladies, but also middle-class women (182).
70. Twining, *Recollections*, 11, 23, 46–48.
71. Jane Senior was the daughter-in-law of economist Nassau Senior, who co-authored the 1834 poor law *Report*, and the sister of novelist Thomas Hughes. "The Late Mrs. Nassau Senior," *Times*, March 29, 1877, 5f.
72. Senior, *Report*, in Smedley, *Boarding-Out*, 52, 53–54.
73. Ibid., 52, 70–76, 63–64, 82–83, 117–19.
74. Dorice Williams Elliott examines the mid-century conflict between male professionals and the female philanthropist Anna Jameson in *The Angel Out of the House: Philanthropy and Gender in Nineteenth-Century England* (Charlottesville: University Press of Virginia, 2002), 111–34.
75. Evidence from Senior's 1874 *Report*, quoted in Edward Carleton Tufnell, *Observations on the Report of Mrs. Senior to the Local Government Board as to the Effect on Girls of the System of Education at Pauper Schools* (London: George E. Eyre and William Spottiswoode, 1875), 1. Also see W.H.T. Hawley, "Reports Related to the Education of Pauper Children," in *Return from Unions in England*

and Wales of the Number of Children in Workhouses, PP (1862) xlix, 536–37; Tufnell, *Observations*, 7, 13; Edwin Chadwick, quoted in Tufnell, *Training of Pauper Children*, 7; Chadwick, manuscript in file, Sickness and death rates in District Schools, Questionnaire for 1883, Papers on sanitation and health in schools, including details of illnesses in District Schools, ca. 1875–88, Papers of Sir Edwin Chadwick, 97, University College London Archives (UCL).

76. Tufnell, *Observations*, 6.
77. See Prochaska, *Women and Philanthropy*, 138–81.
78. Driver, "Discipline Without Frontiers?" 278 and passim. See Foucault, *Discipline and Punish*, 293–96.
79. Driver, "Discipline Without Frontiers?" 286–87; Driver, *Power and Pauperism*, 101.
80. Seth Koven, "Henrietta Barnett, 1851–1936: The (auto)biography of a Late Victorian Marriage," and Standish Meacham, "Raymond Unwin, 1863–1940: Designing for Democracy in Edwardian England," both in *After the Victorians: Private Conscience and Public Duty in Modern Britain*, ed. Susan Pedersen and Peter Mandler (London and New York: Routledge, 1994), 31–53 and 97–100.
81. Henrietta Barnett, *Canon Barnett: His Life, Work, and Friends*, vol. 2 (Boston and New York: Houghton Mifflin Co., 1919), 288–300; Forest Gate District School, *Annual Reports of Managers* (1890), 6–10, and (1894), 5–7, FGSD 19, LMA.
82. *Departmental Committee on Existing Systems for the Maintenance and Education of Children under the Charge of Managers of District Schools and Boards of Guardians in the Metropolis*, PP (1896) xliii, 15. For a detailed criticism of the 1896 Mundella Report, see Chance, *Children under the Poor Law*.
83. See *Barnardo's Annual Reports, 1877–1886* (back covers), D239/A3/10–19, ULLSCA. It is particularly difficult to categorize Barnardo's institutions into barrack and family-based systems. The populations of Barnardo's barrack-style institutions were relatively small compared with the massive poor law schools. Moreover, Barnardo's philanthropic literature describes even his barrack-style institutions with a rhetoric of domesticity that belies their actual spatial organization. For Barnardo's distinction between his barrack schools and cottage homes, which I have used for the discussion above, see PP (1896) xliii, para. 9146–53.
84. PP (1896) xliii, para. 9112–14.
85. *Report on the Home and Cottage System*, PP (1878) lx.
86. PP (1896) xliii, para. 16,180; and *Return on Cottage Homes*, PP (1903) lix.
87. The children in London poor law schools represented 65 percent of all in-care children above two years old chargeable to the metropolitan boards of guardians. See PP (1896) xliii, para. 27.
88. PP (1896) xliii, para. 5–8.
89. List of Metropolitan Poor Law Schools, A Return of the Particulars of Salaries and Emoluments, etc., received by Superintendents and Matrons in Metropolitan Poor Law Schools, directed to be prepared by the Managers, January 8, 1909, Kensington and Chelsea School District, KCSD 171, LMA. The average number of children in the schools during 1909 was 9,562.
90. On the increasing number of female poor law authorities, see M. A. Crowther, *The Workhouse System, 1834–1929* (Athens: University of Georgia Press, 1982), 77–78.
91. "Pauper Girls," *Westminster Review* 93 (1870): 472.

92. See Driver, "Discipline Without Frontiers?" 285–86; F. K. Prochaska, "Female Philanthropy and Domestic Service in Victorian England," *Historical Research* 54 (1981): 79–85; and Prochaska, *Women and Philanthropy*, 148–55.
93. Prochaska, "Female Philanthropy and Domestic Service."
94. Joanna Hill, *Practical Suggestions for the Use of Associates for the Department for G.F.S. Candidates from Workhouses and Orphanages* (London: Hatchards, 1884), 3.
95. "A Lady from Kent," quoted in Barlee, *Friendless and Helpless*, 216.
96. See, for example, Barnardo, "Preventive Homes: A Paper Read before the Social Science Congress at Liverpool, October, 1876," *Night and Day* (January 15, 1877): 4; Frances Power Cobbe, "Workhouse Sketches," *Macmillan's Magazine* 3 (1861): 454; Cobbe, "The Philosophy of the Poor-Laws," *Fraser's Magazine* 66 (1862): 383; Senior, *Report*, in Smedley, *Boarding-Out*, 121, 141; Smedley, *Boarding-Out*, 19; Twining, "Workhouses and Woman's Work," in Twining, *Recollections*, 150–52.
97. As M. Jeanne Peterson's study of Victorian gentlewomen demonstrates, women of the upper middle class did not conceive of themselves as child nurturers until the First World War. Instead, servants were allotted the role of child caretakers, and those servants who did not fit this role were characterized as pathological and unfeminine. See Peterson, *Family, Love, and Work in the Lives of Victorian Gentlewomen* (Bloomington: Indiana University Press, 1989).
98. Florence Hill (1857), quoted in Henrietta Barnett, "The Home or the Barrack for the Children of the State?" *Contemporary Review* 66 (1894): 243.
99. Smedley, "Workhouse Schools for Girls," 28.
100. Synnot, "Little Paupers," 958.
101. Senior, *Report*, in Smedley, *Boarding-Out*, 144.
102. Smedley, *Boarding-Out*, vi.
103. Letter from a worker in a metropolitan female adult ward, quoted in Hill, "Family System for Workhouse Children," 247.
104. Ibid., 248.
105. Senior, *Report*, in Smedley, *Boarding-Out*, 73.
106. Letter from a worker in a metropolitan female adult ward, quoted in Hill, "Family System for Workhouse Children," 247.
107. Ibid., 247.
108. Smedley, *Boarding-Out*, viii, xviii, 15, 44, 49.
109. "Pauper Girls," *Westminster Review* 93 (1870): 472. On the gendered construction of class identity, see Sally Alexander, "Women, Class, and Sexual Differences in the 1830s and 1840s: Some Reflections on the Writing of Feminist History," *History Workshop* 17 (Spring 1984): 125–49, and Joan Wallach Scott, *Gender and the Politics of History* (New York: Columbia University Press, 1988), 53–67.
110. PP (1896) xliii, para. 9250.
111. T. B. Browne, quoted in "Pauper Girls," *Westminster Review* 93 (1870): 472. Also see Browne, quoted in Smedley, *Boarding-Out*, xviii.
112. Crowther, *Workhouse System*, 195–96; Digby, *Pauper Palaces*, 157.
113. Barnett, "Home or the Barrack?" 245.
114. Smedley, *Boarding-Out*, 48.
115. *"Rescue the Perishing,"* xiv.

116. See Hill, "Family System for Workhouse Children," 240–41, and Mouat, "Education and Training of Children of the Poor," 220, 221.
117. PP (1896) xliii, para. 612–14. Proponents of district schools, such as Tufnell and Chadwick, claimed that they were not overcrowded centers of contagious disease. Citing death statistics from the South Metropolitan District School, Chadwick argued that none of the children's deaths "can be attributed to the congregation of numbers." See Edwin Chadwick, manuscript in file, Sickness and death rates in District Schools, Questionnaire for 1883, Papers on sanitation and health in schools, including details of illnesses in District Schools, ca. 1875–88, Papers of Sir Edwin Chadwick, 97, UCL.
118. Smedley, "Pauper Homes," 51; Henrietta Barnett, "The Verdict on the Barrack Schools," *Nineteenth Century* 41 (1897): 57.
119. Hill, *Children of the State*, 27.
120. Smedley, "Pauper Homes," 48; "Pauper Girls," *Westminster Review* 93 (1870): 471; Smedley, "Workhouse Schools for Girls," 30; M. B. Edwards, "English Orphans in Paris," *Good Words* 19 (1878): 598.
121. "Little Paupers," *Cornhill Magazine* 22 (1870): 373.
122. Hill, *Practical Suggestions*, 6; Senior, *Report*, in Smedley, *Boarding-Out*, 73, 84.
123. Driver, "Discipline Without Frontiers?"
124. Forest Gate School District, *Annual Reports of Managers* (1893), 8, FGSD 19, LMA.
125. For criticisms of the artificial nature of cottage homes, which could become "large pauper colonies," see PP (1896) xliii, para. 416–23.
126. Barnardo, "Preventive Homes," *Night and Day* (January 15, 1877): 4 (emphasis in original).
127. See, for example, Bermondsey Board of Guardians (St. Olave's Union), Reference to and Enquiry by General Relieving Officer (February 10, 1896–April 3, 1897), BBG.539/1, LMA: cases no. 17, Edith Simmonds (April 22, 1896); no. 23, Denis McCarthy (May 14, 1896); nos. 25 and 32, William Currier (May 21, 1896, June 30, 1896); no. 50, William Codling (September 9, 1896); no. 66, George and Maud Pugh (January 14, 1897); and no. 68, James Driscoll (January 27, 1897).
128. Barnardo, *"Something Attempted, Something Done"* (1889), 86; "The Village Home, Ilford," *Night and Day* (September 1, 1877): 117. Each girl did have her own bed, which would have been unusual.
129. "Wanted: A Village School," *Night and Day* (April 1891): 61.
130. *The First Annual Report of the Managers of the Kensington and Chelsea School District in Respect of the School at Banstead, Together with an Account of their Proceedings from the Formation of the District in 1876* (London: J. W. Wakeham, 1881), 21, KCSD 201, LMA. For a similar description of cottage "fathers," see Barnett, "Home or Barrack?" 256.
131. Barnardo, "Our Village Home at Ilford," *Night and Day* (March 15, 1877): 28 (emphasis in original). Also see the advertisement for "mothers" at the Girls' Village Home, "To Ladies Seeking Work for Christ," *Night and Day* (June 2, 1879): 68.
132. Barnardo, "Our Village Home at Ilford," *Night and Day* (March 15, 1877): 28.
133. Adams, *Architecture in the Family Way*, 139; Clifford Clark, "Domestic Architecture," 50.

134. Barnardo, *"Something Attempted, Something Done"* (1889), 86.
135. Cheyne Brady, "A Visit to the Village Homes for Girls at Ilford," *Night and Day* (August 1, 1877): 91.
136. Barnardo, "Our Village Home at Ilford," *Night and Day* (March 15, 1877): 28. By 1889, the layout was slightly changed: "*Each cottage now contains* on the ground-floor a Mother's Sitting-room, a Sitting-room and Play-room for the girls, a large Dining-room for the family meals, and a Kitchen, Scullery, Pantry, and Store-room. Upstairs there are either five or six Bedrooms, four of which in the older cottages, and five in the new, contain each from four to six single beds, the remaining one being the 'Mother's' room. There is further, of course, a Bath-room and necessary offices in each building." Barnardo, *"Something Attempted, Something Done"* (1889), 86 (emphasis in original).
137. "A 'Village Home,'" *Chambers's Journal* 14 (July 14, 1877), reprinted in *Night and Day* (August 1, 1877): 101–2; Barnardo, "Preventive Homes," *Night and Day* (January 15, 1877): 4.
138. "A 'Village Home,'" *Night and Day* (August 1, 1877): 102 (emphasis in original).
139. [A Late "Holiday Mother"], *My Cottage*, 4.
140. See chapter 5.
141. Florence Hill, "Family System for Workhouse Children," 240–41.
142. "Little Paupers," *Cornhill Magazine* 22 (1870): 377, 379.
143. "A 'Village Home,'" *Night and Day* (August 1, 1877): 103.
144. Ibid., 102.
145. Evidence of Mary Carpenter (June 24, 1861), *Report from the Select Committee on the Education of Destitute Children; Together with the Proceedings of the Committee, Minutes of Evidence, and Appendix*, PP (1861) vii, 507, para. 2162 (emphasis added). Also see 540, para. 2500, for a similar criticism of the accepted definition of ragged schools. George Higginbotham, the master of Carpenter's school, disagreed with her over the sanctity of the homes of the poor. When asked whether "there would be anything wrong in severing the tie between parents and children" by removing the children, he responded, "Generally speaking, there would be no wrong in it." See ibid., 506, para. 2220–21.
146. PP (1861) vii, 403.
147. Earl of Cairns, "Our Annual Meeting in Exeter Hall," *Night and Day* (October 1883): 56.
148. See Elliott, *Angel Out of the House*; Seth Koven and Sonya Michel, eds., *Mothers of a New World: Maternalist Politics and the Origins of the Welfare State* (New York: Routledge, 1993); and Prochaska, *Women and Philanthropy*.
149. On the Second Reform Act, see Catherine Hall, Keith McClelland, and Jane Rendall, *Defining the Victorian Nation: Class, Race, Gender and the Reform Act of 1867* (Cambridge: Cambridge University Press, 2000).

CHAPTER 3 *The Parents of "Nobody's Children"*

1. W. T. Stead, "Dr. Barnardo: The Father of 'Nobody's Children,'" *Review of Reviews* (New York) 14 (July–December 1896): 188. Barnardo was very fond of Stead's biographical sketch, and he encouraged readers of *Night and Day* to buy it. See *Night and Day* (August 1896): 63.
2. Gillian Wagner traces Barnardo's earliest account of Jim Jarvis to his article "How It All Happened," published in *The Christian* (1872). See Wagner, *Barnardo*, 30–34.

3. See Blake Morrison, "Lost and Found: The Forgotten Legacy of Dr. Barnardo," *The Independent on Sunday*, June 11, 1995, 6–11, and a three-part BBC series (1995) on Barnardo's, covering the society's policies from the early years to the late twentieth century.

4. See Syrie Barnardo and James Merchant, *The Memoirs of the Late Dr. Barnardo* (London: Hodder and Stroughton, 1907); John Herridge Batt, *Dr. Barnardo: The Foster-Father of "Nobody's Children"* (London: S. W. Partridge and Co., 1904); J. Wesley Bready, *Doctor Barnardo: Physician, Pioneer, Prophet* (London: G. Allen and Unwin, 1930); David E. Fessenden, *Father to Nobody's Children* (Fort Washington, PA: Christian Literature Crusade, 1995); A. E. Williams, *Barnardo of Stepney: The Father of Nobody's Children*, 2nd ed. (1953; London: George Allen and Unwin, Ltd., 1966); Norman Wymer, *Father of Nobody's Children: A Portrait of Dr. Barnardo* (London: Hutchinson, 1954).

5. Foreword by Christopher Fry to the second edition (1953) of Williams, *Barnardo of Stepney*, vii.

6. Wagner, *Children of the Empire*, 137. Also see Wagner, *Barnardo*.

7. Rose, *For the Sake of the Children*, 186–87, 262–64, quotation at 287.

8. Wagner, *Barnardo*, 214–36; Wagner, *Children of the Empire*, 143–47.

9. For example, in her introduction to Valerie Lloyd's *The Camera and Dr. Barnardo*, Wagner repeated Barnardo's account of finding Jim Jarvis as a typical example of his work (4), although she later recognized the story to be part of Barnardo's "folklore" (*Barnardo*, 30).

10. Norman Longmate, *The Workhouse: A Social History* (New York: St. Martin's Press, 1974), 179.

11. Crompton, *Workhouse Children*.

12. Goffman defines a "total institution" as "a place of residence and work where a large number of like situated individuals, cut off from the wider society for an appreciable period of time, together lead an enclosed, formally administered round of life" (quoted in Crompton, *Workhouse Children*, 107).

13. Crompton, *Workhouse Children*, 150, 213.

14. Parr, *Labouring Children*; Philip Bean and Joy Melville, *Lost Children of the Empire* (London, Sydney, and Wellington: Unwin Hyman, 1989); Harrison, ed., *Home Children*; Sherington and Jeffery, *Fairbridge*.

15. Parr, *Labouring Children*, 11. See Bean and Melville, *Lost Children of the Empire*, 4, 39.

16. Parr, *Labouring Children*, 64.

17. For an analysis of parents' roles in nineteenth-century child welfare, also see Abrams, *Orphan Country*; Rachel Fuchs, *Poor and Pregnant in Paris: Strategies for Survival in the Nineteenth Century* (New Brunswick: Rutgers University Press, 1992); Ann Rowell Higginbotham, "The Unmarried Mother and Her Child in Victorian London, 1834–1914" (Ph.D. diss., Indiana University, 1985); Ross, *Love and Toil*; and Ward, "Charitable Relationship."

18. Valentina K. Tikoff, "Assisted Transitions: Children and Adolescents in the Orphanages of Seville at the End of the Old Regime, 1681–1831" (Ph.D. diss., Indiana University, 2000).

19. Judith A. Dulberger, *"Mother Donit fore the Best": Correspondence of a Nineteenth-Century Orphan Asylum* (Syracuse: Syracuse University Press, 1996), 10–11, 15.

20. Timothy A. Hacsi, *Second Home: Orphan Asylums and Poor Families in America* (Cambridge, MA: Harvard University Press, 1997). Also see Nurith Zmora, *Orphanages Reconsidered: Child Care Institutions in Progressive Era Baltimore* (Philadelphia: Temple University Press, 1994).
21. Lees, "The Survival of the Unfit: Welfare Policies and Family Maintenance in Nineteenth Century London," in *Uses of Charity*, ed. Mandler, 86–87, and Lees, *Solidarities of Strangers*, 281–87.
22. See in particular Behlmer, *Friends of the Family*; Marguerite Dupree, *Family Structure in the Staffordshire Potteries, 1840–1880* (New York: Oxford University Press, 1995), 325 and passim; Colin Jones, "Recent Trends in the History of Charity," 53–55; Hitchcock, Kind, and Sharpe, eds., *Chronicling Poverty*; Lees, *Solidarities of Strangers*; Mandler, ed., *Uses of Charity*.
23. See Lees, "Survival of the Unfit," 68–91.
24. Children's Admission Registers, 1875–1966, Children's Records, In-care children's records, Barnardo Archive, D239/D/2/2a/2–28, ULLSCA. I sampled entries from 1877 and 1884. Entry spaces are often left blank or used to record other information.
25. Précis Books, 1886–1937, 58 vols., In-care children's records, Barnardo Archive, D239/D/2/2a/104–58, ULLSCA. I sampled more than five hundred entries from 1886, 1887, 1891, and 1895. There are references to several overlapping children's registers for Barnardo's: admission registers, précis books, case histories, and diary entries. If they still exist, the case histories and diary entries are not kept with the Barnardo Archive at the University of Liverpool.
26. On narrative and the interpretation of medical and other case histories, see Rita Charon, "To Build a Case: Medical Histories as Traditions in Conflict," *Literature and Medicine* 11, no. 1 (Spring 1992): 115–32; Ellen Dwyer, *Homes for the Mad: Life Inside Two Nineteenth-Century Asylums* (New Brunswick: Rutgers University Press, 1987); and Steven M. Stowe, "Seeing Themselves at Work: Physicians and the Case Narrative in the Mid-Nineteenth-Century American South," *American Historical Review* 101, no. 1 (February 1996): 41–79.
27. T.K. (admitted January 5, 1877), J.G. (admitted January 19, 1877), and R.M. (admitted January 5, 1877), Barnardo Children's Admission Registers, D239/D/2/2a, ULLSCA.
28. For comparable reports by poor law relieving officers, who investigated custody claims for children among other things, see, for example, Bermondsey Board of Guardians (St. Olave's Union), Reference to and Enquiry by General Relieving Officer (February 10, 1896–April 3, 1897), BBG.539/1, LMA.
29. J.H. (male, age 17), admitted January 8, 1887, Barnardo Précis Books, vol. 1, D239/D/2/2a/104, ULLSCA.
30. Barnardo's Annual Reports, 1898–1925, Barnardo Archive, D239/A3/1/33–60, ULLSCA. For the years 1902 and 1903, see *National Waifs' Magazine and Night and Day* (August–September 1903): 68, and (August 1904): 55. It is logical to assume that the proportion of short-term inmates who were orphans would be significantly smaller, but I do not have the records to confirm this supposition.
31. These case history samples are for all of the children admitted in March 1886 (the first available month with complete entries, including detailed director's remarks), January 1887, January 1891, and January 1895. See Barnardo Précis Books, vols. 1, 5, and 10, D239/D/2/2a/104, 108, 113, ULLSCA.

32. Until the early 1900s, most of the admissions to Barnardo's tended to be older youths. I discuss the age ratio of child admissions in chapter 5 in the context of industrial training.
33. B.S. (male, age 10) and S.S. (female, no age listed), admitted January 12, 1891, Barnardo Précis Books, vol. 5, D239/D/2/2a/108, ULLSCA.
34. A.H. (female, age 7), admitted January 3, 1887, Barnardo Précis Books, vol. 1, D239/D/2/2a/104, ULLSCA.
35. These percentages exclude cases for which information on the mother or father was not reported.
36. *Return of the Number of Orphan and Deserted Pauper Children Boarded Out, Jan. 1877, in Unions in England and Wales with the Number of Pauper Children in District Schools*, PP (1878) lxiv, 21. The percentage of orphaned and deserted children for all nine district schools in England and Wales was slightly higher at 37 percent.
37. Similar cutbacks on outrelief in the United States during the 1870s went hand in hand with the expansion of orphanages. Many families resorted to separation when they lost outrelief. See Dulberger, *"Mother Donit fore the Best,"* 8–9.
38. The total school population was 740; PP (1896) xliii, 304, para. 8493. Guardians were more likely to emigrate orphaned and deserted children. From 1887 to 1894, 207 children in the Kensington and Chelsea School District emigrated to Canada.
39. Admission and Discharge Registers (March 1896–March 1897), Banstead, Kensington and Chelsea School District, KCSD 307, LMA.
40. "Infirmary Visiting Committee, Report" (September 23, 1884), 461–63, Stepney Board of Guardians, Whitechapel Union, St.B.G/Wh/106/1, LMA.
41. "Boards of Guardians," *Times*, October 4, 1889, 7; Florence Davenport Hill, "Letter to the Editor," *Times*, October 7, 1889, 13a.
42. PP (1896) xliii, 304.
43. The recorders of this information may not always have thought it necessary to take down information about the mother.
44. For a discussion of circumstances leading to the admission of children to the Waifs and Strays Society based on case history samples from 1887 to 1894, see Ward, "Charitable Relationship," 191–227.
45. On the history of the NSPCC, see Behlmer, *Child Abuse*, and Behlmer, *Friends of the Family*, 104–16.
46. F.D. (female, age 10), admitted January 3, 1895, Barnardo Précis Books, vol. 10, D239/D/2/2a/113, ULLSCA.
47. F.F. (female, age 9), admitted January 3, 1895, Barnardo Précis Books, vol. 10, D239/D/2/2a/113, ULLSCA.
48. F.F. (female, age 9), admitted January 3, 1895; F.D. (female, age 10), admitted January 3, 1895; B.H. (female, age 11), admitted January 14, 1895; F.T. (male, age 14), admitted January 15, 1895; H.W. (male, age 14), admitted January 18, 1895; R.L. (male, age 11), admitted January 22, 1895, Barnardo Précis Books, vol. 10, D239/D/2/2a/113, ULLSCA.
49. This was a repeated phrase of NSPCC workers, quoted in Behlmer, *Friends of the Family*, 106.
50. Behlmer, *Friends of the Family*, 109. See *The Cruelty Man*, 143–44.
51. "Personal Notes," *Night and Day* (March 1890): 57–60; "The Rev. Benjamin Waugh and the Editor," *Night and Day* (June 1890): 113–17; Wagner, *Barnardo*,

216–17. Barnardo's most hard-fought custody battles with parents involved cases in which he was attempting to prevent the children from being raised as Roman Catholics. See chapter 4 and Wagner, *Barnardo*, 214–36.

52. E.N. (male, age 16), admitted January 2, 1895, and H.S. (male, age 15), admitted January 21, 1895, Barnardo Précis Books, vol. 10, D239/D/2/2a/113, ULLSCA. In a third case of possible abuse, the Barnardo officer dismissed a charge that the father "criminally assaulted" his daughter. The officer thought "the accusation was merely *an excuse to get rid of*" the daughter. See M.M. (female, age 13), admitted January 11, 1895 (emphasis in original).

53. F.T. (male, age 14), admitted January 15, 1895, Barnardo Précis Books, vol. 10, D239/D/2/2a/113, ULLSCA.

54. E.B. (male, age 11), admitted January 9, 1895, Barnardo Précis Books, vol. 10, D239/D/2/2a/113, ULLSCA.

55. Behlmer, *Child Abuse*, 172, 190; Behlmer, *Friends of the Family*, 112.

56. Anthony Wohl, *The Eternal Slum: Housing and Social Policy in Victorian London* (London: E. Arnold, 1977), has analyzed the Victorian housing crisis in vivid detail.

57. Papers on the way of life and working conditions of boys and girls working as street-sellers, Papers of Sir Edwin Chadwick, 99, UCL. Thanks to Anna Davin for this reference.

58. Division E Report (November 10, 1883), Papers of Sir Edwin Chadwick, 99, UCL. Police explained the small number of orphaned and deserted street children by noting that they were generally quickly cared for by "School Board Officers, Relieving Officers, the Clergy, Police and many benevolent persons." See Division L Report (November 9, 1883). Also see Davin, *Growing Up Poor*, 162.

59. Division N Report (November 10, 1883), Papers of Sir Edwin Chadwick, 99, UCL.

60. See the reports of Divisions C, E, G, H, K [Poplar], M, P, and Y (all November 10, 1883), and Division S (November 11, 1883), Papers of Sir Edwin Chadwick, 99, UCL. For an exception, see Division K [Bow] Report (November 10, 1883), which notes that child street vendors did live in lodging houses and were occasionally found in "Outhouses, Cellers, &c but they are generally boys who have run away from home or who have committed some offence, and when found are taken care of by Police." Likewise, the Wandsworth (Division V) police reported that "some [children] occasionally sleep in Outhouses when they have committed themselves & fear to go home, but none are known to do so from actual necessity."

61. Division K [Poplar] Report (November 10, 1883), Papers of Sir Edwin Chadwick, 99, UCL.

62. Reports of Divisions W and Y (both November 10, 1883), Papers of Sir Edwin Chadwick, 99, UCL.

63. Division B Report (November 10, 1883). Also see the reports of Division L (November 9, 1883) and Divisions C, M, N, W, and Y (all November 10, 1883), Papers of Sir Edwin Chadwick, 99, UCL.

64. Division P Report (November 10, 1883), Papers of Sir Edwin Chadwick, 99, UCL.

65. Division C Report (November 10, 1883), Papers of Sir Edwin Chadwick, 99, UCL.

66. Division E Report (November 10, 1883), Papers of Sir Edwin Chadwick, 99, UCL.

67. Division L Report (November 9, 1883), Papers of Sir Edwin Chadwick, 99, UCL. For a similarly detailed description of the furnishings and crowding of a one-room family dwelling, see Arthur Harding, *East End Underworld: Chapters in the Life*

of Arthur Harding, ed. Raphael Samuel (London, Boston, and Henley: Routledge and Kegan Paul, 1981), 22.

68. Case of Florence and Herbert Heard (August 22, 1898), Bethnal Green Board of Guardians, history sheets of children, 1896–1900, Be.BG.301/1, LMA.

69. Application of Emma Pimm (July 15, 1884), 131, Bethnal Green Board of Guardians, Settlement Records and Records Relating to Relief Examinations (rough), February 19, 1884–February 10, 1885, Be.BG.267/35, LMA. Also see Alice Winder's application (May 27, 1884), 89.

70. Information about rent payments and wages is more systematically found in the 1891 and 1895 samples than in the earlier samples.

71. Section 37 of the 1868 Poor Law Amendment Act stated that it was guardians' responsibility to prosecute parents suspected of willful neglect, a responsibility that many local guardians ignored. On this and the 1889 Children's Charter, see Behlmer, *Child Abuse*, 78–110.

72. Case no. 68 (January 27, 1897), James Driscoll, Bermondsey Board of Guardians (St. Olave's Union), Reference to and Enquiry by General Relieving Officer, February 10, 1896–April 3, 1897, BBG.539/1, LMA. For similar recommendations against custody requests based unsanitary or overcrowded housing, see cases 17, 23, 25, and 50.

73. Case no. 66 (January 14, 1897), George and Maud Pugh, Bermondsey Board of Guardians (St. Olave's Union), Reference to and Enquiry by General Relieving Officer, February 10, 1896–April 3, 1897, BBG.539/1, LMA.

74. F.J. (male, age 17), admitted January 12, 1891; T.D. (male, age 9) and G.D. (male, age 7), admitted January 12, 1891, Barnardo Précis Books, vol. 5, D239/D/2/2a/108, ULLSCA.

75. E.W. (male, age 14), admitted January 12, 1891, Barnardo Précis Books, vol. 5, D239/D/2/2a/108, ULLSCA.

76. C.H. (male, age 3), admitted January 7, 1895, Barnardo Précis Books, vol. 10, D239/D/2/2a/113, ULLSCA.

77. T.T. (male, age 17), admitted January 8, 1887, Barnardo Précis Books, vol. 1, D239/D/2/2a/104, ULLSCA.

78. J.B. (male, age 17), admitted January 8, 1887, Barnardo Précis Books, vol. 1, D239/D/2/2a/104, ULLSCA.

79. J.B. (male, age 17), admitted January 10, 1895, Barnardo Précis Books, vol. 10, D239/D/2/2a/113, ULLSCA.

80. A.T. (male, age 10), admitted January 26, 1887, Barnardo Précis Books, vol. 1, D239/D/2/2a/104, ULLSCA.

81. H.L. (age 1), admitted January 14, 1887, Barnardo Précis Books, vol. 1, D239/D/2/2a/104, ULLSCA.

82. M.H. (male, age 17), admitted January 8, 1887, Barnardo Précis Books, vol. 1, D239/D/2/2a/104, ULLSCA.

83. C.S. (male, age 5), admitted January 12, 1887, Barnardo Précis Books, vol. 1, D239/D/2/2a/104, ULLSCA.

84. R.J. (female, age 8), admitted January 27, 1887, Barnardo Précis Books, vol. 1, D239/D/2/2a/104, ULLSCA.

85. G.S (male, age 16) and E.S. (male, age 13), admitted January 20, 1887, Barnardo Précis Books, vol. 1, D239/D/2/2a/104, ULLSCA.

86. See Keir Waddington, *Charity and the London Hospitals, 1850–1898* (Woodbridge, Suffolk: Boydell Press, 2000).
87. A.B. (male, age 5), admitted March 5, 1886, Barnardo Précis Books, vol. 1, D239/D/2/2a/104, ULLSCA.
88. P.R. (male, age 12), admitted March 19, 1886, Barnardo Précis Books, vol. 1, D239/D/2/2a/104, ULLSCA.
89. F.B. (male, age 11), admitted March 26, 1886, Barnardo Précis Books, vol. 1, D239/D/2/2a/104, ULLSCA. Also see, for example, H.M. (male, age 2), admitted March 25, 1886; E.W. (female, age 9), admitted January 8, 1895; H.A. (male, age 9) and F.A. (male, age 4), admitted January 12, 1891, Barnardo Précis Books, vols. 1, 10, 5, D239/D/2/2a/104, 113, 108, ULLSCA.
90. E.W. (female, age 9), admitted January 8, 1895, Barnardo Précis Books, vol. 10, D239/D/2/2a/113, ULLSCA.
91. W.N. (male, age 15), admitted January 8, 1887; T.W. (male, age 17), admitted January 8, 1887; W.L. (male, age 16), admitted January 3, 1895, Barnardo Précis Books, vols. 1 and 10, D239/D/2/2a/104 and 113, ULLSCA. Brief examination of the National Children's Home records indicates similar occupational backgrounds of parents. Of the fourteen admissions listed for 1870, eight of their mothers were listed as having the following occupations: paper flower maker, needlework (two), watercress seller, washerwoman, hawker, charwoman, cinder shifter (six entries were blank). The fathers' occupations were listed as: clerk, soldier, shop blind maker, carpenter, cabman, laborer, engineer (seven entries were blank). National Children's Home Archive, Analytical Registers (1870), D541/H6/1, ULLSCA. On casual labor conditions, see Gareth Stedman Jones, *Outcast London.*
92. See Parr, *Labouring Children,* 17.
93. Lees, "Survival of the Unfit," 87.
94. See entries for Eliza or Elizabeth Bond and Ethel Bond in Whitechapel samples, Stepney Board of Guardians, Whitechapel, Children from Whitechapel at Forest Gate, Roman Catholic Schools, T. S. Exmouth, etc., vol. 1 (1871–1891) and vol. 2 (1892–1899), St.B.G.Wh/138/1–2, LMA. Eliza/Elizabeth Bond's admission and discharge dates: October 22, 1885–November 4, 1885; November 19, 1885–April 5, 1886; April 22, 1886–June 20, 1886; July 29, 1886–January 15, 1887; January 27, 1887–May 19, 1887; June 2, 1887–September 14, 1893. Ethel Bond's admission and discharge dates: December 4, 1884–August 24, 1885; February 25, 1886–April 5, 1886; July 15, 1886–January 15, 1887; May 29, 1889–October 2, 1889 (to infirmary); September 4, 1890–May 10, 1893.
95. There are similar examples in Barnardo's case histories. See the case of R.S. (male, age 12), admitted January 12, 1891, Barnardo Précis Books, vol. 5, D239/D/2/2a/108, ULLSCA: "Received from Mr. Walter Austin's Home, Burdett Road, E.'s Father, A.S., died five years ago. Mother was left with six children, and fell into great distress. Three of her children were, in consequence, admitted in a School in Norfolk, and R. was admitted, soon after his Father's death, to Mr. W. Austin's Home where he has remained four years. Mother is now in more comfortable circumstances. She earns 12/— weekly by washing and charing, and rents 2 rooms, 3/6 weekly. She has one child only at home, A. [female], 10 years of age, and states she is quite able to keep R., who was therefore restored to her on the 26th January 1891."
96. L.E. (female, age 11), admitted March 22, 1886, Barnardo Précis Books, vol. 1, D239/D/2/2a/104, ULLSCA.

97. J.R. (female, age 11), admitted March 16, 1886, Barnardo Précis Books, vol. 1, D239/D/2/2a/104, ULLSCA.
98. E.B. (female, age 9), admitted March 31, 1886, Barnardo Précis Books, vol. 1, D239/D/2/2a/104, ULLSCA.
99. See Behlmer, *Friends of the Family*, 235–37, 372n28, and Lees, *Solidarities of Strangers*, 284.
100. C.S. (male, age 15), admitted January 3, 1895, Barnardo Précis Books, vol. 10, D239/D/2/2a/113, ULLSCA.
101. A.L. (female, age 12) and F.L. (female, age 11), admitted January 12, 1891, Barnardo Précis Books, vol. 5, D239/D/2/2a/108, ULLSCA.
102. A.H. (male, age 17), admitted January 16, 1895, Barnardo Précis Books, vol. 10, D239/D/2/2a/113, ULLSCA.
103. G.W. (male, age 14), admitted January 22, 1895, Barnardo Précis Books, vol. 10, D239/D/2/2a/113, ULLSCA.
104. J.D. (male, age 12), admitted January 12, 1891, Barnardo Précis Books, vol. 5, D239/D/2/2a/108, ULLSCA.
105. B.P. (female, age 10), admitted January 18, 1887, Barnardo Précis Books, vol. 1, D239/D/2/2a/104, ULLSCA. Also see C.F. (male, age 16), admitted January 8, 1887; W.S. (male, age 13), admitted January 12, 1891; C.M. (male, age 16), admitted January 2, 1895, Barnardo Précis Books, vols. 1, 5, and 10, D239/D/2/2a/104, 108, and 113, ULLSCA.
106. W.S. (male, age 13), admitted January 12, 1891; G.M. (male, age 14), admitted January 12, 1891; H.B. (male, age 12), admitted January 12, 1891, Barnardo Précis Books, vol. 5, D239/D/2/2a/108, ULLSCA.
107. M.F. (male, age 17), admitted January 8, 1887, Barnardo Précis Books, vol. 1, D239/D/2/104, ULLSCA.
108. E.P. (male, age 18), admitted January 8, 1887, Barnardo Précis Books, vol. 1, D239/D/2/2a/104, ULLSCA.
109. D.S. (male, age 14), admitted January 8, 1887. Also see C.F. (male, age 16), admitted January 8, 1887, Barnardo Précis Books, vol. 1, D239/D/2/2a/104, ULLSCA.
110. D.D. (male, age 17), admitted January 8, 1887, Barnardo Précis Books, vol. 1, D239/D/2/2a/104, ULLSCA.
111. G.H. (male, age 5), admitted January 24, 1895, Barnardo Précis Books, vol. 10, D239/D/2/2a/113, ULLSCA.
112. The institutional records do not support Barnardo's claim, naively repeated by biographer Gillian Wagner, that 85 percent of the children admitted to his institutions "owed their social ruin to the influence, direct or indirect, of the drinking habits of their parents, grandparents or other relatives." Wagner, *Barnardo*, 55.
113. W.W. (male, age 19), admitted January 8, 1887, Barnardo Précis Books, vol. 1, D239/D/2/2a/104, ULLSCA.
114. C.M. (male, age 8) and F.M. (male, age 5), admitted January 4, 1895; J.M. (male, age 18), admitted January 29, 1895, Barnardo Précis Books, vol. 10, D239/D/2/2a/113, ULLSCA.
115. T.T. (male, age 5), admitted January 4, 1895; E.W. (female, age 9), admitted January 8, 1895; M.N. (female, age 11), admitted January 9, 1895; A.A. (male, age 10), admitted January 10, 1895; H.J. (male, age 3 months), admitted January 10, 1895; G.T. (male, age 7), admitted January 14, 1895; W.S. (male, age 18), admitted January 15, 1895; H.S. (male, age 5), admitted January 18, 1895, Barnardo Précis

Books, vol. 10, D239/D/2/2a/113, ULLSCA. Also see the following Auxiliary Boarding Out Cases: W.P. (male, age 2), E.B. (female, age 3 months), M.T. (female, age 5 months), J.W. (male, age 11 months), A.S. (male, age 1), S.J. (male, age 10 months), G.S. (female, age 2), and D.C. (female, age 1), all January 24, 1895; and H.C. (male, age 5), January 25, 1895. Barnardo Précis Books, vol. 10, D239/D/2/2a/113, ULLSCA.

The flexibility and gendered nature of respectability is notable in a case where a man prosecuted for domestic violence was deemed respectable despite—or likely because of—his actions against his wayward wife: "Father, a labourer (honest, sober, respectable) lives at Wortley. Mother neglected her home and 'went out drinking & carrying on with men.' In June, 1891, she so aggravated the father that he struck her with a hatchet." See E.E. (female, age 10), admitted January 26, 1895, Barnardo Précis Books, vol. 10, D239/D/2/2a/113, ULLSCA.

116. "Orphan, Destitute, or Neglected Girls," *Night and Day* (May 16, 1877): 64. The agreements likely became more uniform in later years. Wagner provides a copy of a general agreement form: "The nearest Friend shall place the said child in the said *Protestant Homes* to be taken care of, maintained and educated therein, or in one of the Branch Establishments named at the head of the paper, or boarded-out in the country for a term of years from the date hereof, or for a less time if the managers for the time being of the said Homes think fit, during that time to be brought up in the *Protestant faith*" (emphasis in original). See Wagner, *Barnardo*, 217.

CHAPTER 4 *"That Most Delicate of All Questions in an Englishman's Mind"*

1. For accounts of the fire, see Forest Gate School District, *Annual Report of Managers* (1890), 6–10, FGSD 19, LMA; Barnett, *Canon Barnett*, 2:291; *Departmental Committee on Existing Systems for the Maintenance and Education of Children under the Charge of Managers of District Schools and Boards of Guardians in the Metropolis*, PP (1896) xliii, quotation at Appendix A, 176. Barnett incorrectly cited the number of pupils killed as twenty-two.
2. "Terrible Calamity at an Industrial School," *Police Chronicle*, January 4, 1890, 7; PP (1896) xliii, Appendix A, 176.
3. PP (1896) xliii, Appendix A, 176.
4. The burning of an early training ship was another of the most deadly accidents to occur at a poor law institution. On December 22, 1875, the *Goliath* was completely destroyed by fire, resulting in the deaths of sixteen or seventeen boys. The *Goliath* had previously suffered damages after colliding with a French schooner and a barge. See Forest Gate School District, Signed Minutes of Ship (Training Ship *Goliath*), (December 26, 1874, February 20 and December 22, 1875, and January 8, 1876), FGSD 17, LMA; R. J. Fenn, *The Burning of the "Goliath"* (London: Shaw and Sons, 1876). The mass outbreak of ptomaine poisoning at Forest Gate in 1893, the result of feeding the children maggot-infested meat, caused the deaths of two children and the illness of hundreds of others. See PP (1896) xliii, Appendix A, 177–78. The death of Elizabeth Clarke, a child at Hackney Union's Brentwood schools (discussed below), sparked the other major late-Victorian investigation involving the abuse of poor law children. Clarke's death revealed horrific cases of abuse by Ella Gillespie, the school nurse. See Longmate, *Workhouse*, 179, and PP (1896) xliii, Appendix A, 178.

5. As of January 1, 1889, the school housed 636 inmates. See "Terrible Fire at Forest-Gate Schools," *East End News*, January 3, 1890, 3.

6. The 1896 Mundella report, which largely condemned barrack schools, discusses the fire in this context. See PP (1896) xliii, 31, para. 116 and Appendix A, 176. There was some criticism of the report's condemnation of the fire as a consequence of the barrack system. See, for example, Chance, *Children under the Poor Law*, 398.

7. "Terrible Fire at Forest-Gate Schools," *East End News*, January 3, 1890, 3. For listings of the deceased children, also see "Terrible Calamity at an Industrial School," *Police Chronicle*, January 4, 1890, 7.

8. "Terrible Calamity at an Industrial School," *Police Chronicle*, January 4, 1890, 7.

9. Forest Gate School District, *Annual Report of Managers* (1890), 8, 9, FGSD 19, LMA.

10. "The Forest Gate Fire," *East End News*, January 10, 1890, 3.

11. "The Forest Gate Fire: Letter to the Editor," *East End News*, January 17, 1890, 2. Also see "The Forest Gate Fire," *East End News*, January 10, 1890, 3.

12. Forest Gate School District, *Annual Report of Managers* (1890), 9–10, FGSD 19, LMA. The children were buried in five communal graves at West Ham Cemetery. The memorial consisted of "five stone slabs upon the five graves, with the names and ages of the children interred in each; the whole space being inclosed by a stone-coping and dwarf railing and the centre containing a monument, in obelisk form, of red polished granite" with the inscription on the base (9).

13. Legislation in 1844 (7 & 8 Vict. c. 101) and 1848 (11 & 12 Vict. c. 82) empowered unions to build district schools combining the children from multiple unions, yet most boards of guardians continued to use schools connected with the workhouse or single-union schools known as separate schools. Still, district schools were used in many urban areas, and they were popularly upheld as the preferred institutions for pauper children until large schools came under increasing attack in the 1870s.

14. *Short History of the North Surrey District School* (n.p., ca. 1908), 7, 3, LMA.

15. See, for example, Behlmer, *Friends of the Family*; Dupree, *Family Structure in the Staffordshire Potteries*; Lees, *Solidarities of Strangers*; Mandler, ed., *Uses of Charity*. For a more typical approach to child welfare that largely ignores parents' roles, see Crompton, *Workhouse Children*.

16. Erving Goffman, quoted in Crompton, *Workhouse Children*, 107.

17. Grant, Birmingham, 1870, quoted in "Summary of Medical Reports by Dr. Bridges and Dr. Mouat, with Special Reference to Opthalmia," in Smedley, *Boarding-Out*, 33. See chapter 2 for a discussion of the rhetoric reformers used to discuss the ins and outs.

18. PP (1896) xliii, 67–68, para. 274, 276, 278. Most schools kept children from the workhouse in probationary quarantine quarters for a period of up to three weeks.

19. Ibid., 68, para. 278. Also see 71–72, para. 290, and 397–98, para. 10,378–440.

20. Ibid., 72, para. 291.

21. As the expectation that children should be removed from workhouses grew with the rise of separate and district schools beginning in the 1840s, many workhouses ceased to provide quarters for children that were separate from adult paupers. See PP (1896) xliii, 69–70, para. 282–86.

22. PP (1896) xliii, 73–74, para. 300–303; Kensington and Chelsea School District, Printed Reports, Copy of Instructional Letter Addressed by the Managers to the

Guardians of the Parishes in the District, with Regard to the Admission of Children to the Branch School at Hammersmith, to be Opened on the 5th March, 1883, Jno. H. Rutherglen, Clerk [to Guardians of St. Mary Abbotts, Kensington and St. Luke's, Chelsea] (printed March 2, 1883, written February 27, 1883), KCSD 157, LMA.

23. The yearly average of more permanent children sent to Banstead from Marlesford Lodge decreased from 215 for the three years ending Michaelmas 1895 to 180 during the three years ending Michaelmas 1898. Henry Aslett, "Report of the Superintendent of the Branch School for the Three Years Ended Michaelmas, 1898," in *The Sixth Report of the Managers of the Kensington and Chelsea School District in Respect of Their Schools at Banstead and Hammersmith, for the Four Years Ended Michaelmas, 1899* (London: J. W. Wakeham, 1899), 79, Volume Containing all the Annual Reports to 1905, Kensington and Chelsea School District, Poor Law School District Records, KCSD 201, LMA.

24. Ibid., 78.

25. PP (1896) xliii, 75, para. 303.

26. Kensington and Chelsea School District, Visitors' Book, February 29, 1909–November 26, 1915, with reports of the Rota Committee [Marlesford Lodge], Report of the Rota Committee (November 18, 1910), KCSD 129, LMA.

27. *Ashford School Magazine* (1906–14), WLSD 472–80, LMA. The cover of the magazine shows a photograph of the school and the Ashford coat of arms, composed of a tree and the motto "We Grow Upright."

28. Evidence of E. C. Tufnell (February 2, 1860), *Report of the Royal Commission to Inquire into the State of Popular Education in England*, PP (1861) xxi, 403, para. 3237, 3239.

29. In his 1890 report, J. H. Bridges, the medical inspector of the Local Government Board, estimated that 36–37 percent of indoor poor law children were of the more permanent class and 63–64 percent were ins and outs. PP (1896) xliii, para. 950.

30. See samples from Stepney Board of Guardians, Whitechapel, Children from Whitechapel at Forest Gate, Roman Catholic Schools, T. S. Exmouth, etc., vol. 1 (1871–1891) and vol. 2 (1892–1899), St.B.G.Wh/138/1–2, LMA. My samples include admissions and discharges of children with last names beginning with B, C, E, H, and W for volume 1 and B, C, E, H, S, and W for volume 2 (N = 1,399 for both volumes). This is my best sample for tracing readmissions, parental information, and length of stay.

31. During the year 1893–94, only two children were admitted to Banstead more than once, compared with forty-five children at Forest Gate, fifty-nine at Sutton, and seventy-five at Ashford. These other schools included cases of the same children being admitted as many as six times during the year. PP (1896) xliii, 73–4, para. 300. The children at Banstead had already first been housed at Marlesford Lodge, so their total time in poor law institutions would have been longer. See yearly samples from Admission and Discharge Registers, Banstead, Kensington and Chelsea School District, Frederick Harston, Superintendent, Poor Law School District Records, KCSD 307 (March 1896–March 1897), KCSD 308 (1901), KCSD 308 (1906), KCSD 309 (1911), LMA. For information about the length of stay for those children who were at Banstead long enough to be registered at the school, see Admission and Discharge Log Book of Banstead School Boys (1881–1910), KCSD 313, LMA. The boys' log book seems to include only those children who

were at Banstead long enough to complete the probationary period and be registered at the school; many children from the general admission and discharge records are not included, and the admission date in the school log is generally later than the admission date in the general log. Most of these children were at Banstead from one to several years.

32. Paper read by Mr. Birkby, superintendent of Swinton schools, North-Western Poor Law Officers' Association (1896), referred to in Chance, *Children under the Poor Law*, 129.

33. In a minority of cases, parents refused to sign these agreements specifying lengths of stay or signed the general agreement but omitted the clauses giving Barnardo permission to emigrate children.

34. Children's complete case records detailing length of stay were not available for this study.

35. Temporary admissions for 1896–1905 ranged from 59 to 67 percent and averaged 62 percent. The percentage of temporarily sheltered children decreased to 29 percent in 1906. The dramatic switch in policy after Barnardo's death corresponded with the organization's admission of infants and young children as opposed to older youths. Chapter 5 will discuss this policy change in more detail. See Barnardo's, *Annual Reports* (1905), 17, D239/A3/40, and (1914), 29, D239/A3/49, ULLSCA.

36. Barnardo's, *Annual Reports* (1874–75), xxxviii, D239/A3/7, ULLSCA (emphasis in original).

37. Barnardo's, *Annual Reports* (1888), 52, D239/A3/21, ULLSCA.

38. C. S. Loch, secretary, *COS leaflet, re. Dr. Barnardo's Homes*, 2, Dr. Barnardo's Homes, Barnardo Correspondence, Press Cuttings, A/FWA/C/D10/6, LMA.

39. *Short History of the North Surrey District School*, 15, LMA. It is unclear whether these notables actually attended the opening.

40. Letter from Anerley chaplain to Edward Tufnell (1851), quoted in *Short History of the North Surrey District School*, 19, LMA.

41. Barnardo, *"The King's Business Requireth Haste,"* 71.

42. Kensington and Chelsea School District Branch School [Marlesford Lodge, Hammersmith], Superintendent's Report and Journal [reports presented to the Rota Committee] (February 25, 1916), KCSD 301, LMA. Also see (March 3, 1916).

43. Interview with Percy Hide (b. 1903), Paul Mersh Orphanage Interviews (Charles Haddon Spurgeon, Stockwell Orphanage), C453/A/A–B, cassette no. F989, National Sound Archive (NSA). During the First World War, a time of extreme disruption in many children's institutions, the numbers of children who ran away from poor law schools increased sharply. See Kensington and Chelsea School District Branch School [Marlesford Lodge, Hammersmith], Superintendent's Report and Journal [reports presented to the Rota Committee], Agnes McEwen, Supt. (January 7, February 18, 25, and March 3, 1916, March 16 and October 5, 1917), KCSD 301, LMA; Kensington and Chelsea School District, Visitors' Book with Reports of the Rota Committee [Marlesford Lodge], Rota Committee Report (September 13, 1918), KCSD 130, LMA; West London School District, Ashford, Minutes of the Board of Managers, Education Committee Report (October 13 and 29, 1916), WLSD 29/1, LMA.

44. Kensington and Chelsea School District Branch School [Marlesford Lodge, Hammersmith], Superintendent's Report and Journal [reports presented to the Rota Committee] (January 7, 1916), KCSD 301, LMA.

45. Ibid. (August 28, 1908), KCSD 299, LMA.
46. Ernest Hull, discharge record (April 1, 1901), Admission and Discharge Registers, Banstead, Kensington and Chelsea School District, Frederick Harston, Superintendent, Poor Law School District Records, KCSD 308, LMA. For cases of children who were returned to Ashford District School and punished after running away, see Punishment Log Book, West London School District, Ashford, 2 vols. (1872–1934), WLSD 438, LMA. Youths also ran away from various training homes, where they were sometimes placed after leaving poor law schools. See, for example, the case of Elizabeth Gough (age fifteen), who ran away from the MABYS Home and eventually went to live with her aunt. Bermondsey Board of Guardians (St. Olave's Union), Reference to and Enquiry by General Relieving Officer, case no. 81 (March 26, 1897), BBG.539/1, LMA.
47. Forest Gate School District, *Annual Report of Managers* (1893), 13, FGSD 19, LMA; Kensington and Chelsea Standing Orders and Regulations to be Observed by Officers and Servants (July 30, 1915), 8–9, KCSD 205, LMA. Hammersmith workhouse inmates who had children at Ashford were allowed to visit the school "about twice a year." Minutes of the Board of Managers, West London School District, Ashford, Visiting Committee (August 1, 1913), WLSD 28/1, LMA.
48. Forest Gate School District, Signed Minutes of Ship (Training Ship *Goliath*), (November 14, 1870), FGSD 16, LMA.
49. Kensington and Chelsea Standing Orders and Regulations to be Observed by Officers and Servants (July 30, 1915), 9, KCSD 205, LMA.
50. Minutes of the Board of Managers, West London School District, Ashford (January 29, 1904), WLSD 23/1, LMA.
51. Ibid. (September 27, 1901), WLSD 22/1, LMA; Kensington and Chelsea Standing Orders and Regulations to be Observed by Officers and Servants (July 30, 1915), 9, KCSD 205, LMA; Forest Gate School District, *Annual Report of Managers* (1893), 13, FGSD 19, LMA.
52. Kensington and Chelsea Standing Orders and Regulations to be Observed by Officers and Servants (July 30, 1915), 8, KCSD 205, LMA.
53. Forest Gate School District, *Annual Report of Managers* (1893), 13, FGSD 19, LMA.
54. Ibid.
55. West London School District, Reports of the Visiting Committee (January 23, 1880), WLSD 13, LMA.
56. West London School District, Ashford, Minutes of the Board of Managers (May 24, 1901), WLSD 22/1, LMA.
57. Ibid. (January 9, 1913), WLSD 28/1, LMA.
58. West London School District, Ashford, Minutes of the Board of Managers (October 29, 1880), reference to a letter from the guardians, St. George's Union, WLSD 6, LMA. Also see Kensington and Chelsea School District, Minutes of the Proceedings of the Managers, vol. 13 (July 31, 1914), reference to a letter from Chelsea guardians re. Ellen Croft, KCSD 26, LMA.
59. West London School District, Ashford, Minutes of the Board of Managers (March 19, 1880), reference to a request from Fulham guardians, WLSD 6, LMA.
60. Hackney Board of Guardians, Applications to the Guardians for Custody, Servants, etc., vol. 1 (September 28, 1904), request by Mr. Fairclough, and (August 11, 1909), request by Annie Day, Ha.BG.227/1, LMA.

61. Bermondsey Board of Guardians (St. Olave's Union), Reference to and Enquiry by General Relieving Officer, case no. 44 (August 14, 1896), BBG.539/1, LMA.

62. Hackney Board of Guardians, Applications to the Guardians for Custody, Servants, etc., vol. 1, Ha.BG.227/1, LMA. The many requests for children to visit the homes of relatives were denied in 1903 and 1904, but they were more likely to be granted by 1906.

63. "News from All the Districts," *East London Observer*, December 16, 1889, 6.

64. Forest Gate School District, *Annual Reports of Managers* (1890), 19, FGSD 19, LMA. In this case, the managers meant to appease the children's relatives by arguing that the prevention of disease was the main reason for the policy. In later statements, however, the managers allowed children to leave the school for holiday trips and visits to Sunday school instructors' homes, but declared that "in very few instances do we consider it would be desirable for them to go to the homes of parents." *Annual Reports of Managers* (1897), 9, FGSD 19, LMA.

65. *Dr. Barnardo's Homes, Girls' Village Home: Visiting Regulations* (n.d.), 2922/A, Barnardo Library.

66. "A Village Home," *Night and Day* (January 1881): 14.

67. Harding, *East End Underworld*, 62. The boys in Barnardo's London homes likely had much more freedom to leave their institutions than the inmates of the Girls' Village Home, which in Ilford was far from the city center. In 1876 the Stepney Union relief officer, John Jones, complained to Barnardo that boys from his home had mixed with a fifteen-year-old girl recently admitted to the Stepney workhouse and that "the state of things [was] rather alarming." The officer warned, "I have witnessed some very irregular doings with some of your Boys and some girls in the Streets." John Jones to Barnardo, July 21, 1876, Dr. Barnardo's Homes, Reynolds-Barnardo Arbitration Correspondence, vol. 1, A/FWA/C/D10/1, LMA.

68. Harding, *East End Underworld*, 62, 12.

69. Charles W. Gough (Old Barnardo Boy), *Apprenticeship for Life* (Goldings, Hertford: Dr. Barnardo Press, n.d.), 1–4, 45, 17, ULLSCA. For an example of a boy temporarily leaving Stepney Boys' Home to visit his relatives in Brighton for Christmas, see ibid., 40. Children at Spurgeon's Stockwell Orphanage were allowed to visit their relatives for the summer holidays. Interview with Percy Hide (b. 1903), Paul Mersh Orphanage Interviews (Charles Haddon Spurgeon, Stockwell Orphanage), C453/4/A–B, cassette no. F989, side 2, NSA.

70. For the history of the police courts' origin and powers, see Behlmer, *Friends of the Family*, 182–90, and Jennifer Davis, "A Poor Man's System of Justice: The London Police Courts in the Second Half of the Nineteenth Century," *Historical Journal* 27, no. 2 (1984): 309–35.

71. See, for example, the records of the Thames Police Court, Part 1, PS/TH/A01/12–16, and Part 2, PS/TH/A02/1–125, LMA.

72. Thames Police Court, uncatalogued series, box 1 of 2 (January 1889), MSJ/CD, LMA.

73. Davis, "Poor Man's System of Justice," 326–30.

74. "Police [Court Reports]," *Times*, November 13, 1876, 11.

75. "Police [Court Reports]," *Times*, November 16, 1876, 11.

76. For examples of missing persons, see *Courier and East London Advertiser*, December 8, 1876, 3; *East End News*, January 31, 1890, 3; *East London Observer*, July 27, 1889, 7; *East London Observer*, August 3, 1889, 7; *East London*

Observer, October 5, 1889, 7; *Illustrated Police News*, July 5, 1890, 3; *Times*, November 6, 1876, 11; and *Times*, November 8, 1876, 11.

77. *Times*, November 17, 1876, 9, and subsequent daily police reports beginning on November 21.
78. *Standard*, December 5, 1889, article in Dr. Barnardo's Homes, Barnardo Correspondence, Press Cuttings, A/FWA/C/D10/6, LMA.
79. *Standard*, April 17, 1890, article in Dr. Barnardo's Homes, Barnardo Correspondence, Press Cuttings, A/FWA/C/D10/6, LMA.
80. *Standard*, April 18, 1890, article in Dr. Barnardo's Homes, Barnardo Correspondence, Press Cuttings, A/FWA/C/D10/6, LMA. As a way to discredit the applicant, Barnardo claimed that the children were illegitimate and that the applicant was not married to the man she called her husband. He refused to give the children over to their parents and said he would await court trials. For Barnardo's explanation of this and similar cases, see "Dr. Barnardo Again!" *Night and Day* (June 1890): 126–28.
81. See Bermondsey Board of Guardians (St. Olave's Union), Reference to and Enquiry by General Relieving Officer, case no. 3 (February 12, 1896), Florence Stone, BBG.539/1, LMA.
82. Bermondsey Board of Guardians (St. Olave's Union), Reference to and Enquiry by General Relieving Officer, case no. 67 (January 25, 1897), Mary Driscall, BBG.539/1, LMA.
83. West London School District, Ashford, Minutes of the Board of Managers (March 24, 1916), WLSD 29/1, LMA.
84. The first Vaccination Act in 1840 made variolation a crime punishable by imprisonment and demanded that all boards of guardians provide free public vaccination. The 1841 Vaccination Act specifically declared that acceptance of free vaccination was "non-pauperizing." The landmark 1853 act made infant vaccination compulsory within three months of birth in England and Wales (six months in Scotland), and declared that noncompliance was punishable by a fine of twenty shillings. The steady refinement of the law with increasing penalties for noncompliance suggests that there was much passive as well as organized resistance. The 1861 act made fines repeatable, and the 1867 act authorized boards of guardians to appoint nonmedical vaccination officers to levy fines and, after the 1871 act, to imprison parents who refused to pay fines. In response to opposition, Parliament began to accept the unfeasibility of compulsory vaccination with the 1898 act, which provided for conscientious objection with the permission of two justices, a stipendiary, or a metropolitan police magistrate. Compulsory vaccination was effectively eroded by the 1907 act, which made conscientious objection a simple matter of stating an oath before a magistrate or a commissioner of oaths. On smallpox vaccination legislation and resistance, see Ann Beck, "Issues in the Anti-Vaccination Movement in England," *Medical History* 4 (December 1960): 310–21; Behlmer, *Friends of the Family*, 76–92; Nadja Durbach, "'They Might as Well Brand Us': Working-Class Resistance to Compulsory Vaccination in Victorian England," *Social History of Medicine* 13, no. 1 (2000): 45–62; Nadja Durbach, *Bodily Matters: The Anti-Vaccination Movement in England, 1853–1907* (Durham: Duke University Press, 2005); Stuart M. F. Fraser, "Leicester and Smallpox: The Leicester Method," *Medical History* 24 (July 1980): 315–32; Anne Hardy, "Smallpox in London: Factors in the Decline of the Disease in the Nineteenth

Century," *Medical History* 27 (1983): 111–38; R. J. Lambert, "A Victorian National Health Service: State Vaccination, 1855–71," *Historical Journal* 5 (1962): 1–18; R. M. MacLeod, "Law, Medicine and Public Opinion: The Resistance to Compulsory Health Legislation, 1870–1907," *Public Law* (1967), part I: 107–28, part II: 189–211; F. B. Smith, *The People's Health, 1830–1910* (London: Croom Helm, 1979); J. R. Smith, *The Speckled Monster: Smallpox in England, 1670–1970, with Particular Reference to Essex* (Chelmsford: Essex Record Office, 1987), 117–41.

85. Mr. Young, quoted in "Anti-Vaccination Demonstration at Leicester," *Times*, March 24, 1885, 10:e. Mary Hume-Rothery, daughter of radical Joseph Hume and ardent campaigner against the Contagious Diseases Acts, similarly wrote in protest of compulsory vaccination: "An Englishman's house is no longer his own. Under favour of the odious Vaccination Acts a poor man's house may be entered by emmissaries of the Medical Star Chamber to ascertain whether his children have been blood-poisoned according to law." Hume-Rothery, *Women and Doctors, or, Medical Despotism in England* (1871), quoted in F. B. Smith, *People's Health*, 166.

86. Lord Salisbury, *Times*, August 5, 1898, quoted in Millicent Garrett Fawcett, "The Vaccination Act of 1898," *Contemporary Review* 75 (March 1899): 334. Britain's imposition of smallpox vaccination on its Indian subjects was much more difficult than Salisbury suggested. See David Arnold, *Colonizing the Body: State Medicine and Epidemic Disease in Nineteenth-Century India* (Berkeley: University of California Press, 1993), 116–58.

87. See Durbach, "'They Might as Well Brand Us.'"

88. Council Minutes, including information on individual children and residency statistics, vol. 3 (February 19, 1902), 99, Council Papers, Barnardo Archive, D239/B1/7, ULLSCA.

89. West London School District, Ashford, Minutes of the Board of Managers, Medical Officer's Report (November 8, 1901), WLSD 22/1, LMA.

90. West London School District, Ashford, Minutes of the Board of Managers (November 22, 1901), WLSD 22/1, LMA. Also see West London School District, Minutes of the Visiting Committee [Ashford] (November 29, 1901) and (December 20, 1901), WLSD 105, LMA. Many boards of guardians opposed compulsory vaccination and refused to enforce penalties. See Fawcett, "Vaccination Act of 1898," 335.

91. West London School District, Ashford, Minutes of the Board of Managers (December 13, 1901), WLSD 22/1, LMA.

92. Kensington and Chelsea School District, General Regulations Issued by the Board of Management for the Management of the "Cottage Homes," and Instructions to the "Fathers and Mothers," and, so far as they are applicable, to the whole of the staff of the school (n.d.), Poor Law School District Records, KCSD 202/1, LMA.

93. *Times*, June 21, 1894, 12:b.

94. *Times*, June 1, 1894, 11:f, and June 7, 1894, 5:e. Also see Longmate, *Workhouse*, 179; PP (1896) xliii, Appendix A, 178; *Times*, June 13, 1894, 4:a, June 21, 1894, 12:b, July 19, 1894, 6:f, July 26, 1894, 13, September 18, 1894, 3:d, September 20, 1894, 7:f.

95. *Times*, September 18, 1894, 3.

96. Bermondsey Board of Guardians (St. Olave's Union), Reference to and Enquiry by General Relieving Officer, case no. 19, John Sharpe (May 6, 1896), BBG.539/1, LMA.

97. West London School District, Ashford, Minutes of the Board of Managers (January 3, 1919), reference to a letter from Mrs. E. L. Molineux (dated December 27, 1918), WLSD 29/4, LMA.

98. West London School District, Ashford, Minutes of the Board of Managers (October 27, 1916), reference to a letter from Mrs. Prince forwarded by Fulham Board of Guardians (dated October 25, 1916), WLSD 29/1, LMA. For similar complaints from parents about the treatment and possible abuse of children, see West London School District, Ashford, Minutes of the Board of Managers (March 21, 1879) and (April 4, 1879), reference to letter to Fulham Board of Guardians from Laura Kendall about her daughter's injury from falling on steam pipes and the following report of the special committee, WLSD 6; West London School District, Reports of the Visiting Committee (February 7, 1879), reference to complaint by Mrs. Walker to Fulham Board of Guardians, WLSD 13, LMA.

99. West London School District, Ashford, Minutes of the Board of Managers (June 23, 1902) and (July 11, 1902), reference to a letter from Mrs. Winfield, Report of the Visiting Committee, and the managers' response, WLSD 22/2, LMA.

100. West London School District, Ashford, Minutes of the Board of Managers (June 28, 1918), reference to a letter from City of Westminster Board of Guardians (dated June 15, 1918), WLSD 29/3, LMA.

101. Reynolds, *Dr. Barnardo's Homes*, 4–11, quotations at 10, 11.

102. "Recent Police Court Complaints," *Supplement to Night and Day* (December 1889): 208. Barnardo complained that the popular press failed to print his rebuttal to accusations brought to the police courts.

103. *Standard*, November 22, 1889, found in Dr. Barnardo's Homes, Barnardo Correspondence, Press Cuttings, A/FWA/C/D10/6, LMA. Also see *Sunday Times*, November 24, 1889. A Mrs. Seeley made similar charges at the Thames Police Court that her two girls were abused at Barnardo's homes. This case was investigated during the 1877 arbitration and dismissed due to lack of evidence. See "Illegal Detention of Children," *Morning Advertiser*, March 15, 1875, reprinted with discussion in Reynolds, *Dr. Barnardo's Homes*, 4–7; Minutes of the Third Special Meeting of the Trustees [COS] (January 29, 1877), re. Mrs. Seeley's case, Dr. Barnardo's Homes; copy of certificates from Dr. E. W. Sullivan, Medical Attendant at Girls' Home, Ilford, Essex (December 22, 1876), Reynolds-Barnardo Arbitration, COS's Dr. Barnardo Sub-Committee Minutes, A/FWA/C/D10/3, LMA; *Night and Day* (November 1, 1877): 127.

104. "Recent Police Court Complaints," *Supplement to Night and Day* (December 1889): 208.

105. De Profundis, *A Plea for Workhouse Children* (London: Burns, Lambert, and Oates, 1866), 5.

106. PP (1896) xliii, 9, para. 24. Guardians also often sent disabled children to special certified schools. The Poor Law (Certified Schools) Act of 1862 established the guidelines for certified schools, and an 1866 act (29 & 30 Vict. ch. 113, s. 14) guaranteed that children would be sent to certified schools of their own denomination.

107. Approximately once every month, for example, the Stepney Board of Guardians transferred Catholic children to the local Catholic certified school. See Stepney Board of Guardians, Whitechapel, Committee Report Book, no. 1 (December 19, 1881), (January 16, 1882), (February 27, 1882), (March 13, 1882), (April 10,

1882), St.B.G./Wh/106/1, LMA. For the placement of Roman Catholic, Jewish, and the few Protestant Dissenter children from Whitechapel, see Stepney Board of Guardians, Whitechapel, Children from Whitechapel at Forest Gate, Roman Catholic Schools, T. S. Exmouth, etc., vol. 1 (1871–1891) and vol. 2 (1892–1899), St.B.G.Wh/138/1–2, LMA. When not sent to certified schools, Catholic children appear more likely than Jewish children to be sent to the Forest Gate poor law district school.

Based on samples of creed and service discharge registers, guardians became more observant about sending children to their proper denominational institutions as the century progressed. A small minority (about 10 percent) of children in the West London School District were Catholic in the early 1870s. In the mid- to late 1880s, it was very rare for any Catholic children to be listed in the Forest Gate School District creed registers. At the end of the nineteenth and beginning of the twentieth century, samples from service registers for 1,015 children leaving Ashford, the West London District School, show that all of the children were Church of England except for one Baptist, one Congregationalist, and one Wesleyan. See West London School District, Religious Creed Register (September 24, 1872–August 12, 1877), WLSD 428, LMA; Forest Gate School District, Creed Register from Various Unions (December 1884–July 1888), FGSD 30, LMA; West London School District Service Register (sample includes 1898, 1900, 1902, 1904, 1906, 1908, 1910, 1912, 1914, 1916, and 1918–23), WLSD 433 and 434, LMA.

108. Bermondsey Board of Guardians (St. Olave's Union), Reference to and Enquiry by General Relieving Officer, case no. 54 (1896), Cornelius Forest and wife, BBG.539/1, LMA.

109. Forest Gate School District, Signed Minutes of Ship (Training Ship *Goliath*), (July 15 and September 23, 1871, July 20, 1872, and November 28, 1874), FGSD 16–17, LMA.

110. The Banstead managers hoped these Catholic cottages would be an alternative to sending Catholic children to certified schools, allowing Catholic as well as Protestant children to benefit from the cottage system. Kensington and Chelsea School District Agenda of Meeting of Managers (February 27 and March 2, 1880), KCSD 77, LMA.

111. Opthalmia Committee Reports (April 24, 1897), Central London School District, CLSD 73, LMA.

112. Kensington and Chelsea School District, Visitors' Book with Reports from the Rota Committee, Rota Committee Report (September 12, 1913), KCSD 129, LMA; West London School District, Ashford, Minutes of the Board of Managers (March 13, 1914), WLSD 28/1, LMA.

113. For a sample agreement form, see Wagner, *Barnardo*, 217.

114. Herbert, Bishop of Salford, "Abuses in Philanthropic Institutions" (letter to the editor responding to Martha Tye case), *Times*, June 10, 1889, article in Dr. Barnardo's Homes, Barnardo Correspondence, Press Cuttings, A/FWA/C/D10/6, LMA.

115. For Barnardo's discussions of the police court cases against him in the 1870s and later complaints sparked by the publicized custody battles, also see "The Editor in the Police Court," *Night and Day* (April 16, 1877): 43, and "Dr. Barnardo Again!" *Night and Day* (June 1890): 126–28. For a summary of nineteenth-century legislation

concerning parental rights, see Ward, "Charitable Relationship," 33–81, and Mary Lyndon Shanley, *Feminism, Marriage, and the Law in Victorian England* (Princeton: Princeton University Press, 1989), 131–55.

116. East End Juvenile Mission, Minutes of Committee Meetings, Children's Statistics, General Committee Meeting of the EEJM (September 5, 1878), 37–38, Barnardo Archive, D239/B1/5, ULLSCA. There is also a reference in the admission register for a six-year-old girl admitted January 8, 1883, who was returned by judge's order in court of appeal, February 18, 1883. Children's Admission Registers, Children's Records, In-care children's records, Barnardo Archive, D239/D/2/2a/2–28, ULLSCA.

117. "Is Philanthropic Abduction Ever Justifiable?" *Night and Day* (November 1885): 149–50 (emphasis in original). Joy Parr estimates that among the children Barnardo emigrated to Canada, 9 percent of the boys and 15 percent of the girls were cases of philanthropic abduction. See Parr, *Labouring Children*, 67.

118. For a detailed summary of the complicated narrative of events and legal proceedings, see Wagner, *Barnardo*, 214–36, and Wagner, *Children of the Empire*, 143–47.

119. "Sold to Organ-Grinders: The True Story of Harry Gossage," *Night and Day* (December 1889): 170–80; "A Mighty Meeting," *Night and Day* (December 1889): 162; letter from Alfred Newdigate, *Standard*, December 5, 1889; Wagner, *Barnardo*, 229.

120. "Kidnapped by a Priest," *Night and Day* (June 1890): 120.

121. "Personal Notes," *Night and Day* (December 1889): 141 (emphasis in original). On anti-Catholicism as a common component of English national identity, see Walter Arnstein, *Protestant versus Catholic in Mid-Victorian England: Mr. Newdegate and the Nuns* (Columbia: University of Missouri Press, 1982); Colley, *Britons*; and Carol Marie Engelhardt, "Victorians and the Virgin Mary: Religion, National Identity, and the Woman Question in England, 1830–1880" (Ph.D. diss., Indiana University, 1997).

122. "The Roman Catholics and My Children," *Night and Day* (November 1889): 124–5.

123. *Times*, December 18, 1889, 13:c. Also see *Times*, December 5, 1889, 3:f, and December 9, 1889, 13:a. W. T. Stead noted that by 1896, Barnardo had been on trial for eighty-eight custody claims. See Stead, "Dr. Barnardo: The Father of 'Nobody's Children,'" *Review of Reviews* (New York) 14 (July–December 1896).

124. *Times*, December 18, 1889, 13:c.

125. *Standard*, December 18, 1889, 2.

126. See the case against Mr. Walter Austin, who ran a children's home in Limehouse, in *Illustrated Police News*, April 5, 1890, 3.

127. *Standard*, April 18, 1890, 3.

128. "Another Application Against Dr. Barnardo," *East End News*, January 17, 1890, 3.

129. Twenty-four percent (fifty) of the discharges were children who went to service, 13 percent (twenty-eight) were transferred to Mile End School, 6 percent (thirteen) entered the army, 5 percent (ten) joined the *Exmouth* training ship, 3 percent (seven) were transferred to a local parish or workhouse, where they may have joined parents, 3 percent (seven) were sent to an infirmary or hospital or placed under the care of a nurse, 1 percent (three) ran away, 1 percent (three) went to live with an aunt, uncle, or sibling, 1 percent (two) emigrated, and 0.5 percent (one) died. Admission and Discharge Registers, Banstead, Kensington and Chelsea School District (March 1896–March 1897), KCSD 307, LMA.

130. Gough, *Apprenticeship for Life*, 45. Joy Parr notes that even many of the Barnardo children who emigrated to Canada managed to maintain contact with parents: "Seventy per cent of the parents of the Barnardo girls who received before-sailing notices remained in contact with their children; almost as high a proportion—60 per cent—of parents who were sent after-sailing notices did so; and 22 per cent of parents who had been deprived of any knowledge of their children's emigration later succeeded in re-establishing communication with them" (*Labouring Children*, 72). Almost one-third of Barnardo's child emigrants to Canada visited Britain in their teens and twenties, and 16 percent permanently returned to Britain as adults (*Labouring Children*, 75).

131. Executive Committee, Committee Minutes (December 4, 1912), Council Papers, Barnardo Archive, D239/B3/1/1, ULLSCA. The committee also discussed returning older girls who were paid for by poor law guardians to their parents and paying parents a subsidy to help with the girls' maintenance. See Committee Minutes (January 4, 1909).

132. See, for example, letter from Elsie B. in *"Something Attempted, Something Done"* (1889), 112; letters from K.M. and B.O., *National Waifs' Magazine* (August 1904): 90–91; letter from Annie Warren (July 23, 1906) and letter from H. Latham (July 15, 1906), *Ashford School Magazine* 1 (1906): cover inset; letter from Private Frederick Wyatt, *Ashford School Magazine* (1915): cover inset; letter from the sisters of Private Thomas Lester notifying the school of his death in battle, *Ashford School Magazine* (1917): cover inset, WLSD 472, 481–82, LMA.

133. Crowther, *Workhouse System*, 69; PP (1896) xliii, para. 256–61; Twining, *Recollections*, 46–48.

134. Prochaska, "Female Philanthropy," 80.

135. Forest Gate School District, *Annual Reports of Managers, Including Report of the Association for Befriending Young Servants*, report for E.B. (Whitechapel) (1888), FGSD 19, LMA.

136. West London School District (Ashford), Metropolitan Association for Befriending Young Servants (MABYS), *Annual Reports*, Maria Poole, Secretary, reports for Agnes Farley (1887–89), WLSD 459, LMA.

137. Forest Gate School District, *Annual Reports of Managers, Including Report of the Association for Befriending Young Servants*, report for J.A. (Poplar) (1888), FGSD 19, LMA.

138. Clara did soon return to service. West London School District (Ashford), MABYS, *Annual Reports*, Maria Poole, Secretary, reports for Mary Ball (1888), Clara Maystone (1888, 1890), WLSD 459, LMA.

139. West London School District (Ashford), MABYS, *Annual Reports*, Maria Poole, Secretary, report for Alice Knowles (1892); also see, for example, reports for Clara Beischer (1890), Annie Lacey (1892), Rose Curtis (1893), Edith Warren (1894), Adelaide Watson (1897), Ada Wilson (1897), Annie Welch (1899), WLSD 459, LMA.

140. West London School District (Ashford), MABYS, *Annual Reports*, Maria Poole, Secretary, report for Ellen Kett (1897), WLSD 459, LMA.

141. Forest Gate School District, *Annual Reports of Managers, Including Report of the Association for Befriending Young Servants*, reports for E.J. (1896–97), FGSD 19, LMA; West London School District (Ashford), MABYS, *Annual Reports*, Maria Poole, Secretary, reports for Minnie Moody (1888), Ada Stallion (1890–95), E.

Jones or Allgate (1891), Annie Woolcock (1892), Jane Lang (1893), Florence Deer (1893, 1898), Ada Carter (1895), Maud Wadsworth (1897), WLSD 459, LMA.

142. This quotation was repeated in the summary report of the 1896 Mundella report, which noted that Louisa Twining "quoted the matron of her home . . . thirty years ago" as the original source. PP (1896) xliii, 85, para. 339.

143. Tufnell, *Observations on the Report of Mrs. Senior*, 7.

144. Senior, *Report*, in Smedley, *Boarding-Out*, 113. For Barnardo's views, see PP (1896) xliii, 83, para. 334.

145. Forest Gate School District, *Annual Reports of Managers, Including Report of the Association for Befriending Young Servants*, report for E.Q. (Poplar) (1893), FGSD 19, LMA.

146. West London School District (Ashford), MABYS, *Annual Reports*, Maria Poole, Secretary, report for Edith Simmonds (1893), WLSD 459, LMA.

147. Forest Gate School District, *Annual Reports of Managers, Including Report of the Association for Befriending Young Servants*, report for C.G. (Poplar) (1891), FGSD 19, LMA.

148. West London School District (Ashford), MABYS, *Annual Reports*, Maria Poole, Secretary, report for Kate Saville (1888), WLSD 459, LMA.

149. *Ashford School Magazine* (October 1917): cover inset, WLSD 482, LMA.

CHAPTER 5 *Training "Street Arabs" into British Citizens*

1. Fenn, *Burning of the "Goliath,"* 1. The Metropolitan Poor Amendment Act of 1869 empowered boards of guardians or school districts to acquire, with the Poor Law Board's consent, ships to train boys for naval careers. See Chance, *Children under the Poor Law*, 30, 248.

2. *Times*, October 1871, quoted in Forest Gate School District, *Annual Reports of Managers* (1888), 7, FGSD 19, LMA.

3. The poor law training ships are another example of how the state modeled its programs on charitable traditions, particularly the work of the Marine Society, founded in 1756, which directed poor boys into naval careers. See Donna T. Andrew, *Philanthropy and Police: London Charity in the Eighteenth Century* (Princeton: Princeton University Press, 1989), 109–15.

4. Donation letter from Florence Nightingale to the Lord Mayor, January 11, 1876, quoted in Fenn, *Burning of the "Goliath,"* 41.

5. "Motto for our Training Ships," *Punch* (December 30, 1876): 287.

6. Kensington and Chelsea School District, General Regulations Issued by the Board of Management for the Management of the "Cottage Homes," and Instructions to the "Fathers and Mothers," 5, 15, KCSD 202/1, LMA, quotation at 5.

7. Edwin Chadwick, rough draft of paper for the National Association for the Promotion of Social Science, Bradford (1859), 27, Papers on military and naval education, including drill in schools, ca. 1859–1880, Papers of Sir Edwin Chadwick (1800–1890), 92, UCL.

8. J. S. Hurt, "Drill, Discipline and the Elementary School Ethos," in *Popular Education and Socialization in the Nineteenth Century*, ed. Phillip McCann (London: Methuen and Co. Ltd., 1977), 172–76. Also see Davin, *Growing Up Poor*, 125.

9. Edwin Chadwick, "The Military and Naval Drill; with Systematised Gymnastics as Part of a National Education," National Association for the Promotion of Social

Science, Education Section, Bradford (1859), 2, Papers of Sir Edwin Chadwick, 92, UCL.

10. Barnardo, *"Something Attempted Something Done"* (1888), 40.

11. Anerley chaplain's letter to Tufnell (1851), quoted in *Short History of the North Surrey District School*, 19, LMA.

12. Evidence of E. C. Tufnell (February 2, 1860), in *Report of the Royal Commission to Inquire into the State of Popular Education in England*, PP (1861) xxi, 396, para. 3164. Also see Hurt, "Drill, Discipline and the Elementary School Ethos," 170.

13. Evidence of E. C. Tufnell (February 2, 1860), PP (1861) xxi, 396, para. 3164.

14. Kensington and Chelsea School District, General Regulations Issued by the Board of Management for the Management of the "Cottage Homes," and Instructions to the "Fathers and Mothers," 16, KCSD 202/1, LMA; *The Third Report of the Managers of the Kensington and Chelsea School District in Respect of Their Schools at Banstead and Hammersmith, for the Six Years Ended Michaelmas, 1890*, 20–24, KCSD/201, LMA; Forest Gate School District, Signed Minutes of Ship (Training Ship *Goliath*), (July 20, 1872), FGSD 16, LMA; John Vincent, "Life on Board the Training-Ship 'Exmouth,'" *Ashford School Magazine* (1909): back cover, WLSD 475, LMA.

15. Forest Gate School District, Signed Minutes of Ship (Training Ship *Goliath*), (April 1871), FGSD 16, and (August 16, 1873), FGSD 17, LMA.

16. Barnardo, *"Something Attempted Something Done"* (1888), 43 (emphasis in original). Also see the interview with Dennis Charles Greenop, Paul Mersh Orphanage Interviews (Charles Haddon Spurgeon, Stockwell Orphanage), C453/2/A–B, cassette no. F986, NSA, for a description of how such housework made him very "domesticated" as an adult.

17. Barnardo, "London Lodging Houses, I. As They Were," *Night and Day* (January 1877): 11.

18. West London School District, Reports of the Visiting Committee (February 6, 1880), WLSD 13, LMA; *The Second Report of the Managers of the Kensington and Chelsea School District in Respect of Their Schools at Banstead and Hammersmith, for the Three Years Ended Michaelmas, 1884* (London: Wakeham and Son, 1884), 9, KCSD/201, LMA. For a sample poor law school daily schedule, see Kensington and Chelsea School District, General Regulations Issued by the Board of Management for the Management of the "Cottage Homes," and Instructions to the "Fathers and Mothers," 15, KCSD 202/1, LMA. For a comparison of the numbers of children in school versus industrial training, see Frederick Harston, Observations of the Superintendent of the "Cottage Home" School at Banstead, . . . presenting Regulations for the Instruction of Children in Workhouses and in Separate District Schools, submitted to the Managers on the 12th February, 1897, KCSD 165, LMA.

19. Ashford Service Register samples, West London School District Service Register (sample includes 1,015 entries for children leaving Ashford for employment in 1898, 1900, 1902, 1904, 1906, 1908, 1910, 1912, 1914, 1916, and 1918–23), WLSD 433 and 434, LMA. On the Homes for Working Boys, see Chance, *Children under the Poor Law*, 309–12. Chance notes that nine of London's thirty poor law unions were subscribers to the Homes for Working Boys in 1897.

20. On the training ships, see Chance, *Children under the Poor Law*, 248–55.

21. Barnardo, "The Continued Necessity for Voluntary Agencies in Reclaiming the Children of the Streets," *Night and Day* (November 1881): 205–6.
22. Children's Admission Registers (January 16 and 24, 1884), Children's Records, In-care children's records, Barnardo Archive, D239/D/2/2a, ULLSCA.
23. Barnardo's, *Annual Reports* (1898), 20, Barnardo Archive, D239/A3/33, ULLSCA.
24. See Barnardo's, *Annual Reports* (1899–1903, 1905, 1907), Barnardo Archive, D239/A3/34–38, 40, 42, ULLSCA.
25. J.S. (male, age 14), admitted March 15, 1887, Précis Books, vol. 1, In-care children's records, Barnardo Archive, D239/D/2/2a/104, ULLSCA.
26. *Report of F. J. Mouat and Capt. J. D. Bowly, On Home and Cottage System of Training and Educating Children of the Poor*, PP (1878) lx (285), 1. The study reported on Princess Mary's Village Home at Addlestone, Surrey; the Home for Little Boys at Farningham, Kent; the Village Home for Orphan, Neglected, and Destitute Girls at Ilford, Essex (Barnardo's Girls' Village Home); the Stockwell Orphanage, Clapham; the Philanthropic Society's Farm School at Redhill, Surrey; and the Children's Home in the Bonner-road, East London.
27. For a summary of technical training provided for boys and girls in fifteen poor law schools (Bethnal Green [Leytonstone], Brighton [Warren Farm], Central London [Hanwell], Farnham and Hartley Wintney [Farnham], Holborn [Mitcham], Kensington and Chelsea [Banstead], Lambeth [West Norwood], Liverpool [Kirkdale], North Surrey [Anerley], St. Marylebone [Southhall], St. Pancras [Leavesden], Shoreditch [Hornchurch], South East Shropshire, Walsall and West Bromwich, and West Ham Union), see West London School District, Ashford, Minutes of the Board of Managers (March 8, 1901), WLSD 22/1, LMA. For specific descriptions of girls' training, see, for example, Tufnell, *Training of Pauper Children*, 11–12; Forest Gate School District, *Annual Reports of Managers* (1888), 11–12, FGSD 19, LMA; Kensington and Chelsea School District, *The Sixth Report of the Managers of the Kensington and Chelsea School District in Respect of Their Schools at Banstead and Hammersmith, for the Four Years Ended Michaelmas, 1899* (London: J. W. Wakeham, 1899), 38–39, KCSD/201, LMA; PP (1896) xliii, 50–53, para. 195–216; "Report of Inspection of Classes, 1907, Ashford, The City and Guilds of London Institute, Margaret Eleanor Pillow" (October 26, 1907) and Ashford Housewifery Syllabus (1907), West London School District (Ashford), Education Committee Reports, WLSD 84, LMA. For descriptions of boys' training, see, for example, Forest Gate School District, *Annual Reports of Managers* (1888), 10, FGSD 19, LMA; Kensington and Chelsea School District, *Second Report of the Managers . . . 1884*, 17–18, *Third Report of the Managers . . . 1890*, 20–24, *The Fifth Report of the Managers . . . for the Three Years Ended Michaelmas, 1895*, 21–31, KCSD/201, LMA; West London School District, *Annual Report of the Board of Managers. Sixth Annual Report . . . for the Year Ended Lady-Day 1874*, WLSD/135, LMA.
28. Barnardo, *"Something Attempted Something Done"* (1888), 40.
29. The North Surrey, Stepney, and Central London poor law schools used grounded ship skeletons for training purposes. See Tufnell, *Training of Pauper Children*, 10.
30. These photographs are representative of what Raphael Samuel termed "industrial photography." See his *Theatres of Memory*, vol. 1, *Past and Present in Contemporary Culture* (London and New York: Verso, 1994), 324.

31. See *Short History of the North Surrey District School*, 73, LMA.
32. Kensington and Chelsea School District, *Sixth Report of the Managers . . . 1899*, 44, KCSD/201, LMA.
33. See chapter 2. Also see Barnardo, "A Thrashing," *Night and Day* (August 1877): 85–87, and *"Something Attempted Something Done"* (1888), 146.
34. Evidence of E. C. Tufnell (February 2, 1860), PP (1861) xxi, 392, para. 3142–43. Louisa Twining likewise claimed in 1859 that "we have already far more tailors and shoemakers than can find employment." See Twining, *On the Supervision and Training of Workhouse Girls* (London: Bell and Daldy, 1860), 23. Also see Chance, *Children under the Poor Law*, 89.
35. Report on Technical Education, summary of school policies, West London School District, Ashford, Minutes of the Board of Managers (March 8, 1901), WLSD 22/1, LMA. The schools that responded to the survey are the same ones listed in note 27 above.
36. West London School District, Education Committee Reports (June 27 and March 20, 1913), WLSD 85, LMA.
37. "Report of Sub-Committee of Children's Committee, respecting the Training of Children at the West London District School who are exempt from attending school" (November 20, 1901), West London School District, Ashford, Minutes of the Board of Managers (December 13, 1901), WLSD 22/1, LMA. Also see PP (1896) xliii, 46, para. 166–69.
38. Report of J. R. Mozley, inspector of poor law schools (June 8, 1903), Ashford Visitors' Book, with short accounts, WLSD 118, LMA; West London School District, Education Committee Reports (April 18, 1912), WLSD 85, LMA. For numbers of children at various types of industrial training at Ashford, see West London School District, Education Committee Reports (January 1906–January 1919), WLSD 84–85, LMA. There were also suggestions that some children viewed their training more as drudgery than as craftsmanship. In the 1870s, children at Anerley took extraordinary measures to be sent to the infirmary, where they received better rations and were exempted from school and work. To become infected with the eye disease ophthalmia, they "went so far as to rub the [highly contagious] matter into their eyes." Others settled for rubbing a mixture of salt and butter into their eyes, which provoked an irritation resembling the disease. *Short History of the North Surrey District School*, 39, LMA.
39. David Rubinstein, "Socialization and the London School Board, 1870–1904: Aims, Methods and Public Opinion," in *Popular Education and Socialization in the Nineteenth Century*, ed. McCann, 232. On the Education Acts and their applicability to poor law schools, also see Chance, *Children under the Poor Law*, 40–41, and PP (1896) xliii, 57, para. 227.
40. Kensington and Chelsea School District, copy of report from Wyndham Holgate, the Local Government Board school inspector, regarding his inspection of the district school at Banstead (August 11, 1884), KCSD 158, LMA.
41. PP (1896) xliii, 54–56, para. 218–21.
42. Correspondence between the managers of the Kensington and Chelsea School District and the Local Government Board, with respect to the application of the board's general order of January 30, 1897, prescribing regulations as to the school attendance and industrial training of children in poor law schools established on the "cottage home" system, 1–4, KCSD 164, LMA.

43. See ibid., and Kensington and Chelsea School District, *Sixth Report of the Managers . . . 1899,* 7–8, KCSD/201, LMA.

44. Frederick Harston, Observations of the Superintendent of the "Cottage Home" School at Banstead, . . . presenting Regulations for the Instruction of Children in Workhouses and in Separate and District Schools, submitted to the Managers on the 12th February, 1897, KCSD 165, LMA (statistics for 1898–1900 were later written in by hand).

45. Kensington and Chelsea School District, *The Seventh Report of the Managers of the Kensington and Chelsea School District in Respect of Their Schools at Banstead and Hammersmith, for the Six Years Ended Michaelmas, 1905* (London: J. Wakeham and Co., Ltd., 1905), 21–22, 24, KCSD 201, LMA.

46. *Annual Report of Dr. Barnardo's Homes: National Incorporated Association* (1907), 15, Barnardo Archive, D239/A3/1/42, ULLSCA.

47. *Annual Report of Dr. Barnardo's Homes: National Incorporated Association* (1905), 19, (1907), 15, (1908), 14, (1911), 23, Barnardo Archive, D239/A3/1/40, 42–43, 46, ULLSCA (emphasis in originals).

48. On how the empire influenced debates on national citizenship in the context of the 1867 Reform Act, see Catherine Hall, "The Nation Within and Without," in *Defining the Victorian Nation,* ed. Hall, McClelland, and Rendall, 179–233.

49. Stephen Heathorn, "'Let us remember that we, too, are English': Constructions of Citizenship and National Identity in English Elementary School Reading Books, 1880–1914," *Victorian Studies* 38, no. 3 (Spring 1995): 397. Also see Davin, *Growing Up Poor,* 201–8, and Stephen Heathorn, *For Home, Country, and Race: Constructing Gender, Class, and Englishness in the Elementary School, 1880–1914* (Toronto: University of Toronto Press, 2000).

50. Schneer, *London 1900.* See especially chapter 5, "Popular Culture in the Imperial Metropolis," 93–115, quotation at 93.

51. Council Minutes including information on individual children and residency statistics, vol. 4 (June 15, 1915), 198 (includes references to earlier Colonial Day celebrations at the Girls' Village Home), Council Papers, Barnardo Archive, D239/B1/7, ULLSCA; Executive Committee, Committee Minutes (June 7, 1916), Council Papers, Barnardo Archive, D239/B3/121, ULLSCA; interview with Dennis Charles Greenop (b. August 15, 1914), Paul Mersh Orphanage Interviews (Charles Spurgeon, Stockwell Orphanage), C453/2/A–B, cassette no. F986, side 2, NSA. Also see Davin, *Growing Up Poor,* 202–3, and MacKenzie, *Propaganda and Empire,* 231–40, for descriptions of Empire Day celebrations.

52. Schneer, *London 1900,* 98.

53. *Ashford School Magazine* (May 1906): 109, (June 1906), and (July 1906): 156–57, 180–81, WLSD 472, LMA. School officials sent free copies of the magazine to youths who emigrated or gained employment; after twelve months, they were expected to pay an annual subscription of one shilling. Ashford officials announced the last issue of the journal in December 1914 and encouraged youths to subscribe to *Work and Play: The Scholars' Own Magazine.* Although the readership of both magazines was likely not specific to Ashford, school officials continued to use the inside of the magazine covers for updates about the school and correspondence from old scholars.

54. See Annie E. Coombes, *Reinventing Africa: Museums, Material Culture and Popular Imagination in Late Victorian and Edwardian England* (New Haven and London: Yale University Press, 1994), and Schneer, *London 1900,* 93–94. The

earliest reference I have found to the Ashford museum is from the *Ashford School Magazine* (November 1907): front cover inset, WLSD 473, LMA.

55. *Ashford School Magazine* (January 1914): front cover inset, WLSD 480, LMA; ibid. (May 1911): back cover inset, WLSD 477, LMA.
56. *Ashford School Magazine* (January 1914): front cover inset, WLSD 480, LMA. Also see ibid. (November 1907), WLSD 473, LMA.
57. *Ashford School Magazine* (May 1911): back cover inset, WLSD 477, LMA.
58. *Ashford School Magazine* (January 1914): front cover inset, WLSD 480, LMA.
59. Ibid.
60. There were thirty-six magic lantern slide shows at Banstead from 1895 to 1899. See Kensington and Chelsea School District, *Sixth Report of the Managers . . . 1899*, 34–35, KCSD 201, LMA.
61. MacKenzie, *Propaganda and Empire*, 32–33.
62. Kensington and Chelsea School District, *Sixth Report of the Managers . . . 1899*, 34–35, KCSD 201, LMA. My analysis is deeply indebted to Edward Said's *Orientalism* (New York: Vintage, 1979).
63. *Ashford School Magazine* (November 1906): back cover inset, WLSD 472, LMA.
64. Schneer, *London 1900*, 97. Also see Michael Pickering, "White Skin, Black Masks: 'Nigger' Minstrelsy in Victorian England," in *Music Hall: Performance and Style*, ed. J. S. Bratton (Milton Keynes: Open University Press, 1986), 70–91.
65. *Ashford School Magazine* (April 1906): front cover inset, WLSD 472, LMA.
66. See Heathorn, "'Let us remember,'" 404, 409, 414.
67. "The Far East, III: Burmah," *Ashford School Magazine* (April 1906): 74, WLSD 472, LMA.
68. "The Far East, IV: Indo-China," *Ashford School Magazine* (May 1906): 99, WLSD 472, LMA.
69. "The Far East, III: Burmah," *Ashford School Magazine* (April 1906): 75, WLSD 472, LMA.
70. "The Far East, IV: Indo-China," *Ashford School Magazine* (May 1906): 99, WLSD 472, LMA.
71. "The Far East, V: Malaysia," *Ashford School Magazine* (June 1906): 81–83, WLSD 472, LMA.
72. Hurt, "Drill, Discipline and the Elementary School Ethos," 170–71.
73. Chadwick, rough draft of "The Military and Naval Drill; with Systematised Gymnastics as Part of National Education" (1859), 19–20, Papers on military and naval education, Papers of Sir Edwin Chadwick, 92, UCL.
74. See the photograph, "The Manufactured Article: A Plea for a Training Ship," in *"Rescue the Perishing,"* facing liv; *Night and Day* (January 1877): 4, and (September 1877): 108. For reprints of pacifist and Quaker objections to Barnardo's plans to train poor children for the army and navy, see *Night and Day* (January 1882): 1–3. In 1891, Barnardo temporarily seemed to abandon his former esteem for training ships. In a veiled attack, he wrote, "We have it from thoroughly competent informants that the *amount of immorality known to exist on board more than one of these ships is positively appalling*; that several ships having a large number of boys on board, are veritable sinks of iniquity. . . . That numbers of young lads are ruined at the very outset on board such Training Ships we have had ourselves lamentable proofs. . . ." "Training Ship Morals: A Call to Attention," *Night and Day* (September 1891): 129 (emphasis in original).

75. *Night and Day* (February 1898): 11.
76. Flower, *Boy Who Did Grow Up*, 55, 60, and passim; *National Waifs' Magazine* (January 1902): 9–12.
77. See, for example, Barnardo's *Annual Report* (1920), 24–25, Barnardo Archive, D239/A3/55, ULLSCA; *Night and Day* (March 1923): back cover photographs of Girls' Village Home. The Girl Guides were first introduced to the Girls' Village Home in 1920.
78. Vice Chairman W. Elliott, quoted in *Ashford School Magazine* (August 1906): back cover inset, WLSD 472, LMA.
79. Eighteenth-century charities also tended to emphasize military service as a means to incorporate poor children into the nation. See Andrew, *Philanthropy and Police*, esp. 109–15.
80. See Cunningham, *Children of the Poor*, 190–217, 228; Harry Hendrick, *Child Welfare: England, 1872–1989* (London and New York: Routledge, 1994), 41–42.
81. *For God and Country, Some Useful Citizens in the Making: Under One Flag, Dr. Barnardo's Homes 45th Annual Report, year 1910*, 18, Dr. Barnardo's Homes, Correspondence and papers, 1911–22, A/FWA/C/D10/9, LMA.
82. See Barnardo's, *Annual Report* (1905), Barnardo Archive, D239/A3/40, ULLSCA.
83. Ashford school song, by Holcombe Ingleby, *Ashford School Magazine* (July 1906): front cover inset, WLSD 472, LMA.
84. See Heathorn, "'Let us remember,'" 408.
85. See, for example, letter from H. Latham, bandsman, *Ashford School Magazine* (October 1906): back cover inset, WLSD 472, LMA; letter from sisters of Thomas Lester, *Ashford School Magazine* (October 1917): cover inset, WLSD 482, LMA; Harding, *East End Underworld*, 68, 74; letter from a mother of two Barnardo boys, *Night and Day* (October 1915): 56.
86. See West London School District, *Annual Report of the Board of Managers: Statement of Accounts . . .* (1888–93), WLSD 142–47, LMA. Other positions were: barber (one), butcher (one), clerk/office boy (three), coach builder (one), dairy boy (three), farm/gardener (four), farrier (one), grocer (two), printer (two), and telegraph boy (one). For later placement data, see West London School District Service Register (1898–1923), WLSD 434, LMA.
87. Kensington and Chelsea School District, *Second Report of the Managers . . . 1884*, 10, and *Third Report of the Managers . . . 1890*, 10, KCSD 201, LMA.
88. Kensington and Chelsea School District, *Second Report of the Managers . . . 1884*, 10; *Third Report of the Managers . . . 1890*, 10; *The Fourth Report of the Managers of the Kensington and Chelsea School District in Respect of Their Schools at Banstead and Hammersmith, for the Two Years Ended Michaelmas, 1892* (London: J. W. Wakeham, 1892), 21; *Fifth Report of the Managers . . . 1895*, 32; *Sixth Report of the Managers . . . 1899*, 47, KCSD 201, LMA.
89. Kensington and Chelsea School District, *Seventh Report of the Managers . . . 1905*, 23, KCSD 201, LMA. Also see annual reports of the Local Government Board, which contain data for all of London, but are not as detailed as individual school district reports.
90. Kensington and Chelsea School District, *Seventh Report of the Managers . . . 1905*, 21, KCSD 201, LMA.
91. "Return of the Local Government Board showing the nature of the employments in which children chargeable to each union or parish were placed, during the year

1884, after education in a pauper school," *Local Government Board: Fourteenth Report, 1884–85*, PP (1884–85) xxxii, Appendix E, no. 59, 182.

92. *Local Government Board: Twenty-fifth Report*, quoted in Chance, *Children under the Poor Law*, 285.
93. Tufnell (20 P.L.B., 134), quoted in Chance, *Children under the Poor Law*, 87–8.
94. Letter from Mrs. Manning, discussed in Kensington and Chelsea School District, Minutes of the Proceedings of the Managers (December 16, 1879), 332, KCSD 1, LMA.
95. See West London School District, Education Committee Reports (April 19, 1912), and "Report of the Sub-Committee on Technical Training of Boys" (April 18, 1913), WLSD 85, LMA; Minutes of the Board of Managers, recommendation of the Education Committee (April 28, 1916), WLSD 29/1, LMA.
96. Order of June 15, 1892, *Local Government Board, Twenty-second Report*, quoted in Chance, *Children under the Poor Law*, 249.
97. Kensington and Chelsea School District, Chairman's Report upon the progress made at the schools during the year ended March 1909, KCSD 173, LMA.
98. Letter from Local Government Board (July 20, 1918), discussed in West London School District, Ashford, Minutes of the Board of Managers (July 26, 1918), WLSD 29/3, LMA.
99. West London School District, Ashford, Minutes of the Board of Managers, Education Committee Report (September 20, 1918), WLSD 29/3, LMA.
100. West London School District, Ashford, Minutes of the Board of Managers, Education Committee Report (January 29, 1915), WLSD 28/3, LMA.
101. Fenn, *Burning of the "Goliath."*
102. Letter from H. Latham, *Ashford School Magazine* (October 1906): back cover inset, WLSD 472, LMA.
103. West London School District, Ashford, Minutes of the Board of Managers (September 19 and October 24, 1919), WLSD 29/4, LMA.
104. See Barnardo's, *Annual Report* (1896), 100, Barnardo Archive, D239/A3/31, ULLSCA; Kensington and Chelsea School District, *Second Report of the Managers . . . 1884*, 10; *Third Report of the Managers . . . 1890*, 10; *Fourth Report of the Managers . . . 1892*, 21; *Fifth Report of the Managers . . . 1895*, 32; *Sixth Report of the Managers . . . 1899*, 47, KCSD 201, LMA; West London School District Service Register (1898–1923), WLSD 434, LMA.
105. Forest Gate School District, *Annual Reports of Managers, Including Report of the Association for Befriending Young Servants*, report for H.M. (Poplar, 1893), FGSD 19, LMA.
106. See for example Forest Gate School District, *Annual Reports of Managers, Including Report of the Association for Befriending Young Servants*, reports for H.M., M.D., E.G., and F.J. (Poplar, 1894), and reports for E.S. and M.I. (Whitechapel, 1894), FGSD 19, LMA.
107. West London School District (Ashford), Metropolitan Association for Befriending Young Servants (MABYS), *Annual Reports*, Maria Poole, Secretary, report for Annie Towle (1891), WLSD 459, LMA. Also see Forest Gate School District, *Annual Reports of Managers, Including Report of the Association for Befriending Young Servants*, report for M.R. (Poplar, 1888), FGSD 19, LMA.
108. Forest Gate School District, *Annual Reports of Managers, Including Report of the Association for Befriending Young Servants*, report for A.D. (Whitechapel, 1888),

FGSD 19, LMA. Also see report for M.G. (Poplar, 1888), who worked at Bryant and May's factory, FGSD 19, LMA.

109. Forest Gate School District, *Annual Reports of Managers, Including Report of the Association for Befriending Young Servants*, reports for H.B. (Whitechapel, 1890), A.B. (Whitechapel, 1890), E.S. (Poplar, 1892), A.S. (Poplar, 1897), FGSD 19, LMA.

110. West London School District (Ashford), MABYS, *Annual Reports*, Maria Poole, Secretary, reports for Margaret Murphy (1886) and Ada Wilson (1898), WLSD 459, LMA.

111. See, for example, Forest Gate School District, *Annual Reports of Managers, Including Report of the Association for Befriending Young Servants*, report for R.L. (Whitechapel, 1892) for tailoring; report for C.C. (Whitechapel, 1892) for shoemaking and (1893) tailoring; report for J.S. (Poplar, 1892) for machine work; report for E.H. (Poplar, 1894) for bookbinding; report for E.F. (Poplar, 1894) for tailoring; report for E.S. (Whitechapel, 1895) for shop work; report for G.B. (Poplar, 1895) for bookbinding; report for E.J. (Poplar, 1896) for work in a jam factory; report for M.I. (Whitechapel, 1896) for work in a restaurant, FGSD 19, LMA; West London School District (Ashford), MABYS, *Annual Reports*, Maria Poole, Secretary, report for Ada Carter (1895) for accounting in a shop, WLSD 459, LMA.

112. West London School District (Ashford), MABYS, *Annual Reports*, Maria Poole, Secretary, reports for Alice Coleman (1891, 1892, 1893), WLSD 459, LMA. For a description of earlier London water shows, see Richard D. Altick, *The Shows of London* (Cambridge, MA: Harvard University Press, 1978), 77–80.

113. Letter from Annie Warren (July 23, 1906), *Ashford School Magazine* (September 1906): back cover inset, WLSD 472, LMA.

CHAPTER 6 *"Their Charge and Ours"*

1. "Their Charge and Ours," Barnardo's 52nd *Annual Report* (1917): 12–13, Barnardo Archive, D239/A3/52, ULLSCA. The image later appeared in *Night and Day*.

2. The before-and-after contrasts do not disappear, although they become less common. The juxtaposition of the "Dreadful Past" with the "Delightful Present" was used as late as 1918 in the film *From Cradle to Citizenship*.

3. *Night and Day* (October 1914): front cover. There were no issues printed between June and October. The new *Night and Day* cover was very similar to the one used on annual reports beginning in 1908.

4. Gullace, *"Blood of Our Sons,"* 7. Also see Neal McCrillis, *The British Conservative Party in the Age of Universal Suffrage* (Columbus: Ohio State University Press, 1998), 18, and Martin Pugh, *Electoral Reform in War and Peace, 1906–18* (London: Routledge and Kegan Paul, 1978). Gullace (4) rightly stresses that the 1918 Representation of the People Act also disenfranchised conscientious objectors.

5. Gullace, *"Blood of Our Sons,"* 4.

6. See, for example, the June 14, 1915, admission order for Henry Winger, whose father was interned and whose mother continued to live in Pimlico. Both parents were members of the Church of England. Kensington and Chelsea School District, *Select Samples of Children's Workhouse School Admission and Discharge Orders*, KCSD 282, LMA.

7. West London School District, Ashford, Minutes of the Board of Managers (July 26, 1918), WLSD 29/3, LMA.

8. Executive Committee, Committee Minutes (September 29, 1915), Council Papers, Barnardo Archive, D239/B3/121, ULLSCA.

9. "Little Air Raid Victims," *Night and Day* (December 1917): 59.

10. *Night and Day* (December 1916): 49; "How are Dr. Barnardo's Homes Helping to Win the War?" *Night and Day* (December 1917): 52; Council Minutes including information on individual children and residency statistics (June 20, 1917), 221, and (October 15, 1919), 388, Council Papers, Barnardo Archive, D239/B1/7, ULLSCA.

11. Barnardo's *Annual Reports*, Barnardo Archive, D239/A3/49–51, ULLSCA. Records for 1917, 1918, and 1919 are unavailable.

12. Director's Report, Council Minutes including information on individual children and residency statistics (June 21, 1916), 161, Council Papers, Barnardo Archive, D239/B1/7, ULLSCA.

13. *Night and Day* (December 1916): 49.

14. West London School District, Ashford, Visiting Committee Report, Minutes of the Board of Managers (January 29 and May 21, 1915), WLSD 28/3, LMA.

15. Kensington and Chelsea School District, Minutes of the Proceedings of the Managers (December 4, 1914), vol. 13, KCSD 26, LMA; *Times*, as quoted in *Night and Day* (March 1915): 7.

16. West London School District, Ashford, Minutes of the Board of Managers (November 20, 1914), WLSD 28/2, LMA.

17. Executive Committee, Committee Minutes (September 29, 1915, and April 12, 1916), Council Papers, Barnardo Archive, D239/B3/121, ULLSCA; *Night and Day* (December 1915): 67–68.

18. West London School District, Ashford, Minutes of the Board of Managers (October 14, 1914, and January 4, 1915), WLSD 28/2, 3, LMA.

19. Higginbotham, "Unmarried Mother and Her Child," xii, 84–85, 168–69, 306ff.

20. Barnardo's *Annual Report* (1892), 19, Barnardo Archive, D239/A3/27, ULLSCA. Also see the *Annual Reports* for 1893–96, Barnardo Archive, D239/A3/28–31, ULLSCA. The Auxiliary Boarding-Out program involved from 100 to 180 children each year in the 1890s. It appears to have declined in the late 1890s for lack of funding, but continued and even expanded in the first decades of the twentieth century. See Barnardo's *Annual Report* (1918), 7, (1920), 13, (1921), 12, Barnardo Archive, D239/A3/53, 55, 56, ULLSCA; Flower, *Boy Who Did Grow Up*, 164–74.

21. Higginbotham, "Unmarried Mother and Her Child," 165.

22. See Deborah Dwork, *War Is Good for Babies and Other Young Children* (London and New York: Tavistock Publications, 1987); Karen Offen, "Depopulation, Nationalism, and Feminism in Fin-de-Siècle France," *American Historical Review* 89 (1984): 649–50; Jay M. Winter and Michael S. Teitelbaum, *The Fear of Population Decline* (New York: Academic Press, 1985). Similar eighteenth-century concerns about England's population and military encouraged charitable support of maternity hospitals and foundling homes. See Andrew, *Philanthropy and Police*, 54–57.

23. Hendrick, *Child Welfare*, 93–103.

24. A number of wartime child welfare groups reported that nine British soldiers and twelve infants died every hour. See "Britain's Greatest Need: The Child

[Barnardo's Appeal]," *Times*, December 17, 1917, 1; J. Cossar Ewart, "The Saving of Child Life," *Nineteenth Century and After* 82 (1917): 118; Mary Scharleib, "The Nation's Children and Our Duty Towards Them," *Nineteenth Century and After* 81 (1917): 1278.

25. A. M. Richardson, "The Professional Classes, the War, and the Birth-Rate," *Nineteenth Century and After* 77 (1915): 603.
26. Robert McNeill, as quoted in "War Babies: Mr. M'Neill and 'An Emergency Question,'" *Observer*, April 18, 1915, 15. Also see Arthur Marwick, *The Deluge: British Society and the First World War* (London: Bodley Head, 1965), 107–9.
27. "War Babies," *Observer*, May 2, 1915, 12. See Behlmer, *Friends of the Family*, 302.
28. McNeill, as quoted in "Moral Problem of the 'War Baby,'" *Literary Digest* 50 (May 22, 1915): 1220.
29. See, for example, "The Unmarried Mother," *Times*, April 22, 1915, 7; "War Morality and the Rights of War-Mothers and War-Babies," *Current Opinion* 59 (July 1915): 44; E. Brown Rowlands, "Legitimation by Subsequent Marriage," *Fortnightly Review* 107 (1917): 514–24. The 1926 act legalizing adoption allowed unmarried mothers to legitimate their children by adopting them. See Behlmer, *Friends of the Family*, 307.
30. "The Unmarried Mother: State of the Law," *Times*, April 20, 1915, 4.
31. Annie E. Barnes, "The Unmarried Mother and Her Child," *Contemporary Review* 112 (November 1917): 557.
32. See Dwork, *War Is Good for Babies*.
33. Angela Woollacott, *On Her Their Lives Depend: Munitions Workers in the Great War* (Berkeley: University of California Press, 1994), 77–78.
34. Higginbotham, "Unmarried Mother and Her Child," 74, 166, 291–93; Woollacott, *On Her Their Lives Depend*, 77.
35. Higginbotham, "Unmarried Mother and Her Child," 293.
36. Council Minutes including information on individual children and residency statistics (April 21, 1915), vol. 5, Council Papers, Barnardo Archive, D239/B1/7, ULLSCA.
37. "The Babies and 'The One Thing Needful,'" *Night and Day* (June 1918): 27; Flower, *Boy Who Did Grow Up*, 164–65, 227–29.
38. Flower, *Boy Who Did Grow Up*, 224–25. On the wartime growth of crèches, see Higginbotham, "Unmarried Mother and Her Child," 291–93.
39. For example, see Executive Committee, Committee Minutes (December 1, 1915; December 12, 1917; January 2, February 27, March 6, 13, April 10, 1918), Council Papers, Barnardo Archive, D239/B3/121, ULLSCA; Council Minutes including information on individual children and residency statistics (December 15, 1915; December 19, 1917; January 23, February 20, March 20, April 14, October 16, 1918; January 19, March 19, 1919), vol. 5, Council Papers, Barnardo Archive, D239/B1/7, ULLSCA. On Vickers, see Woollacott, *On Her Their Lives Depend*, 29, 50–52.
40. "Crèches and Day Nurseries," *Night and Day* (March 1918): 2; *Night and Day* (June 1918): 19; "Mothers Who Are Working on Munitions—And Their Babies," *Night and Day* (December 1918): 56–58; *Night and Day* (March 1919): 67; Council Minutes including information on individual children and residency statistics (October 16, 1918), vol. 5, Council Papers, Barnardo Archive, D239/B1/7, ULLSCA.

41. Barnardo's *Annual Report* (1918), 6, Barnardo Archive, D239/A3/53, ULLSCA. By the summer of 1920, however, the charity had closed all of its crèches except for the Marie Hilton Crèche in Stepney. At the same time, it shifted back to prewar policies concerning unmarried mothers and expanded the Auxiliary Boarding-Out program. See Council Minutes including information on individual children and residency statistics (March 19, 1919), 340, Council Papers, Barnardo Archive, D239/B1/7, ULLSCA; Barnardo's *Annual Report* (1919), 7, (1920), 13, 17, and (1921), 12, Barnardo Archive, D239/A3/54–56, ULLSCA.
42. "Somebody's Bairns.—XXI," *Night and Day* (June 1916): 27.
43. "Somebody's Bairns.—XXII," *Night and Day* (December 1916): 61.
44. See, for example, installments 21–23 of "Somebody's Bairns," in *Night and Day* (June 1916): 27, (December 1916): 61, and (March 1917): 11.
45. See, for example, "The Story of Private Banks," *Night and Day* (March 1917): 12–13; "Victims of War," *Night and Day* (June 1917): 29; "How Are Dr. Barnardo's Homes Helping to Win the War?" *Night and Day* (December 1917): 52–53; Flower, *Boy Who Did Grow Up*, 127, 156, 159–61. For discussion of an actual case history, see Executive Committee, Committee Minutes (June 14, 1916), Council Papers, Barnardo Archive, D239/B3/121, ULLSCA.
46. "How Are Dr. Barnardo's Homes Helping to Win the War?" *Night and Day* (December 1917): 52.
47. "War Babies: Women's Conference in London," *Times*, April 23, 1915, 5. Also see Barnes, "Unmarried Mother and Her Child," 558; and "The Unmarried Mother," *Observer*, April 18, 1915, 7.
48. Council Minutes including information on individual children and residency statistics (June 20, 1917), 221, vol. 5, Council Papers, Barnardo Archive, 239/B1/7, ULLSCA (emphasis in original).
49. *Child Life: The Nation's Greatest Asset* (n.p., [ca. 1915]), 3, 5 (emphasis in original), copy available in Barnardo Archive, ULLSCA.
50. *Night and Day* (June 1917): 27.
51. "Our Hero Boys," *Night and Day* (June 1920): 149.
52. Barnardo's *Annual Report* (1919), 9, Barnardo Archive, D239/A3/54, ULLSCA.
53. *Fair Play* (n.p., n.d.), 7, Barnardo Archive, ULLSCA; "A War-Time Record," *Night and Day* (December 1918): 49.
54. Barnardo's *Annual Report* (1914), 4, Barnardo Archive, D239/A3/49, ULLSCA.
55. For records of youths leaving the Ashford District School, see the West London School District Service Register, WLSD 434, LMA.
56. *Ashford School Magazine* (December 1918): cover inset, and (August 1919): cover inset, WLSD 483–84, LMA.
57. Executive Committee, Committee Minutes (July 4, 1917), Council Papers, Barnardo Archive, D239/B3/121, ULLSCA.
58. *Night and Day* (March 1915): 7, 10.
59. Council Minutes including information on individual children and residency statistics (February 17, 1915), 57–59, vol. 5, Council Papers, Barnardo Archive, D239/B1/7, ULLSCA; Flower, *Boy Who Did Grow Up*, 29.
60. See, for example, the memorial plans at Barnardo's institutions and the Ashford and Banstead poor law schools. *Night and Day* (June 1920): 148; *Ashford School Magazine* (August 1919): cover inset, WLSD 484, LMA; Kensington and Chelsea

School District, Special Committee Book, Meeting of the Memorial Committee (April 22 and November 1920), KCSD 126, LMA.

61. Education Committee Report, Minutes of the Board of Managers (January 3, 1919), West London School District, Ashford, WLSD 29/4, LMA.
62. Letter from Lance Corporal Alfred Twelftree, *Ashford School Magazine* (November 1915): cover inset, WLSD 481, LMA.
63. Letter from Private James Kerr, published in *Night and Day* (June 1915): 29.
64. Letter from Private Frederick Wyatt, *Ashford School Magazine* (November 1915): back cover inset, WLSD 481, LMA.
65. *Ashford School Magazine* (July 1917): cover inset, WLSD 482, LMA.
66. *Ashford School Magazine* (October 1917): cover inset, WLSD 482, LMA.
67. "Jottings from Our Annals—XVIII," *Night and Day* (March 1917): 6. This letter from Private John Shepheard was reprinted in the October 1917 issue of *Night and Day*. Also see the letter from Corporal Arthur Wheelhouse, *Night and Day* (March 1915): 15.
68. Letter from John A. Roberts, *Ashford School Magazine* (April 1917): cover inset, WLSD 482, LMA.
69. Letter from Private C. Francis, *Ashford School Magazine* (August 1915): cover inset, WLSD 481, LMA.
70. Letter from Lance Corporal F. Ivey, *Ashford School Magazine* (August 1917): cover inset, WLSD 482, LMA.
71. West London School District, Ashford, Superintendent's Report, "Behaviour of the Children," in Minutes of the Board of Managers (September 22, 1916), WLSD 29/1, LMA.
72. See, for example, the complaints against Mr. Edmeads, the temporary chargemaster at Ashford, who admitted to striking a boy, in West London School District, Ashford, Superintendent's Report (September 22, 1916), WLSD 29/1, LMA; Mrs. Prince's complaint forwarded to Ashford from the Fulham Board of Guardians that Mr. Ellson, the temporary assistant chargemaster, boxed her son on the ear, Minutes of the Board of Managers (October 25 and 27, 1916), WLSD 29/1, LMA; and a mother's complaints forwarded from the City of Westminster Board of Guardians concerning the abuse of her three sons, William, Arthur, and Harry Payne, at Ashford, Minutes of the Board of Managers (June 28, 1918), WLSD 29/3, LMA.
73. West London School District, Ashford, Education Committee Report, Minutes of the Board of Managers (November 24, 1916, and March 23, 1917), WLSD 29/1–2, LMA; Visiting Committee Report, Minutes of the Board of Managers (December 21, 1917), WLSD 29/2, LMA.
74. Kensington and Chelsea Branch School [Marlesford Lodge, Hammersmith], Agnes McEwen, Superintendent, Superintendent's Report and Journal (October 5, 1917), KCSD 301, LMA.
75. On food rationing, see, for example, Kensington and Chelsea School District Dietary (1891–1922), notes for June 1915, when the managers decided to reduce the meat budget for Banstead by 25 percent, KCSD 186, LMA. On influenza in the schools, see West London School District, Minutes of the Board of Managers (July 26, November 22, December 6, 1918, and January 3, 1919), WLSD 29/3, LMA.
76. J. Victor H. Reade, *Ashford School Magazine* (January 1915): cover inset, WLSD 481, LMA.

77. Letter from J. Victor H. Reade, *Ashford School Magazine* (January 1918): cover inset, WLSD 483, LMA.
78. West London School District, Ashford, Superintendent's Report, "Behaviour of the Children," Minutes of the Board of Managers (September 22, 1916), WLSD 29/1, LMA.
79. West London School District, Ashford, Education Committee, submitting the Superintendent's Report, Minutes of the Board of Managers (October 13, 1916), WLSD 29/1, LMA.
80. West London School District, Ashford, Education Committee, submitting the Superintendent's Report, Minutes of the Board of Managers (October 29, 1916), WLSD 29/1, LMA.
81. See, for example, the cases of the mothers of Edgar and Fredrick Wood and Edward Sowden, who returned their children to Marlesford Lodge; Kensington and Chelsea Branch School [Marlesford Lodge, Hammersmith], Agnes McEwen, Superintendent, Superintendent's Report and Journal (January 7, February 18, 25, March 3, 16, 1916), KCSD 301, LMA.
82. Kensington and Chelsea Branch School [Marlesford Lodge, Hammersmith], Agnes McEwen, Superintendent, Superintendent's Report and Journal (October 5, 1916), KCSD 301, LMA.
83. West London School District, Ashford, Extract from Superintendent's Report Book, in Special Committees (1916), 234, WLSD 96, LMA.
84. J. R. Mozley, inspector of poor law schools, Ashford Visitors' Book (October 30, 1896), WLSD 118, LMA. Mozley wrote, "The point that needs most attention is the intonation of the girls, when they answer questions. . . . They should be made to feel that a wrong answer spoken out with firmness and precision is for the most part better than a right one spoken under the breath and inaudibly—On occasions, they should be encouraged to ask questions themselves; this will tend to cure shyness."
85. West London School District, Ashford, Extract from Superintendent's Report Book, in Special Committees (1916), 234, WLSD 96, LMA.
86. See, for example, West London School District, Ashford, Visiting Committee Report, in Minutes of the Board of Managers (March 24, 1916), WLSD 29/1, LMA; Superintendent's Report and Medical Officer's Report, in Minutes of the Board of Managers (April 14, 1916), WLSD 29/1; Visiting Committee Report on receipt of Medical Officer Report, in Minutes of the Board of Managers (July 28, 1916), WLSD 29/1; Visiting Committee Report on receipt of Medical Officer reports, in Minutes of the Board of Managers (July 27, 1917), WLSD 29/2; Medical Officer (C. Batchelor) Report on Incontinence (October 18, 1917), in Visiting Committee Report, in Minutes of the Board of Managers (October 26, 1917), WLSD 29/2; Visiting Committee Report (November 16, 1917), in Minutes of the Board of Managers (November 23, 1917), WLSD 29/2; Report of the Superintendent within the Education Committee Report, in Minutes of the Board of Managers (March 22, 1917), WLSD 29/3; Report of the Ladies Committee with Reference to Wet-Beds, in Minutes of the Board of Managers (March 22, 1918), WLSD 29/3; Superintendent's Report, "Cases of Incontinence," in Minutes of the Board of Managers (April 26, 1918), WLSD 29/3; Ladies' Committee Report (July 22, 1918), in Minutes of the Board of Managers (July 26, 1918), WLSD 29/3; Medical Officer Report and discussion of incontinent children, Minutes of the Board of Managers (November 22, 1918), WLSD 29/3; and Ladies'

Committee Report, in Minutes of the Board of Managers (May 23, 1919), WLSD
29/4.

87. West London School District, Ashford, Minutes of the Board of Managers
(November 23, 1917), WLSD 29/2, LMA.

88. West London School District, Ashford, Medical Officer (C. Batchelor) Report
(October 18, 1917), in Visiting Committee Report, in Minutes of the Board of
Managers (October 26, 1917), WLSD 29/2, LMA. The medical officer estimated
that of the 119 cases, "21 girls, 9 senior boys, and 13 junior boys may be considered as bad cases." He did not find an immediate physical cause: "Enlarged tonsils
and adenoids are said to be an exciting cause of incontinence, but I was surprised
to find but a very small proportion of these cases."

89. West London School District, Ashford, Superintendent's Report, "Cases of
Incontinence," in Minutes of the Board of Managers (April 26, 1918), WLSD 29/3,
LMA.

90. West London School District, Ashford, "Report of the Ladies Committee with
Reference to Wet-Beds," in Minutes of the Board of Managers (March 22, 1918),
WLSD 29/3, LMA.

91. Ibid.

92. West London School District, Ashford, Punishment Log Books (November 1918),
2 vols., 1872–1934, WLSD 438, LMA. The same boy repeated similar acts twice
in February 1919 and several times in 1920.

93. See, for example, West London School District, Ashford, Punishment Log Books
(May 1918), 2 vols., 1872–1934, WLSD 438, LMA.

94. West London School District, Ashford, "Report of the Ladies Committee with
Reference to Wet-Beds," in Minutes of the Board of Managers (March 22, 1918),
WLSD 29/3, LMA.

95. West London School District, Ashford, Superintendent's Report, in Education
Committee Report, in Minutes of the Board of Managers (March 22, 1918),
WLSD 29/3, LMA.

96. West London School District, Ashford, Visiting Committee, in Minutes of the
Board of Managers (November 23, 1917), WLSD 29/2, LMA.

97. West London School District, Ashford, Superintendent's Report, "Cases of
Incontinence," in Minutes of the Board of Managers (April 26, 1918), WLSD 29/3,
LMA.

98. West London School District, Ashford, "Report of the Ladies Committee with
Reference to Wet-Beds," in Minutes of the Board of Managers (March 22, 1918),
WLSD 29/3, LMA. Also see Ladies' Committee Reports, in Minutes of the Board
of Managers (July 26, 1918, and May 23, 1919), WLSD 29/3–4, LMA.

99. West London School District, Ashford, Medical Reports of Children in Band by
Peter W. de la Motte (November 29, 1912), in West London School District
Education Committee Reports, WLSD 85, LMA.

100. See, for example, "The Treatment of Incontinence of Urine," *Lancet* (September 3,
1904): 739; "The Treatment of Enuresis," *Lancet* (July 29, 1905): 322;
"Manchester Medical Society," *Lancet* (March 20, 1909): 841; "Treatment of
Nocturnal Incontinence of Urine," *Lancet* (October 2, 1909): 1036; Samuel Sloan,
"Electro-Therapeutics in Gynaecology," *Lancet* (February 5, 1910): 347–53; F.
Hernaman-Johnson, "The Treatment of Urinary Incontinence by Electrical

Methods," *Lancet* (June 18, 1921): 1295–96; Mary O'Brien Beadon, "A Note on a Case of Enuresis Treated by Electricity," *Lancet* (February 10, 1923): 283.

101. The Ashford superintendent listed lycopodium as one of the common treatments in 1916, and the school medical officer tried treating special cases with belladonna "without any definite effect" in 1917. See West London School District, Ashford, Superintendent's Report, in Minutes of the Board of Managers (April 14, 1916), WLSD 29/1, LMA; Visiting Committee Report, in Minutes of the Board of Managers (July 27, 1917), WLSD 29/2, LMA. On the various drugs used to treat incontinence, see, for example, "The Treatment of Incontinence of Urine in Children," *Lancet* (October 30, 1897): 1133–34; Leonard Williams, "Adenoids, Nocturnal Incontinence, and the Thyroid Gland," *Lancet* (May 1, 1909): 1245–47; A.C.D. Firth, "Enuresis and Thyroid Extract," *Lancet* (December 9, 1911): 1619–21; W. H. Slingerland, *A Child Welfare Problem: The Care and Cure of Enuresis or Bedwetting in Child-Caring Institutions* (New York: Department of Child-Helping, Russell Sage Foundation, 1917), 6.

102. West London School District, Ashford, Superintendent's Report, in Minutes of the Board of Managers (April 14, 1916), WLSD 29/1, LMA.

103. West London School District, Ashford, Visiting Committee Report, in Minutes of the Board of Managers (March 24, 1916), WLSD 29/1, LMA; Minutes of the Board of Managers (April 14, 1916), WLSD 29/1, LMA.

104. West London School District, Ashford, Medical Officer Report, in Visiting Committee Reports, in Minutes of the Board of Managers (July 27, 1917), WLSD 29/2, LMA; Report of the Superintendent, in Education Committee Report, in Minutes of the Board of Managers (March 22, 1918), WLSD 29/3, LMA.

105. West London School District, Ashford, Education Committee Report, in Minutes of the Board of Managers (March 22, 1918), WLSD 29/3, LMA.

106. West London School District, Ashford, Punishment Log Books (April–September 1918), 2 vols., 1872–1934, WLSD 438, LMA.

107. West London School District, Ashford, "Report of the Ladies Committee with Reference to Wet-Beds," in Minutes of the Board of Managers (March 22, 1918), WLSD 29/3, LMA.

108. West London School District, Ashford, Ladies' Committee Report, in Minutes of the Board of Managers (July 26, 1918), WLSD 29/3, LMA.

109. West London School District, Ashford, Superintendent's Report, in Minutes of the Board of Managers (April 26, 1918), WLSD 29/3, LMA.

110. Ibid.

111. West London School District, Ashford, Ladies' Committee Report, in Minutes of the Board of Managers (May 23, 1919), WLSD 29/4, LMA.

112. In 1926, after visiting Ashford, the Inspection Committee reported: "We noted that several little boys had on smocks in the school and were told that they had been put on as a punishment by Mr. Hanbury for wetting their beds. We believe the Managers decided some time ago, on principle, that such differential punishment should not be given." Reports and Letters of the Visiting Committee to Ashford and Park Schools (November 5, 1926), 2–3, WLSD 450, LMA.

113. E. E. Southard, *Shell-Shock and Other Neuropsychiatric Problems Presented in Five Hundred and Eighty-Nine Case Histories* (Boston: W. M. Leonard, 1919), 476, 719. For cases of soldiers suffering from incontinence, see W.H.R. Rivers,

"The Repression of War Experience," *Lancet* (February 2, 1918): 173–77, and Southard, *Shell-Shock*, 63, 78–79, 476, 536, 561, 705, 806–7.

114. *Index to the Surgeon General's Library*, 2nd ser. (1914), 319–26, and 3rd ser. (1936), 869–72.

115. Committee of the Whole Board on Discipline and Administration of District Schools, in Minutes of the Board of Managers (February 2, 1917), WLSD 29/2, LMA.

116. For reports describing incontinence as stemming from a lack of will power, see, for example, the Superintendent's Report, in Minutes of the Board of Managers (April 14, 1916), WLSD 29/1, LMA; "Report of the Ladies Committee with Reference to Wet-Beds," in Minutes of the Board of Managers (March 22, 1918), WLSD 29/3, LMA; Superintendent's Report, in Minutes of the Board of Managers (April 26, 1918), WLSD 29/3, LMA; Ladies' Committee Report, in Minutes of the Board of Managers (July 26, 1918), WLSD 29/3, LMA.

117. Admiral Stileman, quoted in Rose, *For the Sake of the Children*, 75.

Conclusion

1. Barnardo's still continued to separate children from their parents until after the Second World War. The society's twentieth-century policies were actually more successful at separating parents and children, because the children tended to be admitted at a younger age for long-term stays.

2. "A Public Funeral," *National Waifs' Magazine* (October 1905): 49.

BIBLIOGRAPHY

Special Collections and Archives

Barnardo Photographic and Film Archive, Barkingside, Essex (BPFA)
Barnardo Library, Barkingside, Essex
British Library
Colindale Newspaper Library
Lilly Library, Bloomington, Indiana
London Metropolitan Archives (LMA)
National Archive, Kew, Surrey (NA)
National Sound Archive, London (NSA)
University College London Archive (UCL)
University of Liverpool Library Special Collections and Archives (ULLSCA)

Parliamentary Papers

PP (1861) vii. *Report from the Select Committee on the Education of Destitute Children; Together with the Proceedings of the Committee, Minutes of Evidence, and Appendix.*

PP (1861) xxi. *Report of the Royal Commission to Inquire into the State of Popular Education in England.*

PP (1862) xlix. *Return from Unions in England and Wales of the Number of Children in Workhouses.*

PP (1878) lx. *Report of F. J. Mouat and Capt. J. D. Bowly, On Home and Cottage System of Training and Educating Children of the Poor.*

PP (1878) lxiv. *Return of the Number of Orphan and Deserted Pauper Children Boarded Out, Jan. 1877, in Unions in England and Wales with the Number of Pauper Children in District Schools.*

PP (1884–85) xxxii. *Local Government Board: Fourteenth Report, 1884–85.*

PP (1896) xliii. *Departmental Committee on Existing Systems for the Maintenance and Education of Children under the Charge of Managers of District Schools and Boards of Guardians in the Metropolis.*

PP (1903) lix. *Return on Cottage Homes.*

Periodicals

All the Year Round
Ashford School Magazine
British Medical Journal

Chambers's Journal
Contemporary Review
Cornhill Magazine
The Courier and East London Advertiser
Current Opinion
The East End News and Advertiser
East London Observer
Fortnightly Review
Fraser's Magazine
Good Words
Good Words for the Young
Illustrated Police News
The Independent
Journal of the Statistical Society
Lancet
The Literary Digest
Macmillan's Magazine
Night and Day (continued as *National Waifs' Magazine,* June 1899–January 1906)
Nineteenth Century
The Observer
*Our Log Book: A Monthly Record of the National Refuges for Homeless and Destitute
    Children and Training Ships "Arethusa" and "Chichester"*
Pall Mall Gazette
The Police Chronicle
Punch
Review of Reviews
The Standard
The Times
Westminster Review

Published Primary Sources

Antrobus, Edmund Edward. *Training Schools and Training Ships: For the Training of
    Boys for the Navy, Army, and Mercantile Marine.* London: Staunton and Son, 1875.
Aveling, Henry F. *The Boarding-Out System and Legislation Relating to the Protection
    of Children and Infant Life: A Manual for Poor-Law Guardians, Boarding-Out
    Committees, and Practical Workers.* London: Swan Sonnenschein and Co., 1890.
Barlee, Ellen. *Friendless and Helpless.* London: Emily Faithfull, 1863.
———. *Our Homeless Poor; And What We Can Do To Help Them.* London: James
    Nisbet and Co., 1860.
———. *Pantomime Waifs: or, A Plea for Our City Children.* With an Introduction by the
    Earl of Shaftesbury. London: S. W. Partridge and Co., 1884.
Barnardo, Syrie Louise, and Sir James Marchant. *Memoirs of the Late Dr. Barnardo.*
    London: Hodder and Stroughton, 1907.
Barnardo, T. J. *A Brief Account of the Institutions Known as "Dr. Barnardo's Homes."*
    London, 1879.
———. *China-John: or "What's the Good?"* London: Stepney Causeway, 1902.
    Barnardo Library.

———. *A City Waif: How I Fished For and Caught Her.* London: J. F. Shaw and Co., ca. 1886.

———. *Episodes in Humble Lives.* London: J. F. Shaw and Co., ca. 1894. Barnardo Library.

———. *Kidnapped! A Narrative of Fact.* London: J. F. Shaw and Co., ca. 1885.

———. *"The King's Business Requireth Haste": A Year's Work in "Dr. Barnardo's Homes."* London: J. F. Shaw and Co., 1885.

———. *My First Arab; or How I began My Life-Work.* 1888. Reprint, London: Stepney Causeway, 1917. Barnardo Library.

———. *Never Had A Home: A Very Commonplace History.* London: J. F. Shaw and Co., 1890.

———. *The 1/—Baby: An Incident of the London Slave Trade.* London: Stepney Causeway, ca. 1889. Barnardo Library.

———. *Out of an Horrible Pit.* London: J. F. Shaw and Co., ca. 1892. Originally published in *Night and Day* (November 1891): 149–51. Barnardo Library.

———. *Rescued for Life: The True Story of a Young Thief; To Which Is Added the Testimony of Three Bishops and Three Eminent Nonconformists.* London: J. F. Shaw and Co, ca. 1885.

———. *"The Seed of the Righteous" among the Children of the Poorest.* London: J. F. Shaw and Co., ca. 1887. Barnardo Library.

———. *Shipwrecked at Our Doors!* London: Stepney Causeway, n.d. Reprinted as *Suppose Nobody Cared!* (n.d.). Barnardo Library.

———. *"Something Attempted Something Done, Being the Annual Report of Dr. Barnardo's Homes, East End Juvenile Mission."* London: John F. Shaw and Co., 1888.

———. *"Something Attempted, Something Done": Dr. Barnardo's Homes.* London: John F. Shaw and Co., 1889.

———. *"Taken Out of the Gutter": A True Incident of Child Life on the Streets of London.* London: Haughton and Co., ca. 1881. Barnardo Library.

———. *Two Rescues!* London: Stepney Causeway, n.d. Barnardo Library.

———. *Worse Than Orphans: How I Stole Two Girls and Fought for a Boy.* London: J. F. Shaw and Co., ca. 1885.

———. *A Year's Work in the Institution Known as "Dr. Barnardo's Homes."* London: J. F. Shaw and Co., ca. 1884.

Barnardo's. *Child Life: The Nation's Greatest Asset.* N.p., [ca. 1915].

Barnes, Annie E. "The Unmarried Mother and Her Child." *Contemporary Review* 112 (November 1917): 556–559.

Barnett, Henrietta. *Canon Barnett: His Life, Work and Friends.* 2 vols. Boston and New York: Houghton Mifflin Company, 1919.

———. "The Home or the Barrack for the Children of the State?" *Contemporary Review* 66 (1894): 243–58.

Battersby, C. Maud. *Gaspar: or, The Story of a Street Arab.* London: George Cauldwell, 1891.

Booth, William. *In Darkest England and the Way Out.* New York and London: Funk and Wagnalls, 1891.

Brenda [Mrs. G. Castle Smith]. *Froggy's Little Brother.* Illustrated by Cas. London: John F. Shaw and Co., 1875.

Brooks, S. H. *Select Designs for Public Buildings; Consisting of Plans, Elevations, Perspective Views, Sections, and Details, of Churches, Chapels, Schools, Alms-Houses,*

Gas-Works, Markets, and Other Buildings Erected for Public Purposes. London: Thomas Kelly, Paternoster Row, 1842.

Browne, T. H. Murray. *The Education and Future of Workhouse Children: A Paper Read at the West Midland District Poor Law Conference.* London: Knight and Co., 1883.

Chance, William. *Children under the Poor Law: Their Education, Training and After-Care, Together with a Criticism of the Report of the Departmental Committee on Metropolitan Poor Law Schools.* London: S. Sonnenschein and Co., 1897.

Code, George, ed. *"Waifs and Strays": An Old Fable in a . . . New Setting.* London: National Incorporated Waifs' Association (otherwise Dr. Barnardo's Homes), ca. 1901.

Crockett, S. R. *Cleg Kelly: Arab of the City.* London: Smith, Elder, and Co., 1896.

The Cruelty Man: Actual Experiences of an Inspector of the N.S.P.C.C. Graphically Told by Himself. London: National Society for the Prevention of Cruelty to Children, 1912.

Cunynghame, Henry H. *Street Trading by Boys and Girls: A Paper Read at the York Conference on June 3, 1902.* London: Reformatory and Refuge Union, 1902.

De Profundis. *A Plea for Workhouse Children.* Reprinted from *The Month.* With an introduction by Henry Edward, Archbishop of Westminster. London: Burns, Lambert, and Oates, 1866.

Dickens, Charles. *The Adventures of Oliver Twist.* Oxford: Oxford University Press, 1987.

Evans, Eric T., ed. *Social Policy, 1830–1914: Individualism, Collectivism and the Origins of the Welfare State.* London: Routledge and Kegan Paul, 1978.

Fawcett, Millicent Garrett. "The Vaccination Act of 1898." *Contemporary Review* 75 (March 1899): 328–42.

Fegan, J.W.C. *A Plea for Our Street-Arabs: Grace Triumphant, or the Dying Match-Seller.* London: Boys' Home, 1895.

Fenn, R. J. *The Burning of the "Goliath."* London: Shaw and Sons, 1876.

Fisher, Pearl. *The Harvest of the City, and the Workers of To-day.* With an introduction by H. Sinclair Paterson. London: John F. Shaw and Co., 1884.

Flower, Norman. *The Boy Who Did Grow Up.* With an introduction by J. M. Barrie. London, New York, Toronto, and Melbourne: Cassell and Company, Ltd., 1919.

Fredur, Thor. *Sketches from Shady Places.* London: Smith, Elder, and Co., 1879.

Fry, Danby Palmer. *The Boarding Out of Pauper Children: Containing the General Order of the Poor Law Board, and the Accompanying Circular, with Notes and Introduction.* London: Knight and Co., 1870.

Goldsmith, Howard J. *Dottings of a Dosser: Being Revelations of the Inner Life of Low London Lodging-Houses.* London: T. Fisher Unwin, 1886.

Gough, Charles W. (Old Barnardo Boy). *Apprenticeship for Life.* Goldings, Hertford: Dr. Barnardo Press, n.d.

Greenwood, James. *The True History of a Little Ragamuffin.* London: S. O. Beeton, 1866.

Hall, Wilhelmina L. *Boarding-Out, as a Method of Pauper Education and Check on Hereditary Pauperism.* London: Hatchards, 1887.

Harding, Arthur. *East End Underworld: Chapters in the Life of Arthur Harding.* Edited by Raphael Samuel. London, Boston, and Henley: Routledge and Kegan Paul, 1981.

Haw, George. *From Workhouse to Westminster: The Life Story of Will Crooks, M.P.* With an introduction by G. K. Chesterton. London, Paris, New York, and Melbourne: Cassell and Company, Ltd., 1907.

Hill, Florence Davenport. *Children of the State*. 1868. Reprint, London: Macmillan and Co., 1889.

———. "The Family System for Workhouse Children." *Contemporary Review* 15 (1870): 240–73.

Hill, Joanna. *Practical Suggestions for the Use of Associates for the Department for G.F.S. Candidates from Workhouses and Orphanages*. London: Hatchards, 1884.

Holmes, Thomas. *Pictures and Problems from London Police Courts*. London: Edward Arnold, 1900.

Hopkins, Ellice. *"God's Little Girl": A Truthful Narrative of Facts Concerning a Poor "Waif" Admitted into "Dr. Barnardo's Village Home."* London: J. F. Shaw and Co., ca. 1885.

Humble, Richard. *Boarding-Out of Orphan and Deserted Pauper Children versus Workhouse Schools*. Adel, Leeds: n.p., 1883.

Ingestre, Viscount, ed. *Meliora: or, Better Times to Come*. London: John W. Parker and Son, 1852.

Jane Mansel: The Workhouse Girl. London: Society for Promoting Christian Knowledge, 1872.

Keating, Peter, ed. *Into Unknown England, 1866–1913: Selections from the Social Explorers*. Manchester: Manchester University Press; Totowa, N.J.: Rowman and Littlefield, 1976.

"A Lady." *Five Days and Five Nights as a Tramp among Tramps: Social Investigation by A Lady*. With a preface by the Reverend Canon Hicks. Manchester: John Heywood, 1904.

[A Late "Holiday Mother"]. *My Cottage: A Story of Dr. Barnardo's Village Home for Orphan and Destitute Girls*. London: J. F. Shaw and Co., ca. 1885.

Liefde, John de. *Six Months among the Charities of Europe*. 2 vols. London: Alexander Strahan, 1865.

Macpherson, Annie. *The Little London Arabs*. London: Morgan and Chase, 1870.

———. *The Little Matchbox-Makers*. London: Morgan and Chase, 1870.

Marchant, James, ed. *Tales for the Homes*. London: Chatto and Windus, 1907.

Mayhew, Augustus. *Paved with Gold: or The Romance and Reality of the London Streets*. London: Chapman and Hall, 1857.

Mayhew, Henry. *London Labour and the London Poor*. 1861–62. Reprint, London: Penguin Books, 1987.

Mearns, Andrew. *The Bitter Cry of Outcast London with Leading Articles from the "Pall Mall Gazette" of October 1883 and Articles by Lord Salisbury, Joseph Chamberlain, and Forster Crozier*. Edited by Anthony S. Wohl. New York: Humanities Press, 1970.

Mill, John Stuart. *On Liberty*. Edited by Edward Alexander. Toronto: Broadview, 1999.

Mouat, Federic J. "On the Education and Training of Children of the Poor." *Journal of the Statistical Society* 43 (1880): 183–243.

Nisbet, Hume. "The Life of a Waif." In Marchant, ed., *Tales for the Homes*.

Partridge, J. E. *Ragamuffin Tom*. Illustrated by Helen J.A. Miles. London: Wells Gardner, Darton and Co., 1903.

Peek, Francis. "Hereditary Pauperism and Pauper Education." *Contemporary Review* 31 (1877): 133–43.

Phillips, Watts. *The Wild Tribes of London*. London: Ward and Lock, 1855.

The Photography of O. G. Rejlander: Two Selections. Edited by Peter C. Bunnell. New York: Arno Press, 1979.

Pike, G. H. *Children Reclaimed for Life: The Story of Dr. Barnardo's Work in London.* London: Hodder and Stroughton, 1875.

————[“A London Rambler”]. *The Romance of the Streets.* London: Hodder and Stroughton, 1872.

“Rescue the Perishing”: Being the Report for the Ninth Year of the East-End Juvenile Mission, and for the Fifth Year of the Homes for Reclaiming Destitute Children of Both Sexes: A Statement of Accounts, 1874–75. London: Morgan and Scott; Haughton and Co., 1876.

Reynolds, George. *Dr. Barnardo's Homes, Containing Startling Revelations.* London: n.p., 1877.

Robinson, Henry Peach. *The Elements of a Pictorial Photograph.* 1896. Reprint, New York: Arno Press, 1973.

————. *Picture-Making by Photography.* 5th ed., 1897. Reprint, New York: Arno Press, 1973.

Royce, Mary. *Little Scrigget, the Street Arab.* Leicester: J. and T. Spencer, 1875.

Shakesby, Albert. *From Street Arab to Evangelist: The Life Story of Albert Shakesby, a Converted Athlete, by Himself.* Hull: Burtt Brothers, 1910.

Shephard, J. E. *Mahomet, A. J.: From Street Arab to Evangelist.* With a preface by I. W. Ventnor. 2nd. ed. London: W. H. Tomkins, 1885.

Slingerland, W. H. *A Child Welfare Problem: The Care and Cure of Enuresis or Bedwetting in Child-Caring Institutions.* New York: Department of Child-Helping, Russell Sage Foundation, 1917.

Smedley, Menella B. *Boarding-Out and Pauper Schools Especially for Girls: Being a Reprint of the Principal Reports on Pauper Education in the Blue Book for 1873–4.* London: Henry S. King and Co., 1875.

————. “Pauper Homes.” *Good Words* 17 (1876): 48–52.

————. “Workhouse Schools for Girls.” *Macmillan's Magazine* 31 (1874): 27–36.

Snell, H. Saxon. *Charitable and Parochial Establishments.* London: B. T. Batsford, 1881.

Southard, E. E. *Shell-Shock and Other Neuropsychiatric Problems Presented in Five Hundred and Eighty-nine Case Histories.* Boston: W. M. Leonard, 1919.

Stanley, H. M. [Dorothy Tennant]. *London Street Arabs.* London, Paris, and Melbourne: Cassell and Company, Ltd., 1890.

Synnot, Henrietta. “Little Paupers.” *Contemporary Review* 24 (1874): 954–72.

Twining, Louisa. *A Letter on Some Matters of Poor Law Administration.* [Addressed (by Permission) to the Right Hon. the President of the Local Government Board]. London: William Ridgway, 1887.

————. *On the Supervision and Training of Workhouse Girls.* London: Bell and Daldy, 1860.

————. *Recollections of Workhouse Visiting and Management during Twenty-five Years.* London: C. Kegan Paul and Co., 1880.

Tuckwell, Gertrude M. *The State and Its Children.* London: Methuen and Co., 1894.

Tufnell, Edward Carleton. *Observations on the Report of Mrs. Senior to the Local Government Board as to the Effect on Girls of the System of Education at Pauper Schools.* London: George E. Eyre and William Spottiswoode, 1875.

————. *Training of Pauper Children.* London: Eyre and Spottiswoode, 1880.

Webster, Alphonsus W. *Sunday Schools in the Workhouse and Other Institutions for Poor, Neglected, Refractory, and Criminally Disposed Children. A Paper Read at a Conference of the Sunday School Union, May 2, 1894.* London: Sunday School Union, 1894.

Secondary Sources

Abrams, Lynn. *The Orphan Country: Children of Scotland's Broken Homes from 1845 to the Present Day.* Edinburgh: John Donald Publishers, Ltd., 1998.

Alexander, Sally. "Women, Class, and Sexual Differences in the 1830s and 1840s: Some Reflections on the Writing of Feminist History." *History Workshop* 17 (Spring 1984): 125–49.

Adams, Annmarie. *Architecture in the Family Way: Doctors, Houses, and Women.* Montreal: McGill-Queen's University Press, 1996.

Altick, Richard D. *The Shows of London.* Cambridge, MA: Harvard University Press, 1978.

Andrew, Donna T. *Philanthropy and Police: London Charity in the Eighteenth Century.* Princeton: Princeton University Press, 1989.

Arnold, David. *Colonizing the Body: State Medicine and Epidemic Disease in Nineteenth-Century India.* Berkeley: University of California Press, 1993.

Arnstein, Walter. *Protestant versus Catholic in Mid-Victorian England: Mr. Newdegate and the Nuns.* Columbia: University of Missouri Press, 1982.

Baer, Marc. *Theatre and Disorder in Late Georgian London.* Oxford: Clarendon Press, 1992.

Bakhtin, Mikhail. *Rabelais and His World.* Translated by Helene Iswolsky. Cambridge, MA: MIT Press, 1968.

Batt, John Herridge. *Dr. Barnardo: The Foster Father of "Nobody's Children."* London: S. W. Partridge and Co., 1904.

Bean, Philip, and Joy Melville. *Lost Children of the Empire.* London, Sydney, and Wellington: Unwin Hyman, 1989.

Beck, Ann. "Issues in the Anti-Vaccination Movement in England." *Medical History* 4 (December 1960): 310–21.

Behlmer, George K. *Child Abuse and Moral Reform in England, 1870–1908.* Stanford: Stanford University Press, 1982.

———. *Friends of the Family: The English Home and Its Guardians, 1850–1940.* Stanford: Stanford University Press, 1998.

Berry, Laura C. *The Child, the State, and the Victorian Novel.* Charlottesville: University Press of Virginia, 1999.

Biagini, Eugenio F., and Alastair J. Reid, eds. *Currents of Radicalism: Popular Radicalism, Organised Labour and Party Politics in Britain, 1850–1914.* Cambridge: Cambridge University Press, 1991.

Booth, Michael R. *English Melodrama.* London: Herbert Jenkins, 1965.

Bready, J. Wesley. *Doctor Barnardo: Physician, Pioneer, Prophet.* London: G. Allen and Unwin, 1930.

Bratton, Jacky, Jim Cook, and Christine Gledhill, eds. *Melodrama: Stage, Picture, Screen.* London: British Film Institute, 1994.

Brooks, Peter. "Melodrama, Body, Revolution." In Bratton, Cook, and Gledhill, eds., *Melodrama: Stage, Picture, Screen,* 11–24.

———. *The Melodramatic Imagination: Balzac, Henry James, Melodrama, and the Mode of Excess.* New Haven and London: Yale University Press, 1976.

Burton, Antoinette. *At the Heart of the Empire: Indians and the Colonial Encounter in Late-Victorian Britain.* Berkeley: University of California Press, 1998.

Cannadine, David. *The Rise and Fall of Class in Britain.* New York: Columbia University Press, 1999.

Charon, Rita. "To Build a Case: Medical Histories as Traditions in Conflict." *Literature and Medicine* 11, no. 1 (Spring 1992): 115–32.

Clark, Anna. "The Politics of Seduction in English Popular Culture, 1748–1848." In *The Progress of Romance: The Politics of Popular Fiction,* edited by Jean Radford, 47–70. London: Routledge and Kegan Paul, 1986.

———. "Queen Caroline and the Sexual Politics of Popular Culture in London, 1820." *Representations* 31 (1990): 47–68.

Clark, Clifford E., Jr. "Domestic Architecture as an Index to Social History: The Romantic Revival and the Cult of Domesticity in America, 1840–1870." *Journal of Interdisciplinary History* 7, no. 1 (Summer 1976): 33–56.

Colley, Linda. *Britons: Forging the Nation, 1707–1837.* New Haven: Yale University Press, 1992.

Colomina, Beatriz, ed. *Sexuality and Space.* New York: Princeton Architectural Press, 1992.

Coombes, Annie E. *Reinventing Africa: Museums, Material Culture and Popular Imagination in Late Victorian and Edwardian England.* New Haven and London: Yale University Press, 1994.

Crompton, Frank. *Workhouse Children: Infant and Child Paupers under the Worcestershire Poor Law, 1780–1871.* Stroud: Sutton Publishing, 1997.

Crowther, M. A. *The Workhouse System, 1834–1929.* Athens: University of Georgia Press, 1982.

Cunningham, Hugh. *The Children of the Poor: Representations of Childhood since the Seventeenth Century.* Oxford: Blackwell, 1991.

Curtis, Perry L. *Apes and Angels: The Irishman in Victorian Caricature.* Rev. ed. Washington, DC: Smithsonian Institution Press, 1997.

———. *Jack the Ripper and the London Press.* New Haven and London: Yale University Press, 2001.

Daunton, Martin J. *House and Home in the Victorian City: Working-Class Housing, 1850–1914.* London: Edward Arnold, 1983.

———, ed. *Charity, Self-Interest and Welfare in the English Past.* New York: St. Martin's Press, 1996.

Davidoff, Leonore, and Catherine Hall. *Family Fortunes: Men and Women of the English Middle Class, 1780–1850.* Chicago: University of Chicago Press, 1987.

Davin, Anna. *Growing Up Poor: Home, School and Street in London, 1870–1914.* London: Rivers Oram Press, 1996.

———. "Imperialism and Motherhood." *History Workshop* 5 (1978): 9–65.

———. "Waif Stories in Late Nineteenth-Century England." *History Workshop Journal* 52 (2001): 67–98.

Davis, Jennifer. "A Poor Man's System of Justice: The London Police Courts in the Second Half of the Nineteenth Century." *Historical Journal* 27, no. 2 (1984): 309–35.

Digby, Anne. *Pauper Palaces: The Economy and Poor Law of Nineteenth-Century Norfolk.* London: Routledge, 1978.

————. *The Poor Law in Nineteenth-Century England and Wales.* London: Historical Association, 1982.

————. "The Rural Poor Law." In Fraser, ed., *New Poor Law,* 149–70.

Donzelot, Jacques. *The Policing of Families.* Translated by Robert Hurley. New York: Pantheon Books, 1979.

Driver, Felix. "Discipline Without Frontiers? Representations of the Mettray Reformatory Colony in Britain, 1840–1880." *Journal of Historical Sociology* 3, no. 3 (1990): 272–93.

————. "The Historical Geography of the Workhouse System in England and Wales, 1834–1883." *Journal of Historical Geography* 15, no. 3 (1989): 269–86.

————. "Moral Geographies: Social Science and the Urban Environment in Mid-Nineteenth Century England." *Transactions of the Institute of British Geographers,* n.s., 13 (1988): 275–87.

————. *Power and Pauperism: The Workhouse System, 1834–1884.* Cambridge: Cambridge University Press, 1993.

Duke, Francis. "Pauper Education." In Fraser, ed., *New Poor Law,* 67–86.

Dulberger, Judith A. *"Mother Donit fore the Best": Correspondence of a Nineteenth-Century Orphan Asylum.* Syracuse: Syracuse University Press, 1996.

Dupree, Marguerite. *Family Structure in the Staffordshire Potteries, 1840–1880.* New York: Oxford University Press, 1995.

Durbach, Nadja. *Bodily Matters: The Anti-Vaccination Movement in England, 1853–1907.* Durham: Duke University Press, 2005.

————. "'They Might as Well Brand Us': Working-Class Resistance to Compulsory Vaccination in Victorian England." *Social History of Medicine* 13, no. 1 (2000): 45–62.

Dwork, Deborah. *War Is Good for Babies and Other Young Children.* London and New York: Tavistock Publications, 1987.

Dwyer, Ellen. *Homes for the Mad: Life Inside Two Nineteenth-Century Asylums.* New Brunswick: Rutgers University Press, 1987.

Dyos, H. J., and Michael Wolff, eds. *The Victorian City: Images and Realities.* London: Routledge and Kegan Paul, 1973.

Edwards, Elizabeth, ed. *Anthropology and Photography, 1860–1920.* New Haven and London: Yale University Press, 1992.

Elliott, Dorice Williams. *The Angel Out of the House: Philanthropy and Gender in Nineteenth-Century England.* Charlottesville: University Press of Virginia, 2002.

Elsaesser, Thomas. "Tales of Sound and Fury: Observations on the Family Melodrama." *Monogram* 4 (1972): 2–15.

Engelhardt, Carol Marie. "Victorians and the Virgin Mary: Religion, National Identity, and the Woman Question in England, 1830–1880." Ph.D. diss., Indiana University, 1997.

Evans, Andrew D. "Capturing Race: Anthropology and Photography in German and Austrian Prisoner-of-War Camps during World War I." In *Colonialist Photography: Imag(in)ing Race and Place,* edited by Eleanor M. Hight and Gary D. Sampson, 226–56. London and New York: Routledge, 2002.

Feather, John Waddington. *A Century of Model-Village Schooling: The Salt Grammar School, 1868–1968.* Bingley: T. Harrison and Sons Ltd., 1968.

Fessenden, David E. *Father to Nobody's Children.* Fort Washington, PA: Christian Literature Crusade, 1995.

Finlayson, Geoffrey. *Citizen, State, and Social Welfare in Britain, 1830–1990.* Oxford: Clarendon Press, 1994.

Foucault, Michel. *Discipline and Punish: The Birth of the Prison.* Translated by Alan Sheridan. New York: Vintage Books, 1979.

———. "Of Other Spaces." Translated by Jay Miskowiec. *Diacritics* 16 (Spring 1986): 22–27.

Fraser, Derek. "The English Poor Law and the Origins of the British Welfare State." In Mommsen, ed., *Emergence of the Welfare State,* 9–31.

———. *The Evolution of the British Welfare State: A History of Social Policy since the Industrial Revolution.* London: Macmillan Press, Ltd., 1973.

———. *Urban Politics in Victorian England.* Leicester: Leicester University Press, 1976.

———, ed. *The New Poor Law in the Nineteenth Century.* New York: St. Martin's Press, 1976.

Fraser, Stuart M. F. "Leicester and Smallpox: The Leicester Method." *Medical History* 24 (July 1980): 315–32.

Fuchs, Rachel. *Poor and Pregnant in Paris: Strategies for Survival in the Nineteenth Century.* New Brunswick: Rutgers University Press, 1992.

Gatens, Moira. "Corporeal Representation in/and the Body Politic." In *Writing on the Body: Female Embodiment and Feminist Theory,* edited by Kate Conboy, Nadia Medina, and Sarah Stanbury, 80–89. New York: Columbia University Press, 1997.

Goffman, Erving. *Asylums: Essays on the Social Situation of Mental Patients and Other Inmates.* 1961. Reprint, New York: Doubleday, 1990.

Gordon, Linda. "Family Violence, Feminism, and Social Control." In *Women, the State, and Welfare,* edited by Linda Gordon, 178–98. Madison: University of Wisconsin Press, 1990.

Gorham, Deborah. "The 'Maiden Tribute of Modern Babylon' Re-examined: Child Prostitution and the Idea of Childhood in Late-Victorian England." *Victorian Studies* 21, no. 3 (1978): 353–79.

Green-Lewis, Jennifer. *Framing the Victorians: Photography and the Culture of Realism.* Ithaca and London: Cornell University Press, 1996.

Greenough, Sarah. "The Curious Contagion of the Camera." In *On the Art of Fixing a Shadow: One Hundred and Fifty Years of Photography.* Boston, Toronto, London: National Gallery of Art and Art Institute of Chicago in Association with Bulfinch Press/Little, Brown and Co., 1989.

Grosz, Elizabeth. "Bodies-Cities." In Colomina, ed., *Sexuality and Space,* 241–53.

Gullace, Nicoletta F. *"The Blood of Our Sons": Men, Women, and the Renegotiation of British Citizenship during the Great War.* New York: Palgrave Macmillan, 2002.

Hacsi, Timothy A. *Second Home: Orphan Asylums and Poor Families in America.* Cambridge, MA: Harvard University Press, 1997.

Hadley, Elaine. *Melodramatic Tactics: Theatricalized Dissent in the English Marketplace, 1800–1885.* Stanford: Stanford University Press, 1995.

———. "Natives in a Strange Land: The Philanthropic Discourse of Juvenile Emigration in Mid-Nineteenth-Century England." *Victorian Studies* 33, no. 3 (1990): 411–39.

Hall, Catherine. *Civilising Subjects: Metropole and Colony in the English Imagination, 1830–1867.* Chicago: University of Chicago Press, 2002.

———. *White, Male and Middle Class: Explorations in Feminism and History.* New York: Routledge, 1992.

Hall, Catherine, Keith McClelland, and Jane Rendall. *Defining the Victorian Nation: Class, Race, Gender and the Reform Act of 1867.* Cambridge: Cambridge University Press, 2000.

Hardy, Anne. "Smallpox in London: Factors in the Decline of the Disease in the Nineteenth Century." *Medical History* 27 (1983): 111–38.

Harrison, Phyllis, ed. *The Home Children.* Winnipeg, Manitoba: Watson and Dwyer Publishing Ltd., 1979.

Heathorn, Stephen. *For Home, Country, and Race: Constructing Gender, Class, and Englishness in the Elementary School, 1880–1914.* Toronto: University of Toronto Press, 2000.

———. "'Let us remember that we, too, are English': Constructions of Citizenship and National Identity in English Elementary School Reading Books, 1880–1914." *Victorian Studies* 38, no. 3 (Spring 1995): 395–427.

Heilman, Robert Bechtold. *Tragedy and Melodrama: Versions of Experience.* Seattle and London: University of Washington Press, 1968.

Hendrick, Harry. *Children, Childhood and English Society, 1880–1990.* Cambridge: Cambridge University Press, 1997.

———. *Child Welfare: England, 1872–1989.* London and New York: Routledge, 1994.

Hewitt, Martin. "District Visiting and the Constitution of Domestic Space in the Mid-Nineteenth Century." In *Domestic Space: Reading the Nineteenth-Century Interior,* edited by Inga Bryden and Janet Floyd, 121–41. Manchester: Manchester University Press, 1999.

———. "The Travails of Domestic Visiting: Manchester, 1830–70." *Historical Research* 71 (June 1998): 196–227.

Higginbotham, Ann Rowell. "The Unmarried Mother and Her Child in Victorian London, 1834–1914." Ph.D. diss., Indiana University, 1985.

Himmelfarb, Gertrude. *The Idea of Poverty: England in the Early Industrial Age.* New York: Knopf, 1985.

Hitchcock, Timothy, Peter King, and Pamela Sharpe, eds. *Chronicling Poverty: The Voices and Strategies of the English Poor, 1640–1840.* New York: St. Martin's Press, 1997.

Hochman, Baruch, and Ilja Wachs. *Dickens: The Orphan Condition.* Madison, NJ: Fairleigh Dickinson University Press; London: Associated University Press, 1999.

Houghton, Walter E. *The Victorian Frame of Mind, 1830–1870.* New Haven and London: Yale University Press, 1957.

Hurt, J. S. "Drill, Discipline and the Elementary School Ethos." In McCann, ed., *Popular Education and Socialization in the Nineteenth Century,* 167–91.

Israel, Kali. "French Vices and British Liberties: Gender, Class, and Narrative Competition in a Late Victorian Sex Scandal." *Social History* 22 (1997): 1–26.

Jones, Colin. "Some Recent Trends in the History of Charity." In Daunton, ed., *Charity, Self-Interest and Welfare in the English Past,* 51–63.

Jones, Gareth Stedman. *Outcast London: A Study in the Relationship between Classes in Victorian Society.* 1971. Reprint, New York: Pantheon Books, 1984.

Joyce, Patrick. *Democratic Subjects: The Self and the Social in Nineteenth-Century England.* Cambridge: Cambridge University Press, 1994.

————. *Visions of the People: Industrial England and the Question of Class, 1848–1914.* Cambridge: Cambridge University Press, 1990.

Katz, Michael. *The Undeserving Poor: From the War on Poverty to the War on Welfare.* New York: Pantheon Books, 1989.

Kidd, Alan. *State, Society and the Poor in Nineteenth-Century England.* London: Macmillan Press; New York: St. Martin's Press, 1999.

Kilgarriff, Michael, ed. *The Golden Age of Melodrama: Twelve Nineteenth-Century Melodramas.* London: Wolfe Publishing Ltd., 1974.

Koven, Seth. "Dr. Barnardo's 'Artistic Fictions': Photography, Sexuality, and the Ragged Child in Victorian London." *Radical History Review* 69 (1997): 6–45.

————. "Henrietta Barnett, 1851–1936: The (auto)biography of a Late Victorian Marriage." In Pedersen and Mandler, eds., *After the Victorians,* 31–53.

————. *Slumming: Sexual and Social Politics in Victorian London.* Princeton: Princeton University Press, 2004.

Koven, Seth, and Sonya Michel, eds. *Mothers of a New World: Maternalist Politics and the Origins of the Welfare State.* New York: Routledge, 1993.

Lambert, R. J. "A Victorian National Health Service: State Vaccination, 1855–71." *Historical Journal* 5 (1962): 1–18.

Laqueur, Thomas. "The Queen Caroline Affair: Politics as Art in the Reign of George IV." *Journal of Modern History* 54, no. 3 (1982): 417–66.

Leaver, Kristen. "Victorian Melodrama and the Performance of Poverty." *Victorian Literature and Culture* (1999): 443–56.

Lees, Lynn Hollen. *The Solidarities of Strangers: The English Poor Laws and the People, 1700–1948.* Cambridge: Cambridge University Press, 1998.

————. "The Survival of the Unfit: Welfare Policies and Family Maintenance in Nineteenth Century London." In Mandler, ed., *Uses of Charity,* 68–91.

Leeuwen, Marco H. D. van. "Logic of Charity: Poor Relief in Preindustrial Europe." *Journal of Interdisciplinary History* 24 (1994): 589–613.

Lloyd, Valerie. *The Camera and Dr. Barnardo.* With an introduction by Gillian Wagner. Hertford, England: Barnardo School of Printing, 1974.

Longmate, Norman. *The Workhouse: A Social History.* New York: St. Martin's Press, 1974.

Low, Setha M. "Cultural Meaning of the Plaza: The History of the Spanish-American Gridplan-Plaza Urban Design." In Rotenberg and McDonogh, eds., *Cultural Meaning of Urban Space,* 75–93.

Lynch, Katherine. *Family, Class, and Ideology in Early Industrial France: Social Policy and the Working-Class Family, 1825–1848.* Madison: University of Wisconsin Press, 1988.

MacKenzie, John M. *Propaganda and Empire: The Manipulation of British Public Opinion, 1880–1960.* Manchester: Manchester University Press, 1984.

MacLeod, R. M. "Law, Medicine and Public Opinion: The Resistance to Compulsory Health Legislation, 1870–1907." *Public Law* (1967), part I: 107–28; part II: 189–211.

Mandler, Peter, ed. *The Uses of Charity: The Poor on Relief in the Nineteenth-Century Metropolis.* Philadelphia: University of Pennsylvania Press, 1990.

Marks, Lara. *Model Mothers: Jewish Mothers and Maternity Provision in East London, 1870–1939.* Oxford: Clarendon Press, 1994.

Marwick, Arthur. *The Deluge: British Society and the First World War.* London: Bodley Head, 1965.

Matthew, Colin, ed. *The Nineteenth Century: The British Isles, 1815–1901.* Oxford: Oxford University Press, 2000.

Maza, Sarah. "Domestic Melodrama as Political Ideology: The Case of the Comte de Sanois." *American Historical Review* 94 (1989): 1249–64.

McCann, Phillip, ed. *Popular Education and Socialization in the Nineteenth Century.* London: Methuen and Co. Ltd., 1977.

McCrillis, Neal. *The British Conservative Party in the Age of Universal Suffrage.* Columbus: Ohio State University Press, 1998.

McWilliam, Rohan. "The Licensed Stare: Melodrama and the Culture of Spectacle." *Nineteenth Century Studies,* 13 (1999): 156–61.

———. "Melodrama and the Historians." *Radical History Review* 78 (2000): 59–62.

———. "Radicalism and Popular Culture: The Tichborne Case and the Politics of 'Fair Play,' 1867–1886." In Biagini and Reid, eds., *Currents of Radicalism,* 44–64.

Meisel, Martin. *Realizations: Narrative, Pictorial, and Theatrical Arts in Nineteenth-Century England.* Princeton: Princeton University Press, 1983.

Mommsen, W. J., ed. *The Emergence of the Welfare State in Britain and Germany, 1850–1950.* London: Croom Helm, 1981.

Murdoch, Lydia D. "From Barrack Schools to Family Cottages: Creating Domestic Space for Late Victorian Poor Children." In *Child Welfare and Social Action in the Nineteenth and Twentieth Centuries: International Perspectives,* edited by Jon Lawrence and Pat Starkey, 147–73. Liverpool: Liverpool University Press, 2001.

Nord, Deborah Epstein. "The Social Explorer as Anthropologist: Victorian Travellers among the Urban Poor." In Sharpe and Wallock, eds., *Visions of the Modern City,* 118–30.

———. *Walking the Victorian Streets: Women, Representation, and the City.* Ithaca and London: Cornell University Press, 1995.

Nowell-Smith, Geoffrey. "Minnelli and Melodrama." *Screen* 18 (Summer 1977): 113–18.

Nunes, Jadviga M. Da Costa. "O. G. Rejlander's Photographs of Ragged Children: Reflections on the Idea of Urban Poverty in Mid-Victorian Society." *Nineteenth Century Studies* 4 (1990): 105–36.

Offen, Karen. "Depopulation, Nationalism, and Feminism in Fin-de-Siècle France." *American Historical Review* 89 (1984): 649–50.

Parker, Julia. *Women and Welfare: Ten Victorian Women in Public Social Service.* New York: St. Martin's Press, 1989.

Parr, Joy. *Labouring Children: British Immigrant Apprentices to Canada, 1869–1924.* London: Croom Helm; Montreal: McGill-Queen's University Press, 1980.

Pedersen, Susan, and Peter Mandler, eds. *After the Victorians: Private Conscience and Public Duty in Modern Britain.* London and New York: Routledge, 1994.

Peters, Laura. *Orphan Texts: Victorian Orphans, Culture, and Empire.* Manchester: Manchester University Press, 2000.

Peterson, M. Jeanne. *Family, Love, and Work in the Lives of Victorian Gentlewomen.* Bloomington: Indiana University Press, 1989.

Petro, Patrice. *Joyless Streets: Women and Melodramatic Representation in Weimar Germany.* Princeton: Princeton University Press, 1989.

Pickering, Michael. "White Skin, Black Masks: 'Nigger' Minstrelsy in Victorian England." In *Music Hall: Performance and Style,* edited by J. S. Bratton, 70–91. Milton Keynes: Open University Press, 1986.

Poovey, Mary. *Making a Social Body: British Cultural Formation, 1830–1864.* Chicago: University of Chicago Press, 1995.

Prasch, Thomas. "Fixed Positions: Working-Class Subjects and Photographic Hegemony in Victorian Britain." Ph.D. diss., Indiana University, 1994.

Prochaska, F. K. "Female Philanthropy and Domestic Service in Victorian England." *Historical Research* 54 (1981): 79–85.

———. "A Mother's Country: Mothers' Meetings and Family Welfare in Britain, 1850–1950." *History* 74 (October 1989): 379–99.

———. *Women and Philanthropy in Nineteenth-Century England.* Oxford: Clarendon Press, 1980.

Pugh, Martin. *Electoral Reform in War and Peace, 1906–18.* London: Routledge and Kegan Paul, 1978.

Rahill, Frank. *The World of Melodrama.* University Park and London: Pennsylvania State University Press, 1967.

Rose, June. *For the Sake of the Children: Inside Dr. Barnardo's, 120 Years of Caring for Children.* London: Hodder and Stroughton, 1987.

Rose, Lionel. *The Erosion of Childhood: Child Oppression in Great Britain, 1860–1918.* London and New York: Routledge, 1991.

Rose, Michael. "The Crisis of Poor Relief in England, 1860–1890." In Mommsen, ed. *Emergence of the Welfare State,* 50–70.

Ross, Ellen. *Love and Toil: Motherhood in Outcast London, 1870–1918.* Oxford: Oxford University Press, 1993.

Rotenberg, Robert, and Gary McDonogh, eds. *The Cultural Meaning of Urban Space.* Westport, CT, and London: Bergin and Garvey, 1993.

Said, Edward. *Orientalism.* New York: Vintage, 1979.

Samuel, Raphael. *Theatres of Memory.* Vol. 1, *Past and Present in Contemporary Culture.* London and New York: Verso, 1994.

Schneer, Jonathan. *London 1900: The Imperial Metropolis.* New Haven and London: Yale University Press, 1999.

Scott, Joan Wallach. *Gender and the Politics of History.* New York: Columbia University Press, 1988.

Sekula, Allan. "The Body and the Archive." *October* 39 (Winter 1986): 3–64.

Shanley, Mary Lyndon. *Feminism, Marriage, and the Law in Victorian England.* Princeton: Princeton University Press, 1989.

Sharpe, William, and Leonard Wallock, eds. *Visions of the Modern City: Essays in History, Art, and Literature.* New York: Columbia University Press, 1983.

Sherington, Geoffrey, and Chris Jeffery. *Fairbridge: Empire and Child Migration.* Ilford, Essex: Woburn Press, 1998.

Smith, F. B. *The People's Health, 1830–1910.* London: Croom Helm, 1979.

Smith, J. R. *The Speckled Monster: Smallpox in England, 1670–1970, with Particular Reference to Essex.* Chelmsford: Essex Record Office, 1987.

Smith, Lindsay. "The Shoe-black to the the Crossing Sweeper: Victorian Street Arabs and Photography." *Textual Practice* 10, no. 1 (1996): 29–55.

Spencer, Stephanie. *O. G. Rejlander: Photography as Art.* Ann Arbor: University of Michigan Research Press, 1985.

Stallybrass, Peter, and Allon White. *The Politics and Poetics of Transgression.* Ithaca: Cornell University Press, 1986.

Stange, Maren. "Gotham's Crime and Misery: Ideology and Entertainment in Jacob Riis's Lantern Slide Exhibitions." *Views: The Journal of Photography in New England* 8, no. 3 (Spring 1987): 7–11.

Steinbach, Susie L. "The Melodramatic Contract: Breach of Promise and the Performance of Virtue." *Nineteenth Century Studies* 14 (2000): 1–34.

Stowe, Steven M. "Seeing Themselves at Work: Physicians and the Case Narrative in the Mid-Nineteenth-Century American South." *American Historical Review* 101, no. 1 (February 1996): 41–79.

Tagg, John. *The Burden of Representation: Essays on Photographies and Histories.* Amherst: University of Massachusetts Press, 1988.

———. "Power and Photography: Part One, A Means of Surveillance: The Photograph as Evidence in Law." *Screen Education* 36 (Autumn 1980): 17–55.

Thompson, Dorothy. *The Chartists: Popular Politics in the Industrial Revolution.* New York: Pantheon Books, 1984.

Thompson, F.M.L. *The Rise of Respectable Society: A Social History of Victorian Britain, 1830–1900.* London: Fontana Press, 1988.

Thorne, Susan. *Congregational Missions and the Making of an Imperial Culture in Nineteenth-Century England.* Stanford: Stanford University Press, 1999.

Tikoff, Valentina K. "Assisted Transitions: Children and Adolescents in the Orphanages of Seville at the End of the Old Regime, 1681–1831." Ph.D. diss., Indiana University, 2000.

Turner, Victor. "Social Dramas and Stories about Them." *Critical Inquiry* 7 (Autumn 1980): 141–68.

Upton, Dell. "Lancasterian Schools, Republican Citizenship, and the Spatial Imagination in Early Nineteenth-Century America." *Journal of the Society of Architectural Historians* 55, no. 3 (September 1996): 238–53.

Vernon, James. *Politics and the People: A Study in English Political Culture, c. 1815–1867.* Cambridge: Cambridge University Press, 1993.

Vicinus, Martha. "'Helpless and Unfriended': Nineteenth-Century Domestic Melodrama." *New Literary History* 13, no. 1 (Autumn 1981): 127–43.

Waddington, Keir. *Charity and the London Hospitals, 1850–1898.* Woodbridge, Suffolk: Boydell Press, 2000.

Wagner, Gillian. *Barnardo.* London: Weidenfeld and Nicholson, 1979.

———. *Children of the Empire.* London: Weidenfeld and Nicholson, 1982.

Walker, Pamela J. *Pulling the Devil's Kingdom Down: The Salvation Army in Victorian Britain.* Berkeley: University of California Press, 2001.

Walkowitz, Judith. *City of Dreadful Delight: Narratives of Sexual Danger in Late-Victorian London.* Chicago: University of Chicago Press, 1992.

Ward, Harriet. "The Charitable Relationship: Parents, Children and the Waifs and Strays Society." Ph.D. diss., University of Bristol, 1990.

Williams, A. E. *Barnardo of Stepney: The Father of Nobody's Children.* 1st ed., 1943. 2nd ed., with a foreword by Christopher Fry, 1953. Reprint, London: George Allen and Unwin, Ltd., 1966.

Winter, Jay M., and Michael S. Teitelbaum. *The Fear of Population Decline.* New York: Academic Press, 1985.

Wohl, Anthony S. *The Eternal Slum: Housing and Social Policy in Victorian London.* London: E. Arnold, 1977.

Wood, Peter. *Poverty and the Workhouse in Victorian Britain.* Wolfeboro Falls, NH: Alan Sutton Publishing Inc., 1991.

Woollacott, Angela. *On Her Their Lives Depend: Munitions Workers in the Great War.* Berkeley: University of California Press, 1994.

Wymer, Norman. *Foster Father of Nobody's Children: A Portrait of Dr. Barnardo.* London: Hutchinson, 1954.

Zmora, Nurith. *Orphanages Reconsidered: Child Care Institutions in Progressive Era Baltimore.* Philadelphia: Temple University Press, 1994.

INDEX

Barnardo, Thomas *(continued)*
148, 219n20, 221n41; band training,
122; Barnardo-Reynolds arbitration,
14–15, 17, 22, 206n103; barracks
schools, criticisms of, 57, 59, 187n83;
before-and-after photographs, 37, *37,
38,* 39, 218n2; biographical sketch, 67;
charitable institutions run by, 3–4, 6;
*Child Life: The Nation's Greatest
Asset,* 150; child poverty, account of,
17–18; child prostitution, literature on,
22–24; children and housing, 56, 64,
94, 95, 98–99; children of soldiers,
sheltering, 145; *A City Waif: How I
Fished for and Caught Her,* 19; custody conflicts, 112–15, 119; death,
165–66; depauperization, 35–36; discipline cases, 88; fund-raising efforts,
12–14, 15, 17, 39–41, *39, 40,* 71, 124,
149, 152, 180n124; girls' home, 43,
55, 61–63, 123, 125, 134–35, 152,
161, 190n136; imperial influences, *29,*
131, 134; "Is Philanthropic Abduction
Every Justifiable?" 23; *Kidnapped,* 19;
lodging houses, description of, 47–48;
medical supervision, 107; military
training, 150–52, *151,* 215n74; mortality rates, 146; *My First Arab; or, How
I Began My Life-Work,* 17–18, 25,
173n23; *Out of an Horrible Pit,* 23;
photographs, 3–4, 12–13, 21, *21, 22,*
26, 125, *126,* 127, 168n8, 173n18,
175n44, 179n115; poor children,
description of, 26; professional training, 122–30, 135; records from, 8;
religious instruction, 111–12, 164;
Rescue the Perishing, 22; separation of
children from "dreadful pasts,"
115–16; "street arab," description of,
25–26; studies of homes, 68; tea meetings, 27, *28,* 73, 124; visitation policies, 103–6; war babies, 148; *Worse
Than Orphans: How I Stole Two Girls
and Fought for a Boy,* 19–20
Barnardo Boys, 150, 153
Barnes, Thomas, 22
Barnett, Henrietta, 55, 116
Barnett, Samuel, 55

Barnsbury, 148
barrack schools, 4, 43–44, 52–61. *See
also specific institutions*
bastilles, 4
Battersby, Maud, 26
bedouins, 30
bed-wetting, 157–61
begging, 24
Behlmer, George, 81
Belgian Relief Fund, 145
Belgians, 146
Beni-Zou-Zougs, 30–32
Bentham, Jeremy, 4
Bermondsey, 106, 109
Bethnal Green, 83, 97
Biggs, Robert, 156
Biggs, William, 156
Birmingham, 105
boarding-out, 43, 146, 148, 181n2,
219n20, 221n41
Board of Education, 147, 148
Board of Trade, 56
Bolingbroke, "Georgie," 31
Bond, Eliza, 86–87
Bond, Emily, 86–87
Bond, Ethel, 86–87
Booth, William, 16, 61
Bow, 93
Brentwood school, 102, 108–9
Brisbane, Australia, 73
British East India Company, 53
British Workman, 48
Brooks, Peter, 16, 36, 42
Browne, T. H. Murray, 184n35
Burma, 133

Cairns, Earl of, 64–65
Camberwell, 82
Canada, emigration programs to, 2, 4, 9,
26, 41, 69, 80, 87, 125, 150
Cannadine, David, 182n8
Canterbury, Archbishop of, 99
Carlisle, 148
Carpenter, Mary, 64–65, 66
Carter, Ada, 117
casual children, 50–52, 185–86n57
Catholicism, 111–12, 113–14, 164,
207n107

Sowden, Edward, 100
Spurgeon, Charles, 100
Stallion, Ada, 117
Standard, 105, 110, 114
Stansfeld, James, 54
Stead, William T., 16, 19, 23–24, 67
Stephenson, Thomas Bowman, 3
Stepney, 3, 148
Stepney Board of Guardians, 77, 102
Stepney Boys' Home, 19, 30, 99, 123, 145, 153, 203n67
Stepney Causeway, 32, 39, 56, 110, 124
Stockwell Orphanage, 100
Strand school, 102
strays, 1, 6, 11
street arabs, 1, 6, 24–32, 180n120
street entertainment, 24
suffrage, 7, 143–44. *See also* Reform Acts; Representation of the People Act
Sutton, 84
Swinton, 98, 104

Tasmania, 132
tea meetings, 27, *28,* 73, 124
Tennant, Dorothy, 180n120
Thames Police Court, 12, 14, 105–6, 110–11, 114, 115
theatrical fund-raising events, 15, 17, 39–41, *40*
Thompson, F.M.L., 45
Tikoff, Valentina, 69
Times (London), 105, 114, 120, 145
Tommy's Bairns (pamphlet), 145
Tooting, 53
Tours, France, 55
Towle, Annie, 139
Townshend, E. M., 41
Toynbee Hall, 55
Tufnell, Edward Carleton: absconding, letter about, 100; criticism of tailor and shoemaker training, 128; differences among reformers, 164; district school, population of, 98; poor law school inspector, 49; promotion of military training, 121–23, 134, 138; school style, debates on, 54–55, 60, 117, 189n117; workhouse, characterization of, 50

Tunbridge Wells, 53
Turkey, 30
Turner, Victor, 16
Twelftree, Alfred, 152
Twining, Elizabeth, 53
Twining, Louisa, 53–54, 65, 164, 213n34
Twining, Richard (father), 53
Twining, Richard (son), 53
Tye, Martha, 113–14

undomestic poor, 46–48
unemployment, 84–86
unfeminine masses, 57–61

Vaccination Acts, 107, 204–5n84, 205n85
Vicinus, Martha, 15
Vickers, 148
Victoria, Queen, 93
Victorian child philanthropy. *See* philanthropy
visits between parents and children, 100–106

Wadsworth, Maud, 117
Wagner, Gillian, 68, 69
waifs, 1, 6, 11
Wallbridge, Mrs., 110
war babies, 147–48, 149
War Office, 145
Warren, Annie, 140
Watts, Edmund, 134
Watts Naval School, 134, 135, 150–52
Waugh, Benjamin, 3, 80
West Ham Cemetery, 93, 199n12
West London School District, 101, 128, 131, 145–46, 151
Westminster Review, 59
Whitechapel, 2, 48, 93, 98, 101, 116, 139
Willesden, 148
Williams, A. E., 67
Wilson, Ada, 139–40
Winfield, Fred, 109
Winfield, Mrs., 109
Wood, Edgar, 100
Wood, Fred, 100
Woolcock, Annie, 117

About the Author

Lydia Murdoch is an assistant professor of history at Vassar College in Poughkeepsie, New York.